EVERYDAY SOCIOLOGY READER

RECENT SOCIOLOGY TITLES FROM NORTON

Code of the Street: Decency, Violence, and the Moral Life of the Inner City by Elijah Anderson

Social Problems by Joel Best

You May Ask Yourself: An Introduction to Thinking Like a Sociologist by Dalton Conley

The Real World: An Introduction to Sociology, 2nd Edition by Kerry Ferris and Jill Stein

Introduction to Sociology, 7th Edition, by Anthony Giddens, Mitchell Duneier, Richard P. Appelbaum, and Deborah Carr

Essentials of Sociology, 2nd Edition, by Anthony Giddens, Mitchell Duneier, Richard P. Appelbaum, and Deborah Carr

The Contexts Reader edited by Jeff Goodwin and James M. Jasper

Mix It Up: Popular Culture, Mass Media, and Society by David Grazian

When Sex Goes to School by Kristin Luker

Inequality and Society: Social Science Perspectives on Social Stratification by Jeff Manza and Michael Sauder

Readings for Sociology, 6th Edition, edited by Garth Massey

Families as They Really Are edited by Barbara J. Risman

A Sociology of Globalization by Saskia Sassen

The Sociology of News by Michael Schudson

The Social Construction of Sexuality, 2nd Edition, by Steven Seidman

The Corrosion of Character: The Personal Consequences of Work in the New Capitalism by Richard Sennett

Biography and the Sociological Imagination: Contexts and Contingencies by Michael J. Shanahan and Ross Macmillan

A Primer on Social Movements by David A. Snow and Sarah A. Soule

Six Degrees: The Science of a Connected Age by Duncan J. Watts

More Than Just Race: Being Black and Poor in the Inner City by William Julius Wilson

NORTON CRITICAL EDITIONS

The Souls of Black Folk by W. E. B. Du Bois edited by Henry Louis Gates Jr. and Terri Hume Oliver

The Communist Manifesto by Karl Marx, edited by Frederic L. Bender

The Protestant Ethic and the Spirit of Capitalism by Max Weber, translated by Talcott Parsons and edited by Richard Swedberg

For more information on our publications in sociology, please visit wwnorton.com/college/soc

EVERYDAY SOCIOLOGY READER

Karen Sternheimer
University of Southern California

W. W. Norton & Company
New York ■ London

W. W. Norton & Company has been independent since its founding in 1923, when William Warder Norton and Mary D. Herter Norton first published lectures delivered at the People's Institute, the adult education division of New York City's Cooper Union. The firm soon expanded its program beyond the Institute, publishing books by celebrated academics from America and abroad. By midcentury, the two major pillars of Norton's publishing program—trade books and college texts—were firmly established. In the 1950s, the Norton family transferred control of the company to its employees, and today—with a staff of four hundred and a comparable number of trade, college, and professional titles published each year—W. W. Norton & Company stands as the largest and oldest publishing house owned wholly by its employees.

Printed in the United States of America.
First Edition.

The text of this book is composed in Benton Modern 2
with the display set in Century Gothic
Book design by Deborah Brouwer
Composition by Westchester Book Group
Manufacturing by Worldcolor
Production manager: Eric Pier-Hocking

Library of Congress Cataloging-in-Publication Data

Sternheimer, Karen.
Everyday sociology reader / Karen Sternheimer.
p. cm.
Includes bibliographical references.
ISBN 978-0-393-93429-8 (pbk.)
1. Sociology. I. Title.

HM585.S74 2010
301—dc22

2009033808

W. W. Norton & Company, Inc., 500 Fifth Avenue, New York, N.Y. 10110-0017
wwnorton.com

W. W. Norton & Company Ltd., Castle House, 75/76 Wells Street, London W1T 3QT

4 5 6 7 8 9 0

ABOUT THE EDITOR

Karen Sternheimer teaches in the sociology department at the University of Southern California, where she is also a faculty fellow at USC's Center for Excellence in Teaching. She is the editor and lead writer for the Everyday Sociology Blog (everydaysociologyblog.com), a site devoted to analyzing sociology's relevance in everyday life. She is also the author of *Connecting Social Problems and Popular Culture: Why Media Is Not the Answer* (2009), *Kids These Days: Facts and Fictions About Today's Youth* (2006), and *It's Not the Media: The Truth About Pop Culture's Influence on Children* (2003), and editor of *Childhood in American Society: A Reader* (2009). Additionally, she has provided commentary on CNN, MSNBC, Fox News, the History Channel, and numerous television and radio programs.

CONTENTS

ABOUT *THE EVERYDAY SOCIOLOGY READER*

This reader is designed to help you make connections between major sociological concepts, popular culture, current events, and everyday life. Unlike traditional course readers, this book combines classic and contemporary readings in sociology with blog posts to generate thinking about sociology in your everyday experiences. The blog posts come from everydaysociologyblog.com, a site where sociologists discuss issues from the news and their daily experiences in order to help readers better understand the world from a sociological perspective. I invite you to visit the site, read about current events, and post your thoughts online. The purpose of this book is not simply for you to read about sociology, but for you to actively engage in sociological thinking, writing, and research.

To help you accomplish these goals, this book is divided into ten modules. Each module begins with an objective and includes a brief discussion of the major concepts to consider within the section, as well as questions to think about before you begin reading the module's selections. At the end of each module you will find questions for discussion (under the "Talk About It" heading), and topics for further writing—and perhaps blogging ("Write About It"). Finally, I propose projects for conducting your own research ("Do It")—one of the best ways to learn about sociology and to see its relevance to everyday life.

I invite you to begin the process of seeing the world through sociological lenses. Thinking sociologically will not only help you master the concepts in this book and succeed in your class, but will also enhance your understanding of your experiences and the world around you.

Karen Sternheimer

ACKNOWLEDGMENTS

The *Everyday Sociology Reader* has many parents that deserve thanks and recognition. First and foremost, thanks to Karl Bakeman for inviting me to be the inaugural editor for the Everyday Sociology Blog, and to his predecessors, Melea Seward and Steve Dunn, for laying the groundwork for the blog years ago. Along with Karl, emedia editor Eileen Connell has been vital in shaping the blog and ultimately this book. She has been a terrific partner in creating the character and quality of the blog. Our bloggers have written many of this book's essays, and I am grateful for their excellent sociological imaginations: special thanks to C. N. Le, Kathleen Lowney, Janis Prince Inniss, Sally Raskoff, and Bradley Wright. I would also like to thank the College editorial board at Norton, which supported our new online venture, as well as our reviewers for their feedback and suggestions.

The Norton staff also deserves special recognition. Much thanks to Ben Reynolds for helping with the book's overall structure and copyediting. Assistant editor Kate Feighery was always helpful in a pinch. And thanks also to Rebecca Charney and Sarah Johnson, editorial assistants, Stephanie Romeo, picture editor, and Eric Pier-Hocking, production manager.

I would also like to thank the sociology department staff at the University of Southern California, Melissa Hernandez, Stachelle Overland, Lisa Rayburn-Parks, and Amber Thomas. Their help makes my life easier on a daily basis. I also appreciate the continued support of Tim Biblarz, Barry Glassner, Elaine Bell Kaplan, and Mike Messner, whose advice through the years has culminated in this project.

Lastly, I would like to thank the thousands of readers of the Everyday Sociology Blog. Keep your comments coming—we love hearing from you!

EVERYDAY SOCIOLOGY READER

1

Thinking Sociologically and Doing Sociology

Module Goal: ***Think sociologically, ask sociological questions, and develop a basic understanding of sociological research.***

What does it mean to think sociologically? To do so is often a challenge for those new to sociology because American society encourages us to focus on individuals rather than social systems. The first task in any sociology class is to develop what C. Wright Mills called a "sociological imagination."

Writing in the mid-twentieth century, Mills challenged conventional sociological thought, charging that predominating theories were "not readily understandable" and not "altogether intelligible" (p. 26).[1] Mills encouraged sociologists to look at real people's lives and draw connections between the personal and the social—what he called biography and history. This book is imbued with the spirit of Mills's suggestions, and we encourage you to continually draw connections between your personal experiences and sociology.

In the first selection, "The Promise," Mills details what he means by a sociological imagination. As you read this essay, think about how you might apply current events to sociological concepts.

A sociological imagination can help us create theories, or attempts to explain specific phenomena about the social world. As Sally Raskoff explains in "Fractals, Theories, and Patterns," theories are similar to fractals, geometric shapes that when broken down (or fractured) represent the shape of the whole. Sociological theories seek to provide a clearer understanding of everyday life by describing a persistent pattern.

Because sociology is a science, our theories need to be tested using empirical methods: we must base our conclusions not on mere opinion, but instead on scientific

1. Mills. (1959). *The Sociological Imagination*. New York: Oxford University Press.

inquiry. As Janis Prince Inniss discusses in "Matching Research Methods to Research Questions," even if we think something is true, we must find evidence to support our claims. Even well-known, highly educated people sometimes draw conclusions without adequately testing their hypotheses. Prince Inniss reminds us that in order for us to conclude that our hypothesis is correct, our research methods have to be consistent with our research questions; otherwise, our conclusions will not be supported by evidence.

So how do we begin the research process? In "Where to Sit: Doing Qualitative Research," Bradley Wright describes an example of how to get started. This selection shows that although sociological research is systematic, it isn't necessarily difficult for novice researchers. Sociologists use both qualitative methods—gathering data in the form of observations and interviews—and quantitative methods—gathering numerical information and analyzing statistics—in order to make sociological discoveries.

After gathering and evaluating the data we collect, we present our findings, ideally in a manner that is both clear and honest. As Joel Best's selection "Scary Numbers" reveals, numbers are sometimes misused to gain support for a cause. We are taught that numbers convey authority, so it's important to think critically about statistics. As you read this selection, consider how sociological research is conceived, conducted, and presented. You will then be well on your way to thinking sociologically.

As you begin to think about how sociology applies to everyday life, ask yourself the following questions:

1. What is the sociological perspective? What are your theories about a sociological phenomenon?
2. Think of a sociological question you would like to answer. How would you design a study to answer this question?
3. Are there any "scary numbers" you have heard from friends or in the news that you are skeptical about and would like to study more?

The Promise

(1959)

C. WRIGHT MILLS

The sociological imagination enables its possessor to understand the larger historical scene in terms of its meaning for the inner life and the external career of a variety of individuals. It enables him to take into account how individuals, in the welter of their daily experience, often become falsely conscious of their social positions. Within that welter, the framework of modern society is sought, and within that framework the psychologies of a variety of men and women are formulated. By such means the personal uneasiness of individuals is focused upon explicit troubles and the indifference of publics is transformed into involvement with public issues.

The first fruit of this imagination—and the first lesson of the social science that embodies it—is the idea that the individual can understand his own experience and gauge his own fate only by locating himself within his period, that he can know his own chances in life only by becoming aware of those of all individuals in his circumstances. In many ways it is a terrible lesson, in many ways a magnificent one. We do not know the limits of man's capacities for supreme effort or willing degradation, for agony or glee, for pleasurable brutality or the sweetness of reason. But in our time we have come to know that the limits of 'human nature' are frighteningly broad. We have come to know that every individual lives, from one generation to the next, in some society, that he lives out a biography, and that he lives it out within some historical sequence. By the fact of his living he contributes, however minutely, to the shaping of this society and to the course of its history, even as he is made by society and by its historical push and shove.

The sociological imagination enables us to grasp history and biography and the relations between the two within society. That is its task and its promise. To recognize this task and this promise is the mark of the classic social analyst. . . . And it is the signal of what is best in contemporary studies of man and society.

No social study that does not come back to the problems of biography, of history and of their intersections within a society has completed its intellectual journey. Whatever the specific problems of the classic social analysts, however limited or however broad the features of social reality they have examined, those who have been imaginatively aware of the promise of their work have consistently asked three sorts of questions.

(1) What is the structure of this particular society as a whole? What are its essential components, and how are they related to one another? How does it differ from other varieties of social order? Within it, what is the meaning of any particular feature for its continuance and for its change?

(2) Where does this society stand in human history? What are the mechanics by which it is changing? What is its place within and its meaning for the development of humanity as a whole? How does any particular feature we are examining affect, and how is it affected by, the historical period in which it moves? And this period—what are its essential features? How does it differ from other periods? What are its characteristic ways of history-making?

(3) What varieties of men and women now prevail in this society and in this period? And what varieties are coming to prevail? In what ways are they selected and formed, liberated and repressed, made sensitive and blunted? What kinds of 'human nature' are revealed in the conduct and character we observe in this society in this period? And what is the meaning for 'human nature' of each and every feature of the society we are examining?

Whether the point of interest is a great power state or a minor literary mood, a family, a prison, a creed—these are the kinds of questions the best social analysts have asked. They are the intellectual pivots of classic studies of man in society—and they are the questions inevitably raised by any mind possessing the sociological imagination. For that imagination is the capacity to shift from one perspective to another—from the political to the psychological; from examination of a single family to comparative assessment of the national budgets of the world, from the theological school to the military establishment, from considerations of an oil industry to studies of contemporary poetry. It is the capacity to range from the most impersonal and remote transformations to the most intimate features of the human self—and to see the relations between the two. Back of its use there is always the urge to know the social and historical meaning of the individual in the society and in the period in which he has his quality and his being.

That, in brief, is why it is by means of the sociological imagination that men now hope to grasp what is going on in the world, and to understand what is happening in themselves as minute points of the intersections of biography and history within society. In large part, contemporary man's self-conscious view of himself as at least an outsider, if not a permanent stranger, rests upon an absorbed realization of social relativity and of the transformative power of history. The sociological imagination is the most fruitful form of this self-consciousness. By its use men whose mentalities have swept only a series of limited orbits often come to feel as if suddenly awakened in a house with which they had only supposed themselves to be familiar. Correctly or incorrectly, they often come to feel that they can now provide themselves with adequate summations, cohesive assessments, comprehensive orientations. Older decisions that once appeared sound now seem to them products of a mind unaccountably dense. Their capacity for astonishment is made lively again. They acquire a new way of thinking, they experience a transvaluation of values: in a word, by their reflection and by their sensibility, they realize the cultural meaning of the social sciences.

Perhaps the most fruitful distinction with which the sociological imagination works is between 'the personal troubles of milieu' and 'the public issues of social structure.' This distinction is an essential tool of the sociological imagination and a feature of all classic work in social science.

Troubles occur within the character of the individual and within the range of his immediate relations with others; they have to do with his self and with those limited areas of social life of which he is directly and personally aware. Accordingly, the statement and the resolution of troubles properly lie within the individual as a biographical entity and within the scope of his immediate milieu—the social setting that is directly open to his personal experience and to some extent his willful activity. A trouble is a private matter: values cherished by an individual are felt by him to be threatened.

Issues have to do with matters that transcend these local environments of the individual and the range of his inner life. They have to do with the organization of many such milieux into the institutions of an historical society as a whole, with the ways in which various milieux overlap and interpenetrate to form the larger structure of social and historical life. An issue is a public matter: some value cherished by publics is felt to be threatened. Often there is a debate about what that value really is and about what it is that really threatens it. This debate is often without focus if only because it is the very nature of an issue, unlike even widespread trouble, that it cannot very well be defined in terms of the immediate and everyday environments of ordinary men....

In these terms, consider unemployment. When, in a city of 100,000, only one man is unemployed, that is his personal trouble, and for its relief we properly look to the character of the man, his skills, and his immediate opportunities. But when in a nation of 50 million employees, 15 million men are unemployed, that is an issue, and we may not hope to find its solution within the range of opportunities open to any one individual. The very structure of opportunities has collapsed. Both the correct statement of the problem and the range of possible solutions require us to consider the economic and political institutions of the society, and not merely the personal situation and character of a scatter of individuals.

Consider war. The personal problem of war, when it occurs, may be how to survive it or how to die in it with honor; how to make money out of it; how to climb into the higher safety of the military apparatus; or how to contribute to the war's termination. In short, according to one's values, to find a set of milieux and within it to survive the war or make one's death in it meaningful. But the structural issues of war have to do with its causes; with what types of men it throws up into command; with its effects upon economic and political, family and religious institutions, with the unorganized irresponsibility of a world of nation-states.

Consider marriage. Inside a marriage a man and a woman may experience personal troubles, but when the divorce rate during the first four years of marriage is 250 out of every 1,000 attempts, this is an indication of a structural issue having to do with the institutions of marriage and the family and other institutions that bear upon them.

Or consider the metropolis—the horrible, beautiful, ugly, magnificent sprawl of the great city. For many upper-class people, the personal solution to 'the problem of the city' is to have an apartment with private garage under it in the heart of the city and forty miles out, a house . . . on a hundred acres of private land. In these two controlled environments—with a small staff at each end and a private helicopter connection—most people could solve many of the problems of personal milieux caused by the facts of the city. But all this, however splendid, does not solve the public issues that the structural fact of the city poses. What should be done with this wonderful monstrosity? Break it all up into scattered units, combining residence and work? Refurbish it as it stands? Or, after evacuation, dynamite it and build new cities according to new plans in new places? What should those plans be? And who is to decide and to accomplish whatever choice is made? These are structural issues; to confront them and to solve them requires us to consider political and economic issues that affect innumerable milieux.

In so far as an economy is so arranged that slumps occur, the problem of unemployment becomes incapable of personal solution. In so far as war is inherent in the nation-state system and in the uneven industrialization of the world, the ordinary individual in his restricted milieu will be powerless—with or without psychiatric aid—to solve the troubles this system or lack of system imposes upon him. In so far as the family as an institution turns women into darling little slaves and men into their chief providers and unweaned dependents, the problem of a satisfactory marriage remains incapable of purely private solution. In so far as the overdeveloped megalopolis and the overdeveloped automobile are built-in features of the overdeveloped society, the issues of urban living will not be solved by personal ingenuity and private wealth.

What we experience in various and specific milieux, I have noted, is often caused by structural changes. Accordingly, to understand the changes of many personal milieux we are required to look beyond them. And the number and variety of such structural changes increase as the institutions within which we live become more embracing and more intricately connected with one another. To be aware of the idea of social structure and to use it with sensibility is to be capable of tracing such linkages among a great variety of milieux. To be able to do that is to possess the sociological imagination.

Fractals, Theories, and Patterns

(2007)

SALLY RASKOFF

Have you ever seen fractals? They are designs that show large patterns made up of smaller and smaller versions of that large pattern. They are discussed in mathematics, physics, and other fields where they notice large patterns consisting of the same pattern but in smaller units.

I recently came upon a book, *Heaven & Earth*,[1] which illustrates commonalities between those large and tiny structures through photos taken of tiny or microscopic items. The book progresses to photos of earth's features from aircraft, satellites, and space. I was struck by how those different realms present seemingly identical images. It's intriguing to think that the small writ large is a pattern that also applies to human phenomena.

Most sociological theorists are either micro or macro—they focus either on individual or small group phenomena or entire societies, nation-states, or global phenomena. Herbert Blumer and others who created symbolic interactionist theories focus on how human actions create meanings and how those meanings are modified through people's interpretations and guide people's actions. Although symbolic interactionist theorists note that humans create society by their actions, they often focus on individual actions and meanings rather than on those of society as a whole.

Some recent theorists, such as advocates of postmodern theory, suggest that the disconnect between individuals and society might even be a false concept—because they see "society" as a false concept. They propose that society might be seen so differently by each individual that society is not a reality outside one's own perspective. It is only the individual who might "exist" and society differs for each person based on his or her unique experience and perception.

Rarely does one theorist apply their theories to both types of study. When they do, sometimes they go miserably off the road to understanding.

Émile Durkheim, for example, does a brilliant job of studying societal patterns in *Suicide*.[2] He illustrates how suicide is not necessarily an individual issue—instead, various societies and communities have different rates of suicide because of varying types of social integration and moral regulation. However when he

1. Malin, D., & Roucoux, K. (2007). *Heaven & Earth: Unseen by the Naked Eye*. London: Phaidon. [*Editor's note*]
2. (1897). Bibliothèque de philosophie contemporaine. [*Editor's note*]

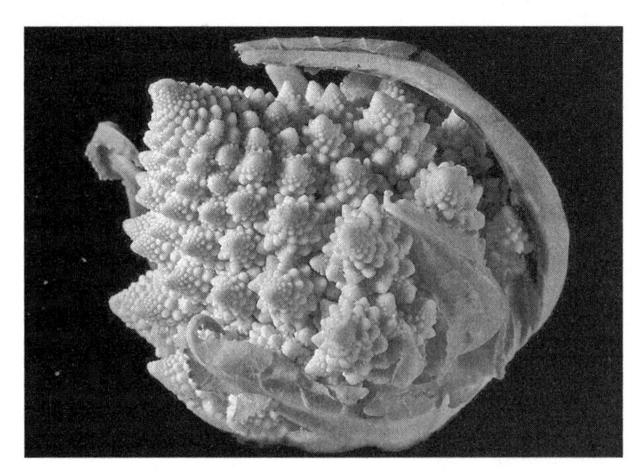

Photograph of broccoli fractal.

also explains four distinct types of suicide and uses individualistic examples for each of them, he loses some explanatory power.

For example, he deals with gender differences in suicide rates by discussing how single men have higher rates than married men and married women have higher rates than single women. He continues to explain that when comparing widows and widowers, "woman can endure life in isolation more easily than man" and that society is "less necessary to [a woman] because she is less impregnated with sociability."[3]

These conclusions are not only incredibly sexist, they also commit an ecological fallacy. This is when one explains individual behaviors with aggregate data (from societies or communities, in essence large groups). One is using one level of analysis (individuals) but uses data gathered from another level of analysis (groups or societies). This is a methodological problem and has an impact upon the theory guiding research.

On the other hand, the social theorist Max Weber created theories that included all levels of analysis. He did not try to apply the same theories to all of those levels. His book *The Protestant Ethic and the Spirit of Capitalism* [1904–5] came from his studies on how religious ethics and economic systems interact. Class, status, and party rest within social groups and help explain the dynamics of power.

His insistence on *verstehen*, or understanding, links the individual and society and suggests that sociologists must understand the meaning that individuals give to social phenomena before they (the researchers) can truly understand those phenomena.

3. Translations are from Spaulding, J. A., trans. (1997). *Suicide: A Study in Sociology*. New York: Free Press.

Taking into account both the contributions and challenges that sociological theorists offer us, fractals may explain natural phenomena but may not be applicable to human research. Social phenomena may be so complex that the sum of the parts are much more than the whole, that human interactions and meanings are building blocks but also create whole new structures that we call society.

Matching Research Methods to Research Questions

(2007)

JANIS PRINCE INNISS

Dr. James Watson, the seventy-nine-year-old American scientist credited with co-discovering the DNA double helix, recently told a reporter that black people are naturally less intelligent than whites, and that although he would like to think we all have the same abilities, "people who have to deal with black employees find this is not true."

At the very least, Watson seems to have a penchant for making outrageous statements, but I refer to him not to discuss the obvious. Instead, I want to focus on the *data* on which he based his headline-grabbing conclusion. Or put another way, how could we attempt to compare intelligence levels of blacks and whites? What would be some reasonable sources of data from which one could conclude that black people are "naturally" less intelligent than whites?

First, we would have to define the two groups of people: whites and blacks. What criteria would we use to define blacks? And whites? Would we apply the "one-drop rule"? Would we use people's self-definitions?

Would we, as researchers, assign people to one of the two groups based on appearance? What if someone "looked" white or self-identified as white, but had a black parent or grandparent? And given that the comparison is of blacks and whites, with no mention of country, we would have to include people from around the world in our study; this can be quite complicated, as conceptions of race vary significantly in different parts of the world. And assuming we could come up with acceptable definitions in any one country, we would have to use these definitions all across the world in order to have common definitions for the study—regardless of how alien they are to others.

Let's say that we managed to come up with a fairly precise definition of blacks and whites that would work in the real world, all over the world. What would be the next step? What research method would we use to answer this empirical question?

If we chose to conduct an ethnography (and do a good job), we could produce rich data, but of what nature? Ethnography includes interviews and participant observation; we could interview people and get their opinions and thoughts about the intelligence levels of blacks and whites. Fascinating as this might be, it would not answer our research question. We could observe blacks and whites and opine about their intelligence, but any conclusions would not address the central question posed by our research. Further, our observations will likely be biased by any preconceived notions we may have, and we might notice examples that justify our beliefs more than those that do not.

Besides ethnography, we could develop a questionnaire to measure intelligence or use an existing IQ (intelligence quotient) test and mail them out to people and/or administer them ourselves. Clearly, administering or mailing the questionnaire to every black and white person in the world, or even in the United States, is an impractical task.

Therefore, we would have to focus on a sample or a fraction of the world's population of blacks and whites. Once the sample is carefully chosen, we could feel confident that it represents and applies to the entire population. In our case, *every* black and white person in the world should have an equal possibility of being involved in our study; then, we would randomly choose our sample.

As an illustration, in order to conduct a study with a random sample of college students at your university, we would obtain a list of all students and then, for example, include every tenth name in the sample. Once we had figured out how to obtain a random sample of the world's population of blacks and whites, we would administer our IQ test to the sample. Managing the cost, resources, and other logistics for a survey of this magnitude is not a responsibility I would sign up for, but I suppose it could be done.

I have devoted more time discussing the definition of black and white, which might suggest that defining intelligence is easy; it is not. What is intelligence? What *kind* of intelligence would we measure? Emotional? Spatial? Conceptual? Mathematical? All of the above and more?

If you are familiar with some of the criticisms of IQ tests, you would have raised an eyebrow at their earliest mention. How would we account for differences in access to formal education, for example, given that less formal education results in lower IQ test scores? How would we sort out social and cultural factors that related to scores?

It is shocking to me that a scientist, a Nobel Laureate, would mention the experiences of unspecified "people" as a source of data regarding anything, including his claim that black people are less intelligent than whites. The claim implies a biological difference between the races and fundamentally would require an ability to differentiate between blacks and whites in some absolute manner; this is difficult to do when race is a socially constructed concept with no biological basis.

I wonder which "people" Watson was referring to. How does he know what "people" believe or think? Did he interview some people about this question? How many such people did he interview? Good, in-depth interviews provide a deep understanding of behavior or beliefs, but no evidence regarding a biologically-based difference between races. Did he send questionnaires to a random sample of "people"? Surveys could provide the opinions of a large number of people, but not some "truth" about blacks and whites. What rigorous research method was Watson employing?

Even a fledgling scientist recognizes that research is a *process*, and that matching the research method to the research question is critical. Sadly, when such a highly regarded scientist makes outrageous claims, those with little understanding of the scientific method (and more than a little prejudice) just might believe that he is right.

Related Links

Article about James Watson:
www.cnn.com/2007/TECH/science/10/18/science.race/index.html
Other statements by Watson:
www.sptimes.com/2007/10/19/Worldandnation/Scientific_icon_sets_.shtml
Related post: nortonbooks.typepad.com/everydaysociology/2007/09/black-and-white.html

Where to Sit

Doing Qualitative Research (2008)

BRADLEY WRIGHT

One of the fun things to do in sociology is to make empirical generalizations. Sometimes in research we start with an idea or a theory, make a hypothesis, and then collect data to test if our idea is correct. This is deductive research, going from large (abstract idea) to small (collecting data about specific people or situations). Deductive research can be very interesting, because we learn if our ideas hold up in the real world, but I don't think that it's as fun as inductive research (and as I am aging—about a year annually—I am placing more weight on research being fun).

Sometimes when we enter a situation, even if we don't know anything about it, we start noticing things. We notice if there are patterns to people's behavior. From these patterns, we create larger explanations about how the social world works. This is inductive because we start with the smaller observation, and from it we build explanations about the larger social world.

Here's a simple example of how to create empirical generalizations. In my social research methods class, I asked my students why they sat where they did. It was a reasonable question because the class itself has about 100 chairs, but there are only 50 students, so they had some choice in where they sat.

After talking for about it for about 10 minutes, we came up with the following ways that students decided where to sit.

1. Look for a friend. When you walk into the classroom, first look for someone that you know reasonably well and feel positively toward and sit next to them if there's an available seat nearby. Or, if you're really close, see if they'll move so that you can sit next to them. Don't sit next to them if you know them well but feel negatively toward them (e.g., an enemy). Also, don't sit next to them, at least too conspicuously, if you feel positively but don't know them (e.g., you're attracted to a stranger).

2. Figure out how close to the front of the room you like to be. If you're right up front, you catch everything that is going on, but it does make it difficult to sleep, text message, or talk with your friends. If you want to goof around a bit, maybe sit in the back.

3. Find a comfortable seat. Classroom seating is usually pretty tight, with the seats being crammed together—just like economy seating on an airplane. The best seats are those on the aisle. Once class starts, students in the aisle seats can stretch out their legs more than those in the interior seats. The first students to arrive in the class tend to take the aisle seats, and as a result the students arriving later have to step past them to get to the middle seats.
4. Keep an empty seat between you and others (unless you know them). When at all possible, pick a seat that has empty seats on both sides. Seating directly next to someone invades their personal space, and it gives you less room as well.
5. Sit in same area each time. Once you find a suitable seat, try to sit in it, or near it, every class period. This way you get the best seat for you each time, and you don't really have to think about it. Of course, you may have to change if someone is sitting too close to that seat.

We came up with some other factors that might be incorporated, such as left-handed desks for left-handed students and not sitting directly behind people, especially if they are tall, but the five criteria listed above represented the main decisions made by the students.

Because students follow these criteria, when I as a professor look out on a classroom, I see alternate seating with only friends sitting next to each other. The aisle seats are always taken. Also, since students tend to sit in the same area each time, I learn to recognize them in part by where they sit. In fact, on test days, when I assign random seating, I have trouble recognizing all of my students.

These seating rules are strong enough that they represent social norms, and it can be considered deviant to violate them. For example, if you have friends in a class, but you go sit by yourself, they would probably be upset. Likewise, if there are plenty of empty seats but you pick one right next to someone, they may take offense.

Obviously where to sit in classrooms is a relatively minor issue in the grand scheme of things. Still, it represents a highly structured social interaction, demonstrating the reach of social norms into every aspect of our lives.

Scary Numbers

(2004)

JOEL BEST

A series of recent polls asked American adults to estimate the percentage of children without health insurance and to describe recent trends in the teenage crime rate, the teenage birth rate, and the percentage of children raised in single-parent families.[1] A clear pattern emerged: on each of these issues, large majorities—between 74 and 93 percent of the respondents—judged that the problems were worse than they actually were. For example, 76 percent responded that the percentage of children living in single-parent families had increased during the previous five years. In fact, the percentage had not changed. Some 66 percent responded that the percentage of teens committing violent crimes had increased during the previous ten years, and another 25 percent said that the percentage had remained about the same; but there had actually been a decrease. What accounts for this tendency to imagine that things are worse than they are?

Because statistics can be confusing, they make most of us a little anxious. In addition, many of the numbers we encounter are intended, if not to scare us, at least to make us anxious about our world. Of course, most of what counts as newsworthy is bad news; our local "happy news" broadcast may end with a forty-five-second piece about a skydiving grandmother, but the lead story often features a reporter at the scene of a fatal convenience store robbery. The same pattern holds for statistics: in general, disturbing, scary statistics get more news coverage than numbers reporting good news or progress. It's no wonder we tend to exaggerate the scope of social problems. We're used to a fairly steady stream of statistics telling us what's wrong, warning that things are much worse than we might imagine.

This tendency to highlight scary numbers reflects the way social problems become noticed in our society. Advocates seeking to draw attention to a social problem must compete with other causes for the notice of the press, politicians, and the public. Amid a cacophony of competing claims, advocates must make the case that their particular problem merits concern. Their claims tend to hit familiar notes: the problem is widespread; it has severe consequences; its victims are vulnerable and need protection; everyone is a prospective victim; the problem is getting worse. Evidence to support these claims often comes from coupling troubling examples with statistics. Advocates seeking to raise concern naturally find it advantageous to accentuate the negative; therefore, they prefer scary statistics that portray the problem as very common or very serious.

But advocates aren't the only ones favoring frightening figures. The media comb the most routine statistical reports, such as the release of census figures, for their most newsworthy—usually understood to mean the most troubling—elements. Even scientists and officials may find that emphasizing scary numbers makes their work seem more important.

DESCRIBING SOCIAL PROBLEMS IN SCARY TERMS

When advocates describe a social problem, the statistic we're most likely to hear is probably some sort of estimate of the problem's size—the number of cases or the number of people affected, for example. Large numbers support claims that the problem is common and therefore serious. Other statistics, such as the number or percentage of people victimized, convey a sense of risk; they offer a rough estimate for the likelihood that the problem will threaten you or someone you love. These figures foster a sense of our vulnerability. Still other statistics, such as rates of growth, project the problem into the future, leading us to believe that what is now bad is likely to become much worse.

Such statistics are most compelling when they portray the world in especially frightening terms. The more widespread the perceived harm and suffering, the more likely it seems that the problem will impinge on our world; and the greater the prospects for things getting worse, the greater our fear. This fear, in turn, makes the advocates' claims seem more compelling and therefore more likely to influence us. Whereas earlier generations of reformers spoke of society's moral obligation to aid its most vulnerable and most wretched members, contemporary claims often encourage people to act out of self-interest. We democratize risk by warning that a problem can touch anyone. . . . If a threat seems to endanger everyone, then we all have a vested interest in doing something about the problem. It is telling that modern persuasion so often invokes self-interest rather than concern for others.

Even when a problem does not appear to pose a direct, immediate threat, it is possible to paint a picture of a future when things will be much worse. Trends are a way of spotting troubling patterns; even if things aren't bad now, we may see signs that they are deteriorating. Of course, the most frightening trends are those that seem to lead inevitably toward catastrophe. Statistical estimates for future social problems are hard to contradict; aside from waiting to see how things turn out, it is difficult to debunk a doomsday scenario. Still, a glance at the recent history of prognostication reveals how cloudy experts' visions of the future can be. The popular magazines of my boyhood predicted that the world of 2000 would feature commuters traveling to work in atomic-powered cars and personal helicopters, yet they made no mention of personal computers. The track record of advocates envisioning the future of social problems is not much better: just recall those Y2K forecasts of the widespread social collapse that would follow the simultaneous failure of the world's computer systems as the calendar shifted from 1999 to 2000.

A tension exists, then, between advocates' need for compelling rhetoric—claims that can move others to address some social problem—and the limitations of the available evidence. Commonly, this is resolved by ignoring those limitations in favor of presenting the most powerful message. For activists, who believe firmly that their cause is right and who may well consider the numbers perfectly reasonable, scary statistics have obvious appeal. For the media, scary numbers seem newsworthy, the stuff of good stories. Such numbers thus encounter remarkably little resistance. . . .

Measuring a Problem's Size

The simplest sort of scary number estimates the size of a social problem—the number of people involved, for example, or the cost in dollars. This seems straightforward: we have all counted things, so we naturally presume that someone must have counted something to come up with these numbers. If someone's count has produced a big number, we tend to assume that there must be a big problem.

But social problems are notoriously tricky to count. Cases may be hard to identify, and it may be difficult to define and measure whatever is being counted. Take recent heavily publicized claims that preventable medical errors kill between forty-four thousand and ninety-eight thousand U.S. hospital patients each year. These are remarkably scary numbers, both because they seem large and because we go to hospitals in the hope of preserving our lives, not ending them. But what, exactly, are medical errors that kill—and how might we identify them and count them? The fact that we are given a fairly wide range of numbers for the death toll reveals that these numbers are estimates, not precise counts. So how did people arrive at these figures?

The answer is a little complicated. These particular estimates were derived from two studies of hospital discharges that reviewed patients' records to identify "adverse events" (injuries caused by medical mistakes); the researchers concluded that about 3 to 4 percent of patients experienced such injuries. However, neither study measured the percentage of adverse events that were preventable or the percentage of preventable adverse events that led to death—both of these figures were later estimated by people who reinterpreted the data from the original studies.[2] These later estimates of deaths, not the original research on adverse events, were the statistics that attracted public attention, despite critics who argued that the basis for those estimates was not made clear.

In addition, the original studies did not consider the overall health of each patient. One later study adopted a more refined analysis that did consider this factor. The results of this research remind us that hospital patients are, after all, often very ill. Imagine a patient who is already seriously ill, who is not expected to live more than a few days. A medical error—even a "preventable adverse event"—might be the immediate cause of that patient's death; in fact, the precarious health of such patients makes them particularly vulnerable to the effects of medical mistakes. But such cases are not likely to be chosen to exemplify the danger of medical mistakes. Advocates and the media favor more melodramatic examples, pointing to patients who, prior to the adverse event, had long life expectancies—for example, a high school athlete whose surgery for a minor injury led to severe brain damage.[3] The study that took into account the overall health of each patient suggested that "optimal [that is, mistake-free] care . . . would result in roughly 1 additional patient of every 10,000 admissions living 3 months or more in good cognitive health."[4] In other words, these researchers argued, medical errors rarely kill patients with good life expectancies.

The point of this example is not to argue that hospitals don't make fatal errors—surely they do. Nor do I mean to dismiss some studies and endorse others. The point is that measures of a problem's size may not be nearly as straightforward as they seem. This example illustrates how tricky it can be to measure what might appear, at first glance, to be an unambiguous phenomenon—patients killed by medical errors. . . .

◇ ◇ ◇

RISKS

Risk statistics have become one of the most common types of scary numbers. We talk about "increased risk," "risk factors," or being "at risk." The watershed in our understanding of risk may have been the 1960s, a decade that included such landmark events as the release of the 1964 surgeon general's report on tobacco and health. While critics had long warned that smoking damaged health, the tobacco industry had insisted that no convincing evidence made this causal link. The surgeon general's report had great impact precisely because it seemed authoritative (although few Americans could have explained in any detail how the surgeon general had drawn the conclusions in the report) and because it claimed to offer a comprehensive overview of a large body of evidence that led to one conclusion: overall, smoking increased one's risk of contracting various diseases.

Many of the trappings of modern life—seat belts; automobile air bags; bicycle helmets; foods produced without fat, caffeine, or pesticides; smoke-free restaurants and workplaces; safe sex; daily baby aspirins; assorted medical check-ups—reflect our current understanding of, and efforts to minimize, various risks. There is a comic quality to some of this, as we try to adjust our lives to the latest news story about the latest study. Is drinking bad for your health, or is a daily drink beneficial, or is it just red wine that's good for you? (Personally, I'm clinging to the notion that dark chocolate prolongs life, and if you have convincing evidence to the contrary, I don't want to hear it.)

When we try to translate these words into numbers, we enter the realm of probability. A risk is the chance, the probability, that something might occur. Thus, when we say that smokers have a higher risk of developing lung cancer, we are not saying that every smoker will develop lung cancer, nor are we saying that no nonsmoker will develop the disease. Rather, the notion of increased risk implies comparing probabilities; if X of every 1,000 nonsmokers eventually develop lung cancer, and if smokers develop the disease at a higher rate, then the number of lung cancer cases per 1,000 smokers should be markedly higher than X. The idea seems simple, but the numbers quickly lead to confusion.

Probability is not well understood. (This explains why casinos flourish.) We tend to recognize patterns and assume that they are meaningful. If we flip a fair coin four times and get four straight heads, some people assume that the next flip will be tails (because this outcome is somehow "overdue"), while others assume that it will be heads (because there is a "streak" going). A mathematician would say that both assumptions are wrong because each coin flip is independent of the others; that is, what happens on the next flip is not influenced by what happened on the previous flip. After four straight heads, the odds of heads on the fifth flip remain fifty-fifty. Should we get a fifth consecutive heads, the odds of heads on the sixth flip are still fifty-fifty. If we flip a coin a total of six times, we have sixty-four possible sequences of results. Six consecutive heads (HHHHHH) is one of those results; HTHTHT is another. We tend to notice the former and consider it remarkable, while the latter seems routine, but the odds of getting either pattern are exactly the same: one in sixty-four. This is not to say that the odds of getting six heads are the same as the odds of getting three heads and three tails; twenty of the sixty-four possible sequences involve three heads and three tails (HHHTTT, HHTHTT, and so on), whereas only one of the sixty-four sequences involves six heads. But any particular sequence is equally likely to occur, and the fact that some sequences seem to form recognizable patterns does not make them any more or less likely to occur.

Once we realize this, we can understand that all sorts of apparently unusual combinations—the sorts of things we might consider remarkable coincidences—can be expected to occur on occasion. If about 10 percent of people are left-handed, then the odds that the next person we see will be left-handed are one in ten (or .1), the odds are one in a hundred that the next two people will both be left-handed ($.1 \times .1 = .01$), and one in a thousand that the next three people will be lefties ($.1 \times .1 \times .1 = .001$). Despite these odds, if we meet lots of people, we will occasionally run into two or even three consecutive left-handers. Even rare things can be expected to happen—it's just that they will happen rarely.

Converting these principles into statistics—risk calculations—routinely leads to confusion. . . .

◇ ◇ ◇

It also helps to put risks in some larger context. Every time we get in a car and drive to work, we take a risk. We all understand that traffic accidents kill people. To some degree, we can minimize our risk by obeying the traffic laws and wearing our seat belts, but the risk never becomes zero, although the chance of being killed on any particular journey is very low. Still, such routine risks—the sorts of things we take for granted—may be far greater than the highly publicized risks that suddenly become the focus of public attention. When we are frightened, we tend to focus on what scares us rather than on the actual risk of our being affected, a reaction that has been termed "probability neglect."[5]

We can see a good example of this in the public's alarmed reaction to the news that a sniper was killing people in the region around Washington, D.C., during the fall of 2002. Because our ordinary, day-to-day assumption is that the risk of being shot by a sniper is zero, the news that some risk existed frightened people. Still, in a region containing millions of people, the risk of being shot remained very low. Even during the weeks when individuals died at the hands of the sniper, people were at much greater risk of dying in traffic accidents in greater Washington—yet traffic deaths were not headline news. Following the mundane advice we've heard all our lives—don't smoke, wear seat belts, eat sensibly, and exercise—is likely to increase our life expectancies far more than ducking to keep out of a sniper's sights or avoiding that food additive that figures so prominently in this week's headlines.

The Risk of Divorce

Another reason that the notion of risk leads to confusion is that we're not always sure how best to calculate risks. Consider an apparently simple question that turns out to be somewhat complicated: what proportion of marriages end in divorce? No official agency keeps track of particular marriages and is therefore able to identify precisely which ones end in divorce—which is the sort of information one would like to have to answer this question. Lacking complete and perfect data, analysts are forced to use the numbers that are available. Since filing a marriage license and obtaining a divorce are both legal steps, official agencies do keep records of these events, and various jurisdictions tally the marriages and divorces they record. Therefore, analysts have long divided the number of divorces during a particular year by the number of marriages during that year to get a rough measure of the likelihood of marriage ending in divorce. Since roughly 1960, the number of divorces has been nearly half that of marriages, and commentators often refer to this as the "divorce rate."

The problem is that when we speak of a rate, we are usually dividing some number of events (such as deaths or crimes) by the population at risk. Thus, both death rates and crime rates are usually presented as the number per 100,000 people in the population; for example, the FBI reported that the murder rate was 5.5 murders for every 100,000 people in the United States in 2000. But who makes up the population at risk when we try to calculate a divorce rate? Obviously, it does not include only those who married during the same year; in fact, we know that relatively few couples get divorced during the calendar year in which they marry. Rather, the population at risk is all married couples—a very large number indeed. If we calculate the rate of divorce by dividing the number of divorces during a particular year by the total number of married couples, regardless of the length of their marriages, then the divorce rate must be far less than 50 percent. All manner of commentators have made this point, insisting that marriage is therefore a more stable institution and divorce is less common than we might have imagined.

But let's examine this assertion. Imagine a community that records two marriages each year—and one of those new marriages ends in divorce during that same year. In this case, it is true that half of all new marriages end in divorce; yet it is also true that, with each passing year, the total number of married couples will grow by one. Thus, after the first year, dividing the current year's lone divorce by the total number of married couples will produce a rate lower than 50 percent in spite of the fact that half of marriages end in divorce. This reasoning suggests that the standard critique used to dismiss high divorce rate statistics must be flawed.

Clearly, measuring the risk of divorce is a tricky problem, one that requires both careful thought and, it turns out, a lot of data. In 1996, investigators interviewed a very large sample, nearly seventy thousand people at least fifteen years old, living in some thirty-seven thousand households. The respondents were asked about all marriages and divorces in their personal histories. For instance, one person might report marrying once, forty years earlier, and remaining married to the same spouse; whereas another respondent, currently unmarried, might report marriages in 1970 and 1985 that ended in 1980 and 1992, respectively.[6] These data allowed the investigators to identify cohorts of marriages that had occurred during different periods (for example, first marriages that took place in 1945–1949) and to calculate the proportion of marriages in each cohort that had ended in divorce by 1996. (It is always possible that a couple still married at the time of the interview could later decide to divorce.) Although these data are not complete, because they come from a sample rather than from the population as a whole, the sample is a good one—about as good as samples get—and the data give a glimpse of what happens to particular marriages over time (which was, remember, the sort of data we wished for at the beginning of this discussion).

Alas, these data suggest that about half of current marriages can be expected to end in divorce. The researchers found important cohort differences that reveal how society has changed; basically, people in each cohort were likely to have remained married longer than those in the cohort that followed. Thus, only about 34 percent of sixty-year-old men had had their first marriage end in divorce, but the comparable figure for fifty-year-old men was 40 percent. Of the women who first married during 1945–1949, 70 percent were still married thirty years later; but among those whose first marriage occurred during 1960–1964, only 55 percent (just over half!) remained married. It is too soon to tell what proportion of couples first married during 1980–1985 will celebrate their thirtieth anniversaries, but we can make projections based on the record so far: only 73 percent of the women who wed during those years were still married ten years later, compared to the 90 percent of those first married in 1945–1949 whose marriages lasted at least ten years. Based on these data, the investigators projected that, while a larger proportion of earlier marriages remained intact, about half of recent marriages will indeed end in divorce.

Thus, answering an apparently simple question—what is the likelihood that a marriage will end in divorce?—turns out to be a fairly complicated matter. But this sort of complexity is glossed over in media reports that glibly report on the risk of this or that—an observation that should give us pause. It is all too easy to be frightened by risk statistics. We need to keep in mind the difficulties of calculating risks as we digest today's warning about a newly discovered threat.

Notes

1. Lina Guzman, Laura Lippman, Kristin Anderson Moore, and William O'Hare, "How Children Are Doing: The Mismatch Between Public Perception and Statistical Reality," *Child Trends Research Brief* (July 2003).
2. On the history of this issue, see Harold C. Sox Jr. and Steven Woloshin, "How Many Deaths Are Due to Medical Error? Getting the Number Right," *Effective Clinical Practice* 3 (2000): 277–282.
3. Warren Wolfe, "Reporting Hospital Errors Seen as Good Idea," *Minneapolis Star Tribune*, December 1, 1999, p. 3B. After citing the estimates of forty-four thousand to ninety-eight thousand annual deaths, this article notes that "medical accidents caused or contributed to 26 deaths in Minnesota hospitals between 1994 and 1997" but does not address the gulf between the very large national estimates and that state's vastly smaller number of deaths attributed to errors.
4. Rodney A. Hayward and Timothy P. Hofer, "Estimating Hospital Deaths Due to Medical Errors," *Journal of the American Medical Association* 286 (July 25, 2001): 418. This study was based on patients at veterans' hospitals, who may be older than—or otherwise differ from—patients in other hospitals.
5. Cass R. Sunstein, "Probability Neglect: Emotions, Worst Cases, and Law," *Yale Law Journal* 112 (2002): 61–107.
6. Rose M. Kreider and Jason M. Fields, "Number, Timing, and Duration of Marriages and Divorces, 1996," Bureau of the Census, *Current Population Reports*, P70–80 (Washington, D.C., February 2002). For a study based on a different sample that reaches similar conclusions, see Matthew D. Bramlett and William D. Mosher, "First Marriage Dissolution, Divorce, and Remarriage: United States," *Advance Data from Vital and Health Statistics* 323 (May 31, 2001).

TALK ABOUT IT

1. How would you describe what it means to have a sociological imagination?
2. Discuss how your generation might be affected by current national or global events.
3. Are there any "scary statistics" you hear frequently that you suspect are overstated? Do any claims seem mismatched with the information on which they are based?
4. Construct your own theory on what shapes social forces.
5. What challenges might make answering sociological questions difficult? How would you approach studying sociological issues to best answer your questions?

WRITE ABOUT IT

1. Why do some people misuse statistics? How and why is misinformation sometimes easily taken to be true?
2. Describe the intersection between your biography and history. What sociological factors have shaped your life so far? What factors have shaped your parents' lives?
3. Where do people sit in your sociology class? Is there a persistent pattern? If so, hypothesize why people sit where they do.
4. Discuss your reaction to Prince Inniss's article on a renowned scientist making generalizations about race. What can the sociological imagination teach us about this incident?
5. What sociological patterns have you observed since becoming a college student? Based on these patterns, propose a theory to explain why they occur.
6. Mills describes the difference between private troubles and public issues. Choose examples of each and discuss how each represents a trouble or public issue.

DO IT

1. Interview family members about historical events that happened during their lives, such as a war or the Great Depression. How do they say this event affected their experiences and shaped their life decisions? Analyze how this incident might have affected them and others of their generation.
2. Look in the newspaper or in a magazine for a fear-inducing story that uses statistics. Next, look up the original source of the statistics. Does the word choice and tone of the story alter the meaning of the data from the original source? Can you identify any exaggerations?

3. Find a picture or illustration like the one in Raskoff's article about fractals. How does this picture reflect a sociological pattern you have read about or identified? Draw your own illustration of a social pattern.
4. Conduct a study based on a pattern you have noticed in one of your classes, such as where people sit. Interview your classmates about your observation. How do they explain this pattern?
5. Think about a sociological question like the one Prince Inniss explores in her article. What would be the best method to answer this question? What limitations would your results have? What kinds of conclusions could you draw? What kinds of conclusions could you *not* make based on your data?

2

Culture, Consumption, and Media

Module Goal: ***Understand the contemporary meanings of culture, consumption, and the role of various media in everyday life.***

Culture encompasses our beliefs, practices, and traditions. This very broad concept is vital to understanding society. Sometimes our cultural practices are rooted in our family backgrounds or ethnic heritage, and some of our cultural practices are based on our social class or our age. This module represents a small cross section of examples of the importance of culture in everyday life.

The selections here mostly represent examples of *material* culture—the physical forms of our culture. Material culture includes products we buy, such as clothing, cars, and electronic technology. In the twenty-first century, we have seen an explosion of new forms of material culture, from iPods to smart phones to GPS devices. We can we learn a great deal about society by examining how and why we use these forms of culture, as well as the meanings we ascribe to them.

The multitude of new media products has led some contemporary critics to become concerned about *hyperconsumption*—purchasing products we cannot afford because we think they will make us happy or impress others. The term *consumption* has many interrelated meanings, from making a purchase and using a product to physically ingesting something and literally making it a part of our body. Consumption was once the common term for tuberculosis because the disease would ravage the body and patients could physically waste away. Some people fear that product consumption is like a disease taking over our culture.

Analyses of consumption date back more than a century. Thorstein Veblen wrote our first selection, "Conspicuous Consumption," an excerpt from his book *The Theory of the Leisure Class*, in 1899. As you read this selection, you should notice similarities between his nineteenth-century observations and your own in the twenty-first.

The next selection, Juliet Schor's "The Visible Lifestyle: American Symbols of Status," elaborates on the concept of *aspirational consumption.* Schor analyzes why many people choose to purchase expensive products with well-known labels in the quest to build their social status. Consumption may be personal, but it is also profoundly social. With the proliferation of unscripted television providing glimpses into the lives of the famous (and those in search of fame), wealth and consumption often take center stage. My essay "Reality Life" examines the contradictory nature of these shows; many of them both celebrate and denigrate their subjects.

All these displays of wealth and consumption don't mean that we consumers are simply brainwashed zombies. The next essay, "Beauty Myths and Magazines," explores how we don't need to let go of the pleasure of consumption in order to think critically about the products we buy or the media we consume.

While most Internet users don't believe everything they read online, the Internet has become a central information clearinghouse. As Janis Prince Inniss writes in "Marketing Ideas and Fears through Email: Pass Along Hoaxes and Urban Legends," the Internet enables "viral consumption" of information as people forward messages to one another. These messages often contain warnings to get our attention and sometimes try to sell us things, but as Prince Inniss notes, they can also be used to convey status to people we know, since we presumably have information they do not.

As you read about culture, consumption, and media in everyday life, keep the following questions in mind:

1. What motivates you to purchase and consume the items you buy? What do your consumption habits tell others about you?
2. How do the television programs or movies you have watched promote the consumption of expensive products? Do they also offer critiques of consumption?
3. What forwarded emails have you received recently? Sociologically speaking, what motivated the sender and the original creator of the message?

Conspicuous Consumption

(1899)

THORSTEIN VEBLEN

In what has been said of the evolution of the vicarious leisure class and its differentiation from the general body of the working classes, reference has been made to a further division of labor—that between different servant classes. One portion of the servant class, chiefly those persons whose occupation is vicarious leisure, come to undertake a new, subsidiary range of duties—the vicarious consumption of goods. The most obvious form in which this consumption occurs is seen in the wearing of liveries and the occupation of spacious servants' quarters. Another, scarcely less obtrusive or less effective form of vicarious consumption, and a much more widely prevalent one, is the consumption of food, clothing, dwelling, and furniture by the lady and the rest of the domestic establishment.

But already at a point in economic evolution far antedating the emergence of the lady, specialized consumption of goods as an evidence of pecuniary strength had begun to work out in a more or less elaborate system. The beginning of a differentiation in consumption even antedates the appearance of anything that can fairly be called pecuniary strength. It is traceable back to the initial phase of predatory culture, and there is even a suggestion that an incipient differentiation in this respect lies back of the beginnings of the predatory life. This most primitive differentiation in the consumption of goods is like the later differentiation with which we are all an intimately familiar, in that it is largely of a ceremonial character, but unlike the latter it does not rest on a difference in accumulated wealth. The utility of consumption as an evidence of wealth is to be classed as a derivative growth. It is an adaptation to a new end, by a selective process, of a distinction previously existing and well established in men's habits of thought.

In the earlier phases of the predatory culture the only economic differentiation is a broad distinction between an honorable superior class made up of the able-bodied men on the one side, and a base inferior class of laboring women on the other. According to the ideal scheme of life in force at that time it is the office of the men to consume what the women produce. Such consumption as falls to the women is merely incident to their work; it is a means to their continued labor, and not a consumption directed to their own comfort and fullness of life. Unproductive consumption of goods is honorable, primarily as a mark of prowess and a perquisite of human dignity; secondarily it becomes substantially honorable in itself, especially the consumption of the more desirable things. The consumption of choice articles of food, and frequently also of rare articles of adornment, becomes tabu to the women and children; and if there is a base (servile) class of men, the tabu holds also for them. . . .

The ceremonial differentiation of the dietary is best seen in the use of intoxicating beverages and narcotics. If these articles of consumption are costly, they are felt to be noble and honorific. Therefore the base classes . . . practice an enforced continence with respect to these stimulants, except in countries where they are obtainable at a very low cost. . . .

The consumption of luxuries, in the true sense, is a consumption directed to the comfort of the consumer himself, and is, therefore, a mark of the master. Any such consumption by others can take place only on a basis of sufferance. In communities where the popular habits of thought have been profoundly shaped by the patriarchal tradition we may accordingly look for survivals of the tabu on luxuries at least to the extent of a conventional deprecation of their use by the unfree and dependent class. This is more particularly true as regards certain luxuries, the use of which by the dependent class would detract sensibly from the comfort or pleasure of their masters, or which are held to be of doubtful legitimacy on other grounds. . . . With many qualifications—with more qualifications as the patriarchal tradition has gradually weakened—the general rule is felt to be right and binding that women should consume only for the benefit of their masters. The objection of course presents itself that expenditure on women's dress and household paraphernalia is an obvious exception to this rule; but it will appear in the sequel that this exception is much more obvious than substantial.

During the earlier stages of economic development, consumption of goods without stint, especially consumption of the better grades of goods—ideally all consumption in excess of the subsistence minimum—pertains normally to the leisure class. This restriction tends to disappear . . . with private ownership of goods and an industrial system based on wage labor or on the petty household economy. But during the earlier quasi-peaceable stage, when so many of the traditions through which the institution of a leisure class has affected the economic life of later times were taking form and consistency, this principle has had the force of a conventional law. It has served as the norm to which consumption has tended to conform, and any appreciable departure from it is to be regarded as an aberrant form, sure to be eliminated sooner or later in the further course of development.

The quasi-peaceable gentleman of leisure, then, not only consumes of the staff of life beyond the minimum required for subsistence and physical efficiency, but his consumption also undergoes a specialization as regards the quality of the goods consumed. He consumes freely and of the best, in food, drink, narcotics, shelter, services, ornaments, apparel, weapons and accoutrements, amusements, amulets, and idols or divinities. In the process of gradual amelioration which takes place in the articles of his consumption, the motive principle and the proximate aim of innovation is no doubt the higher efficiency of the improved and more elaborate products for personal comfort and well-being. But that does not remain the sole purpose of their consumption. The canon of reputability is at hand and seizes upon such innovations as are, according to its standard, fit to survive. Since the consumption of these more excellent goods is an evidence of wealth, it becomes honorific; and conversely, the failure to consume in due quantity and quality becomes a mark of inferiority and demerit.

This growth of . . . discrimination as to qualitative excellence in eating, drinking, etc., presently affects not only the manner of life, but also the training and intellectual activity of the gentleman of leisure. . . . In order to avoid stultification he must also cultivate his tastes, for it now becomes incumbent on him to discriminate with some nicety between the noble and the ignoble in consumable goods. He becomes a connoisseur in creditable viands of various degrees of merit, in manly beverages and trinkets, in seemly apparel and architecture, in weapons, games, dances, and the narcotics. This cultivation of the æsthetic faculty requires time and application, and the demands made upon the gentleman in this direction therefore tend to change his life of leisure into a more or less arduous application to the business of learning how to live a life of ostensible leisure in a becoming way. Closely related to the requirement that the gentleman must consume freely and of the right kind of goods, there is the requirement that he must know how to consume them in a seemly manner. His life of leisure must be conducted in due form. . . . High-bred manners and ways of living are items of conformity to the norm of conspicuous leisure and conspicuous consumption.

Conspicuous consumption of valuable goods is a means of reputability to the gentleman of leisure. As wealth accumulates on his hands, his own unaided effort will not avail to sufficiently put his opulence in evidence by this method. The aid of friends and competitors is therefore brought in by resorting to the giving of valuable presents and expensive feasts and entertainments. Presents and feasts had probably another origin than that of naïve ostentation, but they acquired their utility for this purpose very early, and they have retained that character to the present; so that their utility in this respect has now long been the substantial ground on which these usages rest. Costly entertainments . . . are peculiarly adapted to serve this end. The competitor with whom the entertainer wishes to institute a comparison is, by this method, made to serve as a means to the end. He consumes vicariously for his host at the same time that he is a witness to the consumption of that excess of good things which his host is unable to dispose of singlehanded, and he is also made to witness his host's facility in etiquette.

In the giving of costly entertainments other motives, of a more genial kind, are of course also present. The custom of festive gatherings probably originated in motives of conviviality and religion; these motives are also present in the later development, but they do not continue to be the sole motives. The latter-day leisure-class festivities and entertainments may continue in some slight degree to serve the religious need and in a higher degree the needs of recreation and conviviality, but they also serve an invidious purpose. . . . But the economic effect of these social amenities is not therefore lessened, either in the vicarious consumption of goods or in the exhibition of difficult and costly achievements in etiquette.

As wealth accumulates, the leisure class develops further in function and structure, and there arises a differentiation within the class. There is a more or less elaborate system of rank and grades. This differentiation is furthered by the inheritance of wealth and the consequent inheritance of gentility. With the inheritance of gentility goes the inheritance of obligatory leisure; and gentility of a sufficient potency to entail a life of leisure may be inherited without the complement of wealth required to maintain a dignified leisure. Gentle blood may be transmitted without goods enough to afford a reputably free consumption at one's ease. Hence results a class of impecunious gentlemen of leisure, incidentally referred to already. These half-caste gentlemen of leisure fall into a system of hierarchical gradations. Those who stand near the higher and the highest grades of the wealthy leisure class, in point of birth, or in point of wealth, or both, outrank the remoter-born and the pecuniarily weaker. These lower grades, especially the impecunious, or marginal, gentlemen of leisure, affiliate themselves by a system of dependence or fealty to the great ones . . . So many of them, however, as make up the retainers and hangers-on of the patron may be classed as vicarious consumers without qualification. Many of these again, and also many of the other aristocracy of less degree, have in turn attached to their persons a more or less comprehensive group of vicarious consumers in the persons of their wives and children, their servants, retainers, etc.

The Visible Lifestyle

American Symbols of Status (1998)

JULIET B. SCHOR

Clothes, cars, wristwatches, living room furniture, and lipsticks are well-known purveyors of social position. Furnaces, mattresses, bedroom curtains, foundation powders, and bank accounts, on the other hand, are not. What separates the items in the first list from those in the second? Where we use them. Competitive spending revolves around a group of socially visible products.

You probably know the type of car a friend drives, whether she wears designer clothes (perhaps even which designers), and how large her house is. What you probably do not know is the kind of furnace in her basement, the brand of mattress she sleeps on, and how much life insurance she has. You're aware of the visible status items, but not the invisibles. Visible products become status goods for an obvious reason: their ownership can be easily verified. What you drive, wear, or have on your wrist is almost instantaneously known by observers. This is not to say that products hidden from view cannot become status items. They can, but we must work to make them so. We need to let others know, either directly or indirectly, what's in the basement, where we ate, or that we went to particular destinations. However, there is always an element of doubt involved: it is far easier for someone to exaggerate the size of his bank account or life insurance policy than to claim to have a Jaguar in the garage, especially if he's usually seen driving a Tercel. We do relay information about our consumption, and this is increasingly important as certain invisibles become new status symbols, a point I return to later. But doing so always carries risks. It must be believable. And it must be subtle. If you tell the people in your office about your fabulous trip to the South of France, you'll need to be careful about that fine line between casually conveying information and boasting; crossing over to the point where you are obviously trying to gain status can undermine the object. One of the features of status games is that trying too hard doesn't work. "Brand name-dropping" carries its own opprobrium.

Of course, social visibility is not something that is purely inherent in goods. Companies expend enormous effort to *make* products identifiable, through branding, packaging, marketing, and advertising. Twenty years ago, who would have thought that Americans would be drinking designer water or wearing underwear with Calvin Klein's name on it? But once people started undressing in front of each other more often (courtesy of the sexual revolution and the popularity of health clubs) and carrying water around in public (courtesy of growing informality in the social space), these products became fair game. The desire to turn invisibles into visibles can also explain why many computers bear a sticker on the outside reading "Intel inside," or why automobile companies now advertise on the back of the car what's going on under the hood. Ever notice those metal logos indicating that it's a four-wheel drive? Who needs to know? One wonders whether all this free advertising has contributed to the rage for four-wheel-drive vehicles, even in parts of the country that hardly ever get snow. Or consider the large letters printed across the back of Volvos—"Side Impact Protection System." Arguably a visual impediment themselves, they're there because Volvo is trying to "sell" safety. Advertising on the outside of the car can both increase awareness and turn something inside the door into a visible commodity.

The importance of visibility can be seen in the rise of designer logos. In the era when only the rich bought from designers, logos were unnecessary. The number of people involved in the market was small, and participants could not only tell what clothes were designer but identify individual styles. As a larger, middle-class market developed, the fashion industry gained millions of buyers and observers, but ones with little knowledge of the different designer lines and their relative standing. To get her money's worth in terms of status, the middle-class purchaser needed to make sure that others knew what she had bought—hence, the visible logo. By the 1990s, the logo had become essential. According to the designer Tommy Hilfiger: "I can't sell a shirt without a logo. If I put a shirt without a logo on my selling floor next to a shirt with a logo—same shirt, same color, same price—the one with the logo will blow it out. It will sell 10 times over the one without the logo. It's a status thing as well. It really is." And what does a Tommy Hilfiger logo symbolize? Interpreters of the Hilfiger craze have this to say: "These clothes, traditionally associated with a white, upper middle class sporting set, lend kids from backgrounds other than that an air of traditional prestige." "Upper income fashion is about success and that's what people are buying into." The clothes, quite simply, say, "We aspire." By contrast, the most expensive designer clothes carry far fewer outside labels. In haute couture, we never see them. Why should we? These bizarre outfits are immediately recognized as expensive, cutting-edge, and outside the range of ordinary incomes. They are dazzling status markers without the labels.

A TEST OF STATUS CONSUMPTION: WOMEN'S COSMETICS

A few years ago, a student and I designed a test that can differentiate between consuming with and without a "status" element. We look at buying patterns across products that are similar in most respects but differ in their social visibility. We test to see whether people pay more for products with higher social visibility. The reason: visible goods give status that invisibles do not. For example, we predict that people will spend more money on furnishings for the living room than for the bedroom. Or that they will buy a notch above their usual price range for a coat (the most visible apparel item), or that they are more likely to wear underwear than shirts from Wal-Mart. In tests of this sort, it is important to control for differences in quality and functional requirements. So, in looking at home furnishings, we would compare purchasing patterns for two functionally similar items, such as living room and bedroom curtains. (When discussing this project with a colleague, he reported that he decided not to buy curtains for the bedroom at all, because no one would know they were missing!)

Our test is from women's cosmetics, a multibillion-dollar business. This industry provides a fascinating look into the workings of appearance, illusion, and status. In many ways, the cosmetics companies are not too different from the snake oil peddlers of the nineteenth century. Despite the white coats of the salespeople (to make them look scientific), the hype about company "laboratories," and the promises made in the advertising, it's hard to take the effectiveness claims too seriously. Names like "Eye Repair Diffusion Zone," "Ceramide Time Complex Capsules," and "Extrait Vital, Multi-Active Revitalizer with Apple Alpha-Acids" don't help the products' credibility either.

But despite its dubious effectiveness, women keep on buying the stuff. They shell out hundreds, even thousands, for wrinkle cream, moisturizers, eye shadows and powders, lipsticks, and facial makeup. And why? One explanation is that they are looking for affordable luxury, the thrill of buying at the expensive department store, indulging in a fantasy of beauty and sexiness, buying "hope in a bottle." Cosmetics are an escape from an otherwise all too drab everyday existence.

While there is undoubtedly truth in this explanation, it is by no means the whole story. Even in cosmetics—which is hardly the first product line that comes to mind as a status symbol—there's a structure of "one-up-womanship." It turns out that women *are* looking for prestige in their makeup case. Why do they pay twenty dollars for a Chanel lipstick when they could buy the same product for a fraction of the cost? They want the name. . . . Crude as it may sound, many women want or need to be seen with an acceptable brand. A caption describing a Chanel lipstick in a recent newspaper article puts it bluntly: "A classic shade of scarlet, scented with essential oil of roses, in Chanel's signature black and gold case. *Perfect for preening in public.*" . . .

The status component in cosmetics purchasing comes out clearly in our research. We have looked at brand purchasing patterns for four cosmetics products: lipsticks, eye shadows, mascaras, and facial cleansers. Facial cleansers are the least socially visible of the four because they are almost always used at home in the bathroom. After a woman applies makeup in the morning, she doesn't clean her face again until she takes the makeup off. Eye shadows and mascaras are in an intermediate category. Women do reapply them during the day, typically in semipublic "powder rooms" (note the name). Lipsticks are the most visible of the four products. They are applied not only in the semipublic rooms but in public itself, at the end of a meal, in an elevator, on an airplane. The visibility difference can also be seen in the packaging strategies of the companies. Lipstick containers are quite distinctive and recognizable from across a table, while containers for mascara and facial cleansers are less so. (Eye shadows are often packaged to match lipsticks.) If you are skeptical, try this experiment, possible only with upscale women, and most naturally done over dinner. When the lipsticks start appearing after the dessert, ask each person how many of the brands they can recognize from across the table. When I tried this, the level of recognition was impressive.

To test our assumptions about the relative visibilities of the four products, my former Harvard student and coauthor Angela Chao conducted an informal survey among Harvard students, who reproduced our rankings nearly to a woman. Lipsticks are most visible, facial cleansers are least visible, and eye shadows and mascaras are intermediate. Having established the differences in social visibility across this group of cosmetics products, we then tested two propositions. The first was that socially visible products deliver less quality for a given price. And the second was that people buy top-end brands of visible products far more than high-quality invisible ones. Both these propositions are strongly supported by the data.

Independent quality tests conducted by *Consumer Reports* reveal that among a range of brand lipsticks consumers did not find systematic quality differences. Of course, there are different types of lipsticks. But within types, the lipsticks tend to be chemically similar, and users rated none of them better than any other in terms of quality, despite prices ranging from a few dollars to twenty-five dollars. By contrast, users *can* distinguish between the qualities of facial cleansers, thereby supporting our prediction that with visible products price is less connected to quality. . . . Women are far more likely to buy expensive lipsticks than they are to buy expensive facial cleansers. In fact, with lipsticks, the higher the price, the *more* consumers tend to purchase them. This finding flies in the face of the received wisdom that a higher price discourages buyers.

This perverse relation between price and demand has been called the snob effect, to highlight the role of social status in such purchasing. How else can we explain the results of the cosmetics study? If women were merely in search of quality, attractive packaging, the chance to buy something at a swanky department store, the illusion that they could look like a model, or any of the many other explanations that have been offered for the success of this industry, we would not have found the patterns of purchasing across these four products that we did. Women would be buying expensive facial cleansers at the same rate that they buy expensive lipsticks. They would be getting all their cosmetics in the department store and not picking up the facial cleanser at the local druggist. Buying patterns across the four products would not differ.

◇ ◇ ◇

WHO CARES?

Of course, there are plenty of Americans who refuse to spend for labels, who purchase their lipsticks in drugstores, and who shun brand names altogether. Many will pay the premium for some commodities and not for others. Others attempt to achieve a certain consumer position without paying full price, frequenting discount houses that sell designer merchandise. Although my research confirms the presence of status buying, it does not lead to the conclusion that everyone engages in it.

In the cosmetics study, we found that women with higher education levels and higher incomes did more status purchasing. We found that urban and suburban women did much more status buying than those from rural areas. And we found that Caucasian women were much more likely to engage in status purchasing than African American or non-Caucasian Hispanics. . . .

CONSUMPTION AND THE CONSTRUCTION OF IDENTITY

The possibility of private status seeking immediately raises the issue of identity, and the connection between what you consume and who you are. The attempt to tie individual personal characteristics to consumer choice was once very popular in marketing research. Tremendous efforts have been made to figure out what kind of woman buys instant coffee rather than regular grind, who's behind the wheel of a Ford instead of a Chevy, and what Marlboro men are really like.

It is now widely believed that consumer goods provide an opportunity for people to express themselves, display their identities, or create a public persona. The chairman of one of the world's largest consumer products multinationals well understands that "the brand defines the consumer. We are what we wear, what we eat, what we drive. Each of us in this room is a walking compendium of brands. The collection of brands we choose to assemble around us have become amongst the most direct expressions of our individuality—or more precisely, our deep psychological need to identify ourselves with others." As the popular culture would have it, "I shop, therefore I am."

Through the strong personal connections people come to feel toward products, our possessions become, in the words of Russell Belk, our "extended" selves. "That we are what we have is perhaps the most basic and powerful fact of consumer behavior."

THE COSTS OF STATUS

How does status seeking affect our quality of life and well-being? What does status consumption *cost*?

There are a variety of ways to think about this question. One way is to calculate the price differential between a generic and a branded version of a product, controlling for quality. With lipsticks, the differential would be any excess in price above the $4 or $5 drugstore brand. Taking the price differential for each lipstick and multiplying by the total number sold would give us an overall figure for the amount spent on status in the lipstick market.

With such a method, the key is to control for quality. But doing so is difficult with many products, because status and quality are often intertwined. How do you separate the functional and status components of houses and their furnishings, or restaurant meals, or vacations? It's especially difficult in today's world, where quality has become a status item for upscale consumers. But the difficulties of measurement should not lead us to ignore the thousands of four-wheel-drive vehicles sold to people who almost never use the feature or the extra fee paid to flash a gold (or platinum) credit card (above and beyond the value of whatever services it comes with). With a wide variety of visible commodities, we are shelling out billions for status.

We can also think about the costs of status by considering the money that companies spend to turn identical or virtually identical products into differentiated goods. Savants in advertising know this is what the game is about, although we consumers are often resistant to the idea. Nike buys $150 million of ads annually to convince us to don the Swoosh, but in many ways its shoes are no different from those of archrival Reebok or plenty of no-name brands. Drug companies spend huge sums promoting branded drugs that are the same as generics. Cosmetics companies market identical products under different lines that vary only in their packaging, positioning, and, of course, price. (Insiders know that Bourjois—owned by Chanel—markets last-season Chanel products, in plain cases, at a fraction of the price.) Kellogg's shells out millions to convince us that its corn flakes are better than the other guy's, and we pay through the nose for them. (Ever wonder why cereal is so expensive?) Many of the nation's vitamins come from a single company but are sold in different bottles at a wide range of prices. Fashion companies spend more than $1 billion a year on advertising, trying to keep us from noticing that a hefty segment of that market is also for identical or similar goods at different prices. (For example, a large worldwide manufacturer reports selling jeans with essentially the same manufacturing costs to mass-market chains such as Wal-Mart, mid-market outlets like JC Penney, and high-end designers and department stores, such as Calvin Klein, at retail prices ranging from about $15 to $65.) Not only jeans but many other virtually indistinguishable items of clothing are sold in different retail outlets with wide price differentials. (Designer hosiery is another good example.) Let's not forget that these stores are doing business with the same overseas suppliers, whose products often vary only or mainly by the label. An educated shopper can find bargains this way. But many consumers don't know what they're looking for.

These claims may be hard to digest. It just doesn't seem possible that so many (most?) branded goods are not actually different from other branded goods. Or that their differences are sufficiently small that most consumers don't know which is which, or which they like better, when the labels are removed. Our daily experience tells us something else, often leading us to be fiercely loyal to brands or fashion labels. Tide really *is* better. But don't forget the classic studies, one of which tells us that beer drinkers rated all beer identically without the labels and weren't even able to pick out their favorite brew. Or the lipstick test I reported earlier. I grew up believing that Royal Crown Cola was actually the drink of choice over Pepsi and Coke in blind taste tests. (Can that really be true?) And by the way, remember that local bottling means these soft drinks aren't even identical in different parts of the country. Have you ever done a taste test with bottled water? (I have, and I still can't believe that I didn't choose Evian, to which I have a classic brand attachment.)

I do not mean to imply, by the way, that there are *no* quality differences between goods. There certainly are. Colleagues report that IKEA's veneer bookshelves apparently do not last too long, but solid wood will. Toyotas have better repair records than Hyundais. Rather, my point is twofold: first, for a significant number of branded and highly advertised products, there are no quality differences discernible to consumers when the labels are removed; and second, variation in prices typically exceeds variation in quality, with the difference being in part a status premium.

While a numerical estimate is difficult to settle on, it is clear that the costs of status consumption in the U.S. economy are considerable. In most of the major expenditure categories—housing, furnishings, automobiles, apparel, cosmetics, footwear, travel, and an increasing large group of food items—some fraction of our consumption is addressed to positional concerns. The extra money we spend could arguably be better used in other ways—improving our public schools, boosting retirement savings, or providing drug treatment for the millions of people the country is locking up in an effort to protect the commodities others have acquired. But unless we find a way to dissociate what we buy from who we think we are, redirecting those dollars will prove difficult indeed.

Reality Life

(2008)

KAREN STERNHEIMER

Confession: I am fascinated by reality shows. Not the game show kind, where there is a contest or people get eliminated (although I was into them at first). My weakness is for the ones that follow people around and promise to give us a glimpse into their everyday lives. I don't admit this very often, but I have often thought about the significance of shows like *The Osbournes*, *Hogan Knows Best*, *Hey Paula*, *My Life on the D-List*, and *Newlyweds*. (Yes, I have watched several episodes—okay, every episode—of all of these shows . . . and others like them).

Most of these programs feature the daily lives of people at various levels of celebrity, or people who become celebrities based on their appearance on their show. We get an inside glimpse of what it is like to be one of "them" and temporarily feel like members of their inner circle. There's a bit of a paradox working here: on the one hand the shows present their everyday behaviors that make them seem more like "us," but the fact that they even have a reality show reinforces (or creates) their celebrity.

If you've ever seen the Geico insurance ad, you might have noticed that in spots like this one they pair a "real person" with a celebrity, as if the terms were mutually exclusive.

Even though some of the shows, like *The Real Housewives of Orange County*, *The Hills*, and *My Super Sweet Sixteen* focus on people who are not famous (at first), they do have one thing in common with "celebreality": all the people we are watching are rich.

Are the lives of wealthy people really more interesting than everyone else's?

It all depends on what a large number of people find interesting. And it just so happens that living in a fabulous home in an exclusive community filled with great stuff is interesting to a lot of people (myself included). This has something to do with how we currently define the American Dream: having financial independence and, of course, fame. What is it like to have all that? What's it like to be the child of somebody rich and famous?

The flip side of all this should be lost on no one who has ever seen one of these shows, which are edited in such a way to help us feel a bit superior to them. Now, I would not say that the people on the shows are just "made to look bad," as some reality show participants later complained, and that it is *only* because of the editing. But in addition to watching reality denizens bask in their high tax bracket status, we get to judge them too. Remember how Jessica Simpson seemed to be, er, intellectually challenged? Or all the dog doo lying around the Osbourne house? The temper tantrums when the "sweet" sixteen-year-old didn't have her way?

The wealthy people we see on television aren't always admirable, either. Often shows like *The Real Housewives of Orange County* (which don't really feature "housewives" since nearly of the women work outside the home and some aren't married, but that's the topic for another essay) highlight the excesses and superficiality of their subjects. So in a way these shows both celebrate wealth and criticize the wealthy. If we're not in the exclusive club of being wealthy, watching them might make us feel better about our relatively modest lives.

All of these examples point to the combined fascination and disgust that celebrities often generate. They have come to define what sociologist Thorstein Veblen called the "leisure class" in America. The real upper crust, whose money is not nearly as new, would probably not allow cameras in their home or want to call any attention to themselves, so they remain largely invisible. This helps to maintain the illusion of a completely open society, since it appears that anyone with an interesting personality can be famous, and perhaps rich. As of 2006, only 17 percent of American household earned $100,000 or more, and the wealthiest one percent of Americans hold about one-third of all wealth.

The continued focus on the newly minted rich serves to mask how the *real* elite got that way. CEOs of major corporations, families with multi-generational wealth and power are off of the pop culture radar screen. Sociologist C. Wright Mills called these people the "power elite."

Are they less interesting than the Hogan family of wrestling fame? Who knows. But one thing is for sure: no matter how wealthy (and strong) the Hulk might be, he has a whole lot less power than the invisible rich in the grand scheme of things. And our continued focus on wealth coming from hard work, talent, and being on a reality show masks the reality of where wealth mostly comes from in America.

Beauty Myths and Magazines

(2008)

KAREN STERNHEIMER

I've recently reverted back to an old teenage habit. Last year I got a letter saying that my frequent flyer miles would soon expire and that I could easily convert them to magazine subscriptions. I hadn't subscribed to a magazine in years, so I went nuts. I ordered magazines about politics, technology, business, travel, and fashion.

In my teen years I devoured fashion magazines like *Glamour, Cosmopolitan, Vogue*, and the now defunct *Mademoiselle*, and swapped them with friends to make sure no beauty advice would pass without my knowledge. I saved old issues in my closet for years just in case I would ever want to look at them again, like the reference books that are on my shelves today. When my old house went up for sale years later, my mother told me to take them or toss them. I tossed them.

After I graduated from high school I stopped reading the magazines cold turkey. I don't remember exactly why, but it probably had something to do with a lack of time to read them and (more to the point) the lack of disposable income to buy them. When the first fashion mag showed up in my mailbox last year it was like reuniting with an old friend that I hadn't talked to in years. Yes, I had perused a magazine or two while waiting to have my hair cut, but it's not the same if you can't tear out the samples and dog-ear the particularly relevant advice about hair products to revisit later. Unlike the other magazines I ordered, the beauty ones required very little concentration or commitment to read since they are mostly filled with ads. They could be my secret escape.

As a sociologist, I am also deeply aware of the very narrow version of beauty these magazines typically promote. Yes, most of the women are impossibly thin, white or near-white in complexion, tall and blonde. Many of the articles are about getting/keeping/pleasing/marrying a man, and more than anything, they promote the idea that women's worth is forever linked to how we look. If that's not enough, in the world of most fashion magazines, beauty is something that comes from consumption, not necessarily from character.

That said, I think we often sell readers of these magazines short when we presume that they are merely victims of the beauty industry. I have known a fashion victim or two in my years (and spot them regularly on the streets of Los Angeles), but let's not presume that all women and girls simply read these magazines passively. In a now classic 1984 cultural studies text, *Reading the Romance: Women,*

Patriarchy, and Popular Literature[1] author Janice Radway interviewed women who read romance novels and found that rather than just internalizing the messages of idealized romance they contain, readers used them to escape the drudgery of everyday life. Likewise, we cannot presume that fashion magazine readers just mindlessly adopt the perspectives of the magazines. How readers make meaning of texts—a central goal of cultural studies research—often depends on the social context that each person lives within.

Looking back on my own relationship with fashion magazines, I read them more as a fantasy about what my impending adult life might be like, and for instruction about how to best be ready for that life. The magazines I read in the 1980s, like many today, provided advice about careers and living independently in cities. They told stories about having grown-up relationships with men, which my friends and I had no real frame of reference for (and let's be honest, most seventeen-year-olds would rather not talk to mom and dad much about this topic!).

So why my excitement today? I have had enough experience with being a grown-up to know that the magazines' advice is just a guess, as much advice often is. Fashion magazines offer the promise of self-improvement, or as historian Joan Jacobs Brumberg describes, a body project. Brumberg's study of adolescent girls throughout the twentieth century[2] reveals that these projects continually shift. Unlike the nineteenth century, when girls wrote in their diaries about being better morally, most of the projects today focus on the external.

Why did this happen? We can't blame fashion magazines for the changes, since the ones that existed then bore little resemblance to those of today. Brumberg argues that as women have gradually gained more political power and experienced less external regulation, that they have been encouraged to regulate themselves *internally*. For instance, nineteenth-century women were often discouraged from exercise, but wore binding corsets. Starting in the 1920s women shed these physically restricting undergarments, but took up "slimming" in order to restrict their body size.

So the magazines both reflect and reproduce images of beauty—if we took them away, girls and women wouldn't necessarily feel better about how they look. From my personal experience, I read the magazines from the perspective that I was one of "them." Although not tall, tan, or blonde, as many models in the magazines I bought were, I saw myself as like them in some strange way. And the advice in the magazines about makeup tips and products to try helped me feel part of this thing called beauty. Yes, Marx might say I was experiencing false consciousness—you might say I was deluded. And certainly there might be people who read the magazines and feel inadequate, but we can't make generalizations either way.

1. Chapel Hill: University of North Carolina Press. [*Editor's note*]

2. (1997). *The Body Project: An Intimate History of American Girls*. New York: Random House. [*Editor's note*]

That said, I can't say that I disagree with many of the critiques of the beauty industry author Naomi Wolf offers in her book *The Beauty Myth*[3] or with Jean Kilbourne's analysis of advertising in her book *Killing Us Softly*.[4] But we can't analyze magazines and presume to know how people make sense of them. Sometimes we think that criticizing things we like makes us hypocrites or killjoys. We don't have to be either; we can both enjoy and deconstruct forms of media culture we consume creating the best of both worlds: critical consumers who can have fun reading a magazine once in a while. And learn new makeup tips.

Related Link

www.thebodyproject.com

3. Wolf, N. (1991). *The Beauty Myth: How Images of Beauty Are Used Against Women*. New York: William Morrow. [*Editor's note*]
4. (2000). New York: Henry Holt & Co. [*Editor's note*]

Marketing Ideas and Fears through Email

Pass Along Hoaxes and Urban Legends (2008)

JANIS PRINCE INNISS

I love email! I have been exchanging emails with one aunt in Toronto since 1995—long before most people I knew had email. But what drives me absolutely nuts are forwarded emails designed to scare us. You know the ones that offer safety tips and supposed health information? Very few are true or correct. So why do so many people forward those emails, propelling the crazy ideas even faster around the world?

Today, it seems that everybody uses the Internet. The reality is that there are great disparities in computer use: Europe, North America, and Australia/Oceania are the only areas of the world where Internet usage has penetrated about half or more of the population. Within these countries *who* has computer access varies; for example, in the United States those who are over age 65, have less education, or are African American are less likely to use the internet.

Email is the number one Internet activity in which we engage. On a typical day in 2004, 58 million people in the United States alone used email. Ever think about how many people receive the same loopy emails that crowd your inbox? In 2001, MIT graduate student Jonah Peretti sent an email to 12 friends about his attempts to personalize his Nike shoes with the word "sweatshop." The email made its way around the world and into international media; the story was profiled in large media outlets such as the *Los Angeles Times*, *Wall Street Journal*, and NBC's *Today* show. In less than a three-month period, Peretti received 3,655 inquiries about his email! He got responses from every continent, and his email was translated into several languages. As Peretti writes: "You send an email to 10 friends, and each friend forwards the email to 10 of their friends. If this process continues just 6 steps the message will reach a million people. After 10 steps, the message would hypothetically reach more people than the total population of the earth."

Emails help us maintain social networks and build social capital. They allow us to stay in contact with ever growing networks. As people's networks grow it becomes increasingly difficult for them to stay in contact, except with the use of emails. With email, people are able to stay in contact with more people, more easily. Forwards are one way that people do this. We can forward one note to many people, therefore staying in touch with that many people all at once.

I really like the terms that researchers have come up with to describe some of this: "viral marketing" and "viral consumers." Business researchers examine the ways that consumers become marketers of products and services through the use of emails to spread—hence the term *viral*—information to friends and family. Avoiding these forwards feels a lot like I'm dodging a real virus! They are the marketing of ideas and fears through email. How does this happen? One aspect of this phenomenon is that we do not automatically delete forwarded emails from people we know, although we might do so very easily with notes from strangers. Emails from people we know are more persuasive than those from strangers. Many forwarded emails take a dash of truth and embellish the core with scary details, add names and places, along with an emotional aspect guaranteed to scare us. These urban legends and hoaxes often include details that are possible, but highly unlikely. The details make the claims appear legitimate.

Further, email is quick, and cheap or free. Those passing them along don't have to write or type anything. They simply hit the forward button. The fact that those forwarding emails mostly don't write anything means that the messages are passed on unchanged, unlike the "telephone game." Sometimes there are versions of the same forward, so there is "tampering" at some point. However, because we don't think of our friends or relatives as note originators, they may appear more authentic. It is not Aunt Mary who said this; it's some really knowledgeable, albeit unknown, person. We know the immediate sources of these emails—the people who send them to us—and we assume that if someone we know sends a note, it must be okay. People may not realize that they can check the veracity of emails at websites such as Snopes and figure they are doing more good than harm passing on warnings. None of this is a recipe to discontinue the practice of passing along emails. Indeed, researchers found people pass along emails to be altruistic, and to share what seems to be good information regarding warnings about health and safety. There may also be a degree of impression management in passing along forwards; it is a chance to subtly convey to others what we know, and presumably, they do not.

Related Links

Stats on email use: www.internetworldstats.com/stats

Pew studies on Internet use: www.pewinternet.org

Article on MIT graduate student Jonah Peretti's viral email: www.thenation.com/doc/20010409/peretti

Snopes urban legends page: www.snopes.com

TALK ABOUT IT

1. What are "beauty myths"? Why do they persist in popular culture?
2. Do you have a favorite form of popular culture that is frequently thought to have negative effects, such as video games, reality TV shows, or music downloading? Why do critics focus so much on this particular form of media as potentially harmful?
3. Veblen wrote in 1899 that "unproductive consumption of goods is honorable" for women of the leisure class. Is this still true today? How might this explain the lure of beauty magazines?
4. Have you received emails that encourage you to be afraid of something? Based on Prince Inniss's essay, why are such emails so frequent?
5. Can you think of other forms of media that are as effective as email for spreading misinformation? Why is email such an effective way to promote fear?

WRITE ABOUT IT

1. Based on Veblen's and Schor's selections, what might they think about beauty images in magazines as well as the critical reaction to them?
2. Think of a reality show that you enjoy. In what ways does that program illustrate Schor's ideas about status and consumption?
3. Examine some of your own possessions. How might they convey symbols of status among your peers?
4. Why do so many people aspire to great wealth, or at least enjoy seeing those that are wealthy? How does this reflect our broader culture and economic system?
5. Veblen notes that if items consumed are "thought to be costly, they are felt to be noble." Do you agree with this idea? Do you think others agree? If so, why?

DO IT

1. Using recent fashion magazines, consider what images of beauty the magazines promote. What qualities are implicitly *not* beautiful, based on their absence from these representations? Interview three readers of this magazine to find out how they make sense of beauty images in the magazine. Are their responses similar to your own analysis of the magazines?
2. Ask your friends and family to forward any emails they get that include warnings or hoaxes. Analyze the word choice in the emails, as well as any suggestions provided to prevent the danger the email warns of; then, watch

your local evening news broadcast. Are the topics at all similar? Is the word choice? The suggestions for safety?

3. Go to a shopping mall in two neighborhoods, one that is significantly more affluent than the other. Study the stores in the mall, the products sold, and any information about prices and sales. Also note the patrons in each mall and assess how status is constructed in each setting. Are the differences dramatic? What would Schor say about your findings?
4. Interview five of your friends about the products they own, and why they prefer certain brands over others. Are their visible items more status-oriented than those that no one ever sees, as Schor found in her study?
5. Look up American consumer spending patterns archived in the Statistical Abstract of the United States (www.census.gov/compendia/statab/). How have these patterns changed in the last decade?

3

Self and Interaction

Module Goal: ***To recognize how our individual behavior and identities are constructed through interactions with others.***

Who are you? While this might seem a psychological question, it is a sociological question too. As we will see in this section, we construct our sense of self in conjunction with others. The reactions of other people—the praise and criticism we receive—shape our behavior and how we think about ourselves, whether we like to admit it or not.

Consider this example: you have to make a speech for a class. You don't look forward to this, but you do your best. After your speech, the class bursts into applause. Many of your classmates tell you what a great job you did, and your professor tells you that you have a unique talent for public speaking.

After this experience, you might change the way you think about giving speeches and about yourself. If the next time you give a speech it also goes well, you might even think about how you can incorporate this talent into other parts of your life. Your perception of your self is the direct result of your interactions with others.

Erving Goffman, a major figure in sociological thinking about the self, describes social life as akin to a performance. In our selection from his seminal text *The Presentation of the Self in Everyday Life*, Goffman uses theatrical metaphors to help us understand how we attempt to present ourselves to others in various contexts. He describes how our behavior changes if we think we are visible to others—*frontstage*, as he says—in contrast to how we act in more private, *backstage* settings. First published in 1959, Goffman's classic book has guided many sociologists' work in understanding how the concept of the self is social.

We develop our public selves based on our perception of how others might respond to us, usually presenting ourselves to others in a way that maximizes our likelihood of social acceptance, even among strangers. When we break unwritten rules of social behavior, called *norms*, we invite disapproval. You might have found yourself in a situation where you unwittingly violated a norm; norms shift and change and vary from situation to situation. And sometimes, as Bradley Wright points out, people intentionally violate norms. His "Grocery Shopping, Ordering Whoppers, and Borat" details several norm-breaching experiments and the consequences that follow.

While we strive for the approval of others by attempting to put our best face forward, our private selves sometimes differ from our public presentation. This doesn't necessarily make us phonies or liars—after all, there are some things that other people probably don't want to see or know about us. A problem can arise when parts of our lives we'd like to keep private, or backstage, move frontstage. This is a particularly big problem for politicians and others in the public eye who rely on the approval of others to keep their jobs. Sally Raskoff describes this challenge in her selection "Stand By Our Man." Faced with sex scandals, public figures often manage the stigma of public embarrassment by revealing even more private information, which can forever tarnish their reputations.

Sometimes people struggle privately to manage their sense of identity. We don't have to experience public humiliation to feel shame; in some cases, the conflict has more to do with an internal belief that something is wrong with us. Meika Loe and Leigh Cuttino interviewed college students diagnosed with attention deficit hyperactivity disorder (ADHD). As you read the results of their study, "Grappling with the Medicated Self: The Case of ADHD College Students," consider why ADHD might create a special identity challenge for college students.

On the other hand, we might feel that our self-worth is a commodity, something to exchange in order to maximize our personal gains. *Social exchange theory* posits that relationships are the result of a cost-benefit analysis; if the costs are too high in contrast with the benefits of a relationship, we are less likely to pursue or remain in such an arrangement. As you read Bradley Wright's "Romantic Exchanges," consider what exchanges you or people you know make in relationships, and how those exchanges reflect one's sense of self.

As you analyze the construction of the self and identity in everyday life, ask yourself the following questions:

1. How is the construction of the self a social process?
2. How do people manage the negative reactions of others, or the fear of potential social rejection?
3. What social factors influence how individuals place value on who they are?

[Impression Management]

(1959)

ERVING GOFFMAN

Information about the individual helps to define the situation, enabling others to know in advance what he will expect of them and what they may expect of him. Informed in these ways, the others will know how best to act in order to call forth a desired response from him.

For those present, many sources of information become accessible and many carriers (or "sign-vehicles") become available for conveying this information. If unacquainted with the individual, observers can glean clues from his conduct and appearance which allow them to apply their previous experience with individuals roughly similar to the one before them or, more important, to apply untested stereotypes to him. They can also assume from past experience that only individuals of a particular kind are likely to be found in a given social setting. They can rely on what the individual says about himself or on documentary evidence he provides as to who and what he is. If they know, or know of, the individual by virtue of experience prior to the interaction, they can rely on assumptions as to the persistence and generality of psychological traits as a means of predicting his present and future behavior.

The expressiveness of the individual (and therefore his capacity to give impressions) appears to involve two radically different kinds of sign activity: the expression that he *gives*, and the expression that he *gives off*. The first involves verbal symbols or their substitutes which he uses admittedly and solely to convey the information that he and the others are known to attach to these symbols. This is communication in the traditional and narrow sense. The second involves a wide range of action that others can treat as symptomatic of the actor, the expectation being that the action was performed for reasons other than the information conveyed in this way. As we shall have to see, this distinction has an only initial validity. The individual does of course intentionally convey misinformation by means of both of these types of communication, the first involving deceit, the second feigning.

Let us now turn from the others to the point of view of the individual who presents himself before them. . . . Regardless of the particular objective which the individual has in mind and of his motive for having this objective, it will be in his interests to control the conduct of the others, especially their responsive treatment of him. This control is achieved largely by influencing the definition of the situation which the others come to formulate, and he can influence this definition by expressing himself in such a way as to give them the kind of impression that will lead them to act voluntarily in accordance with his own plan. . . .

I have said that when an individual appears before others his actions will influence the definition of the situation which they come to have. Sometimes the individual will act in a thoroughly calculating manner, expressing himself in a given way solely in order to give the kind of impression to others that is likely to evoke from them a specific response he is concerned to obtain. Sometimes the individual will be calculating in his activity but be relatively unaware that this is the case. Sometimes he will intentionally and consciously express himself in a particular way, but chiefly because the tradition of his group or social status require this kind of expression and not because of any particular response (other than vague acceptance or approval) that is likely to be evoked from those impressed by the expression. Sometimes the traditions of an individual's role will lead him to give a well-designed impression of a particular kind and yet he may be neither consciously nor unconsciously disposed to create such an impression. . . .

For example, in gaining admission to a tight social circle, the participant observer may not only wear an accepting look while listening to an informant, but may also be careful to wear the same look when observing the informant talking to others; observers of the observer will then not as easily discover where he actually stands. . . .

In everyday life, of course, there is a clear understanding that first impressions are important. Thus, the work adjustment of those in service occupations will often hinge upon a capacity to seize and hold the initiative in the service relation, a capacity that will require subtle aggressiveness on the part of the server when he is of lower socio-economic status than his client.

◇ ◇ ◇

When the interaction that is initiated by "first impressions" is itself merely the initial interaction in an extended series of interactions involving the same participants, we speak of "getting off on the right foot" and feel that it is crucial that we do so. . . .

Given the fact that the individual effectively projects a definition of the situation when he enters the presence of others, we can assume that events may occur within the interaction which contradict, discredit, or otherwise throw doubt upon this projection. When these disruptive events occur, the interaction itself may come to a confused and embarrassed halt. Some of the assumptions upon which the responses of the participants had been predicated become untenable, and the participants find themselves lodged in an interaction for which the situation has been wrongly defined and is now no longer defined. At such moments the individual whose presentation has been discredited may feel ashamed while the others present may feel hostile, and all the participants may come to feel ill at ease, nonplussed, out of countenance, embarrassed, experiencing the kind of anomy that is generated when the minute social system of face-to-face interaction breaks down.

In stressing the fact that the initial definition of the situation projected by an individual tends to provide a plan for the co-operative activity that follows—in stressing this action point of view—we must not overlook the crucial fact that any projected definition of the situation also has a distinctive moral character. It is this moral character of projections that will chiefly concern us in this report. Society is organized on the principle that any individual who possesses certain social characteristics has a moral right to expect that others will value and treat him in an appropriate way. Connected with this principle is a second, namely that an individual who implicitly or explicitly signifies that he has certain social characteristics ought in fact to be what he claims he is. In consequence, when an individual projects a definition of the situation and thereby makes an implicit or explicit claim to be a person of a particular kind, he automatically exerts a moral demand upon the others, obliging them to value and treat him in the manner that persons of his kind have a right to expect. He also implicitly forgoes all claims to be things he does not appear to be[1] and hence forgoes the treatment that would be appropriate for such individuals. The others find, then, that the individual has informed them as to what is and as to what they *ought* to see as the "is."

One cannot judge the importance of definitional disruptions by the frequency with which they occur, for apparently they would occur more frequently were not constant precautions taken. We find that preventive practices are constantly employed to avoid these embarrassments and that corrective practices are constantly employed to compensate for discrediting occurrences that have not been successfully avoided. When the individual employs these strategies and tactics to protect his own projections, we may refer to them as "defensive practices"; when a participant employs them to save the definition of the situation projected by

1. This role of the witness in limiting what it is the individual can be has been stressed by Existentialists, who see it as a basic threat to individual freedom. See Jean-Paul Sartre, *Being and Nothingness*, trans. by Hazel E. Barnes (New York: Philosophical Library, 1956), p. 365 ff.

another, we speak of "protective practices" or "tact." Together, defensive and protective practices comprise the techniques employed to safeguard the impression fostered by an individual during his presence before others. It should be added that while we may be ready to see that no fostered impression would survive if defensive practices were not employed, we are less ready perhaps to see that few impressions could survive if those who received the impression did not exert tact in their reception of it.

In addition to the fact that precautions are taken to prevent disruption of projected definitions, we may also note that an intense interest in these disruptions comes to play a significant role in the social life of the group. Practical jokes and social games are played in which embarrassments which are to be taken unseriously are purposely engineered.[2] Fantasies are created in which devastating exposures occur. Anecdotes from the past—real, embroidered, or fictitious—are told and retold, detailing disruptions which occurred, almost occurred, or occurred and were admirably resolved. There seems to be no grouping which does not have a ready supply of these games, reveries, and cautionary tales, to be used as a source of humor, a catharsis for anxieties, and a sanction for inducing individuals to be modest in their claims and reasonable in their projected expectations. The individual may tell himself through dreams of getting into impossible positions. Families tell of the time a guest got his dates mixed and arrived when neither the house nor anyone in it was ready for him. Journalists tell of times when an all-too-meaningful misprint occurred, and the paper's assumption of objectivity or decorum was humorously discredited. Public servants tell of times a client ridiculously misunderstood form instructions, giving answers which implied an unanticipated and bizarre definition of the situation.[3] Seamen, whose home away from home is rigorously he-man, tell stories of coming back home and inadvertently asking mother to "pass the fucking butter."[4] Diplomats tell of the time a near-sighted queen asked a republican ambassador about the health of his king.[5]

To summarize, then, I assume that when an individual appears before others he will have many motives for trying to control the impression they receive of the situation. This report is concerned with some of the common techniques that persons employ to sustain such impressions and with some of the common contingencies associated with the employment of these techniques. The specific content of any activity presented by the individual participant, or the role it plays in the interdependent activities of an on-going social system, will not be at issue; I shall be concerned only with the participant's dramaturgical problems

---

2. Goffman, "Communication Conduct in an Island Community" (unpublished Ph.D. dissertation, Department of Sociology, University of Chicago, 1953.)

3. Peter Blau, "Dynamics of Bureaucracy" (Ph.D. dissertation, Department of Sociology, Columbia University. University of Chicago Press, 1963), pp. 127–29.

4. Walter M. Beattie, Jr., "The Merchant Seaman" (unpublished M.A. Report, Department of Sociology, University of Chicago, 1950), p. 35.

5. Sir Frederick Ponsonby, *Recollections of Three Reigns* (New York: Dutton, 1952), p. 46.

of presenting the activity before others. The issues dealt with by stagecraft and stage management are sometimes trivial but they are quite general; they seem to occur everywhere in social life, providing a clear-cut dimension for formal sociological analysis.

It will be convenient to end this introduction with some definitions that are implied in what has gone before and required for what is to follow. For the purpose of this report, interaction (that is, face-to-face interaction) may be roughly defined as the reciprocal influence of individuals upon one another's actions when in one another's immediate physical presence. *An* interaction may be defined as all the interaction which occurs throughout any one occasion when a given set of individuals are in one another's continuous presence; the term "an encounter" would do as well. A "performance" may be defined as all the activity of a given participant on a given occasion which serves to influence in any way any of the other participants. Taking a particular participant and his performance as a basic point of reference, we may refer to those who contribute the other performances as the audience, observers, or co-participants. The pre-established pattern of action which is unfolded during a performance and which may be presented or played through on other occasions may be called a "part" or "routine."[6] These situational terms can easily be related to conventional structural ones. When an individual or performer plays the same part to the same audience on different occasions, a social relationship is likely to arise. Defining social role as the enactment of rights and duties attached to a given status, we can say that a social role will involve one or more parts and that each of these different parts may be presented by the performer on a series of occasions to the same kinds of audience or to an audience of the same persons.

REGIONS AND REGION BEHAVIOR

Given a particular performance as a point of reference, it will sometimes be convenient to use the term "front region" to refer to the place where the performance is given.

It may also be noted that while decorous behavior may take the form of showing respect for the region and setting one finds oneself in, this show of respect may, of course, be motivated by a desire to impress the audience favorably, or avoid sanctions, etc. . . .

In the study of social establishments it is important to describe the prevailing standards of decorum; it is difficult to do so because informants and students

6. For comments on the importance of distinguishing between a routine of interaction and any particular instance when this routine is played through, see John von Neumann and Oskar Morgenstern, *The Theory of Games and Economic Behaviour* (2nd ed.; Princeton: Princeton University Press, 1947), p. 49.

tend to take many of these standards for granted, not realizing they have done so until an accident, or crisis, or peculiar circumstance occurs.

It was suggested earlier that when one's activity occurs in the presence of other persons, some aspects of the activity are expressively accentuated and other aspects, which might discredit the fostered impression, are suppressed. It is clear that accentuated facts make their appearance in what I have called a front region; it should be just as clear that there may be another region—a "back region" or "backstage"—where the suppressed facts make an appearance.

A back region or backstage may be defined as a place, relative to a given performance, where the impression fostered by the performance is knowingly contradicted as a matter of course. . . . It is here that the capacity of a performance to express something beyond itself may be painstakingly fabricated; it is here that illusions and impressions are openly constructed. Here stage props and items of personal front can be stored in a kind of compact collapsing of whole repertoires of actions and characters.

Very commonly the back region of a performance is located at one end of the place where the performance is presented, being cut off from it by a partition and guarded passageway. By having the front and back regions adjacent in this way, a performer out in front can receive backstage assistance while the performance is in progress and can interrupt his performance momentarily for brief periods of relaxation. In general, of course, the back region will be the place where the performer can reliably expect that no member of the audience will intrude.

Since the vital secrets of a show are visible backstage and since performers behave out of character while there, it is natural to expect that the passage from the front region to the back region will be kept closed to members of the audience or that the entire back region will be kept hidden from them. This is a widely practiced technique of impression management. . . .

Service personnel so commonly take for granted the right to keep the audience away from the back region that attention is drawn more to cases where this common strategy cannot be applied than to cases where it can. For example, the American filling station manager has numerous troubles in this regard. If a repair is needed, customers often refuse to leave their automobile overnight or all day, in trust of the establishment, as they would do had they taken their automobile to a garage. Further, when the mechanic makes repairs and adjustments, customers often feel they have the right to watch him as he does his work. If an illusionary service is to be rendered and charged for, it must, therefore, be rendered before the very person who is to be taken in by it. Customers, in fact, not only disregard the right of the station personnel to their own back region but often also define the whole station as a kind of open city for males, a place where an individual runs the risk of getting his clothes dirty and therefore has the right to demand full backstage privileges. . . .

Another interesting example of backstage difficulties is found in radio and television broadcasting work. In these situations, back region tends to be defined as all places where the camera is not focused at the moment or all places out of range of "live" microphones. Thus an announcer may hold the sponsor's product up at arm's length in front of the camera while he holds his nose with his other hand, his face being out of the picture, as a way of joking with his teammates. Professionals, of course, tell many exemplary tales of how persons who thought they were backstage were in fact on the air and how this backstage conduct discredited the definition of the situation being maintained on the air. For technical reasons, then, the walls that broadcasters have to hide behind can be very treacherous, tending to fall at the flick of a switch or a turn of the camera. Broadcasting artists must live with this staging contingency.

A final example of backstage difficulties may be cited from the contingencies of being an exalted person. Persons may become so sacred that the only fitting appearance they can make is in the center of a . . . ceremony; it may be thought improper for them to appear before others in any other context, as such informal appearances may be thought to discredit the magical attributes imputed to them. Therefore members of the audience must be prohibited from all the places the exalted one is likely to relax in . . .

While some of these examples of back region difficulty are extreme, it would seem that no social establishment can be studied where some problems associated with backstage control do not occur.

Throughout Western society there tends to be one informal or backstage language of behavior, and another language of behavior for occasions when a performance is being presented. The backstage language consists of reciprocal first-naming, co-operative decision-making, profanity, open sexual remarks, elaborate griping, smoking, rough informal dress, "sloppy" sitting and standing posture, use of dialect or sub-standard speech, mumbling and shouting, playful aggressivity and "kidding," inconsiderateness for the other in minor but potentially symbolic acts, minor physical self-involvements such as humming, whistling, chewing, nibbling, belching, and flatulence. The frontstage behavior language can be taken as the absence (and in some sense the opposite) of this. In general, then, backstage conduct is one which allows minor acts which might easily be taken as symbolic of intimacy and disrespect for others present and for the region, while front region conduct is one which disallows such potentially offensive behavior. . . .

Grocery Shopping, Ordering Whoppers, and *Borat*

(2007)

BRADLEY WRIGHT

Every once in a while sociologists go bad—but for a good purpose. We call it a "breaching experiment."

There are some things in life that everyone knows are wrong, such as murder, arson, robbery, etc. . . . (Well, just about everyone. There are a few exceptions we call psychopaths). Society outlaws these activities and pays people to enforce these laws.

There are a lot of other things, however, that society considers wrong but that are not officially illegal (though they can get you into trouble). Defining these wrong things are countless unwritten rules about what we should and shouldn't do in everyday life, and violating these rules might get us laughed at or punched in the nose. These unwritten rules are social norms, and they guide just about every possible activity a human being can do.

Unwritten rules guide every social situation. For example, let's take a simple behavior—a student walking into class. What are you supposed to do? Enter somewhat quietly, maybe talk with someone else. Keep a relatively neutral look on your face. Walk to your seat, keeping a mostly even pace, and sit down.

There are a lot of things that you should not do. You shouldn't run as fast as you can, skip like a little kid on the playground, walk backwards, or crawl (unless you're begging for something from the professor).

You shouldn't yell at people across the room, bark like dog, or pretend to be a train steaming down the track. You shouldn't stick your tongue out at the professor, sob loudly, or have a maniacal "I'm an axe murderer" grin on your face. If you violate these rules, you'll probably get laughed at.

At this point you're probably thinking "duh"—you already know all these rules and you're beginning to wonder why sociologists get paid to spell out the obvious. (We sometimes wonder the same thing ourselves.) The fact that you already know these rules is an important point. Society trains people (via parents and teachers and friends and strangers on the street) to do the "right" thing in every situation so that not long past our toddler days we're all walking encyclopedias of the rules of everyday life. Do you think the rules of hockey are complicated? The laws of quantum mechanics? They are nothing compared to everyday social situations.

Now let's have some fun. An easy way to demonstrate the prevalence and power of social norms is to do a "breaching" experiment in which you *intentionally* break social norms and see how strongly people react. (This methodology was developed by Harold Garfinkel in the 1960s and '70s.)

A classic "breaching" experiment involved shopping. Researchers would go to a grocery store, and then instead of pulling the items off the shelf, they would pull them out of other people's carts. When other shoppers noticed this behavior, they would expect the researcher to say something like, "Oh, I thought that was my cart," but instead the researcher just explained that it was easier to reach the items in the other person's cart. While grocery stores do not post signs forbidding this behavior, it clearly violated the unwritten rules of shopping and the shoppers reacted with anger.

In another experiment, the researcher would go into McDonald's, step up to the counter, and order a Whopper (the hamburger made by McDonald's rival Burger King). The clerk behind the register would explain that it's McDonald's, and then the researcher would again order a Whopper. At this point the clerk would look around to see if anyone else heard this breach, and they would start trying to figure out what was happening. Maybe the customer was joking? Maybe they were deluded? Either way, it was breaking norms.

Have you seen the movie *Borat: Cultural Learnings of America for Make Benefit Glorious Nation of Kazakhstan* [2006]? In addition to being side-splittingly funny (and rather gross), it is one long breaching experiment. The character Borat is from Kazakhstan, and he travels around the United States pretending that he doesn't know our social norms, and he breaks many of them. In one scene he walks the streets of New York City and starts talking to strangers. Some of the strangers get so unnerved that they literally run away from him. Then—as passersby gasp in horror—he squats down in the bushes in front of Trump Tower to go to the bathroom.

What's the take-home message of this line of research? Norms are as much a part of social life as air and water are of physical life—they are everywhere, and we can't live without them.

In fact, I can't think of any social behavior that is not guided by norms. Can you? That's why there will always be room for sociologists and our breaching experiments.

Stand By Our Man

(2008)

SALLY RASKOFF

Have you noticed that when politicians get into trouble for something they've done, more often than not their wives appear with them for the public apology? This is particularly evident when the trouble is sexual. (Whether the husbands of politicians in trouble would show up isn't clear since we don't have as many women in office, let alone getting into trouble.)

Eliot Spitzer, former governor of New York, had his wife by his side when he acknowledged hiring prostitutes. Jim McGreevey, former governor of New Jersey, had his wife by his side when he acknowledged having an affair with a man and that he was gay. Hillary Clinton appeared on *60 Minutes* with her husband during his 1992 campaign for president when he was accused of having an affair.

We hold our elected officials to a very high standard. We require those who hold power in this country to display a "normal" life where they look and behave in accordance with our societal expectations. Historically and even now, most (nationally) elected officials, are male, white, Protestant, heterosexual, married, and from the middle or upper class.

When these politicians deviate from these norms, typically through sexual activities with someone other than their wives, we call into question their character, their ability to hold office and to be effective leaders. Especially if politicians do not disclose this information prior to taking office and we find out about it later, they are not likely to keep their position, and/or their political aspirations are severely impaired.

Jim McGreevey and Eliot Spitzer both resigned their governorships. Senator Larry Craig resigned from his committee positions after public disclosure of his legal troubles stemming from public bathroom behaviors observed by an undercover cop during a sting operation. Detroit Mayor Kwame Kilpatrick acknowledged an affair with his female chief of staff (who subsequently resigned), pled guilty to obstruction of justice, and eventually resigned. (Mayor Kilpatrick and President Clinton both faced legal action, not for their infidelity, but for lying under oath. However, their lies were in reference to their sexual liaisons.) Jack Ryan lost his candidacy for Senate in Illinois when his atypical sexual activities were disclosed during divorce proceedings. Los Angeles Mayor Antonio Villaraigosa admitted an affair with a reporter and, although he kept his job, his divorce is pending and there is no longer talk of a run for governor.

Looking at these and the many other politicians whose sexual activities have ended or limited their careers, it is fascinating that upon first disclosure, the wives are there for the public apology, yet later they may distance and/or divorce themselves from their partner. They stand by their man for the media frenzy, yet after the public attention fades, they may not stay with their man.

When the wives appear, it is comforting to the public and reassures us that he may not be all bad since she's staying with him. When the wife doesn't appear, as with Mayor Villaraigosa's situation, it can signal bigger problems that then may derail the politician's career entirely.

Erving Goffman's concepts of *frontstage* and *backstage* can be helpful for understanding this dynamic. In this theory, we have frontstage behavior to manage what we show to others and backstage behaviors to prepare the frontstage and/or to deal with what we really feel or think. Backstage issues may be shared with others or they may play out with the one person alone.

The politician and his wife have a lot of experience with the frontstage; they need to perform their political roles no matter what happens. Backstage is another story. If the politician is having sexual affairs with people other than his spouse, the same may be true for the politician's wife—although since their backstages are not public, we can speculate but we may never know for sure. In the cases above, we do find this out—yet they are both compelled to maintain the frontstage as devoted companion and spouse.

Let's think about the politicians who have had sexual affairs with other women, those who paid prostitutes for sex, and those who allegedly had affairs with men.

Both politicians who prefer same-sex partners and their wives might suffer the greatest tension between their front- and backstages. They feel that homophobia prohibits them from living their lives "out" and maintaining public office. They therefore have to do a lot of backstage work to keep the public (and their wives) from finding out and moving the behavior to the frontstage.

Those who pay prostitutes get into trouble for illegal activity and work to keep this backstage (and from their wives). Politicians who have affairs with other women may keep their office although they may lose their wives. On the other hand, there may not be as large a difference between what both spouses know backstage. Theirs may be a political marriage in which one or both partners seek any sexual liaisons outside the relationship.

If, however, sexual behaviors outside marriage or other non-normative behaviors are disclosed before taking office, do the dynamics change? It seems that they may, since then the non-normative behavior is already public, not secret, and not subject to surprise disclosure or legal action (for perjury).

David Paterson, the new governor of New York, admitted upon Spitzer's resignation that he and his wife both had affairs, received counseling, and have repaired their marriage. During his first presidential campaign, George W. Bush admitted his alcoholism and many polls found that this increased support for his leadership. His drinking and poor grades in college resonated with some and made him seem more accessible to them.

If politicians admit to non-normative behaviors that are relatively common or otherwise familiar to us *before* they take office, we may respond by supporting them rather than condemning them. The difference seems to lie in whether or not they have been keeping such information secret or not and just how acceptable such behavior is in the public eye.

We elect our politicians to use the power we give them wisely and do what we think is right. Thus when they behave outside those expectations, they act in ways to calm our responses, to let us know they have problems much like our own. Their frontstage presentation is meant to reassure us that they are human and aren't different from us and/or people we know—and not to question the job they do wielding the power we give them.

What other sociological theories can you apply to these situations of politicians in trouble for sexual activity and the ubiquity of wives standing by the men whom we elect?

Related Links

Story about former New York governor Eliot Spitzer:
www.cnn.com/2008/POLITICS/03/10/spitzer/

Story about former New Jersey governor Jim McGreevey:
nymag.com/news/politics/21340/

Story about Idaho senator Larry Craig:
abcnews.go.com/Politics/story?id=3538964&page=1

Story about former Detroit mayor Kwame Kilpatrick:
www.wzzm13.com/news/news_article.aspx?storyid=89533

Grappling with the Medicated Self

The Case of ADHD College Students (2008)

MEIKA LOE AND LEIGH CUTTINO

Over the past two decades an astonishing number of children, adolescents, and, more recently, adults in the United States have been diagnosed with attention-deficit/hyperactivity disorder (ADHD) and prescribed treatment in the form of medications such as Ritalin and Adderall.[1] In 1998 over five million children had prescriptions for Ritalin—a fivefold increase over eight years and an extension of a social phenomenon that Lawrence Diller (1999:2–3), the author of *Running on Ritalin*, calls "a white middle class suburban phenomenon." Nearly eight million children have been diagnosed with ADHD, and the demographics cut across traditional race and class lines (CDC 2004). The picture is clearly gendered: almost 10 percent of ten-year-old boys in the United States take stimulants for ADHD, while only about 5 percent of ten-year-old girls do (CDC 2004; Nissen 2006). It is an age-based phenomenon as well, with ADHD generally diagnosed in childhood or early adolescence, although this may be changing as the adult ADHD market expands. And the phenomenon remains uniquely American; the United States consumes between 80 and 90 percent of the Ritalin available in the world (DeGrandpre 1999).

The present analysis is focused on the case of ADHD college students as they negotiate medicated selfhood. Specifically, we ask, "How do elite college students come to terms with selfhood in the context of pharmaceutical use?" While a significant amount of sociological scholarship is focused on identity and its renegotiation in the context of illness, our case study focuses on identity in the context of pharmaceutical use, which can be much more salient for students than medical diagnosis or illness.... For ADHD college students, questions about identity revolve around psychostimulant use in relationship to self, body, and performance.

Many children who took Ritalin are now enrolled in college, an environment in which they encounter new freedoms and responsibilities, as well as new demands and expectations. For them, stimulant medication can become central to their abilities to manage performance and avoid the perceived threat of failure and possible stigmatization.[2] In this way, prescription medication can be . . . a cultural strategy utilized to ensure academic success (Lareau 2003). At the same time, they must actively confront the fact that they are shaped by medicine (Karp 2006). While the use of medication may ease the pressures that accompany their pursuit of academic success, it prompts new questions and strategies in regard to identity and selfhood, particularly in light of a larger antimedication bias in society.

METHODS

Interviews were conducted to understand how college students construct and manage identity in the context of pharmaceutical use. . . . Our sixteen student informants attend a selective private liberal arts college in the Northeast; eight are male and eight are female. . . . [A]ll informants have been diagnosed with ADHD and prescribed treatment in the form of prescription stimulants at some point in their lives; fourteen have active prescriptions. . . . During each interview, students were asked to reflect on their experiences with diagnosis and treatment for ADHD, as well as on their educational background and understanding of success. . . .

While this sample is not generalizable to all ADHD students attending colleges, our data reveal patterns in identity construction that may likely resonate with similar sample populations, including middle and upper-class ADHD students attending elite schools, as well as the larger population of adults taking psychotropic medication (Karp 2006). Like the majority of college students currently diagnosed with ADHD (CDC 2004; Diller 1999), our informants self-identify as white and middle, upper middle, or upper class.[3] These students are in advantageous positions; their economic resources have given them the ability to seek out physicians, obtain medical treatment, and engage in consumption-based body projects.[4] This location in medicalized worlds means that these students have defined their own bodies as deficient or have been diagnosed as such by medical experts. These students have also chosen to take stimulants in college, while we presume that some members of the Ritalin generation with access to these same resources elect not to use medication in this context.

Another point of consideration about our informants is that they have access to extensive educational resources. Many have had their own academic tutors, and more than half of them attended private secondary school for more than four years. With few exceptions, the rest attended public schools in wealthy communities. Access to education of this caliber has given them early exposure to an "academic ethic" that has set high standards for success and achievement. Given that they were all accepted into a competitive liberal arts college and elected to enroll in this college, it is clear that this academic ethic has been and is central to their precollege and current college lives.[5]

In summary, our ADHD informants have been raised with a sense of great opportunity and relatively few external limits. With a significant degree of access to medical and educational resources, these students risk shame if their bodies do not perform in accordance with the collegiate academic ethic. . . .

ADHD AND THE ACADEMIC ETHIC

The legitimacy of ADHD diagnosis and treatment remains a topic of debate among physicians, psychologists, government officials, and the general public (Rafalovich 2004). The purpose of this discussion, however, is not to debate the legitimacy of ADHD as a biologically based disorder or to refute the use of stimulants as treatment. The complex of symptoms that make up ADHD has been designated a disorder and deemed treatable; as a result, a portion of the U.S. population has received medical diagnosis and treatment (Conrad and Schneider 1992; Diller 1999; Rafalovich 2004). In our contemporary health-care context, treatment for ADHD via psychostimulants is common; psychotherapy is rare (Rafalovich 2004).

In most cases, diagnosis and treatment cannot be separated from an educational context. Students face great expectations to be committed to their studies through regular, methodical, and disciplined work, especially when attending a competitive liberal arts college. This set of behaviors and learning styles, otherwise known as the "academic ethic," is learned and achieved in the context of a research-driven university, where faculty model and set narrow standards (Rau and Durand 2000; Shils 1997). However, students rarely, if ever, entirely adhere to this ethic, as it is characterized by ideal behaviors (Rau and Durand 2000). Students who have been diagnosed with ADHD are perceived to be in a position that hinders them from achieving the academic ethic, and pharmaceutical treatment can be seen as integral to the student's ability to meet these expectations.[6] As ADHD students enter colleges with prescriptions in hand, how do they actively construct selfhood and manage performance in the context of academic ideals?

STRATEGIC PHARMACEUTICAL USE AND CONSTRUCTION OF THE SELF

. . . Rather than struggle with biological disruption because of illness (Bury 1982), ADHD college students are more likely to grapple with the costs and benefits of pharmaceutical disruption in the context of self-dosing. In sum, for ADHD college students, the answer to the question "Who am I?" in college is as much about diagnosis as it is about treatment, and it is inseparable from ideas about academic success.

In interviews, students describe how they can teach or discipline their bodies to correct for aberration and perform academically through stimulant medication (and through perfecting study skills, auditory and visual learning styles, and work ethic). . . .

Identity . . . is the meanings a person attributes to self as an object in role situations (Reitzes and Burke 1980:22). In a contemporary context of biomedicalization where medical technology is used to fix, normalize, and enhance the self, psychostimulants can be central to the optimization project and identity construction (Clarke et al. 2003; Rose 2007; Rothman and Rothman 2003).

However, while students may approach the academic ethic strategically, with biomedical tools for enhancement, many remain conflicted when it comes to identity and self. The most common metanarrative that emerged in our student interviews involved concern about the loss of a "natural" self in the context of pharmaceutical use. In this way, the process of identity maintenance and verification can be interrupted or "broken" in the context of pharmaceutical use, resulting in stress (Burke 1991).

If an individual's goal is always "authenticity," the phenomenological emotional experience of feeling true to oneself (Taylor 1992; Vannini 2006), then medicine can create a sense of inner conflict as the gap widens between perceived "authentic" and "ideal" identities. . . . [S]ymbolic interactionists remind us that the self continues to prosper as an important "inner beacon" for actors in the social world and "the leading experiential project of our era" (Gubrium and Holstein 2000:96). Students use language of the authentic self to discuss what it means to be "real," juxtaposed against their medicated (sometimes described as temporary, artificial, or even ideal) selves. In this way, these students' narratives reflect the "quest to establish continuity" of the self (Pierret 2003).

UNDERSTANDING MEDICATED IDENTITY IN THE COLLEGIATE SETTING

. . . In general, many [ADHD students] express some awareness of the interplay between body and society; while they believe that they are biologically different from others, they also realize that their environment plays a crucial role in the construction of self. [The following quote is from Matt, a senior diagnosed in college, an environment that he implies creates disordered bodies . . . the individual implies that diagnoses and subsequent treatment may emerge from an inability to meet the demands of social environments.]

> The thing with having ADHD . . . I don't really believe in it that much, even. I think Adderall helps, but I think it helps everyone. . . . I don't know if ADHD is one of those things that you have [biologically] so that you *need* to take medicine. I didn't need it before . . . and now that I'm taking it I'm just as with it . . . the situation just changed. Maybe people are situationally ADD.

If their bodies are deficient or dysfunctional, social environments are to blame. [Respondents] also blame themselves for not being able to keep up with social expectations. However, while they may see ADHD as a product of social expectations, they may not go far enough in analyzing how they themselves interact with and contribute to these environments through their pharmaceutical use.

In every interview, informants note the challenges of the college environment. . . . When individuals enter new environments, they are often faced with new challenges and situations that they may not be equipped to overcome. Identity may feel threatened, in that a once well-defined and capable self is suddenly questioned by the perceived threat of failure or the inability to perform as that self was once able to. The transition to college requires that students reevaluate selfhood in the context of new demands and expectations. Some have found that medication can smooth a difficult transition.

Diagnosed with learning disabilities at a young age, Mary was not officially diagnosed with ADHD until after her second semester of college. She discusses here how a demanding college academic ethic led to a reevaluation of her self-identity:

> It was a combination of me no longer being at home with my parents over me. And I mean, I was pretty much trying to get by the same way I did in high school . . . not reading until tests . . . and I couldn't, I mean I was staying up for like three nights straight, two nights straight trying to read like, astronomy . . . the entire textbook for a test but I couldn't . . . and then I was failing the tests. So, basically it was. . . . I was pretty much the same but the school demanded that much more of me so I couldn't . . . get by.

. . . Mary's narrative suggests a stable sense of self in a changing context. She describes herself as "pretty much the same," but in an environment that holds her to a new level of expectation. Her new ADHD identity seems to emerge from a sense of inadequacy, a realization that she was unable to handle the challenges that college presented. In the campus context, she is ADHD, and she self-medicates to meet academic expectations. But outside the classroom and the library, Mary retains her "authentic" self, a self that is not considered disordered.

The challenge of handling a rigorous course load, creating a new work ethic, and establishing independence away from parental support is often unsettling to the student entering college. As in the following quote from Sean, medication is something he leans on in the absence of parent- or school-imposed structure.

> Everything is so much more on us. That *we're* in control and *we* have to manage our time and *we* have to get it done, and there are no teachers there. You know, your professors tell you it's due on a specific date and that's about it. But yeah, you don't have [parents around]. Like my parents . . . were always there . . . to help me along. But now, it's all on us, or on me. . . . I've sort of realized how helpful the treatment can be. And at least for me, how necessary it is to get things done.

[Our interviewees] suggest that pharmaceuticals make it easier to manage new (sometimes unrealistic) demands and expectations placed on the college student, and thus diagnosis and treatment are rationalized in this context of perceived academic necessity. Therefore, for the ADHD student, prescription medication serves as a tool to discipline behavior and enhance a sense of self-control (Loe et al. 2006). Perceived self-control is central to students' belief in the possibility of achievement; the greater the sense of perceived self-control, the greater the belief in the possibility of achievement (Ross and Broh 2000:273). . . .

MANAGING IDENTITY AND THE PARADOX OF MEDICAL CONTROL

. . . For [ADHD students] to "fit" with what they see as the academic ethic, they are willing to at least temporarily allow a foreign substance to control their behaviors and discipline their bodies. In other words, in order to *have* control, they must allow themselves to *be* controlled. As a result, their words convey a level of ambivalence about their relationship with prescription medicine:

> *Sean*: I guess since I sort of . . . control it myself . . . that I only take it when I think I need to . . . I guess, I don't know. I like it I guess. I think I like it. I don't like the fact that I need it, but I like the fact that I have it."

> *Mary*: It kind of sucks [needing] medication . . . to do well in school. But the fact that I know I can do it, on medication. . . . I just feel like, it's kind of . . . give or take, almost. It's like, . . . fine, but now I'm . . . just as smart. So . . . take it with a grain of salt.

> *Kristin*: There are pros and cons. Because like . . . certain things in terms of my school work . . . that are kind of . . . out of control enough that . . . without a sort of support system, without doctors helping me, I don't know how I'd . . . take that. I don't know if I would be able to . . . be in school.

Fear of drug dependency is only heightened for students caught up in college performance culture who see ADHD bodies as limiting success and future prospects. In an attempt to confront ambivalence, many of our informants have created approaches to constructing selfhood by attempting to maximize self-determination and minimize medical control. In these ways, ADHD students are managing what they perceive as fragmented identity: the division of the medicated and nonmedicated self. These strategies allow students to believe they are protecting their "authentic" selves and minimizing the need for medicated identities. Students report using three strategies to manage ambivalence and drug dependency (and in turn, preserve a sense of one's "true self"): self-dosing, avoidance of academic risk, and going off the drugs.

The vast majority of students we spoke with manage pharmaceutical dependency by asserting control of their medication and related bodily regimes. Many times this requires taking the doctor and parent out of the equation and self-medicating in ways that protect their sense of coherent selfhood. . . . For some, this means segregating their work and social lives, self-medicating and acknowledging ADHD only "when necessary" in the context of academic success, while purposefully not medicating or identifying as "deficient" in the context of social success, as Sean suggests above. Many see this approach as achieving success in both realms, protecting their authentic self and "personality" and leveraging this at times to achieve academic success.

For example, Kate makes a distinction between her academic and her social self, insisting that her Ritalin self (which is achieved only when necessary) feels "fake" in contrast to her authentic and familiar "social" self. In this way she temporarily trades on her sense of authenticity in order to feel good about herself academically.

> I guess like I'm happier with who I am when I'm not on drugs like Ritalin. . . . I feel better about myself like academically, like when I'm on it, but, not like, you know, socially. To me [the effect of Ritalin] is like—feeling physically drained and like almost fake 'cause it's not like who I am, you know?

. . . Most student informants seem to construct their nonmedicated bodies as primary, normal, and essential (natural), despite having spent years (sometimes the majority of their lives) on medication. . . .

Students seem to enjoy the ability to pick and choose when they take their medication, as it means that they can assume their "medicated identity" only as needed. . . .

Self-dosing allows students . . . to preserve a sense of authentic selfhood (Charmaz 1997) when not playing the role of the student. Below, Nathan explains why he chooses to take his prescription medication only in certain contexts. Being "himself" is preferable and synonymous with being off medication. However, Nathan is willing to shift identity for the purpose of work:

> I feel like I'm kind of different. . . . like I'm more subdued and . . . more concentrating on things, rather than being like, myself and being spontaneous. I feel like it's more like, focused energy. It's good for working but . . . I don't really feel like being on it all the time I guess.

While self-dosing minimizes the length of time that individuals are "controlled" by medication, it also means that they are constantly shifting between their medicated and nonmedicated identities. The question follows: Why not stop treatment? If it causes identity conflict or distress, the answer seems simple enough. However, giving up treatment means scaling down aspirations, which can be perceived as a form of failure. Further, many informants have taken medication so long that they are equally as attached to their medicated self as they are to their "authentic" self. Doug, who was diagnosed at the age of seven, speaks to this point:

> I don't like the idea . . . that the person I'm most like is the person who I am when I am taking medication . . . when there's chemicals that are running through my . . . that aren't naturally there. But I find more and more, that when I don't take it, I don't act as someone that I think that I am or who I'd like to be . . . that I feel like I can't do anything. So . . . I don't know what to do about that.

As his narrative implies, Doug has been on medication so long that he has become more comfortable with his medicated identity than with his nonmedicated one—so much so that he has actually begun to question and even dislike the latter. Rather than feel physiologically "disrupted" because of illness, Doug grapples with medical disruption and its effect on his body. . . . Ali, who was also diagnosed at seven, expresses a similar form of medicated body ambivalence, stating that her sense of self is challenged and changed on medication. She tries to "deal with" the fact that her medicated "personality" is more normal than not.

> I think it's messed up and twisted that I've been on study medications since first grade. I think it's . . . I can't say really a moral debate but, just a debate internally about how I feel about it because I know . . . there's no way I would be at [this school] without it. . . . And at the same time . . . [just thinking] how much [taking a pill] can change your personality . . . who you are is . . . challenged.

> I mean I can deal with it. It's easy for me to rationalize it in the sense that I've taken it for so long I can just not think about it . . . which is what a lot of people do.

As a sense of identity conflict heightens, some students have chosen alternative, nonmedical routes to managing their performance and avoiding failure . . . :

> I pretty much know my strengths and weaknesses. So I know I can't take a history course because I'm not at all oriented in history. I'm pretty good in math . . . I'm pretty math-oriented. And I love education courses and I love sociology courses and [I'm] taking classes I know I'll be fine in. . . . I'm not going to go and throw myself in a Poly Sci course when I know nothing about it. So, . . . I don't really push myself to take courses that I'm not going to do well in. I take courses that I'm interested in that I expect myself to do well in.

Mary's strategy is to orient her choices around that which she perceives she will be able to accomplish. By avoiding certain subjects, she is able ensure performance, guard against failure, and gain a sense of control in the context of her surrounding environment. . . .

In this context of strategic avoidance, the academic ethic is reinforced and rarely questioned. Although Mary has strategically avoided certain classes, it is clear that she still resorts to her prescription medication as a tool to meet demands and expectations. However, . . . as she perceives her nonmedicated self as more capable of excelling in other areas.

Perhaps the easiest way to reconcile ambivalent identities is to stop using prescription medication altogether—a strategy that is particularly courageous and rare while students are still in college. . . . Homer struggle(s) with what (he) describe(s) as stimulant drug dependency, largely because of self-dosing habits and perhaps unknowingly violating "normal dosage" amounts. (He has) since sworn never to go back to these prescription drugs. Instead, (he) trained himself to reverse ADHD symptoms by using study skills or various relaxation techniques. . . .

> *Homer*: I refuse to take the drug now—[so] I've had to come up with like techniques. Like I have to take breaks incessantly, if I don't then I will burn out. Like if I'm reading something, I have to, if I really wanna retain it, like I've gotta write, like, underline things—and then write next to it reminder words. . . . and that's been real helpful.

For . . . Homer, training the ADHD body to fulfill the academic ethic doesn't require medication. In (his) case, medication made things worse. Medicine-free, (he) report(s) feeling more in control of (his body) and "healthier than ever."

EMBRACING MEDICATED SELFHOOD: A CONTRARY CASE

Unlike the rest of the informants who choose to self-dose and take themselves off of medication during school vacations and in between periods of work, Lauren has chosen to follow her prescription every day of her life, including weekends and holidays. This way, there appears to be no conflict with what she perceives as her authentic self and her medicated self. Bury (1982) called this coping process "normalization," or fully integrating illness into one's sense of self. For Lauren, embracing illness goes with embracing treatment; for her medicated selfhood is a way to reconcile identity conflict:

> It's kind of offensive to me actually, when people ask me for it . . . and then people get mad if you won't sell it to them . . . or give it to them. And I'm like, "This is my drug. I take this every day. . . . This isn't like, "Oh I'm going to study and do work now. This is a like a part of . . ." it's like if somebody wakes up in the morning and takes [medicine for] cholesterol everyday. I take my Adderall everyday. But . . . I feel like . . . it's become such a study drug that . . . a lot of people just assume that you take it when you do work or whatever, but . . . I take it Saturdays, Sundays. . . . if I just feel like sitting around. Just 'cause . . . then you are regular. And then you function the same way every day.

Lauren implies a certain comfort in maintaining a "regular" and steady identity, instead of having to accommodate both a medicated and nonmedicated self. . . .

After years of debate, she found that the best way to resolve her identity struggle was to fully assume the new identity or, as she says, become "a different person." Interestingly, Lauren was one of the only informants to discuss her ADHD as having an effect across her everyday activities and roles. However, like our other informants, Lauren expresses discomfort in the idea of taking medication for the rest of her life. The question follows: what will students do with their medicine when they graduate from college? Answers to this question reveal quite a lot about medicine and the ongoing project of self-construction in late modernity.

LOOKING TO THE FUTURE

As ADHD students look to the future, many believe they would not have made it in (or even to) college without their medication. Following college graduation, they face a postindustrial world where flexibility, adaptability, and optimization can be central to success (Martin 1994; Rose 2007). At the same time, as they enter the work world, many want to leave behind the drugs they associate with years of schooling and academic performance. This means embracing and entering the world with (unmedicated) ADHD bodies and finding work that fits with one's sense of self. For example, Lauren, who has embraced her ADHD diagnosis, describes her body not as "deficient" but as overly ambitious, wanting to do a billion things at once. Thus, she feels she is a perfect fit for her career choice, an ER doctor. Nathan is looking for a career and a lifestyle that suits someone with his unique attributes, perhaps in finance. He says, "Having ADD really makes me . . . ready to go for like, a city kind of lifestyle. Very fast-paced." Matt says that choosing a routinized, structured job will eliminate his need for a stimulant.

In the context of pharmaceutical use, ADHD students face a difficult situation in the pursuit of a coherent sense of self. To some, giving up their perceived "authentic" identity means being permanently controlled by medicine that blots out their own unique personalities. Giving up the "medicated" identity means losing the ability to manage performance and achievement. Willing to relinquish neither one nor the other, pharmaceutical ambivalence persists for ADHD college students. To manage this conflict, many students accept and rationalize situational medical control while employing strategies designed to emphasize agency and preserve a sense of authentic selfhood. In this context, what we call strategic pharmaceutical use becomes a way to occupy a middle ground between medical optimization and authenticity. Not unlike workers who engage in emotion management on the job (Hochschild 1983), many ADHD college students attempt to manage the job of "student" with medication to achieve instrumental ends while aiming to protect their "true selves." Interestingly, while students justify strategic pharmaceutical use in the context of an academic ethic, they may not see how, by using prescription drugs to normalize, enhance, or fix themselves, they are contributing to the social expectations to which they are responding.

Notes

1. The number of youths in this country taking prescribed psychotropic drugs—in other words, drugs that alter behavior, emotion, or perception—increased by as much as 300 percent overall from 1987 to 1996. Youths (defined by the study as being under the age of twenty) use psychotropic drugs almost as often as adults do now. The most pronounced increases—700 percent among youths on Medicaid and 1,400 percent among youths enrolled in HMOs—came in the use of amphetamines (mainly dextroamphetamine sulfate, which is used to treat attention deficit disorder). Antidepressants were the second most-commonly prescribed medication. See "Psychotropic Practice Patterns for Youth: A 10-Year Perspective," *Archives of Pediatrics and Adolescent Medicine* 157 (2003): 17–25.
2. As Goffman (1963) reminds us, stigma arises from the "special discrepancy" between an individual's "authentic" identity and the role that he

or she is expected to perform. College students may believe that pharmaceutical intervention can enable them to fulfill their roles as students; however, it may not eliminate the "disgrace" they experience either for not meeting what is expected of them (in a premedicated state) or for using medication for optimization (although this is increasingly acceptable in the student body and society at large). Despite a medical excuse that shifts blame from the person to the body (Conrad and Potter 2000:573), many ADHD students feel they must resort to strategies to save face and preserve selfhood in the face of possible stigmatization, for example, choosing to hide their pills or to publicly rejecting their diagnoses.

3. Recent data from the National Health Interview Survey (CDC 2004:17–25) reveal how the ADHD profile is changing across traditional race, class, and gender lines. In 2001–4, about 8 percent of children ages five to seventeen were reported to have been diagnosed with ADHD; 9 percent of white non-Hispanic children, 8 percent of black non-Hispanic children, 2 percent of Asian non-Hispanic children, and 4 percent of Hispanic children were reported to have ADHD. Almost 13 percent of white non-Hispanic children living in families with incomes below poverty level were reported to have ADHD—the highest of any group. In addition, two to three times more boys than girls were diagnosed with ADHD (CDC 2004). Similarly, Gross (2006) reported in the *New York Times* that equal amounts of psychiatric medication were consumed at low-income and high-income summer camps in 2006, where an estimated one-quarter of campers were medicated for ADHD.
4. The term "body projects" in the United States has centered more on shape, size, and form, not internal body. See, e.g., Joan Jacobs Brumberg's *Body Project: An Intimate History of American Girls.*
5. Interestingly, many of our informants suggested that as ADHD students, they purposely chose to attend a small liberal arts school because of the emphasis on structured learning and individual attention captured in the low student/teacher ratio, small class sizes, and engaged participatory teaching styles.
6. In contrast to other disorders that negatively affect the individual in all aspects of daily life (such as depression), the set of behaviors and tendencies that make up ADHD may only inhibit the performance of specific roles (such as the role of the student). For example, a number of researchers have found that ADHD is highly context-specific; many subjects reveal virtually no symptoms when performing activities they enjoy, are novel, or are very stimulating (Barkley 1990; Jacob, O'Leary, and Rosenblad 1978; Sleator and Ullman 1981). Most informants acknowledge that it is primarily in the context of the academic ethic that their ADHD challenges their desired performance and thus creates a need for

medication. In other contexts, such as social settings. ADHD can be enabling and sometimes described as a source of personality, fun, creativity, and eccentricity.

References

Barkley, R. A. 1990. "Attention Deficit Hyperactivity Disorder: A Handbook for Diagnosis and Treatment." New York: Guilford.

Bell, Susan E. 2000. "Experiencing Illness in/and Narrative." Pp. 184–99 in *Handbook of Medical Sociology*, edited by C. E. Bird, P. Conrad, and A. M. Fremont. Upper Saddle River, NJ: Prentice Hall.

Burke, Peter. 1991. "Identity Processes and Social Stress." *American Sociological Review* 56:836–49.

Bury, Michael. 1982. "Chronic Illness as Biographical Disruption." *Sociology of Health and Illness* 13(4):451–68.

Centers for Disease Control (CDC). 2004. "Summary Health Statistics for US Children." *National Health Interview Survey* 17–25.

Charmaz, Kathy. 1997. "Identity Dilemmas of Chronically Ill Men." Pp. 35–63 in *Grounded Theory in Practice*, edited by A. L. Strauss and J. Corbin. Thousand Oaks, CA: Sage.

Clarke, Adele E., Janet Shim, Jennifer Fishman, Jennifer Fosket, and Laura Mamo. 2003. "Biomedicalization: Technoscientific Transformations of Health, Illness, and U.S. Biomedicine." *American Sociological Review* 68:161–94.

Conrad, Peter and Deborah Potter. 2000. "From Hyperactive Children to ADHD Adults: Observations on the Expansion of Medical Categories." *Social Problems* 47(4):559–82.

Conrad, Peter and Joseph Schneider. 1992. *Deviance and Medicalization: From Badness to Sickness*. Philadelphia: Temple University Press.

DeGrandpre, Richard. 1999. *Ritalin Nation: Rapid-Fire Culture and the Transformation of Human Consciousness*. New York: Norton.

Diller, Lawrence. 1999. *Running on Ritalin: A Physician Reflects on Children, Society, and Performance in a Pill.*. New York: Bantam Books.

Gubrium, Jaber and James A. Holstein. 2000. "The Self in a World of Going Concerns." *Symbolic Interaction* 23(2):95–115.

Hochschild, Arlie. 1983. *The Managed Heart*. Berkeley: University of California Press.

Jacob, R. G., K. D. O'Leary, and C. Rosenblad. 1978. "Formal and Informal Classroom Settings: Effects on Hyperactivity." *Journal of Abnormal Child Psychology* 6(1):47–59.

Kadison, Richard and Theresa DiGeronimo. 2004. *College of the Overwhelmed: The Campus Mental Health Crisis and What to Do about It*. San Francisco: Jossey-Bass.

Karp, David A. 2006. *Is It Me or My Meds? Living with Antidepressants*. Cambridge, MA: Harvard University Press.

Lareau, Annette. 2003. *Unequal Childhoods: Class, Race, and Family Life*. Berkeley: University of California Press.

Loe, Meika, Carrie DeWitt, Cassie Quirindongo, and Rebecca Sandler. 2006. "Medically Disciplined Bodies: College Students Managing Performance Pressures in the Pharmaceutical Era." (Unpublished).

Martin, Emily. 1994. *Flexible Bodies*. Boston: Beacon.

Nissen, Steven. 2006. "ADHD Drugs and Cardiovascular Risk." *New England Journal of Medicine* 354:1445–48.

Pierret, Janine. 2003. "The Illness Experience: State of Knowledge and Perspectives for Research." *Sociology of Health and Illness* 25(2):4–22.

Rafalovich, Adam. 2004. *Framing ADHD Children: A Critical Examination of the History, Discourse, and Everyday Experience of Attention Deficit/Hyperactivity Disorder*. Lanham, MD: Lexington Books.

———. 2005. "Exploring Clinician Uncertainty in the Diagnosis and Treatment of Attention Deficit Hyperactivity Disorder." *Sociology of Health and Illness* 27(3):305–23.

Rau, William and Ann Durand. 2000. "The Academic Ethic and College Grades: Does Hard Work Help Students to 'Make the Grade'?" *Sociology of Education* 73(1):19–38.

Reitzes, Donald and Peter Burke. 1980. "College Student Identity: Measurements and Implications." *Pacific Sociological Review* 23(1):45–66.

Rose, Nikolas. 2007. *The Politics of Life Itself*. Princeton, NJ: Princeton University Press.

Ross, Catherine and Beckett Broh. 2000. "The Roles of Self-Esteem and the Sense of Personal Control in the Academic Process." *Sociology of Education* 73(4):270–84.

Rothman, Sheila M. and David J. Rothman. 2003. *The Pursuit of Perfection: The Promise and Perils of Medical Enhancement*. New York: Pantheon.

Shils, Edward. 1997. *The Calling of Education*. Chicago: University of Chicago Press.

Sleator, E. K. and R. L. Ullman. 1981. "Can the Physician Diagnose Hyperactivity in the Office?" *Pediatrics* 67(11):13–17.

Smith, Davis and Bessie Oster. 2006. "Prescription Drug Misuse on Campus." Paper presented at American College Health Association annual meetings, New York, May 31.

Swidler, A. 1986. "Culture in Action: Symbols and Strategies." *American Sociological Review* 51:273–86.

Taylor, Charles. 1992. *The Ethics of Authenticity*. Cambridge, MA: Harvard University Press.

Vannini, Philip. 2006. "Dead Poets' Society: Teaching, Publish-or-Perish, and Professors' Experiences of Authenticity." *Symbolic Interaction* 29(2):235–57.

Romantic Exchanges

(2007)

BRADLEY WRIGHT

Romantic love is the thing of poets, songwriters, college students text-messaging, and—sociologists. One way that sociologists explain love is from the perspective of exchange theory. According to this theory, people think about relationships in terms of the various benefits and costs available to them, and they choose the relationships with the most benefits.

Think about the relationships that you've been in. What are some of the benefits that you received? They can make you feel loved and special. It's fun to have somebody to do things with—you feel less lonely. They can also offer sexual gratification.

What are some of the costs? They can take a ton of time and money, even when you don't have much of either. They can be full of conflict. They can produce a lot of anxiety, and there's the always-present threat of rejection.

Once we have become aware of these benefits and costs, how do we use them to figure out what to do? Two decision-making standards have been proposed. The first is called *comparison level.* We figure out what we have to gain from a relationship and then we compare it to what we have had in the past. If the potential relationship is better than our previous ones were, we go for it. If it's not, we don't. The idea here is that we want something better than we've had before.

The other decision-making standard is *comparison level of alternatives.* We evaluate a current or future relationship not against past relationships but against other options that we think are available to us. The operating principle here is "can you do better?" Should you get involved with a particular person? Well, it depends on your other options.

These decision standards apply to both getting into a new relationship and to staying in an existing relationship. Should you ask someone out? Do you think that a relationship with that person will provide you more benefits than your past relationships did (i.e., comparison level)? Do you think that you would do better asking someone else out instead (i.e., comparison level of alternatives)? Likewise, if you are already in a relationship, how long should you stay in it? You might stay as long as it's better than what you've had in the past or until you think you can do better.

Now that you understand this sociological perspective on relationships, I would recommend being careful with how you use it. Specifically, society has rules and guidelines about how we present our decisions to potential romantic partners.

When you're at the local bar this weekend and see a very attractive person, don't go up to them and tell them that they exceed both your comparison level and comparison level of alternatives. Even saying that the benefits of hooking up exceed the costs probably won't work. This is where poets and songwriters come in—they provide much more useful advice on how to enact our romantic lives.

Being 100% honest about the exchange aspect of relationships, even if you're being truthful, can make you sound rather coldhearted and calculating. Consider the following exchange in a personal ad on Craigslist. In it, a beautiful woman discusses her problems meeting her ideal mate, and in response a wealthy man subjects her to a rather brutal cost-benefit analysis. White this online exchange may or may not reflect a real conversation, it is still an interesting example of exchange theory.

Personal Ad

What am I doing wrong?

Okay, I'm tired of beating around the bush. I'm a beautiful (spectacularly beautiful) 25 year old girl. I'm articulate and classy. I'm not from New York. I'm looking to get married to a guy who makes at least half a million a year. I know how that sounds, but keep in mind that a million a year is middle class in New York City, so I don't think I'm overreaching at all.

Are there any guys who make 500K or more on this board? Any wives? Could you send me some tips? I dated a business man who makes average around 200–250. But that's where I seem to hit a roadblock. 250,000 won't get me to central park west. I know a woman in my yoga class who was married to an investment banker and lives in Tribeca, and she's not as pretty as I am, nor is she a great genius. So what is she doing right? How do I get to her level?

Here are my questions specifically:

- Where do you single rich men hang out? Give me specifics—bars, restaurants, gyms
- What are you looking for in a mate? Be honest guys, you won't hurt my feelings
- Is there an age range I should be targeting (I'm 25)?
- Why are some of the women living lavish lifestyles on the upper east side so plain? I've seen really 'plain jane' boring types who have nothing to offer married to incredibly wealthy guys. I've seen drop dead gorgeous girls in singles bars in the east village. What's the story there?
- Jobs I should look out for? Everyone knows—lawyer, investment banker, doctor. How much do those guys really make? And where do they hang out? Where do the hedge fund guys hang out?
- How you decide marriage vs. just a girlfriend? I am looking for MARRIAGE ONLY

Please hold your insults—I'm putting myself out there in an honest way. Most beautiful women are superficial; at least I'm being up front about it. I wouldn't be searching for these kind of guys if I wasn't able to match them—in looks, culture, sophistication, and keeping a nice home and hearth.

Response

I read your posting with great interest and have thought meaningfully about your dilemma. I offer the following analysis of your predicament. Firstly, I'm not wasting your time, I qualify as a guy who fits your bill; that is I make more than $500K per year. That said here's how I see it.

Your offer, from the prospective of a guy like me, is plain and simple a crappy business deal. Here's why. Cutting through all the B.S., what you suggest is a simple trade: you bring your looks to the party and I bring my money. Fine, simple. But here's the rub, your looks will fade and my money will likely continue into perpetuity . . . in fact, it is very likely that my income increases but it is an absolute certainty that you won't be getting any more beautiful!

So, in economic terms you are a depreciating asset and I am an earning asset. Not only are you a depreciating asset, your depreciation accelerates! Let me explain, you're 25 now and will likely stay pretty hot for the next 5 years, but less so each year. Then the fade begins in earnest. By 35 stick a fork in you!

So in Wall Street terms, we would call you a trading position, not a buy and hold . . . hence the rub . . . marriage. It doesn't make good business sense to "buy you" (which is what you're asking) so I'd rather lease. In case you think I'm being cruel, I would say the following. If my money were to go away, so would you, so when your beauty fades I need an out. It's as simple as that. So a deal that makes sense is dating, not marriage.

Separately, I was taught early in my career about efficient markets. So, I wonder why a girl as "articulate, classy and spectacularly beautiful" as you has been unable to find your sugar daddy. I find it hard to believe that if you are as gorgeous as you say you are that the $500K hasn't found you, if not only for a tryout.

By the way, you could always find a way to make your own money and then we wouldn't need to have this difficult conversation.

With all that said, I must say you're going about it the right way. Classic "pump and dump." I hope this is helpful, and if you want to enter into some sort of lease, let me know.

So, what's the lesson here? While it might be a good idea to know why we make romantic decisions, we might want to be discreet about how we discuss them with potential or existing romantic partners.

That being said, let's get out there this weekend and maximize comparison levels!

■ TALK ABOUT IT

1. How does people's "frontstage" behavior differ from their behavior "backstage"? What happens when these regions aren't carefully maintained?
2. As a college student, how do you work to manage your identity? How do others you have observed attempt to construct impressions about their identities?
3. Can you think of other examples of people making social exchanges, as Wright describes in "Romantic Exchanges"? Do we judge those people as severely as people who are forthcoming about wanting to exchange looks for wealth? Why or why not?
4. How does the public respond to political spouses who remain with their mates after infidelity? Why do people have such strong opinions about what might otherwise be a private family decision?
5. Can you think of other examples of people breaching unwritten social rules? How do people respond to the "breacher"?

■ WRITE ABOUT IT

1. Drawing on Goffman's and Raskoff's selections, describe what benefits social "actors" derive from keeping certain information "backstage." What commonplace behavior could be damaging for people in the public eye if it were to appear "frontstage"?
2. Consider your own perception of yourself as a student. In what way can you relate to some of the comments of Loe and Cuttino's respondents, setting aside the issue of ADHD? How have you found that establishing a sense of identity differs from when you were in high school?
3. Have you ever accidentally breached a norm, as Wright discusses in "Grocery Shopping, Ordering Whoppers, and Borat"? Describe the incident—the reaction of others, as well as your own. Did you attempt to "save face"? If so, how?
4. How would you describe yourself? List several of your best attributes, and discuss how social interactions with others have come to shape what you think about yourself.
5. Think about a romantic relationship (it can be your own or someone else's; don't feel the need to disclose the identities of the people involved). Aside from money and looks, what exchanges did the partners made? How did their involvement with one another benefit them materially and/or socially?

DO IT

1. Observe the behavior of a roommates or family members. How does their behavior change when they are "frontstage" in the public arena, compared to "backstage," in private? Note even minor details and write a report of your findings.
2. Go to any online dating forum. What details do people choose to share about themselves? What presumably holds "exchange value" on the dating market?
3. Go to the center of your campus, a shopping mall, or any other public place where you will see lots of people. Observe passersby for an hour. Do you observe any breaching, as Wright described in his article? How do others respond to the individual violating a norm?
4. Interview five of your friends about how they might have changed since entering college. Has the workload required them to alter their perceptions of themselves? Has any experience created a shift in how they think about themselves?
5. Watch *Borat*, *Brüno*, *Jackass*, or some other film that contains examples of norm-breaching. What norms are violated? How do people in the films respond to this violation? What message are the performers in the film trying to convey by violating these unwritten rules?

4

Community, Organizations, and Social Groups

Module Goal: ***Achieve a better understanding of how organizations operate and what motivates people to get involved in their communities.***

As social beings, humans must find ways to manage and organize their interactions with each other. Sociologists study how, when, and why groups come together for a common purpose. Sometimes this purpose is to help another group within the population. Other groups form along lines of worship. Still others are created purely for fun.

While reading the selections in this section, think of the organizations you belong to. Do you go to meetings with this group, or contribute your time in support of this organization? If you have a job, you are exchanging your time to further the goals of the organization. If you are part of a club, what purpose does it play in your life?

The German social theorist Max Weber, who wrote during the late nineteenth and early twentieth centuries, focused on how organizations are structured, among other sociological topics. Written at a time when capitalism was growing more complex and many modern-day corporations were born, Weber's essay on bureaucracies describes how such organizations organize themselves for maximum efficiency. Although today the word bureaucracy implies inefficiency, Weber describes how organizations divide labor in ways that are hierarchical, making the chain of decision making clear. He notes that bureaucracies have written rules that guide participants in achieving the organization's goals, and that people in authority positions often derive status from their positions.

But bureaucracies can also be resistant to change, and sometimes rules actually *impede* the smooth functioning of an organization. Think about some of the bureaucracies you have encountered: if you are enrolled in college now, you surely are familiar with at least one.

Janis Prince Inniss describes one particular challenge she faced in dealing with an organization set up for a good cause: to transport people needing medical treatment to and from the hospital. Though grateful that this service exists to help her mother, Inniss describes how the transport service's bureaucracy occasionally made her mother's treatment more difficult.

Sometimes charitable organizations are staffed by volunteers who have little authority to challenge existing rules. Have you ever volunteered for an organization? Robert Putnam, author of "Civic Participation," examines long-term trends in American participation in community-based groups. Fewer people seem willing to show up for community activities today, Putnam concludes.

Sally Raskoff, in "Beyond Bowling Alone," challenges Robert Putnam's conclusions by arguing that many newer forms of civic engagement include forming online communities. For example, President Barack Obama's election came in large part from his campaign's ability to organize supporters online. Raskoff encourages us to redefine the concept of community involvement; twenty-first-century involvement might not look like it did a generation ago, but it still exists.

Because our time and money are limited, organizations sometimes need to compete for our attention and our contributions. In "Social Movements and Your Attention Span," Bradley Wright provides one example of the lengths some organizations will go to in order to get public support—and to reduce it from other causes.

As you analyze communities, organizations, and social groups in everyday life, ask yourself the following questions:

1. How do the bureaucracies you are familiar with compare with Weber's description?
2. How do Putnam's arguments about the decline of civic engagement contrast with Raskoff's discussion about shifts in public participation?
3. Why are bureaucracies sometimes inefficient, and why do they often struggle for survival?

Bureaucracy

(1946 [1922])

MAX WEBER

CHARACTERISTICS OF BUREAUCRACY

Modern officialdom functions in the following specific manner:

I. There is the principle of fixed and official jurisdictional areas, which are generally ordered by rules, that is, by laws or administrative regulations.

1. The regular activities required for the purposes of the bureaucratically governed structure are distributed in a fixed way as official duties.
2. The authority to give the commands required for the discharge of these duties is distributed in a stable way and is strictly delimited by rules concerning the coercive means, physical, or otherwise, which may be placed at the disposal of officials.
3. Methodical provision is made for the regular and continuous fulfilment of these duties and for the execution of the corresponding rights; only persons who have the generally regulated qualifications to serve are employed.

In public and lawful government these three elements constitute 'bureaucratic authority.' In private economic domination, they constitute bureaucratic 'management.' Bureaucracy, thus understood, is fully developed in political and ecclesiastical communities only in the modern state, and, in the private economy, only in the most advanced institutions of capitalism. Permanent and public office authority, with fixed jurisdiction, is not the historical rule but rather the exception. . . .

II. The principles of office hierarchy and of levels of graded authority mean a firmly ordered system of super- and subordination in which there is a supervision of the lower offices by the higher ones. Such a system offers the governed the possibility of appealing the decision of a lower office to its higher authority, in a definitely regulated manner. . . . The principle of hierarchical office authority is found in all bureaucratic structures . . . It does not matter for the character of bureaucracy whether its authority is called 'private' or 'public.'

III. The management of the modern office is based upon written documents ('the files'), which are preserved in their original or draught form. There is, therefore, a staff of subaltern officials and scribes of all sorts. The body of officials actively engaged in a 'public' office, along with the respective apparatus of material implements and the files, make up a 'bureau.' In private enterprise, 'the bureau' is often called 'the office.'

In principle, the modern organization of the civil service separates the bureau from the private domicile of the official, and, in general, bureaucracy segregates official activity as something distinct from the sphere of private life. Public monies and equipment are divorced from the private property of the official. . . .

IV. Office management, at least all specialized office management . . . usually presupposes thorough and expert training. This increasingly holds for the modern executive and employee of private enterprises, in the same manner as it holds for the state official.

V. When the office is fully developed, official activity demands the full working capacity of the official, irrespective of the fact that his obligatory time in the bureau may be firmly delimited. In the normal case, this is only the product of a long development, in the public as well as in the private office. Formerly, in all cases, the normal state of affairs was reversed: official business was discharged as a secondary activity.

VI. The management of the office follows general rules, which are more or less stable, more or less exhaustive, and which can be learned. Knowledge of these rules represents a special technical learning which the officials possess. . . .

The reduction of modern office management to rules is deeply embedded in its very nature. The theory of modern public administration, for instance, assumes that the authority to order certain matters by decree—which has been legally granted to public authorities—does not entitle the bureau to regulate the matter by commands given for each case, but only to regulate the matter abstractly. This stands in extreme contrast to the regulation of all relationships through individual privileges and bestowals of favor, which is absolutely dominant in patrimonialism, at least in so far as such relationships are not fixed by sacred tradition.

THE POSITION OF THE OFFICIAL

Whether he is in a private office or a public bureau, the modern official always strives and usually enjoys a distinct *social esteem* as compared with the governed. His social position is guaranteed by the prescriptive rules of rank order . . .

The actual social position of the official is normally highest where, as in old civilized countries, the following conditions prevail: a strong demand for administration by trained experts; a strong and stable social differentiation, where the official predominantly derives from socially and economically privileged strata because of the social distribution of power: or where the costliness of the required training and status conventions are binding upon him. The possession of educational certificates is usually linked with qualification for office. Naturally, such certificates or patents enhance the 'status element' in the social position of the official. For the rest this status factor in individual cases is explicitly and impassively acknowledged; for example, in the prescription that the acceptance or rejection of an aspirant to an official career depends upon the consent ('election') of the members of the official body. . . .

Usually the social esteem of the officials as such is especially low where the demand for expert administration and the dominance of status conventions are weak. This is especially the case in the United States; it is often the case in new settlements by virtue of their wide fields for profit-making and the great instability of their social stratification.

Bureaucracy: Resistance to Change and Adaptation

(2008)

JANIS PRINCE INNISS

As I have discussed on everydaysociologyblog.com, my mother has been undergoing treatment for cancer. With hospitals stays behind her, once Mum began daily radiation therapy and chemotherapy treatments, transportation became a new challenge for her. She was recovering from major surgeries and receiving treatments that, while ultimately expected to be beneficial, are rather punishing. She would need transportation. Turns out that having cancer qualified her for Tampa's HARTplus door-to-door bus service for people with disabilities. We were thrilled that she would be picked up at home and taken to her appointments, but that elation did not last for long as the dysfunctions of the bureaucracy soon rivaled the gratitude I felt for this service.

According to Google Maps, the trip from Mum's home to the location of her appointments is 13.3 miles and takes 22 minutes. Indeed, that's about the time it takes me when I can take her. But with HARTplus, all bets are off! Once it took her three hours on their van to get home. Hungry and thirsty, but abiding by the HARTplus rules, she ate or drank nothing for the entire time; due to her surgeries and treatments she eats small meals, so this was particularly punishing and added to her fatigue.

Every day for one week drivers were to pick her up at a treatment center on a hospital campus, but they routinely went to the main hospital entrance. This kept happening, although at the time of booking Mum gave the street address and the name—clearly visible outside—of the building where she would be. A few times the drivers left, saying that she was not there! Not only did this leave her stranded, but it also counted as a no-show, essentially a demerit that could ultimately cause her to be expelled from the service.

Add to this a rather peculiar scheduling system in which she must book transportation for an hour prior to an appointment, but must be ready half an hour earlier than that; in other words, she has to be ready to leave an hour and a half before any appointment, but may have to wait an hour for the van to arrive. As inconvenient as that might be, I thought that meant she would always be on time. Wrong. She has missed several appointments because she arrived late!

Another challenge has been rescheduling the time that she would be picked up when a procedure took longer than expected. Recently when a nurse called HARTplus to say that she would not be ready at her scheduled time, the nurse was told that she had to call one hour before the scheduled pickup time—as opposed to the longer notice she was trying to give them! The nurse got busy and called less than an hour before the appointed time, so the van went to pick her up. Mum was not ready, so she was deemed a no-show and received a demerit!

There is more. HARTplus does not allow passengers to book their return trips less than an hour and a half after their appointments. So although the *longest* her appointment lasts is 15 minutes when she goes for a sometimes daily shot to boost her white blood cells, Mum cannot hope to wait less than an hour for a return ride! She has to assume that she'll spend about four hours each day—most of it waiting for her van—to get one shot. Her description of one recent trip is unfortunately not unusual:

> I was picked up at 4:40, despite being scheduled for 4:00. We were zipping along nicely on [the appropriate freeway]; the heavy rush-hour traffic was in the opposite direction. The driver left the freeway two exits before mine, got on another freeway for a short while, and then got off near downtown into the afternoon traffic and long lines at the traffic lights. We then went on a toll road that put us into downtown at rush hour! Because of this circuitous route, without picking up or dropping off anyone else, I got home at 5:45.

The work of the sociologist Robert Merton can help us make sense of this. Merton pointed out that bureaucrats are rule-bound. They are trained to depend on policies. Commonsense and flexibility are anathema to bureaucrats. There is no reward for creativity in bureaucracies either. The reasons and benefits of having rules are many, and I assume that there are good reasons for the HARTplus rules; however, they do not fit the needs of cancer patients. When HARTplus decided to include cancer patients in their system, mid- to high-level bureaucrats should have considered how their system would need to be adapted to serve this new clientele. They should have learned some basics about the needs of cancer patients and trained their drivers about the pertinent issues.

Regardless of the disability, but certainly because of the side effects that chemotherapy produces (nausea, vomiting, and fatigue, to name a few), a priority would be the prompt transportation of these clients. In fact, what Merton called bureaucratic ritualism—holding on to rules even when they prevent the stated goals—seems to be operating given that these services do not exemplify the company's stated mission to be "safe, dependable, and cost effective." Merton recognized that a major weakness of bureaucracies is that they have trouble serving our needs; perhaps given the requirement for change and adaptability in transporting this population, it is not surprising that bureaucracy can render the service ineffective.

Civic Participation

(2000)

ROBERT D. PUTNAM

> Americans of all ages, all stations in life, and all types of disposition are forever forming associations. There are not only commercial and industrial associations in which all take part, but others of a thousand different types—religious, moral, serious, futile, very general and very limited, immensely large and very minute. . . . Nothing, in my view, deserves more attention than the intellectual and moral associations in America.[1]

These lines from Alexis de Tocqueville, a perceptive French visitor to early-nineteenth-century America, are often quoted by social scientists because they capture an important and enduring fact about our country. Today, as 170 years ago, Americans are more likely to be involved in voluntary associations than are citizens of most other nations; only the small nations of northern Europe outrank us as joiners.[2]

The ingenuity of Americans in creating organizations knows no bounds. Wandering through the *World Almanac* list of 2,380 groups with some national visibility from the Aaron Burr Society to the Zionist Organization of America, one discovers such intriguing bodies as the Grand United Order of Antelopes, the Elvis Presley Burning Love Fan Club, the Polish Army Veterans Association of America, the Southern Appalachian Dulcimer Association, and the National Association for Outlaw and Lawman History. . . . Many Americans today are actively involved in educational or school service groups like PTAs, recreational groups, work-related groups, such as labor unions and professional organizations, religious groups (in addition to churches), youth groups, service and fraternal clubs, neighborhood or homeowners groups, and other charitable organizations. Generally speaking, this same array of organizational affiliations has characterized Americans since at least the 1950s.[3]

Official membership in formal organizations is only one facet of social capital, but it is usually regarded as a useful barometer of community involvement. What can we learn from organizational records and social surveys about Americans' participation in the organized life of their communities? Broadly speaking, American voluntary associations may be divided into three categories: community based, church based, and work based. Let us begin with the most heterogeneous, all those social, civic, and leisure groups that are community based—everything from B'nai B'rith to the Parent-Teacher Association.

The record appears to show an impressive increase in the sheer number of voluntary associations over the last three decades. The number of nonprofit organizations of national scope listed in the *Encyclopedia of Associations* more than doubled from 10,299 to 22,901 between 1968 and 1997. Even taking account of the increase in population during this period, the number of national organizations per capita has increased by nearly two-thirds over the last three decades. Excited by this fact, some observers speak, perhaps too hastily, of a "participation revolution" in American politics and society. This impression of a rapid growth in American organizational life is reinforced—but also qualified—by numerous recent studies of the explosion of interest groups represented in Washington since the 1960s. What these studies reveal is ever more groups speaking (or claiming to speak) on behalf of ever more categories of citizens.[4]

In fact, relatively few of the tens of thousands of nonprofit associations actually have mass membership. Many, such as the Animal Nutrition Research Council, the National Conference on Uniform Traffic Accident Statistics, and the National Slag Association, have no individual members at all. A close student of associations in America, David Horton Smith, found that barely half of the groups in the 1988 *Encyclopedia of Associations* actually had individual members. . . . [O]ver this quarter century the number of voluntary associations roughly tripled, but the average membership seems to be roughly one-tenth as large—more groups, but most of them much smaller. The organizational eruption between the 1960s and the 1990s represented a proliferation of letterheads, not a boom of grassroots participation.

The headquarters of the nation's largest organization and one of the most rapidly growing, the American Association of Retired Persons (AARP), however, is not in Florida or California or Arizona (where its constituents are concentrated), but at 6th and E Streets in Washington, a few minutes' walk from Capitol Hill. Similarly, the most visible newcomers to the national associational scene are headquartered within ten blocks of the intersection of 14th and K Streets in Washington: the Children's Defense Fund, Common Cause, the National Organization for Women, the National Wildlife Federation, Greenpeace, Friends of the Earth, the National Gay and Lesbian Task Force, the National Trust for Historic Preservation, the Wilderness Society, the National Right to Life Committee, and Zero Population Growth. The "new associationism" is almost entirely a denizen of the Washington hothouse.[5] The proliferating new organizations are professionally staffed advocacy organizations, not member-centered, locally based associations.[6] The newer groups focus on expressing policy views in the national political debate, not on providing regular connection *among* individual members at the grass roots.

◇ ◇ ◇

From the point of view of social connectedness, however, the new organizations are sufficiently different from classic "secondary associations" that we need to invent a new label—perhaps "tertiary associations."[7] For the vast majority of their members, the only act of membership consists in writing a check for dues or perhaps occasionally reading a newsletter.[8] Few ever attend any meetings of such organizations—many never have meetings at all—and most members are unlikely ever knowingly to encounter any other member. The bond between any two members of the National Wildlife Federation or the National Rifle Association is less like the bond between two members of a gardening club or prayer group and more like the bond between two Yankees fans on opposite coasts (or perhaps two devoted L. L. Bean catalog users): they share some of the same interests, but they are unaware of each other's existence. Their ties are to common symbols, common leaders, and perhaps common ideals, but *not* to each other.

So the vigor of the new Washington-based organizations, though they are large, proliferating, and powerful, is an unreliable guide to the vitality of social connectedness and civic engagement in American communities. . . .

Trends in numbers of voluntary associations nationwide are not a reliable guide to trends in social capital, especially for associations that lack a structure of local chapters in which members can actually participate. What evidence can we glean from organizations that *do* involve their members directly in community-based activity? The membership rolls of such associations across the twentieth century reveal a strikingly parallel pattern across many different civic associations. This pattern is summarized in figure 1, which is a composite of the changing membership rates for thirty-two diverse national, chapter-based organizations throughout the twentieth century, ranging from B'nai B'rith and the Knights of Columbus to the Elks club and the Parent-Teacher Association.[9] . . .

For most of the twentieth century growing numbers of Americans were involved in such chapter-based associations.[10] Of course, the U.S. population was growing, too, but our analysis here eliminates that inflation factor by considering the membership rate as a percentage of the relevant population. So the long upward wave in this figure reflects the fact that more and more women belonged to women's clubs, more rural residents belonged to the Grange, more youths belonged to the Scouts, more Jews belonged to Hadassah and B'nai B'rith, and more men belonged to service clubs. Probably one important factor in this steady growth was the continuing rise in educational levels, but in the aggregate the increase in membership exceeded even that. As the decades passed, America seemed more and more to fit Tocqueville's description.

The sharp dip in this generally rising line of civic involvement in the 1930s is evidence of the traumatic impact of the Great Depression on American communities. The membership records of virtually every adult organization in this sample bear the scars of that period. In some cases the effect was a brief pause in ebullient

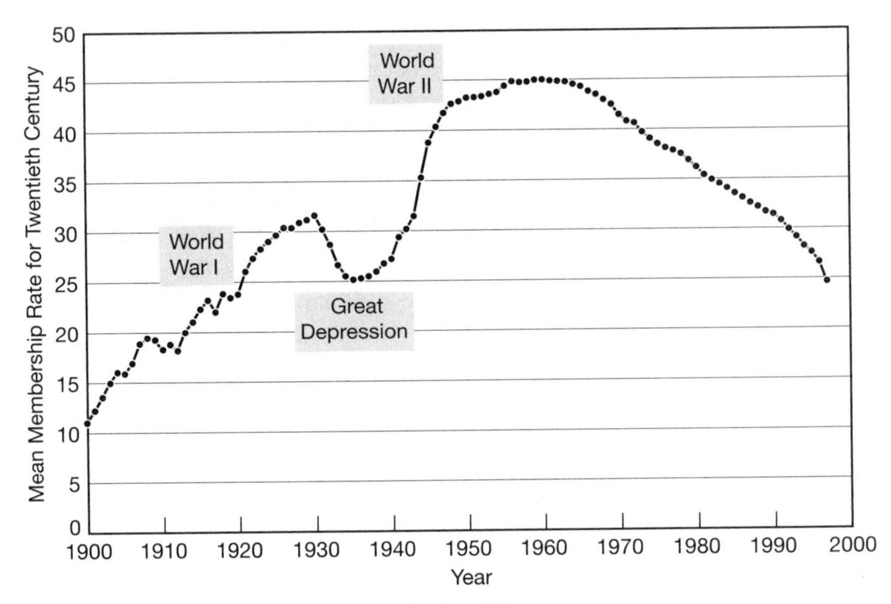

Source: Putnam, Robert. "Civic Participation," from *Bowling Alone*. 2000.

FIGURE 1 Average Membership Rate in Thirty-two National Chapter-Based Associations, 1900–1997

growth, but in others the reversal was extraordinary. Membership in the League of Women Voters, for example, was cut in half between 1930 and 1935, as was membership in the Elks, the Moose, and the Knights of Columbus. This period of history underlines the effects of acute economic distress on civic engagement.

Most of these losses had been recouped, however, by the early 1940s. World War II occasioned a massive outpouring of patriotism and collective solidarity. At war's end those energies were redirected into community life. The two decades following 1945 witnessed one of the most vital periods of community involvement in American history. As a fraction of potential membership, the "market share" for these thirty-two organizations skyrocketed. Because of growing population, the increase was even more dramatic. . . .

By the late 1950s, however, this burst of community involvement began to tail off, even though absolute membership continued to rise for a while. By the late 1960s and early 1970s membership growth began to fall further behind population growth. . . . As the decline deepened, absolute membership began to slip and then to plummet. By century's close the massive postwar boom in membership rates in these organizations had been eliminated.[11]

One useful illustration is provided by the Parent-Teacher Association (PTA). In the middle years of the twentieth century the local PTA was among the most common of community organizations. For example, one grassroots survey of associa-

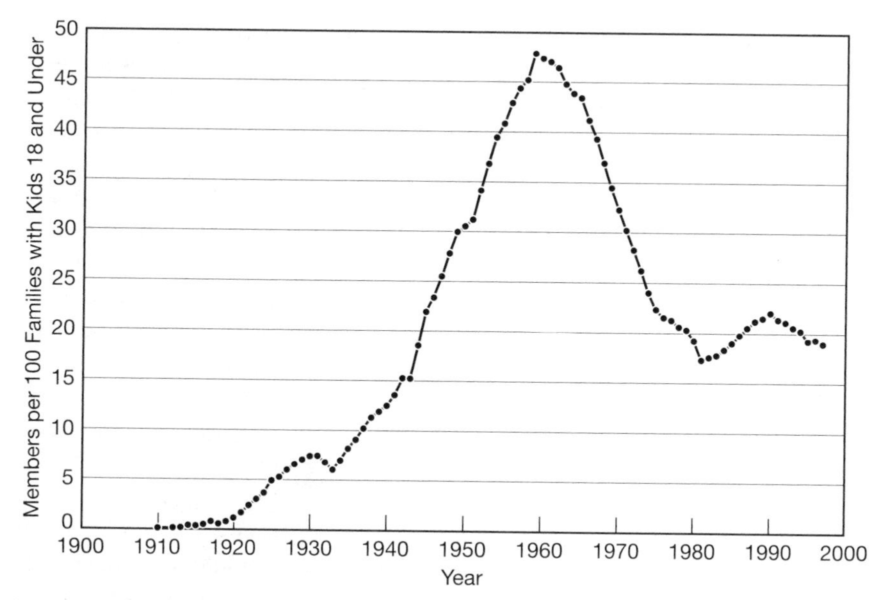

Source: Putnam, Robert. "Civic Participation," from *Bowling Alone*. 2000.

FIGURE 2 The Rise and Fall of the PTA, 1910–1997

tional membership in the early 1960s found that the PTA had more members than any other secular organization. More than one in every six adult Nebraskans reported membership in their local PTA.[12] That the absolute number of PTA members was relatively high during the baby boom is, of course, no surprise at all—more parents, more PTA members. What is more striking, however, is that the *percentage* of parents nationwide who joined the PTA more than doubled between 1945 and 1960, continuing the vertiginous and almost uninterrupted growth of this organization since its founding in 1910. On average, every year throughout the quarter century up to 1960 another 1.6 percent of all American families with kids—more than 400,000 families a year—was added to the PTA membership rolls. Year after year, more and more parents became involved in this way in their children's education.

The reversal of six decades of organizational growth—captured graphically in figure 2—came with shocking suddenness in 1960. When the subsequent decline finally leveled off two decades later, membership in the PTA had returned to the level of 1943, utterly erasing the postwar gains. A brief rebound in the 1980s had all but vanished by the late 1990s. On average, every year throughout the quarter century after 1960 another 1.2 percent of all American families with kids—more than 250,000 families a year—dropped out of the PTA. . . .

The PTA's collapse in the last third of the century is no less sensational than its earlier growth. What could account for this dramatic turnaround? Some part of the decline in rates of membership in the PTA is an optical illusion. Parental involvement in local school service organizations (not all of which are affiliated with the national Parent-Teacher Association) did not fall as rapidly as membership in PTA-affiliated groups. First, during the 1970s, following disagreements about school politics, as well as about national dues, some local parent-teacher organizations disaffiliated from the national PTA either to join competing organizations or to remain wholly independent. As a result, many of the missing local PTAs reappeared as local PTOs (parent-teacher organizations unaffiliated with the national PTA), although many of these now independent local associations themselves subsequently withered. Moreover, bitter battles over school desegregation in the 1960s caused wholesale disaffiliation from the national PTA in several southern states. . . .

In two important respects, membership figures for individual organizations are an uncertain guide to trends in Americans' involvement in voluntary associations. First, the popularity of specific groups may wax and wane quite independently of the general level of community engagement. Even though our historical analysis so far has cast as wide a net as possible in terms of different types of organizations, it is certainly possible that newer, more dynamic organizations have escaped our scrutiny. If so, the picture of decline that we have traced may apply only to "old-fashioned" organizations, not to all community-based organizations. . . .

Second, formal "card-carrying" membership may not accurately reflect actual involvement in community activities. An individual who "belongs to" half a dozen community groups may actually be active in none. What really matters from the point of view of social capital and civic engagement is not merely nominal membership, but active and involved membership. To address these two issues, we need to turn from formal organizational records to social surveys, which can encompass organizational affiliations of all sorts and can distinguish formal membership from actual involvement.

Several reviews of national surveys conducted between the early 1950s and the early 1970s found evidence of steady and sustained growth in organizational memberships of all sorts.[13] . . . In 1957 a team of University of Michigan researchers conducted a careful nationwide survey on behalf of the National Institute of Mental Health (NIMH), and in 1976 a group led by one of the earlier researchers replicated the 1957 study, taking great care to make the studies as nearly identical as possible.[14] . . .

In many respects, the Michigan-NIMH study found considerable stability in the life experiences of Americans across these two turbulent decades. Nevertheless, one of their central findings was a "reduced integration of American adults into the social structure."[15] Over these two decades informal socializing with friends and relatives declined by about 10 percent, organizational memberships fell by 16 percent, and church attendance declined by 20 percent. Examined more closely, these surveys found significant declines in membership in unions; church groups; fraternal and veterans organizations; civic groups, such as PTAs; youth groups; charities; and a catch-all "other" category.[16] . . .

How has group membership in general changed over the last quarter century? The GSS [General Social Survey] provides the most comprehensive measure of trends in Americans' formal membership in many different types of groups. The short answer is that formal membership rates have not changed much, at least if we ignore rising educational levels. The percentage of the public who claim formal membership in at least one organization has fallen a bit, but that trend has been glacial so far, from a little less than 75 percent in the mid-1970s to a little less than 70 percent in the early 1990s.[17] Membership in church-related groups, labor unions, fraternal organizations, and veterans groups has declined, but this decline has been mostly offset by increases in professional, ethnic, service, hobby, sports, school fraternity, and other groups. To be sure, the only substantial increase is in the domain of professional organizations, and that growth has barely kept pace with occupational growth in the professions themselves. . . .

This ambiguous conclusion, however, is drastically altered when we examine evidence on more active forms of participation than mere card-carrying membership. Service as an organizational officer or committee member is very common among active members of American organizations. In 1987, 61 percent of all organization members had served on a committee at some time or other, and 46 percent had served as an officer.[18] Among self-described "active" members—roughly half of the adult population—73 percent had served at some time as a committee member, 58 percent had served at some time as an officer, and only 21 percent had never served as either an officer or a committee member. Sooner or later, in short, the overwhelming majority of active members in most voluntary associations in America are cajoled into playing some leadership role in the organization.

How has the number of Americans who fit this bill changed over the last few decades? Between 1973 and 1994 the number of men and women who took *any* leadership role in *any* local organization—from "old-fashioned" fraternal organizations to new age encounter groups—was sliced by more than 50 percent.[19] This dismaying trend began to accelerate after 1985: in the ten short years between 1985 and 1994, active involvement in community organizations in this country fell by 45 percent. By this measure, at least, nearly half of America's civic infrastructure was obliterated in barely a decade.

Eighty percent of life, Woody Allen once quipped,[20] is simply showing up. The same might be said of civic engagement, and "showing up" provides a useful standard for evaluating trends in associational life in our communities. . . . In 1975–76 American men and women attended twelve club meetings on average each year—essentially once a month. By 1999 that figure had shrunk by fully 58 percent to five meetings per year. In 1975–76, 64 percent of all Americans still attended at least *one* club meeting in the previous year. By 1999 that figure had fallen to 38 percent. In short, in the mid-1970s nearly two-thirds of all Americans attended club meetings, but by the late 1990s nearly two-thirds of all Americans *never* do. By comparison with other countries, we may still seem a nation of joiners, but by comparison with our own recent past, we are not—at least if "joining" means more than nominal affiliation.

In community life, as in the stock market, past performance is no guarantee of future performance, so it is hazardous to assume that trends over the next several decades will mirror those over the last several. Nevertheless, the downtrend has been more or less uninterrupted for more than a quarter century, and if the current rate of decline were to continue, clubs would become extinct in America within less than twenty years. Considering that such local associations have been a feature of American community life for several hundred years, it is remarkable to see them so high on the endangered species list.

Notes

1. Tocqueville, *Democracy in America*, 513–517.
2. A Gallup poll in 1981 ranked America at the top of twelve industrialized democracies in the frequency of membership in voluntary associations; the 1991 World Values Survey found that among thirty-five nations, the United States tied with Norway for fourth, lagging behind Sweden, Iceland, and the Netherlands. See Sidney Verba, Kay Lehman Schlozman, and Henry E. Brady, *Voice and Equality: Civic Voluntarism in American Politics* (Cambridge: Harvard University Press, 1995), 80, and Robert D. Putnam. "Bowling Alone: America's Declining Social Capital," *Journal of Democracy* 6 (January 1995): 65–78.
3. Murray Hausknecht, *The Joiners* (New York: Bedminster Press, 1962); Nicholas Babchuk and Alan Booth, "Voluntary Association Membership: A Longitudinal Analysis," *American Sociological Review* 34 (February 1969): 31–45.
4. Gale Research Company, *Encyclopedia of Associations*, as quoted in the Statistical Abstract of the United States (various years); Allan J. Cigler and Burdett A. Loomis, eds., *Interest Group Politics*, 3rd ed. (Washington, D.C.: CQ Press, 1991), 11; Kay Lehman Schlozman and John T. Tierney, *Organized Interests and American Democracy* (New York: Harper & Row, 1986); Jack L. Walker, *Mobilizing Interest Groups in America: Patrons, Professions, and Social Movements* (Ann Arbor: University of Michigan Press, 1991); Frank R. Baumgartner and Beth L. Leech, *Basic Interests: The Importance of Groups in Politics and in Political Science* (Princeton, N.J.: Princeton University Press, 1998), esp. 102–106.

5. In 1971, 19 percent of all national nonprofit associations had their headquarters in Washington; by 1981 29 percent did, according to Robert H. Salisbury, "Interest Representation: The Dominance of Institutions," *American Political Science Review* 78 (March 1984): 64–76. See also Cigler and Loomis, *Interest Group Politics*, 3rd ed., and Smith, "National Nonprofit, Voluntary Associations."
6. Theda Skocpol, "Advocates without Members: The Recent Transformation of American Civic Life," in *Civic Engagement in American Democracy*, eds. Theda Skocpol and Morris P. Fiorina (Washington, D.C.: Brookings Institution Press, 1999), 461–509.
7. Sociologists use the term *primary associations* to refer to one's most intimate connections—the family and intimate friends—and *secondary associations* to refer to less intimate connections, such as churches, unions, and community organizations. For a prescient analysis, see Bernard Barber, "Participation and Mass Apathy in Associations," in *Studies in Leadership*, ed. A. W. Gouldner (New York: Harper, 1950).
8. Some of these organizations, of course, provide their members with commercial services, like group insurance or high-fashion T-shirts, but in this role they are indistinguishable from other mail-order firms.
9. Figure 2 is intended only as a rough summary of the experiences of more than thirty separate organizations. Given the inevitable uncertainty about membership data extending across an entire century and the unavoidable arbitrariness about which groups to include, the details of figure 2 should not be overinterpreted. I have sought to encompass all large national chapter-based civic organizations in the 1950s and 1960s plus any that came into existence thereafter (none did) plus a selection of smaller "niche" organizations, like Hadassah, NAACP, Optimists, and the 4-H. . . . See Theda Skocpol, with the assistance of Marshall Ganz, Ziad Munson, Bayliss Camp, Michele Swers, and Jennifer Oser, "How America Became Civic," in *Civic Engagement in American Democracy*, eds. Skocpol and Fiorina, 27–80.
10. Though quantitative data on nineteenth-century associationism are scarce, it appears that the only period of unambiguous decline in associational activity between 1865 and 1965 was from 1930 to 1935. For some evidence and relevant historiography, see Gerald Gamm and Robert D. Putnam, "The Growth of Voluntary Associations in America, 1840–1940," *Journal of Interdisciplinary History* 29 (spring 1999), 511–557. John Harp and Richard J. Gagan, "Changes in Rural Social Organizations: Comparative Data from Three Studies," *Rural Sociology* 34 (1969): 80–85, report that organizational density was unchanged between 1924 and 1936 and then increased by 50 percent by 1964—independent confirmation of figure 1.

11. American civic life also quickened after 1865 and after 1918, but both those postwar booms proved reasonably durable, even in the face of substantial economic dislocation, whereas the slump after 1960 began and persisted in periods of prosperity. In other words, the post-1960 slump should not be interpreted as merely some reversion to prewar "normalcy."
12. Nicholas Babchuk and Alan Booth, "Voluntary Association Membership: A Longitudinal Analysis," *American Sociological Review* 34 (1969): 31–45.
13. Frank R. Baumgartner and Jack L. Walker, "Survey Research and Membership in Voluntary Associations," *American Journal of Political Science* 32 (November 1988): 908–928; Smith, "Trends in Voluntary Group Membership."
14. Joseph Veroff, Elizabeth Douvan, and Richard A. Kulka, *The Inner American: A Self-Portrait from 1957 to 1975* (New York: Basic Books, 1981).
15. Veroff, Douvan, and Kulka, *Inner American*, 17.
16. Only the rubric of "social groups" (ranging from country clubs to sports teams), which accounted for roughly one membership in five, did not decline over these two decades; the rate of membership in this category rose from 13 percent to 16 percent.
17. In fifteen separate surveys between 1974 and 1994 the General Social Survey asked Americans "whether or not you are a member of" each of fifteen specific types of groups, from "fraternal groups" to "church-related groups," as well as a catch-all category of "other." Only limited subsamples of the GSS in 1993 and 1994 were asked the relevant question, so the results from those years are less reliable.
18. These data are drawn from the 1987 General Social Survey. A 1973 Louis Harris survey (study number 2343 at the University of North Carolina Institute for Research in the Social Sciences) found that 48 percent of all organizational members had served at one time as a club officer, virtually identical to the 1987 GSS figure.
19. Author's analysis of data from Roper Social and Political Trends archive.
20. William Safire, "On Language," *New York Times*, August 13, 1989.

Beyond Bowling Alone

(2009)

SALLY RASKOFF

Nine years ago Robert Putnam, a professor at Harvard University, wrote *Bowling Alone*, a book that pointed out declining participation rates in bowling leagues and other social phenomena as a harbinger of declining civic engagement and volunteering.

Many years before that book appeared, the Frenchman Alexis de Tocqueville toured the United States in the early 1800s and pointed out in his book *Democracy in America* that America is a "nation of joiners." He was amazed at the number of voluntary associations we had in which we provided services for each other.

In noting an apparent decline in volunteering behavior, the Putnam book created concern since volunteering is a very important mechanism for creating positive social change; it is how we solve our most intractable problems. The concern is that if Americans are less engaged in the public sphere, our society will suffer.

Over the last couple of decades we have transferred some former government services to the nonprofit sector, which depends on volunteers and philanthropy. Many people have moved into gated communities and segregated ourselves into enclaves based on social class. Thus if fewer of us are giving our money and time to community issues, our communities will no longer be able to thrive or even to solve the most basic problems when they occur. Declines in donations are likely to increase as the economy struggles, too.

I've been thinking about these issues in recent days as our new president called for each of us to participate in solving the country's woes. The Obama campaign's success lay in its organizing capacity, technological savvy, quick communication, and mobilization of tremendous numbers of people, which broke new ground for political campaigns. More people than we've seen in a long time have been involved in political action in a very public way.

Research shows varying patterns of volunteering, yet the definition rests on giving time to formal nonprofit organizations. This is problematic enough considering cultural variations and definitions of what constitutes "volunteering." For example, is helping a neighbor with groceries volunteering?

Many people give time and energy to help and socialize with those beyond their own family in a variety of ways, including bowling in a community league, serving meals at the local shelter, giving out blankets for the Red Cross, and helping out at the church or temple or mosque bake sale. As you can see in the figure on the following page, the volunteer rate is actually higher in the early 2000s than it was in the two benchmark years before.

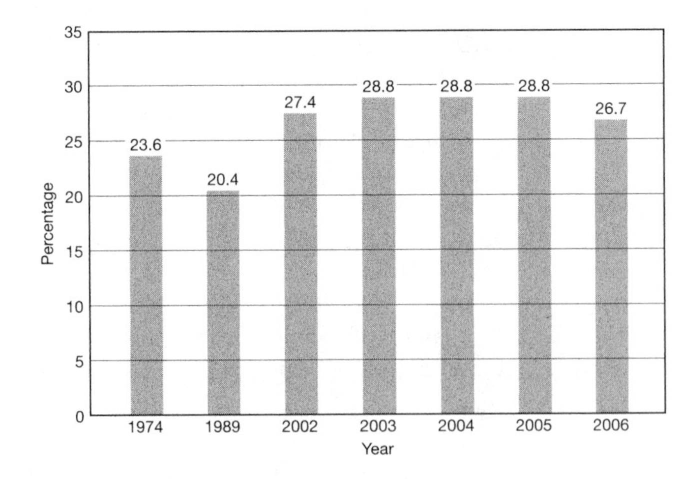

Source: From volunteeringinamerica.gov

National Adult Volunteer Rate, Ages 16 and Older, 1974 to Present.

The organization MoveOn.org is one recent example of a new kind of social involvement—though clicking through sites online is not necessarily equivalent to physical participation when it comes to civic engagement. (Neither is "shopping" for the cause in my opinion.) However, online "mobilizers" such as MoveOn .org bring people together in very efficient ways.

These days, "virtual" volunteering often fosters the communication and mobilization that are essential for the formation and success of social movements. Because of the speed and efficiency of technological communication, new organizations can be formed quickly.

In the early 1900s, an amazing number of nonprofit organizations were founded to help address issues that our country was facing. Nonprofit organizations exist to provide services when government and private for-profit organizations won't or can't—government or private for-profit services may be available to all or to select groups who are most in need of those services. The American Red Cross was congressionally chartered in 1905, the National Association for the Advancement of Colored People (NAACP) was founded in 1909, the Boy Scouts of America and the National Urban League in 1910, the Girl Scouts of America in 1912.

As the Obama presidency begins, I wonder if we won't see another spurt of organizational generation in which new (maybe virtual) nonprofits will emerge as we address our problems through this newer form of organizing—one that may not be accurately captured by the research on volunteering. We might not be bowling in leagues as much as we used to, but that doesn't mean we aren't involved in our communities. Civic engagement looks different today than it might have just a few years ago.

How much civic engagement do you see in your own circle of friends and in your community? Are you a member of any groups on Facebook that get people together in nonvirtual ways to do service activities?

Social Movements and Your Attention Span

(2008)

BRADLEY WRIGHT

There are countless social movements in society, and they all want you to pay attention.

In a social movement, a group of ordinary people come together to advance a social cause. In the early twentieth century, women activists banded together to promote women's suffrage—the right to vote. In the 1960s, the civil rights movement promoted justice for African-Americans. The anti-nuclear movement protests the development of nuclear energy. Mothers Against Drunk Driving advocate tougher laws against drunk driving.

A common goal of most social movements, whatever their focus, is to get the public's attention. Sociologists understand this via resource mobilization theory—how being in the public's eye helps movements accomplish their goals. It brings in workers for the cause, it helps collect money, and it might result in changed laws. In fact, more than a few social movements have as their explicit goal raising public awareness about their cause. For example, the National Children's Cancer Society (NCCS—a worthy cause if ever there was one) explicitly states the importance of raising public awareness. They write:

> Take action against a disease that has been ignored for too long. Raising awareness in your community about childhood cancer and the survivorship issues surrounding it is critical to our mutual mission. Awareness can inform and change minds. It can change public policy and raise more funds for crucial patient services. Awareness of the programs of the NCCS can give hope to families facing the chaos of a diagnosis of childhood cancer.

As a result, social movements work hard at having distinctive approaches. The movement for breast cancer awareness has the ubiquitous pink ribbons. Not to be outdone, other movements have adopted their own ribbon colors. For example, white ribbons are for lung cancer and violence against women. Yellow ribbons are for deployed soldiers and suicide awareness. Blue ribbons are for child abuse and the victims of Hurricane Katrina. Purple is for lupus and showing religious tolerance. Green is for environmental awareness and Lyme disease. Puzzle-piece ribbons are for autism. Ribbons with the words "publish me" are for untenured faculty—okay, I made up that last one.

(As an aside, some have criticized ribbons and wristbands as "slacktivism"—doing things that make us feel good about helping others without actually spending any of our time or money in doing so.)

In addition to distributing ribbons, social movements do lots of other things. They can hold demonstrations. The Million Man March in 1995 brought hundreds of thousands of demonstrators to Washington, D.C. to promote unity and political participation among black men. They also get celebrity endorsements. For example, People for the Ethical Treatment of Animals (PETA) regularly features actors and actresses in its commercials who sometimes take off their clothes (a time-honored method of getting attention). Sometimes PETA just advertises on television and in print, similar to a business seeking customers.

There's a problem, however—there is only so much public attention to go around, and there are a lot more movements wanting attention than there is attention to give. As such, movements compete with each other for the public's attention. In this sense, groups like the National Children's Cancer Society are fighting against not only the disease but also other disease-related groups. If, for example, the Juvenile Diabetes Research Foundation does a particularly good job of raising awareness, then there may be less to give the NCCS.

This puts social movements in a bind. On one hand, they are probably sympathetic to the causes behind their competing social movements. I suspect that members of the NCCS are also against juvenile diabetes. On the other hand, these other groups are their competitors, taking resources from them.

For example, a group called Pandarescue.org is group dedicated to saving wild pandas and their habitat. It's a small group—I'd never heard of them before seeing a commercial, and so I imagine that they struggled with how to get their message out. They came up with their commercial that explicitly recognizes the resource mobilization model described above. But the problem for pandas is not just deforestation and poaching, but also the public support for whales. Yes, Greenpeace and others portray whales as beautiful, noble creatures, but the Pandarescue.org commercial shows whales violently attacking cute baby seals—the shocking truth! (My guess is that baby harp seals and cute little kittens are also harmful for pandas. Hopefully future commercials will get at that as well.)

In a way, I appreciate its honesty because I imagine that a lot of social movements think that they are more important than other movements. Still, it is so, so tacky. It certainly does exemplify the social mobilization theory of social movements.

Related Link

Watch the Pandarescue.org commercial at www.youtube.com/watch?v=ORjOmiluonc

TALK ABOUT IT

1. Discuss your experiences within a large bureaucracy. What did they have in common with Weber's examples, or Prince Inniss's?
2. What are some positive and negative aspects of the organization of the bureaucracies you have experienced? What would large institutions be like without bureaucracy, as Weber defines it?
3. Have you gotten involved with a club or community group like one Putnam mentions? Did you feel more connected to your community?
4. Have you gotten involved in an online community, like one Raskoff describes? Did you feel a greater sense of connection with other participants? Did this involvement lead to any in-person meetings or activities?
5. Raskoff describes nontraditional ways of organizing online. Discuss how the Internet has altered the meaning of community.

WRITE ABOUT IT

1. Think about your experiences with large and sometimes inefficient bureaucracies. Describe how you would reorganize them to work better. Include a flow chart showing the chain of command.
2. Think about your experience with a bureaucracy. List the rules that might govern that particular organization, drawing from Weber's list. Why do those particular rules persist? How difficult or easy would it be to change them?
3. Charities compete with each other for volunteer time and donor money. Choose one cause, real or fictitious, and write a brief description about why this charity is important for society and merits support.
4. Think about the community or communities you grew up in. Discuss how people got involved in the neighborhood—for example, in schools, religious organizations, or political groups. What impact did these groups have on your community? If these groups had not existed, what would have been different in your community?
5. Choose one social problem or challenge in your community. Describe an organization that could work on solving this problem. Explain how the group will be organized and run, how it will recruit members, and how it will help the community.

DO IT

1. Interview a friend or family member who works in what Weber would define as a bureaucracy. Using Weber's points, create questions to learn more about how the organization operates: its hierarchical nature, its structure, and so

forth. Does your interviewee have any suggestions to make the bureaucracy more efficient?

2. Join a campus-based community group. From your experience, does the group create a greater sense of community? In what ways does it reflect—or not reflect—Putnam's ideas, and Raskoff's ideas?
3. Start your own group that seeks to provide a needed service or assistance to your community. What challenges do you face in getting members and resources?
4. Look up a company online that you might want to work for someday. Based on the information on their website, how is the company structured? Describe its hierarchical chain of command as best you can from the information online. Where do you see yourself fitting into this organization, based on its current structure?
5. Find information online about three or four charities with similar goals. How do they frame their cause differently from one another? Are there any overt attempts to disparage a "competing" organization, as Wright details?

5

Crime and Deviance

Module Goal: ***Consider how crime is measured, why crime and deviance happen, and how people respond to crime and deviance.***

Crime, any violation of the law, is a central area of study within sociology. Nearly every community has a special organization designated to prevent and respond to crime, and state and federal budgets devote significant resources to law enforcement. Billions of dollars are spent each year preventing and punishing crime, and a great deal of research is conducted to understand why crime happens.

The first step to understanding crime is figuring out what kinds of crimes are taking place, and how many crimes are occurring. Collecting data and reporting on the number of crimes is an imperfect science; each crime needs to be defined and agreed on by the different agencies that compile data. For instance, different jurisdictions might disagree on what constitutes a hate crime, and report their numbers accordingly. Even with a general consensus on how to define a crime, the data can sometimes be misinterpreted and minor increases might be exaggerated by media reports. In "Murder and Statistics," I examine homicide trends from the Federal Bureau of Investigation's annual Uniform Crime Reports and compare the data with news coverage on the same report. The actual statistics tell a slightly different story from the one on the news.

Sociologists have developed many theories to explain crime and why it increases and decreases at certain times and places. No single theory can explain all of crime's causes, nor is any theory without its limitations. Still, some theories, such as James Q. Wilson and George L. Kelling's "Broken Windows" explanation, can become popular with policymakers and the general public. Yet, many sociologists have challenged the Broken Windows hypothesis. Bradley Wright explores the shortcomings of Wilson and Kelling's theory in "Beyond Broken Windows."

The words *crime* and *deviance* are sometimes used interchangeably, but they are distinct concepts. Whereas crime refers to a specific violation of a law, deviance can be any behavior that draws a significantly negative response; and whereas some acts might be considered both criminal and deviant, sometimes "deviant" behavior violates no law. For example, someone who bathes only once a month is not doing anything illegal but will likely experience rejection among people who bathe more frequently.

Sometimes deviance can garner a lot of attention. Patrick F. Parnaby and Vincent F. Sacco consider whether some people are drawn toward deviance in order to become famous. They include a discussion of Robert Merton's strain theory, which posits that all societies have celebrated goals that all members are encouraged to strive for. As you read this piece, consider whether one of our celebrated goals today is to become famous, and whether people will even encourage derision to achieve this goal.

What explains those who are already famous but become infamous? Sally Raskoff's "Rehab, Labeling, and Deviance" focuses the reality show *Celebrity Rehab* to explore how people manage a damaged sense of self in a public way. Her piece highlights how people labeled "deviant" attempt to deal with social stigma.

As you analyze crime and deviance in everyday life, consider the following questions:

1. Is violent crime is getting worse, better, or staying the same? What has shaped your impression of crime trends?
2. Why does crime happen? Under what circumstances does your theory work best? Under what circumstances does your theory *not* explain why crime happens?
3. Is deviance just about getting noticed? What factors make people behave in ways considered deviant? How do people cope with the judgments of others if labeled deviant?

Murder and Statistics

(2007)

KAREN STERNHEIMER

People who watched the national news on June 4, 2007, heard a frightening story. The FBI released their preliminary report of crimes that occurred in 2006. According to the report, murder was on the rise—up 6.7 percent in America's biggest cities. Experts warned we could be in for a new crime wave, and offered explanations for the upswing. Should we be afraid?

Maybe. Or maybe not.

Let's consider the basic implication when we hear grim statistics like this: things really *are* getting worse, and there is a number to prove it. But in this case, and in many others, we hear only some of the numbers—maybe just one if it seems to tell a dramatic story. What else should we consider before deciding that America really is a more dangerous place?

First, fortunately, murder is one of the rarest crimes. Of all violent crimes reported to police in 2005, including rape, assault, and robbery, only 1.2 percent of those were homicides. But we have a fascination with murder—what would become of network television dramas if shows like *CSI* or *Law & Order* weren't on the air? We are attracted to popular culture that helps us to deal with the scariest parts of the human experience from a safe distance. But sometimes this focus can make us think that the world is a more dangerous place than it actually is.

Second, let's get back to the 6.7 percent rise that the major news networks grimly reported. Based on ten cities with populations over one million, this number reflects approximately 194 more homicides than in 2005. No doubt, every homicide is a tragedy and has a ripple effect that goes way beyond the victims themselves, but this is a relatively small number when you consider the combined populations of those ten cities.

Just over 25 million people live in the nation's largest cities, and according to these early reports in 2006, 3,085 people were killed, or one-tenth of one percent of the population.

By contrast, nearly 95 million Americans live in smaller cities that experienced *reductions* in homicide. Cities with 50,000 to 99,000 residents actually experienced a 6.9 percent *decline* in 2006, but this rarely made it into news reports.

Why the omission? Could it be that fewer people would be affected in smaller cities, and the national news media wouldn't report on something that affects

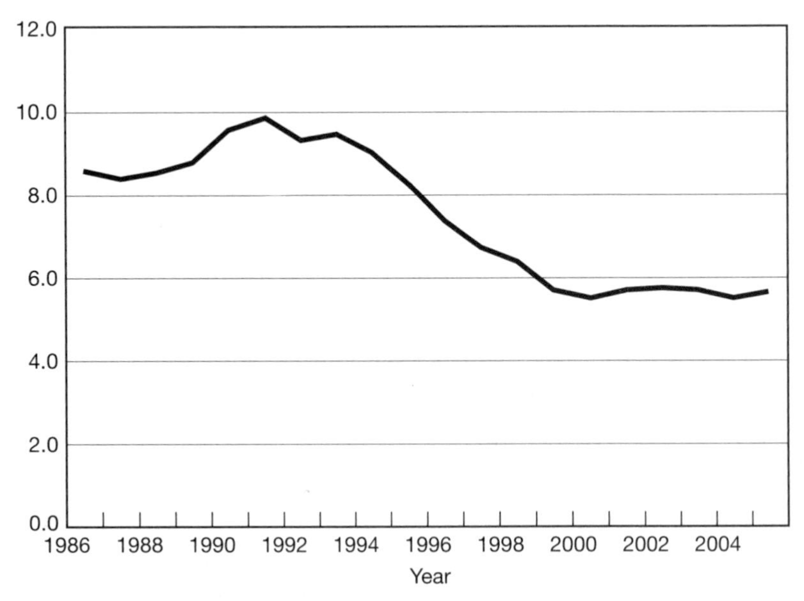

Source: FBI Uniform Crime Reports, www.fbi.gov/ucr/cius2006/data/table_01.html

FIGURE 1 Murder and Nonnegligent Manslaughter Rate, 1986–2005

only a small group? Actually, more people live in midsized cities than those with more than one million residents.

Bad news gets our attention. Consider this headline: MURDER RISES THREE-TENTHS OF A PERCENT! Not impressed? Apparently news organizations weren't either, but that's the overall change from 2005 to 2006 nationwide. This change translates to about fifty more homicides in a population of 300 million. Again, each murder is a tragedy, but three-tenths of a percent raise hardly suggests a major upward trend.

Hearing about rises in crime from year to year, no matter how remote, is still frightening—sort of like a reverse lottery you don't want to win. News reports have a way to stoke this fear. They are not lying when they say that we have experienced increases in homicides in three of the last four years. That sounds like an ominous trend, no matter how small.

But since spiking in 1991, both murder and violent crimes in general have plummeted. Even with the estimated increase in 2006, nearly 8,000 fewer people were murdered in 2006 compared with the period when homicide rates were highest. The graph above gives you a visual perspective of the long-term trends, and how the mostly good news has been distorted.

It's also important to keep in mind that we are not all at equal risk for being the victims of homicide. Murder victims are overwhelmingly male; despite the long-held beliefs of female vulnerability, fully 79 percent of those killed are male.

Nearly half of all of these mostly male victims are African American, yet African Americans comprise only about eleven percent of the total population. This means that African Americans are four times more likely to be killed than we would expect by chance. The odds of an African American male becoming a homicide victim (33.4 per 100,000 people) is six times greater than the general population (5.6 per 100,000), and eight times greater than for white males (4.4 per 100,000).

In addition to masking racial inequality, a big drawback to national data is that homicide is a local rather than a national problem. Some cities experienced major declines in homicides, while others, such as New Orleans, had large increases. Especially since the hurricanes of 2005, this city has faced many well-documented problems that can't be generalized to the country as a whole.

New Orleans has traditionally been a city with a high poverty rate. Within cities, homicide rates also tend to be higher within areas with large concentrations of people living in poverty. While the FBI data contains information about the race of the victim and offender (but still uses the categories "white," "black," "other," an issue for another essay), there is no information on the income levels of those involved.

So do national murder rates matter at all? On many levels, not really. The numbers help us overlook the very real disparities in safety in our country, and they elide some of the major causes for these differences—such as racial segregation and the lack of opportunity many Americans experience.

National numbers aren't totally useless, though. We can compare our figures to those of other industrialized nations to see that far more people are killed in the United States than in many countries around the world.

Seemingly simple numbers, like those presented in June 2007 news reports, actually create more sociological questions than they answer. And the answers are invariably complex and varied, and probably don't make easy-to-digest soundbites. What do you think the answers are?

Related Link

FBI Uniform Crime Reports: www.fbi.gov/ucr/ucr.htm

Broken Windows

The Police and Neighborhood Safety (1982)

JAMES Q. WILSON AND GEORGE L. KELLING

In the mid-1970s the State of New Jersey announced a "Safe and Clean Neighborhoods Program," designed to improve the quality of community life in twenty-eight cities. As part of that program, the state provided money to help cities take police officers out of their patrol cars and assign them to walking beats. The governor and other state officials were enthusiastic about using foot patrol as a way of cutting crime, but many police chiefs were skeptical. Foot patrol, in their eyes, had been pretty much discredited. It reduced the mobility of the police, who thus had difficulty responding to citizen calls for service, and it weakened headquarters control over patrol officers.

Many police officers also disliked foot patrol, but for different reasons: it was hard work [and] it kept them outside on cold, rainy nights. . . . In some departments, assigning officers to foot patrol had been used as a form of punishment. And academic experts on policing doubted that foot patrol would have any impact on crime rates; it was, in the opinion of most, little more than a sop to public opinion. But since the state was paying for it, the local authorities were willing to go along.

Five years after the program started, the Police Foundation, in Washington, D.C., published an evaluation of the foot-patrol project. Based on its analysis of a carefully controlled experiment carried out chiefly in Newark, the foundation concluded, to the surprise of hardly anyone, that foot patrol had not reduced crime rates. But residents of the foot patrolled neighborhoods seemed to feel more secure than persons in other areas, tended to believe that crime had been reduced, and seemed to take fewer steps to protect themselves from crime (staying at home with the doors locked, for example). Moreover, citizens in the foot-patrol areas had a more favorable opinion of the police than did those living elsewhere. And officers walking beats had higher morale, greater job satisfaction, and a more favorable attitude toward citizens in their neighborhoods than did officers assigned to patrol cars.

These findings may be taken as evidence that the skeptics were right—foot patrol has no effect on crime; it merely fools the citizens into thinking that they are safer. But in our view, and in the view of the authors of the Police Foundation study (of whom Kelling was one), the citizens of Newark were not fooled at all. They knew what the foot-patrol officers were doing, they knew it was different from what motorized officers do, and they knew that having officers walk beats did in fact make their neighborhoods safer.

But how can a neighborhood be "safer" when the crime rate has not gone down—in fact, may have gone up? Finding the answer requires first that we understand what most often frightens people in public places. Many citizens, of course, are primarily frightened by crime, especially crime involving a sudden, violent attack by a stranger. This risk is very real, in Newark as in many large cities. But we tend to overlook another source of fear—the fear of being bothered by disorderly people. Not violent people, nor, necessarily, criminals, but disreputable or unpredictable people: panhandlers, drunks, addicts, rowdy teenagers, prostitutes, loiterers, the mentally disturbed.

What foot-patrol officers did was to elevate, to the extent they could, the level of public order in these neighborhoods. Though the neighborhoods were predominantly black and the foot patrolmen were mostly white, this "order-maintenance" function of the police was performed to the general satisfaction of both parties.

One of us (Kelling) spent many hours walking with Newark foot-patrol officers to see how they defined "order" and what they did to maintain it. One beat was typical: a busy but dilapidated area in the heart of Newark, with many abandoned buildings, marginal shops (several of which prominently displayed knives and straight-edged razors in their windows), one large department store, and, most important, a train station and several major bus stops. Though the area was run-down, its streets were filled with people, because it was a major transportation center. The good order of this area was important not only to those who lived and worked there but also to many others, who had to move through it on their way home, to supermarkets, or to factories.

. . . Disreputable regulars observed some informal but widely understood rules. Drunks and addicts could sit on the stoops, but could not lie down. People could drink on side streets, but not at the main intersection. Bottles had to be in paper bags. Talking to, bothering, or begging from people waiting at the bus stop was strictly forbidden. If a dispute erupted between a businessman and a customer, the businessman was assumed to be right, especially if the customer was a stranger. . . . Persons who broke the informal rules, especially those who bothered people waiting at bus stops, were arrested for vagrancy. Noisy teenagers were told to keep quiet.

A determined skeptic might acknowledge that a skilled foot-patrol officer can maintain order but still insist that this sort of "order" has little to do with the real sources of community fear—that is, with violent crime. To a degree, that is true. But two things must be borne in mind. First, outside observers should not assume that they know how much of the anxiety now endemic in many big-city neighborhoods stems from a fear of "real" crime and how much from a sense that the street is disorderly, a source of distasteful, worrisome encounters. The people of

Newark, to judge from their behavior and their remarks to interviewers, apparently assign a high value to public order, and feel relieved and reassured when the police help them maintain that order.

Second, at the community level, disorder and crime are usually inextricably linked, in a kind of developmental sequence. Social psychologists and police officers tend to agree that if a window in a building is broken and is left unrepaired, all the rest of the windows will soon be broken. This is as true in nice neighborhoods as in rundown ones. Window-breaking does not necessarily occur on a large scale because some areas are inhabited by determined window-breakers whereas others are populated by window-lovers; rather, one unrepaired broken window is a signal that no one cares, and so breaking more windows costs nothing. . . .

Philip Zimbardo, a Stanford psychologist, reported in 1969 on some experiments testing the broken-window theory. He arranged to have an automobile without license plates parked with its hood up on a street in the Bronx and a comparable automobile on a street in Palo Alto, California. The car in the Bronx was attacked by "vandals" within ten minutes of its "abandonment." The first to arrive were a family—father, mother, and young son—who removed the radiator and battery. Within twenty-four hours, virtually everything of value had been removed. Then random destruction began—windows were smashed, parts torn off, upholstery ripped. Children began to use the car as a playground. Most of the adult "vandals" were well-dressed, apparently clean-cut whites. The car in Palo Alto sat untouched for more than a week. Then Zimbardo smashed part of it with a sledgehammer. Soon, passersby were joining in. Within a few hours, the car had been turned upside down and utterly destroyed. Again, the "vandals" appeared to be primarily respectable whites.

Untended property becomes fair game for people out for fun or plunder and even for people who ordinarily would not dream of doing such things and who probably consider themselves law-abiding. Because of the nature of community life in the Bronx—its anonymity, the frequency with which cars are abandoned and things are stolen or broken, the past experience of "no one caring"—vandalism begins much more quickly than it does in staid Palo Alto, where people have come to believe that private possessions are cared for, and that mischievous behavior is costly. But vandalism can occur anywhere once communal barriers—the sense of mutual regard and the obligations of civility—are lowered by actions that seem to signal that "no one cares."

We suggest that "untended" behavior also leads to the breakdown of community controls. A stable neighborhood of families who care for their homes, mind each other's children, and confidently frown on unwanted intruders can change, in a few years or even a few months, to an inhospitable and frightening jungle. A piece of property is abandoned, weeds grow up, a window is smashed. Adults stop scolding rowdy children; the children, emboldened, become more rowdy. Families move out, unattached adults move in. Teenagers gather in front of the corner store. The merchant asks them to move; they refuse. Fights occur. Litter accumulates. People start drinking in front of the grocery; in time, an inebriate slumps to the sidewalk and is allowed to sleep it off. Pedestrians are approached by panhandlers.

At this point it is not inevitable that serious crime will flourish or violent attacks on strangers will occur. But many residents will think that crime, especially violent crime, is on the rise, and they will modify their behavior accordingly. They will use the streets less often, and when on the streets will stay apart from their fellows, moving with averted eyes, silent lips, and hurried steps. . . .

Such an area is vulnerable to criminal invasion. Though it is not inevitable, it is more likely that here, rather than in places where people are confident they can regulate public behavior by informal controls, drugs will change hands, prostitutes will solicit, and cars will be stripped. That the drunks will be robbed by boys who do it as a lark, and the prostitutes' customers will be robbed by men who do it purposefully and perhaps violently. . . .

In response to fear people avoid one another, weakening controls. Sometimes they call the police. Patrol cars arrive, an occasional arrest occurs but crime continues and disorder is not abated. Citizens complain to the police chief, but he explains that his department is low on personnel and that the courts do not punish petty or first-time offenders. To the residents, the police who arrive in squad cars are either ineffective or uncaring: to the police, the residents are animals who deserve each other. The citizens may soon stop calling the police, because "they can't do anything."

The process we call urban decay has occurred for centuries in every city. But what is happening today is different. . . . [I]n the period before, say, World War II, city dwellers—because of money costs, transportation difficulties, familial and church connections—could rarely move away from neighborhood problems. When movement did occur, it tended to be along public-transit routes. Now mobility has become exceptionally easy for all but the poorest or those who are blocked by racial prejudice. Earlier crime waves had a kind of built-in self-correcting mechanism: the determination of a neighborhood or community to reassert control over its turf. Areas in Chicago, New York, and Boston would experience crime and gang wars, and then normalcy would return, as the families for whom no alternative residences were possible reclaimed their authority over the streets.

. . . The citizen who fears the ill-smelling drunk, the rowdy teenager, or the importuning beggar is not merely expressing his distaste for unseemly behavior; he is also giving voice to a bit of folk wisdom that happens to be a correct generalization—namely, that serious street crime flourishes in areas in which disorderly behavior goes unchecked. The unchecked panhandler is, in effect, the first broken window. Muggers and robbers, whether opportunistic or professional, believe they reduce their chances of being caught or even identified if they operate on streets where potential victims are already intimidated by prevailing conditions. If the neighborhood cannot keep a bothersome panhandler from annoying passersby, the thief may reason, it is even less likely to call the police to identify a potential mugger or to interfere if the mugging actually takes place.

Our experience is that most citizens like to talk to a police officer. Such exchanges give them a sense of importance, provide them with the basis for gossip, and allow them to explain to the authorities what is worrying them (whereby they gain a modest but significant sense of having "done something" about the problem). You approach a person on foot more easily, and talk to him more readily, than you do a person in a car. Moreover, you can more easily retain some anonymity if you draw an officer aside for a private chat. Suppose you want to pass on a tip about who is stealing handbags, or who offered to sell you a stolen TV. In the inner city, the culprit, in all likelihood, lives nearby. To walk up to a marked patrol car and lean in the window is to convey a visible signal that you are a "fink."

The essence of the police role in maintaining order is to reinforce the informal control mechanisms of the community itself. The police cannot, without committing extraordinary resources, provide a substitute for that informal control. On the other hand, to reinforce those natural forces the police must accommodate them. And therein lies the problem.

Even in areas that are in jeopardy from disorderly elements, citizen action without substantial police involvement may be sufficient. Meetings between teenagers who like to hang out on a particular corner and adults who want to use that corner might well lead to an amicable agreement on a set of rules about how many people can be allowed to congregate, where, and when.

Where no understanding is possible—or if possible, not observed—citizen patrols may be a sufficient response. There are two traditions of communal involvement in maintaining order: One, that of the "community watchmen," is as old as the first settlement of the New World. Until well into the nineteenth century, volunteer watchmen, not policemen, patrolled their communities to keep order. They did so, by and large, without taking the law into their own hands—without, that is, punishing persons or using force. Their presence deterred disorder or alerted the community to disorder that could not be deterred. There are hundreds of such efforts today in communities all across the nation. Perhaps the best known is that of the Guardian Angels, a group of unarmed young persons in distinctive berets and T-shirts, who first came to public attention when they began patrolling the New York City subways but who claim now to have chapters in more than thirty American cities. Unfortunately, we have little information about the effect of these groups on crime. It is possible, however, that whatever their effect on crime, citizens find their presence reassuring, and that they thus contribute to maintaining a sense of order and civility.

Though citizens can do a great deal, the police are plainly the key to order maintenance. For one thing, many communities . . . cannot do the job by themselves. For another, no citizen in a neighborhood, even an organized one, is likely to feel the sense of responsibility that wearing a badge confers. Psychologists have done many studies on why people fail to go to the aid of persons being attacked or seeking help, and they have learned that the cause is not "apathy" or "selfishness" but the absence of some plausible grounds for feeling that one must personally accept responsibility. Ironically, avoiding responsibility is easier when a lot of people are standing about. On streets and in public places, where order is so important, many people are likely to be "around," a fact that reduces the chance of any one person acting as the agent of the community. The police officer's uniform singles him out as a person who must accept responsibility if asked. . . .

Above all, we must return to our long-abandoned view that the police ought to protect communities as well as individuals. Our crime statistics and victimization surveys measure individual losses, but they do not measure communal losses. Just as physicians now recognize the importance of fostering health rather than simply treating illness, so the police—and the rest of us—ought to recognize the importance of maintaining, intact, communities without broken windows.

Beyond Broken Windows

(2008)

BRADLEY WRIGHT

A funny thing happens in our kitchen sink. Sometimes it doesn't have any dirty dishes in it (okay, not that often, but it does happen). When the sink is empty, my family and I usually put our dishes straight into the dishwasher. At other times, however, there are dirty dishes sitting in the sink. When this happens, we all put any additional dishes straight into the sink, not even considering the extra several seconds it takes to put them into the dishwasher. Why in the world am I writing about my kitchen sink? It turns out that what happens with the sink is a reasonable analogy for one of the more important crime-prevention theories: the theory of broken windows.

The theory of broken windows originated in a 1982 article by James Q. Wilson and George L. Kelling in *The Atlantic Monthly*. They started with the idea that some broken windows in a building invite more broken windows. As Wilson wrote in the foreword to *Fixing Broken Windows*:

> If a factory or office window is broken, passersby observing it will conclude that no one cares or no one is in charge. In time, a few will begin throwing rocks to break more windows. Soon all the windows will be broken, and now passersby will think that, not only is no one in charge of the building, no one is in charge of the street on which it faces. Only the young, the criminal, or the foolhardy have any business on an unprotected avenue, and so more and more citizens will abandon the street to those they assume prowl it. Small disorders lead to larger and larger ones, and perhaps even to crime.[1]

According to Wilson and Kelling, the same holds true for neighborhoods and crime. Just as broken windows invite rocks, and dirty sinks get more dishes, so too certain characteristics of neighborhoods attract and promote crime. A neighborhood that is riddled with vandalism, litter, abandoned buildings, and cars signals that no one is taking care of the neighborhood. A neighborhood that has lots of petty crime, such as public drunkenness, pickpockets, and traffic violations, signals that crime is accepted. In both cases the neighborhood is sending out a signal that crime is tolerated if not outright accepted. This encourages

1. James Q. Wilson, foreword to George L. Kelling and Catherine M. Coles, *Fixing Broken Windows: Restoring Order and Reducing Crime in Our Communities* (New York: Free Press, 1996), xv.

crime among residents of the neighborhood and it attracts criminals from other neighborhoods as well.

The importance of this theory is its implications for crime prevention. The way to cut down on crime in a given location, according to the broken-window theory, is to change its physical and social characteristics. This can be done by repairing buildings, sidewalks, and roads, and fixing anything that makes a neighborhood look rundown. It also means enforcing the law for even the smallest infractions. Police should ticket and/or arrest people for things as small as jaywalking, illegal panhandling, and public disorder. The logic is that by cracking down on small problems, the police are preventing more serious crimes.

The best-known application of the broken-window theory occurred in New York City, and depending on who you talk to, it was either a smashing success in preventing crime, an irrelevant policy, or an invasion of individuals' rights.

In 1993, Rudy Giuliani—who was briefly a 2008 presidential candidate—was elected mayor of New York City based on his "get tough on crime" platform. He hired William Bratton as the police chief. Bratton, who was heavily influenced by George Kelling, applied the principles of the broken-window theory. Bratton initiated a program of zero tolerance in which the NYPD cracked down on all sorts of minor infractions, including subway fare dodging, public drinking, urinating in public, and even the squeegee men—people who would wipe the windows of stopped cars and demand payment. A friend of mine who lived in New York City at that time even saw police telling people they could not sit on milk crates on the sidewalk—apparently that was against the law as well.

Almost immediately, rates of both petty and serious crimes dropped substantially. In the first year alone, murders were down 19% and car thefts fell by 15%, and crime continued to drop every year for the following ten years.

So, was this application of "broken windows" an unqualified success? Some critics say no.

In the same time period, crime dropped significantly in other major cities around the country—cities that had *not* adopted broken windows policy (see the figure on page 118). Crime dropped nationwide in the 1990s, and various reasons have been given for this overall crime drop. The crack epidemic of the 1980s was subsiding, and there were fewer people in the fifteen- to twenty-five-year-old age group, which accounts for so much crime. As such, the declines seen in New York City might not have resulted from new police policies but may have happened anyway.

Other critics argue that regardless of the effectiveness of broken windows, it was too costly in terms of individual rights. They claim that the police, emboldened by the mandate to enforce even the smallest of laws, frequently crossed over into harassment of individuals, especially racial minorities and the poor. The application of broken windows, with its zeal for reducing crime, produced unacceptable police behavior.

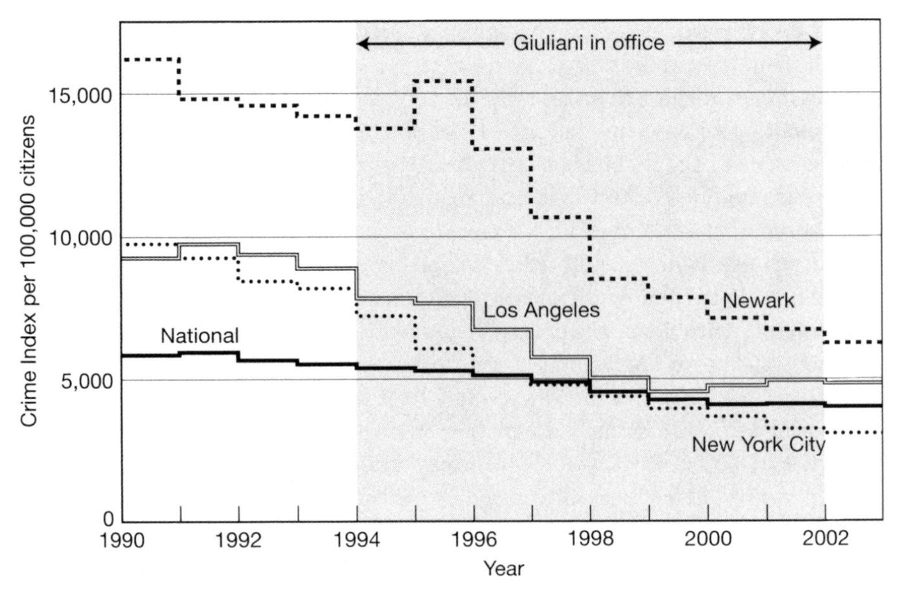

Source: http://en.wikipedia.org/wiki/File:Giuliani_crime_rate.png

Nonetheless, the results in New York City were sufficiently interesting that various police departments around the country have adopted principles of broken-window theory. In fact, William Bratton later served as the police chief of Los Angeles before becoming a consultant.

P.S. This essay shows that sociology covers everything of social importance, including the kitchen sink.

[The Relationship Between Celebrity and Deviant Behavior]

(2003)

PATRICK F. PARNABY AND VINCENT F. SACCO

This article revisits Merton's (1938 [1957, 1968]) original work(s) on the relationship between social structure, anomie, and deviant behavior. Specifically, it is argued that Merton's means/goals gap theory can be adapted to not only better reflect the contemporary normative character of post-industrial society, but also to illuminate how forms of deviant behavior have become adaptive responses to the structurally anomic condition that has emerged out of an incessant emphasis on fame at the level of popular culture and the structurally limited means by which it can be legitimately achieved.

A Mertonian analysis of the relationship between celebrity culture and deviant and criminal outcomes would seem to rest upon the empirical validity of three inter-related propositions. First, the desirability of fame and celebrity status is extremely widespread and thus approximates, in a Mertonian sense, a universal success goal. Secondly, the means to achieve fame and celebrity status are unequally distributed across the social structure. By implication, this disjuncture between, on the one hand, the pressure to achieve fame and personal celebration and, on the other the lack of structural opportunities to do so, creates strain for those seeking a reconciliation of this means/goals gap. The third proposition is that a variety of seemingly unrelated forms of nonnormative conduct exists that reflect attempts to resolve this kind of social strain. Following an outline of Merton's original thesis, each of these propositions will be considered more fully.

In the West, popular culture has become obsessed with fame (Braudy 1986). Moreover, the socially acceptable means by which renown is to be achieved remain tacitly characterized by shifting degrees of emphasis spread across three essential components: individual struggle (or hard work), personal accomplishment and/or a rare talent, and as Gamson (2000) argues, a certain amount of "dumb luck." However, these elements simply do not converge for every aspirant looking for his or her place in the spotlight. Thus, with few legitimate opportunities by which fame and celebrity status can be legitimately achieved, deviant behavior has now become an adaptive response to these structural conditions.

THE ORIGINS AND DESIRABILITY OF FAME

When British or European aristocrats visited America's theaters in the mid 19th century, they were utterly shocked by what they observed. American theater goers were unkempt, boorish, rowdy, and odorous, seldom displaying even a shred of decency (Gabler 2000). Americans had succumbed to the temptations of sensuality and, by way of their appreciation for a budding entertainment culture, had shirked the obligations of high-brow "art." Embracing popular culture had become a form of pseudo-resistance for the working and middle classes, who seemed to have little time for the staunchness of higher civilization. According to Gabler:

> Nothing could have been more democratic than entertainment. Everyone had access to it, the majority ruled it, and no one's aesthetic judgement of it was deemed better than anyone else's . . . And that is what nineteenth-century Americans understood when they raised the entertainment banner. (Gabler 2000:30)

Fueled by the technological advances of modernity—including the telegraph and the newswire—the mass distribution of magazines, newspapers, and penny press novels sent the entertainment industry (and the film industry, in particular) reeling into unbridled competition (Gamson 1994). Over the course of this unprecedented growth, and as the century came to a close, mass entertainment came to reflect the very democratic ideals that often seemed out of reach as America (and North America more generally) faced profound difficulties relating to the spread of social and economic inequality (see, for example, Wiebe 1995).

By the turn of the century, America had become the "republic of entertainment" (Gabler 2000:31–51) as movies and other entertainment paraphernalia engendered both a sense of fantasy and possibility in the hearts and minds of consumers. . . .

The latter half of the 20th century witnessed a unique shift in the nature of entertainment culture. According to Gabler (2000), the massive social, cultural, and economic influence wielded by the entertainment sector began forcing "everything to turn itself into entertainment in order to attract media attention" (Gabler 2000:96). Life's mundane events are now being increasingly lived for the media, the intent of the "actors" being to capture even a small portion of the celebrity status that such crafted events may stimulate. These "pseudo-events," as Boorstin (1961) refers to them, have become the specialty of public relations practitioners who choreograph everything from product launches to hunger strikes. Reality is, therefore, staged according to the values, needs, and precepts of media organizations. Though we are often provided with a glimpse of what lies behind the manufacturing of the celebrity spectacle, it remains, in its entirety, a powerful symbolic acknowledgment of the prospects of democratic individualism as underscored by the validating forces of consumer choice.

Escaping the value-laden imagery of today's celebrity culture is now virtually impossible. In many ways, celebrity imagery, and the desire to be famous, have become part of the normative framework that now defines many of life's most mundane moments. For example, there exists a large amount of evidence that suggests that recognition—even within more narrowly defined social networks—is highly valued. For example, to be mentioned in the company newsletter, to be chosen as employee of the month (while having one's photo on public display), or to have one's achievements publicly noted all represent important, nonmaterial forms of reward or, in a sense, fleeting encounters with fame.

Not surprisingly, perhaps, the significance of these narrowly defined encounters with fame is heightened even further when the media becomes involved. In an early theoretical assessment of the power of the mass media, Lazarsfeld and Merton (1964) described the "status conferral" function of the media. They argued that, irrespective of what one has done or said, a mere appearance in mass media is sufficient to confer a certain degree of social status. Specifically:

> The mass media bestow prestige and enhance the authority of individuals and groups by *legitimating their status.* Recognition by the press or radio or magazines or newsreels testifies that one has arrived, that one is important enough to have been singled out from the large anonymous masses, that one's behavior and opinions are significant enough to require public notice [italics in original]. (Lazarsfeld and Merton 1964:101)

Whether it be during crowded public events (such as parades, demonstrations, or baseball games) or more socially intimate settings (such as the presence of a television news camera), individuals often desperately seek to place themselves in the eye of the camera, eventually revelling in their brief encounter with fame. . . . Recognition in and of itself is wonderful, but recognition with the added benefits of the mass media is generally understood to be even better.

Thus, our cultural preoccupation with fame and celebrity status has manifested itself even in the minutiae of daily living. This infusion of a "celebrity sensibility" has been made possible, in part, by rapid changes in information and communications technologies. . . . Fiber-optic cables, satellite technology, and the Internet, for example, provide the electronic gateways through which celebrity culture now flows with unparalleled ease. As Gitlin (1998) argues, the celebrity is now what the members of the global village have in common. . . . The message is: It is all worth striving for, and all one has to do is desire, tune in, and consume appropriately. As Braudy (1986) argues, "Not everyone can be famous. But much of our daily experience tells us that we should if we possibly can, because it is the best, perhaps the only, way *to be* [italics in original]" (Braudy 1986:6).

ACCESS TO FAME IS RESTRICTED

It is almost axiomatic that access to fame and celebrity status would be restricted. As a form of social currency, fame derives its value from its own scarcity. Yet, the structural distribution of blocked opportunities have, presumably, changed over both time and space. In earlier periods, fame and accomplishment were more closely related. According to Boorstin (1961), historically, the heroic and the famous were virtually indistinguishable. Heroism would have been the result of civic leadership, royal birth, extreme acts of bravery, or even divine designation. Yet, one could only become a hero if one was in a position to do great things to begin with; a servant or a member of the "common folk" would have faced more blocked opportunities than, for example, a military general. Throughout most of history, fame was, in a sense, rationed out in very small portions and the eligibility criteria were much more rigorous by comparison. . . .

Today, however, some might dispute the claim that access to fame is in any way restricted. Indeed, a popular critique of contemporary culture is that fame is all too easily achieved. The common wisdom (first articulated by Andy Warhol) that we could all be famous for 15 minutes would seem to undercut observations about blocked opportunity and celebrity status. It is often suggested that the sheer power and ubiquity of celebrity culture, in combination with the disseminating effects of today's information technologies, has increasingly provided interested parties with myriad means of becoming famous. . . .

However, this observation risks misstating a fundamental element of Merton's theory of deviance and strain. It is precisely the putative, democratized availability of the goals that creates the very problem to which Merton drew our attention in the first place. Thus, while reports of Guinness Book of Records entrants, the number of lottery winners, and the number of so-called average people who "make it big" on shows like *Survivor* or *American Idol* increase, access to fame appears to be that much more of a possibility—that much more tangible.

Yet, the apparent ease with which fame is supposedly achieved is actually a distortion of reality. Most people will not—and if fame is to continue to have value, cannot—become famous. In reality, if the culture of celebrity is to remain truly vibrant, only a small number of us can become famous for 15 minutes. Proportionately, there can only ever be a small number of lottery winners, Guinness Book of World Records record holders, or reality show contestants. The ease with which fame can be acquired is the culturally constructed, normative guise that overshadows a fundamental structural contradiction. Fame, no less than the material success toward which Merton originally directed our attention, has a structure of opportunity that allows some, but certainly not all, to have access to the very ends that we are encouraged to desire.

CRIME, DEVIANCE, AND CELEBRITY

As stated, traditional interpretations of Merton's thesis have focused quite exclusively on the importance of materialist sensibilities in contemporary culture.... It is generally assumed that in the behavior of the "rational" offender who robs, kills, or markets illicit goods we see a behavioral manifestation of anomic structural relations—an attempted reconciliation of structural contradiction via deviant conduct. It is, however, just as reasonable to argue that it may be not only a desire for material success, but also a desire for fame recognition that attends to the kinds of behavior which Merton outlined.... [W]hen the race for stratification outcomes is focused on fame rather than material success, the content of these adaptations changes while the forms remain largely the same.

Al Capone's various biographers have commented extensively on the degree to which he appeared driven to achieve, not only material success, but also the notoriety that the xenophobic social order would have normally denied an uneducated child of immigrant parents (Bergreen 1994; Kobler 1992; Schoenberg 1993). In this sense, as the historians of crime Mark Haller (1971) and others (see, for example O'Kane 1992), have written, crime as an illegitimate route to upward mobility has, historically, been bound up with the social and cultural dynamics of politics, sports, and entertainment. The ward boss, the boxing champion, and the vaudeville performer not only had ready access to financial rewards, but also to fame and recognition.

For example, on September 16, 1952, the North York Township Police (a small police force with a jurisdiction that included what is now North York, a suburb of Toronto, Ontario) arrested the notorious bank robber Edwin Alonzo Boyd and his associates in a hay barn without incident. Boyd had been responsible for numerous bank robberies in the Toronto area. His unwillingness to use force or firearms, in addition to his "matinee-idol good looks and gymnastic ability to leap bank counters at a single bound," brought him a reputation for being a daring "gentlemanly bandit" (Edwards 2002:B2). Most importantly, Boyd looked good in the papers and that was "enough to make him a celebrity of sorts.... [Y]oung women [who lined] the entrances to the jail and courthouse squealed for him as if he were Frank Sinatra" (Edwards 2002:B2).

Such processes are not necessarily rooted in the peculiarities of the prohibition or mid-century era, however. The gangster-as-celebrity phenomenon has had its more recent incarnations in Joey Gallo and John Gotti (one biography of whom is playfully entitled *Mob Star*). Even more recently, the rise of rap music has facilitated an even stronger fusion of fame and criminality. The "gangsta" lifestyle is expressed in both fashion and music as many rap artists have moved easily, it seems, in both directions across whatever line might may have been thought to separate the media celebrity from the criminal (George 1999; Shaw 2000). This state of affairs has not escaped the observations of many rappers themselves, including Tupac Shakur and Eminem, both of whom have rapped about the relationship between violence and criminality on the one hand, and fame and celebrity on the other, a particular dynamic that routinely finds its fertile ground on the streets of North American cities.

Urban streets themselves have become the canvas upon which the relationship between deviant behavior and celebrity status is articulated, most notably in the form of graffiti. "Tagging," as it is often called, is as much about establishing notoriety and recognition through street art as it is about establishing urban territorial boundaries. For the artist, the process is often risky (more elaborate tags are even more so, given the considerable time required for their completion) as property owners and law enforcement officials struggle to keep the spread of graffiti contained. But it is precisely this willingness to risk it all—especially when coupled with notable artistic talent—that helps establish one's reputation on the streets as being one who routinely, and covertly, flirts with the law while showing contempt for the sanctity of private property (Ferrell 1993). The successful street artist, therefore, enjoys a certain degree of fame and notoriety for as long as his or her work continues to lay claim to particular areas of the urban landscape.

On a more melodramatic and dangerous level, some killers have described their actions as being rooted in a search for celebrity status, a level of recognition that eluded them in more conventional pursuits (see, for example Braudy 1986). In Gabler's (2000) study of how entertainment has conquered reality, the "killer as celebrity" convergence is cast into sharp relief:

> John C. Salvi III, who was accused (and later convicted) of murdering two receptionists on December 30, 1994, at two different abortion clinics, told his attorney that he wanted to be interviewed by Barbara Walters. . . . The so-called Unabomber, who killed three and wounded twenty-three in sixteen separate bombing attacks, not only delivered a manifesto to the *New York Times* and *Washington Post* that he demanded be published—else he would kill again—but was clearly concerned about his image, confiding to his journal that if he were caught . . . he would be wrongly dismissed as a "sickie." (Gabler 2000: 183)

Of course, even with such highly visible cases it may be that fame and celebrity status are unintended and unanticipated outcomes of criminal lifestyles. . . . It would suggest that fame is actively sought by some groups of offenders because, in many cases, it is the lack of access to the means by which recognition is achieved that prompts the pursuit of a criminal lifestyle in the first place. Certainly the idea that some forms of crime and violence result from a perception that one has not received a certain degree of respect, esteem, or acknowledgment for one's accomplishments is an old one. Employees who feel cheated by a system that does not recognize or reward their achievements (and who seek violent reprisal) suggest the process in which we are interested writ small.

Of course, the conflation of the criminal type with that of the celebrity is, in part, facilitated by the disseminating effects of the news media. Alongside its truly global reach, the news media's relentless search for all that is dramatic and novel essentially channels the criminal-as-entertainer into the homes of millions under the rhetorical and symbolic pretense of media altruism—while "looking out for the people" the media simultaneously focuses the proverbial spotlight on the deviant(s) in question. That criminals are mindful of the recognition they can achieve under these conditions, therefore, should not be surprising—at one point serial killers found themselves on the face of trading cards in the United States.

The point here is a general one. The innovator engages in criminal conduct, not only to achieve material success, but also to gain social recognition—the cultural goals being thoroughly internalized, yet the socially acceptable means being vehemently rejected. Barring access to other resources, therefore, a deviant lifestyle . . . is now capable of providing the means by which fame and celebrity status can be negotiated in post-industrial society.

Confronted by what appear to be insurmountable barriers to success, the ritualist scales down the goals such that the aspirations can be more readily fulfilled (Merton 1957). Although a belief in the institutionally prescribed means remains somewhat intact, the goals are subjected to revision. . . .

Yet, similar social dynamics unfold vis-à-vis the goal of fame and celebrity status as well. As the very possibility of becoming a bonafide celebrity becomes increasingly remote for the aspirant, the goal itself may be scaled down considerably (such as) the struggling actor or actress who abandons his or her dreams of mainstream Hollywood for the pornography industry; the cover band that dedicates itself to the remaking of famous songs when the multimillion-dollar record deal becomes more fiction than fact; and the struggling dancer who eventually settles for a life as a coach when dreams of the National Ballet of Canada or the New York City Ballet are thwarted.

SUMMARY AND CONCLUSION

. . . The widespread desirability of fame and celebrity status now challenges, or at least parallels, that of material success. The proliferation of information and communications technologies over the past three decades has helped to extend the reach of the West's cultural structure even further, thereby allowing the virtues of fame and celebrity status to be espoused the world over.

Yet, to suggest that communications technologies have somehow democratized the availability of celebrity status (see, for example Gamson 2000) is to misunderstand the structural relationships that underlie and, in a sense, maintain the celebrity phenomenon. If fame or celebrity status are to maintain their level of social currency—their noteworthiness and desirability—there can only ever be a limited number of successful aspirants. In that sense, while such technology has certainly broadened the pool of potential celebrities, one must remember that fame, by its very nature, must remain a rare phenomenon.

The intent here was to explore two interrelated theoretical arguments. First, Merton's classic thesis on social structure and anomie must be understood in a generic sense. . . . The concepts of opportunity and cultural structure can be used to analyze social phenomena across both time and space precisely because they are so well formed at the level of the abstract. . . . The narrowing of Merton's ideas—which the persistent materialist interpretation of his work implies—is unfortunate in so far as Merton's ideas are capable of elucidating so much more in the sociology of crime and deviant behavior.

Secondly, given the generic nature of Merton's original thesis, we argue that Merton's ideas can be effectively used to account for the ways in which forms of deviant behavior are linked to much broader cultural axioms that emphasize the desirability of fame and celebrity status. . . . [D]eviant adaptive forms emerge as a result of a contradiction between a cultural structure that emphasizes fame and celebrity status, and an opportunity structure that fails to provide the proportionate means by which it can be legitimately achieved.

References

Bergreen, L. 1994. *Capone: The Man and the Era*. New York: Simon & Schuster.

Boorstin, Daniel J. 1961. *The Image: A Guide to Pseudo-Events in America*. New York: Harper & Row.

Braudy, Leo. 1986. *The Frenzy of Renown: Fame & Its History*. New York: Oxford University Press.

Edwards, Peter. "Cops and Robbers and Front Page Scoops," *The Toronto Star*, November 7, 2002, P. B1–B2.

Ferrell, Jeff. 1993. *Crimes of Style: Urban Graffiti and the Politics of Criminality*. New York: Garland.

Gabler, Neal. 2000. *Life: The Movie: How Entertainment Conquered Reality*. New York: Vintage.

Gamson, Joshua. 1994. *Claims to Fame: Celebrity in Contemporary America*. Berkeley: University of California Press.

———. 2000. "The Web of Celebrity." *The American Prospect* 11(20) 40–1.

George, Nelson. 1999. *Hip Hop America*. New York: Penguin Group.

Gitlin, Todd. 1998. "The Culture of Celebrity." *Dissent* 45:81–3.

Haller, M. 1971. "Organized Crime in Urban Society: Chicago in the Twentieth Century." *Journal of Social History* 5:210–30.

Kobler, J. 1992. *Capone: The Life and World of Al Capone.* Cambridge, MA: Da Capo.

Lazarsfeld, Paul F. and Robert K. Merton. 1964. "Mass Communication, Popular Taste, and Organized Social Action." pp. 95–118 in *The Communication of Ideas,* edited by Lyman Bryson. New York: Cooper Square Publishers, Inc.

Merton, Robert K. 1938. "Social Structure and Anomie." *American Sociological Review* 3:672–82.

———. 1957. *Social Theory and Social Structure.* Toronto: Collier-Macmillian Canada Ltd.

———. 1968. *Social Theory and Social Structure.* New York: Free Press.

O'Kane, R. M. 1992. *Crooked Ladder: Gangsters, Ethnicity and the American Dream.* New Brunswick, NJ: Transaction Press.

Schoenberg, R. J. 1993. *Mr. Capone: The Real and Complete Story of Al Capone.* New York: William Morrow and Co.

Shaw, W. 2000. *Westside: Young Men & Hip Hop in L.A.* New York: Simon & Schuster.

Wiebe, Robert H. 1995. *The Search for Order: 1877–1920.* New York: Hill and Wang.

Rehab, Labeling, and Deviance

(2008)

SALLY RASKOFF

Your favorite television shows can be useful for applying sociological concepts and theories. Sometimes it's easier to look at other people's lives than it is to analyze something in your own life.

This occurred to me as I watched the beginning episodes of the second season of *Celebrity Rehab with Dr. Drew* on VH1. We all know people who struggle with addiction, whether it be caffeine, alcohol, other drugs, chocolate, sex, shopping, or gambling, yet using those personal examples can be difficult, as our emotions may cloud our perceptions of what is occurring.

Since sociology courses are not "therapy," it may be wise to use examples that are further from one's own life. *Celebrity Rehab* provides many opportunities for us to develop our sociological imaginations.

On this "reality" show, actors, models, musicians, and other celebrities come to Dr. Drew Pinsky and rehab and attempt to kick their habits. In this second season, actor Jeff Conaway has returned—he had been a participant in season 1, but left the program—and his girlfriend Vikki has checked herself in as well. Actor Gary Busey has a mission and has come to share his tales of sobriety to inspire others. Model Amber Smith is also among the second-season participants. Like Sean Stewart, son of the famous singer Rod Stewart, she has come to quit her opiate addiction.

Self-perception is a particularly salient concept to analyze here since many of these people have agreed to come to rehab because they have realized that they can no longer live with their addictions. Charles Horton Cooley's "looking-glass self"—that our self-perception rests partially on how we think others perceive us—is fascinating to consider for these celebrities. They are volunteering to be on television to share their addictions, therapy, and many other personal details with the public. The show airs long after it is filmed, so they have no idea how they will be depicted or what will air, and they have no control over that. Like our own "looking-glass selves" we never really know how others perceive us, but we make internal judgments, and those assessments are based on our own perceptions, thoughts, and feelings about ourselves and others.

This process is rarely conscious; if we feel shame, then our assessments are likely to fuel this shame and guilt and all other such negative emotions that accompany low self-esteem.

Many of these celebrities are living out what Robert K. Merton called "self-fulfilling prophecies," or false assessments and beliefs that can become true if we believe them and act as if they were true.

To some extent we expect actors, models, and children of famous people to abuse drugs and alcohol. The mantra "Sex, Drugs, & Rock 'n' Roll" makes addiction almost a job requirement. Thus, for many who go into these lines of work, or who are members of famous families, the addiction cycle becomes fulfilled as life continues.

Each participant in *Celebrity Rehab* gives different reasons for why they became addicted to their particular drug of choice. Yet most have in common traumatic childhood events, neglectful or abusive histories, and plenty of emotional and physical pain—commonalities with all addicts and many other people. Most of them also mention specifically their social context as part of the reason for their addiction: the actors speak of drugs offered to them on their jobs, the model speaks of drugs to stay thin and alert for work then to bring them down to sleep, and the child actor says that partying was the only vocation expected of him.

People who use or abuse illegal drugs (or misuse prescription drugs) are violating a norm and exemplify primary deviance. When Gary and Jeff talk of earlier cocaine use and Amber mentions her prescription drug use, it's obvious they know this is problematic or deviant behavior. Amber mentions that her mother taught her how to use—and they used together—which makes you wonder if she was aware of the deviant nature of drugs when she first began to abuse them.

Secondary deviance moves a step beyond primary deviance: As a result of breaking a norm, an individual is labeled as deviant and then conforms to that label and thinks of him or herself as deviant. (Or others think that they are.) For example, the Celebrity Rehabbers talk about themselves as addicts and the problems they have as a result of those addictions.

Gary talks frankly about his cocaine addiction and seems proud that he is "thirteen years sober." Jeff talks about his back pain and subsequent painkiller addiction, and in the first season of the show he discloses early childhood abuses that provide another level of rationale for numbing himself (albeit ineffectively). Amber and Sean are upfront about identifying themselves as addicts who are there to break the cycle of addiction. While they all accept the label of drug addict, Gary is adamant about identifying his problem as in the past.

Jeff's girlfriend Vikki seems to move from primary deviance into secondary deviance when she admits that she needs help for her problems related to drug use. In the first season, it was clear she was using but wasn't aware that it was a problem. When she checked into rehab, she seemed to accept that label. On the other hand, perhaps this decision had more to do with staying with Jeff as he participated on the show.

Gary's insistence on his sobriety is a great example of tertiary deviance—when we reject or transform the stigma associated with the deviant label and redefine it as a positive phenomenon. He sees himself as a member of the therapeutic team who is there to inspire and redeem. That he "uses medicinal marijuana for his asthma" among other substances doesn't seem to bother him. Dr. Drew tries to point out, carefully, that any substance use means he is not sober and that Gary is a patient, not an employee, but this message doesn't sink in.

While Gary's brain damage due to earlier events could be a factor in his thinking, his repeated insistence on this role suggests that he has redefined his addiction as an experience through which he can inspire others—thus turning this negative identity into a positive role. He visibly bristles at being equated with the others who are there to kick their addictions, as he firmly believes he has already done so himself.

Television shows like *Celebrity Rehab* can provide some ways to both practice applying sociological concepts and to identify how these concepts and theories can be of use. What other TV shows would you recommend for fleshing out sociological theories and concepts?

TALK ABOUT IT

1. Have you ever been in a neighborhood where you felt afraid? What specifically scared you?
2. Discuss what might reduce crime in a community.
3. What factors need to be taken into account to understand why crime happens and what can prevent crime?
4. Think about someone who became a household name from committing a crime or another deviant activity. Did the person benefit in any way from his or her behavior?
5. Have you ever watched a show featuring celebrities in a negative light? What does this show teach us about deviance?

WRITE ABOUT IT

1. Briefly explain the broken-window theory. Discuss its strengths and weaknesses, drawing from Wright's critique.
2. What factors make homicide "local" rather than "national," according to Sternheimer? Nevertheless, what can we learn about our society from looking at long-term national homicide trends?
3. Define and discuss Merton's strain theory. What other social factors beyond the strain toward fame and fortune can strain theory explain?
4. Parnaby and Sacco discuss how deviance can sometimes lead to celebrity. What other "benefits" do some people get from crime and deviance? What does this tell us about the nature of our society?
5. Based on Raskoff's essay, what is primary, secondary, and tertiary deviance? Apply these concepts to another example of your choice.

DO IT

1. Conduct field research in two communities: one with a low crime rate and one with a higher crime rate. (You can find out about crime rates by visiting your local law enforcement agency's website.) Observe one major street in each community and describe what you see. Does it reflect Wilson and Kelling's broken-window theory?
2. Look up crime statistics in your community, on your campus (http://ope.ed.gov/security/), or in the United States (www.fbi.gov/ucr/ucr.htm). Choose one form of crime and analyze its long-term trends, relation to race and gender, and any other related information you can find. What are your results? Do they surprise you?

3. Find a news story (online, in your local newspaper, or on television news) that mentions a crime statistic. Now look for the original source of that statistic and compare how the news organization reported on that form of crime with the actual data. Did the news report shape your perspective differently from looking at the actual data? If so, how?
4. Collect reports from magazines, websites, or newspapers that portray infamous people who have committed crimes. Look at the word choice, imagery, and other storytelling techniques. Does this coverage encourage others to seek fame? If so, how?
5. Watch a celebrity reality show. What are your initial impressions about the celebrities? Now watch the same episode again. How do the celebrities on the show attempt to shape their identities through the program, and, if applicable, the struggles they go through? How does this exemplify Cooley's concept of the looking-glass self, as Raskoff describes it?

6

Stratification

Module Goal: ***To examine how class divisions are created, maintained, and conceptualized.***

Social class, sometimes referred to as socioeconomic status (SES), comprises a variety of factors, including family income, education, and occupational prestige. In the United States, social class is a central system of *stratification*, the systematic hierarchy that provides more privilege to those at the top and more barriers to those at the bottom. Despite our widespread belief in equal opportunity, some people face significant obstacles to achieving economic success.

The ability to rise to a higher level in the hierarchy is called *social mobility*, an idea fostered by the American Dream that hard work will yield success. How easy is it to move up in America today? Robert Perrucci and Earl Wysong address this question in "Class in America." As you read it, consider how popular culture supports the idea of limitless mobility, and note any resistance you might feel to their challenge to commonly held beliefs about class in America.

In the United States, we have a much greater awareness of racial and ethnic divisions than class divisions, which sometimes overshadows the importance of social class. Racial inequality is deeply intertwined with economic inequality. In "Class and Race," Janis Prince Inniss discusses how racial inequality exacerbates existing economic divisions.

We often see social class divisions as something for those at the bottom to overcome, rather than as a permanent pattern of inequality. Think about some of your own experiences interacting with people from different social class backgrounds. In "Class Consciousness," I relate a personal experience of when social class lines became visible.

Because our everyday interactions are often with people of similar class backgrounds, much of what we know about differing social classes comes from the news and other forms of popular culture. Diana Kendall's "Class Action in the Media" analyzes patterns in the representation of class in newspapers and on television.

Kendall found that the homeless are frequently maligned in news coverage, characterized as a nuisance and general menace to the "normal" population. But how do people become homeless? In "The Disaster of Homelessness," Sally Raskoff considers how our perceptions of homelessness differ by cause. Under what circumstances can you imagine being homeless yourself? We tend to think such a disaster could never happen to us, but Raskoff's piece suggests otherwise.

As you read about the construction of social class divisions in everyday life, consider the following questions:

1. What limitations make it more difficult for some to achieve the American Dream? What privileges make it easier for others?
2. What beliefs do you have about social class, stratification, and social mobility? What has shaped your beliefs?
3. What factors enable people to move up the ladder of social class? What factors can push people *down* the ladder?

Class in America

(2003)

ROBERT PERRUCCI AND EARL WYSONG

My momma always said that life is like a box of chocolates. You never know what you're gonna get. —*Forrest Gump*, 1994

The lead character of the popular film *Forrest Gump* illustrates that despite limitations of intellect, his pure heart, guileless character, sincerity, hard work, and positive mental attitude enable him to prevail over life's hardships. Gump's disarming qualities defrost the cynicism of a heartless world and open the path to material success, social respect, and personal fulfillment. His achievements appear to affirm his momma's homily, reinforce belief in the American Dream, and give testimony to the pervasive ideological belief that all men are created equal.

However, movie ideals often clash with social realities. Is life really like a box of chocolates—unpredictable and capricious in detail but essentially rewarding to the pure of heart? Consider the contrast between the fictional Forrest Gump and the real-life experiences of Jim Farley.

> Jim Farley's fellow workers at Federal Mogul Corporation's roller bearing plant on the east side of Detroit called him Big Jim—not so much because of the size of his body, they said, as because of the size of his heart.
>
> They liked the soft-spoken yet tough manner in which he represented them as a union committeeman. And they liked his willingness to sit down over a shot and a beer at the nearby Office Lounge and listen to the problems they had with their jobs, their wives, or their bowling scores.
>
> Jim Farley had come North from eastern Kentucky, because mechanization of the mines and slumping demand for coal made finding work there impossible. The idea of leaving behind the mountains where he had grown up for the punch-in, punch-out factory life in a big city like Detroit didn't appeal to him much—but neither did the thought of living on relief, like so many unemployed miners in his hollow and most others in Pike County. . . .
>
> Federal Mogul announced that it would be phasing out its Detroit operations by early 1974 and moving bearing production to a new plant in Alabama. Farley, say those who knew him, became a different man almost overnight—tense, moody, withdrawn. A month after the announcement he suffered a heart attack. Physically, he recovered rapidly. Mentally, things got worse. His family and friends called it "nerves." . . .

With close to 20 years at Federal Mogul, the thought of starting all over again—in an unfamiliar job, with no seniority and little hope for a decent pension—was not pleasant. But Farley had little choice. Three times he found work, and three times he failed the physical because of his heart problem. The work itself posed no difficulty, but none of the companies wanted to risk high workers' compensation and health insurance premiums when there were plenty of young, strong workers looking for jobs.

As Farley's layoff date approached, he grew more and more apprehensive. He was 41 years old: what would happen if he couldn't find another job? His wife had gone to work at the Hall Lamp Company, so the family would have some income. But Farley's friends were being laid off, too, and most of them hadn't been able to find work yet either—a fact that worsened his outlook.

Farley was awake when Nancy left for work at 6:15 A.M. on January 29, but he decided to stay home. His nerves were so bad, he said, that he feared an accident at work. His sister-in-law Shirley stopped by late that morning and found him despondent. Shortly before noon he walked from the kitchen into his bedroom and closed the door. Shirley Farley recalls hearing a single click, the sound of a small-bore pistol. She rushed to the bedroom and pounded on the door. There was no response.

Almost 20 years to the day after Jim Farley left the hills of eastern Kentucky, his dream of a secure life for his family was dead. And so was he.[1]

Most people would see Jim Farley's death as an unnecessary personal tragedy. Here was a man with severe psychological problems who simply could not cope with the stress of job loss. "Millions of people lose a job in this lifetime, but they don't commit suicide" might be the typical response. There is a strong tendency to see unemployment as individual failure and the inability to "bounce back" as further evidence of that failure.

But there is another way to look at Jim Farley's death, one that recognizes a long chain of life experiences that produce patterns of predictable hardship and limited opportunities. Farley's chances in life are powerfully shaped by his social-class location, which constrains opportunities. His life is like that of millions of others who barely finish high school and move through half a dozen different jobs hoping to find one that will provide a decent wage and long-term security. Yet, just as the class structure constrains the lives of people like Jim Farley, it confers numerous advantages and opportunities on others. The same class structure that shapes laws denying workers a right to a job gives companies like Federal Mogul the right to do what they wish with their property. They can close a plant with little or no consideration of their workers or the community. In fact, tax laws may provide incentives for closing plants and building new ones in countries with lower-wage workers. The conditions leading to Jim Farley's death some twenty-five years ago have now spread across the land. Millions of workers in stable, high-wage jobs in America's basic industries have been told they are no longer needed. Thousands of plants are closed and sit empty in steel towns along the rivers of the Monongahela Valley in Pennsylvania. They were among the first to go in the dramatic reshaping of America's class structure which eliminated the middle-class worker, and they were soon followed by similar dislocations in the auto, textiles, glass, and electronics industries.

After the flight of manufacturing to foreign shores, corporate America's appetite for profits began to turn to its white-collar labor force. Suddenly, the giant corporations like IBM, AT&T, and GM discovered "downsizing" or "rightsizing" or "restructuring," in which the use of new technology and new work organization resulted in a 10–20 percent reduction in employees. The 1990s brought the global economy, and it became the corporate "bogeyman," disciplining workers with the constant threat of further shutdowns and layoffs to allow American firms to compete with other firms and other workers across the globe.

What are we to make of America's love affair with Forrest Gump? Why the attraction to the Gump myth in the face of the harsh realities? Maybe believing that life is like a box of chocolates leads to an expectation of sweet (but mixed) outcomes and makes predictable class-based disappointments and hardships easier to bear. After all, during the Great Depression of the 1930s, Hollywood produced some of its most upbeat and fanciful films.

To make sense of Jim Farley's death (and maybe even the popularity of Forrest Gump) we need to recognize that the American class structure in the past thirty years has been dramatically altered. What we are seeing is not a temporary aberration that will be soon put right but a fundamental shift in the distribution of economic and political power that constitutes the class structure. To understand the declining fortunes of millions of Jim Farleys and the corporate decisions of thousands of Federal Moguls, it is necessary to examine the workings of class structure and how it shapes the lives of workers, the decisions of politicians, and the actions of corporations.

INEQUALITY

> The real news is that the median wage—the take-home pay of the worker smack in the middle of the earnings ladder—is still less than it was before the last recession. At the same time the upper reaches of America have never had it so good.
>
> —Robert B. Reich, *Nation*, February 16, 1998

Most Americans have a keen sense of the presence of inequality. We learn about it in many ways on a daily basis, from our observations of people, homes, cars, neighborhoods, and news accounts of the "rich and famous." There is good evidence that we start to learn about inequality at a very early age and accumulate additional knowledge throughout our lives.[2]

◇ ◇ ◇

Most Americans are aware of different forms of inequality. They know about income inequality and the patterns of discrimination against women and racial and ethnic groups. This awareness can be traced to stories in the mass media or what they may have learned in courses in high school or college. Knowledge of inequality is often conveyed in stories about the gender gap in salary, or the homeless, or the number of children or older Americans living below the poverty line. But what about the social arrangements that produce inequality and are responsible for its persistence? A pervasive form of inequality cuts across age, race, ethnicity, and gender to confer privilege on a minority of Americans while relegating the rest to varying degrees of insecurity, need, or despair. This is class inequality, a structured system of unequal rewards that provides enormous advantages to a small percentage of people in the United States at the expense of the overwhelming majority. Inequality is contained within a class system that resembles a game of monopoly that is "rigged" so that only certain players have a chance to own Park Place, and a great many others go directly to jail.

The discussion of class in America is a taboo subject because of the national reluctance to examine how the class system of the United States operates on a day-to-day basis. We do not learn from our schools or media how a privileged but organized minority of Americans is able to amass a disproportionate share of our national wealth and to transmit that privilege across generations to create a permanent economic, political, and social elite class. This structured class inequality is both the cause and the consequence of the ability to control important resources such as money, education, votes, or information. And for this system to work, the majority of disadvantaged Americans must be persuaded to believe that the way things work out for people is fair. This is done by distracting attention from class inequality and focusing the national spotlight on conflict between Blacks and Whites, women and men, gays and straights, pro-choice and anti-abortion partisans.

The day-to-day operation of this society is made possible by the 130 million Americans who are in the labor force. The work they do is described in the ten thousand occupations listed in the *Dictionary of Occupational Titles*. The economy, often described as if it were separate from the rest of society, is made up of thousands of establishments where people make a living, from the multinational General Motors with 386,000 employees worldwide (in 2000) to the family-owned Korean grocery in Brooklyn.

[One] way to look at American society is a view that is rarely presented in newspapers, discussed on television, or taught to our school children. This view says that it is possible to understand how society works and how the pursuit of happiness becomes available to some but not to others; that amid all the complexity, one can find stable and enduring patterns in our collective lives.

CLASS STRUCTURE AND CLASS SEGMENTS

The combination of capital and power can be used to describe the class structure of American society. One popular way of describing the class structure of a society is with a physical or geometric shape or image. The shape or image conveys the relative proportions of people in a society who have some valued thing, like money or education. The pyramid, for example, illustrates a class structure in which a small percentage of a society (10 percent) has a great deal of the commodity, another 30 percent has a little less, and the majority (60 percent) has the least amount of the valued commodity.

Another frequently used image is the diamond, which provides a different picture of the way valued things are distributed. The diamond image says that a small percentage (10 percent) of a society has a lot of something, another small percentage (10 percent) has very little of something, and most of the people (80 percent) are in the middle, with moderate amounts of the valued commodity.

In each of these class structures, the class positions of people can be simply designated as upper class, middle class, or lower class. Thus, the pyramid image represents a society in which most persons are lower class, and the diamond image represents a middle-class society. If asked to choose between the two societies depicted here, most people would probably choose the society represented by the diamond image, because most of the people are in the middle class. If you chose to live in the pyramid society, you would have a 60 percent chance of being in the lower class.

[T]he image of a society as pyramidal or diamond-shaped provides an overall view of how people in that society are distributed on some valued characteristic or attribute. But it does not tell about the society's "rules" for determining or changing their class position.

Let us try to make all this a little more concrete by examining American society. Most efforts to portray the American class structure have focused on occupations as the main determinant of the class structure and of people's positions in that structure. Occupations have been classified according to the public's opinion of the social standing or prestige associated with being a public school teacher, or a dentist, or a mechanic, or a machine operator. . . .

However, if you look behind these prestige rankings to ask what it is that people are actually ranking, you will find that what is being evaluated is not simply the prestige of an occupation but also its income and power. In our society, the occupational structure as embedded in organizations is the key to understanding the class structure, and a person's occupation is one aspect of class position. But how do the hundreds of different occupations combine to create a structure of distinct classes with different amounts of economic, political, and social power? What aspects of occupations determine their position in the class structure?

People often speak of their occupation or their job as what they do for a living. An occupation or job describes how a person is related to the economy in a society or what one does in the process of the production of goods and services. An occupation or job provides people with the means to sustain life ("to make a living"); and the sum total of the work done by people in their occupations or jobs is the wealth generated by the economic system. . . . The more people in a society are working at making a living, the better the economic health of the total society. . . . Some people contribute more to the total wealth than they receive for their work, as in the case of some workers whose wages are a fraction of the value of their products when they are sold. And some people may receive ten or twenty times more in income for their work than that received by others. So although there may be 130 million Americans involved in occupations and jobs for which they are compensated, their amount of compensation varies widely according to how they are related to the production process. There are a variety of ways in which people are related to the production process in today's economy.

The Privileged Class

The activity of some people in the system of production is focused on their role as owners of investment capital. Such a person may be referred to colloquially as the "boss" or, in more respectful circles, as a "captain of industry," an "entrepreneur," or a "creator of wealth," but in the language of class analysis they are all owner-employers. The owner may actually be the sole proprietor of the XYZ Corporation and be involved in the day-to-day decisions of running that corporation. But ownership may also consist in the possession of a large number of shares of stock in one or several corporations in which many other persons may also own stock. However, the ownership of stock is socially and economically meaningful only when (1) the value of shares owned is sufficient to constitute "making a living," or (2) the percentage of shares of stock owned relative to all shares is large enough to permit the owner of said shares to have some say in how the company is run. Members of this group (along with the managers and professionals) control most of the wealth in America. The point of this discussion is to distinguish owners of investment capital from the millions of Americans who own shares of stock in companies, who own mutual funds, or whose pension funds are invested in the stock market. The typical American stock owner does not make a living from that ownership and has nothing to say about the activities of the companies they "own."

On the lower rungs of the owner-employer group are the proprietors of small but growing high-tech firms that bring together venture capital and specialized knowledge in areas involving biomedical products or services and computer software forms. These are "small" businesses only in Department of Commerce classifications (less than $500,000 in sales), for they bear no resemblance to the Korean grocer, the Mexican restaurant owner, or the African American hair salon found in many American cities. They are more typically spin-off firms created by technical specialists who have accumulated some capital from years of employment in an industrial lab or a university and have obtained other investment capital from friends, family, or private investors.

A second activity in the system of production is that of manager, the person who makes the day-to-day decisions involved in running a corporation, a firm, a division of a corporation, or a section within a company. Increasingly, managers have educational credentials and degrees in business, management, economics, or finance. Managers make decisions about how to use the millions of dollars of investment capital made available to them by the owners of investment capital.

The upper levels of the managerial group include the top management of the largest manufacturing, financial, and commercial firms in the United States. These managers receive substantial salaries and bonuses, along with additional opportunities to accumulate wealth. Table 1 presents a typical pattern of "modest" compensation for the officers of a large firm in 2000. We refer to this compensation as "modest" because it is far below the multimillion-dollar packages of compensation for CEOs at IBM, AT&T, Disney or Coca-Cola (which range from $20 million to $50 million). But such distinctions are probably pointless, because we are describing executives whose wealth is enormous in comparison with others not in their class. For example, the top CEO in the group just listed also owns

TABLE 1 Compensation for Corporate Executives (2000)

Position	Annual Compensation	Bonus	Stock Awards
President and CEO	$745,385	$450,000	$2,028,125
Executive vice president	299,897	119,000	745,000
Executive vice president	273,846	120,000	558,750
Senior vice president and General Counsel	242,885	34,000	447,000
Senior vice president and CFO	275,192	128,000	558,750
Vice president	342,029	174,760	–
Executive vice president	322,400	5000	–

Source: Based on data from the Annual Report and Proxy Statements, Great Lakes Chemical Corporation, 2001, Indianapolis, Ind.

100,000 shares of stock and has options for another 100,000 shares in the corporation he heads. The value of these shares fluctuates with the market value of the stock, which in the summer of 2001 was $31 a share, or about $3 million for the 100,000 shares.

The lower levels of the managerial group carry out the important function of supervising the work done by millions of workers who produce goods and services in the economy. The success of this group, and their level of rewards, is determined by their ability to get workers to be more productive, which means to produce more at a lower cost.

Professionals carry out a third activity in the economic system. This group's power is based on the possession of credentialed knowledge or skill, such as an engineering degree, a teaching degree, or a degree in public relations. Some may work as "independent professionals," providing service for a fee, such as declining numbers of doctors, dentists, and lawyers. But most professionals work for corporations, providing their specialized knowledge to enhance the profit-making potential of their firm or of firms that buy their services. The professional group is made up of university graduates with degrees in the professional schools of medicine, law, business, and engineering and in a variety of newly emerging fields (e.g., computer sciences) that serve the corporate sector. The possession of credentialed knowledge unifies an otherwise diverse group, which includes doctors who may earn $500,000 a year and computer specialists who earn $60,000 a year.

Professors at elite universities who are in selected fields like law, medicine, business, biomedical engineering, or electrical engineering have opportunities to start high-tech firms and to consult for industry in ways that can significantly enhance income. Even "modest" activities, like becoming an outside director for a bank or industrial firm, can be very rewarding. A colleague in a business school at a Big Ten university who is a professor of management has been on the board of directors of a chemical corporation for twenty years. His annual retainer is $26,000. He gets an additional $1,000 a day for attending meetings of the board or committee meetings and $500 a day for participating in telephone conference meetings (the board meets six times a year, and committees convene from one to six times a year). . . .

Professionals in elite settings not only make six-figure salaries, but they have enough "discretionary time" to pursue a second line of activity that may double or triple their basic salaries. Not a bad deal for the professional class.

Not everyone with a credentialed skill is in the privileged professional class. We exclude from this group workers like teachers, social workers, and nurses, who despite their professional training and dedication fail to get the material rewards accorded to other professionals. Moreover, they are usually labeled as "semiprofessions," implying that they somehow fall short of the full professionals. This may be due to the fact that most of these "semiprofessionals" are women, and that their services do not provide direct benefits to the privileged class. They deal with people in nonproductive roles as students, patients, or human service clients, and they deal mostly with people without much in the way of consumption or investment capital. We also exclude university professors at nonelite schools. They are excluded because of the large number of faculty at hundreds of nonelite colleges and universities who make modest salaries; and many of them are not even employed in tenure track positions. We also exclude the thousands of attorneys working for legal services agencies, franchise law firms, and in public defender positions. Professionals in these positions are excluded because of limited job security, modest levels of income, and little investment capital. Thus, we distinguish between elite and marginalized professional groups, with only the former being in the privileged class.

The New Working Class

Finally, there is the large majority of Americans—employees who sell their capacity to work to an employer in return for wages. This group typically carries out their daily work activities under the supervision of the managerial group. They have limited skills and limited job security. Such workers can see their jobs terminated with virtually no notice. The exception to this rule is the approximately 14 percent of workers who are unionized; but even union members are vulnerable to having their jobs eliminated by new technology, restructuring and downsizing, or the movement of production to overseas firms.

This working group also consists of the many thousands of very small businesses that include self-employed persons, and family stores based on little more than "sweat equity." Many of these people have been "driven" to try self-employment as a protection against limited opportunities in the general labor market. But many are attracted to the idea of owning their own business, an idea that has a special place in the American value system: It means freedom from the insecurity and subservience of being an employee. For the wage worker, the opportunities for starting a business are severely limited by the absence of capital. Aspirations may be directed at a family business in a neighborhood where one has lived, such as a dry-cleaning store, a beauty shop, a gas station, or a convenience store. Prospects for such businesses may depend upon an ethnic "niche" where the service, the customer, and the entrepreneur are tied together in a common cultural system relating to food or some personal service. The failure rate of these small businesses is very high, making self-employment a vulnerable, high-risk activity.

Another sizable segment of wage earners, perhaps 10–15 percent, has very weak links to the labor market. For these workers, working for wages takes place between long stretches of unemployment, when there may be shifts to welfare benefits or unemployment compensation. This latter group typically falls well below official poverty levels and should not be considered as part of the "working poor." The working poor consists of persons who are working full time at low wages, with earnings of about $12,000 a year—what you get for working full time at $6.00 an hour.

These segments of the class structure are defined by their access to essential life-sustaining resources and the stability of those resources over time. As discussed earlier, these resources include consumption capital, investment capital, skill capital, and social capital. The class segments differ in their access to stable resources over time, and they represent what is, for all practical purposes, a two-class structure, represented by a double-diamond. The top diamond represents the privileged class, composed of those who have stable and secure resources that they can expect will be available to them over time. This privileged class can be subdivided into the superclass of owners, employers, and CEOs, who directly or indirectly control enormous economic resources, and the credentialed class of managers and professionals with the knowledge and expertise that is essential to major industrial, financial, commercial, and media corporations and key agencies of government. The bottom diamond is the new working class, composed of those who have unstable and insecure resources over time. . . .

It is important to keep in mind that a person's location in the double-diamond class structure is related to his or her occupation but not determined by that occupation. Some lawyers are in the top diamond, and some in the bottom. Some engineers, scientists, and professors are in the privileged class, and some in the new working class. It is not occupation that determines class position but access to generative capital—stable, secure resources over time.

THE NEW AMERICAN CLASS STRUCTURE DEFINED

> The gap between the haves and have-nots is greater now than at any time since 1929. —Edward N. Wolf, *Top Heavy: The Increasing Inequality of Wealth in America and What Can Be Done about It*, 1996

. . . [The] two-class structure is composed of approximately 20 percent privileged Americans and 80 percent non-privileged Americans. Members of the employer, managerial, and professional classes have a stable income flow, employment stability, savings, pensions, and insurance. Their positions in the economy enable them to use their resources to accumulate more resources and to ensure their stability over time. The new working class has little in the way of secure resources.

Their jobs are unstable, as they can be eliminated by labor-replacing technology or corporate moves to offshore production. Only marginal professionals and craft workers possess some skills that provide short-term security, but even their skills are being eroded by new technology, the reorganization of work, and the decline of union power.[3]

This image of class structure in American society is based on three important principles that define the new American class structure and how it works in practice.

Class Structure Is Intergenerationally Permanent

One of the most significant aspects of class structures is their persistence over time. The inequality that a person experiences today provides the conditions that determine the future. This aspect of class structure is rarely discussed by the media or even by scholars devoted to the layer-cake image of inequality. In fact, most discussion of class structure views that structure, and one's place in it, as temporary and ever changing. The belief in equality of opportunity states that regardless of where a person starts out in life it is possible to move up through hard work, motivation, and education. Similarly, the overall structure is viewed as changing, as revealed in statistics on the median income, the expanding middle class, or the declining percentage of the population living below the poverty line. In short, the popular image of class differences is that they are temporary and constantly changing. But in fact, nothing could be further from the truth when it comes to the new class system in the United States.

The "rules of the game" that shape the class structure are designed to reproduce that structure. Let's consider a few of those "rules" and how they work.

First, our legal system gives corporations the right to close down a plant and move the operation overseas, but it does not give workers a right to their jobs. Owners and employers have property rights that permit wide latitude in making decisions that impact on workers and communities. But workers' jobs are not viewed as a property right in the law. The protected right to a secure job would provide workers with a stable resource over time and modify their vulnerable situation in the class system.

Second, people in privileged classes have unrestricted opportunities to accumulate wealth (i.e., extensive consumption capital and investment capital). The accumulation process is based on tax laws that favor the rich, a variety of loopholes to avoid taxes, and an investment climate that enables the rich to get richer. The share of net worth and financial wealth going to the top 20 percent of the population is staggering. One out of five Americans owns almost everything, while the other four are on the outside looking in.[4]

This extraordinary disparity in wealth not only provides a clear picture of the polarized two-class structure; it also provides the basis for persistence of that structure. Because inheritance and estate laws make it possible to do so, wealth is transmitted across generations, and privilege is thereby transmitted to each succeeding generation. At the end of May 2001, the United States Congress passed a new tax bill that included the elimination of the federal estate tax, thereby enabling the privileged class to transmit their wealth without tax penalty. This was part of President Bush's tax reform proposal that will provide significant tax reduction for people with six-figure earnings, but only modest reductions for middle- and low-income families. Moreover, there were no reductions in payroll taxes, including those supporting Social Security and Medicare, which account for a much higher percentage tax on lower-income families than on those in upper-income brackets.

Another feature of the American class structure that contributes to its permanence is the sheer size of the privileged class. It consists of approximately 20 million households, or between 40 million and 50 million people. A class of this numerical size, with its associated wealth, is able to fill all the top positions across the institutional spectrum. Moreover, it is able to fill vacant positions or newly created positions from among its own members. Thus, recruitment of talented women and men from the nonprivileged class will become increasingly rare.

Third, the so-called equality of opportunity in America is supposed to be provided by its system of public education. Yet everyone who has looked at the quality of education at the primary and secondary levels knows that it is linked to the class position of parents. Spending per pupil in public schools is tied to property taxes, and therefore the incomes of people in school districts. Schools in poor districts have the poorest physical facilities, libraries, laboratories, academic programs, and teachers.[5] Some of the children who survive this class-based public education are able to think about some sort of postsecondary education. But even here the game is stacked against them.

Going to college is based on the ability to pay the costs of tuition, and, unless living at home, room and board. Even at low-cost city colleges or state universities, the expenses exceed what many working-class families can afford. On the other hand, even if college attendance were not tied to ability to pay, it is not likely that many youngsters from low-income families would think of college as a realistic goal, given the low quality of their educational experience in primary and secondary grades.

Thus, the "rules of the game" that are the foundation for the class structure are designed primarily to transmit advantage and disadvantage across generations. This persistence of structure exists even when there are instances of upward social mobility—the sons and daughters of working-class families who move into the professional classes. This upward mobility occurs in a very selective way and without changing the rules of the game. For example, when the birthrates among the privileged class fail to produce enough children to fill all the high-level, organizationally based professional positions for doctors, lawyers, engineers, computer specialists, and managers, it may become necessary to recruit the most talented young men and women from the working class. The most talented are identified through special testing programs and curriculum tracking and are encouraged to consider advanced education. "Elite" colleges and universities develop special financial and academic programs for talented working-class students, and a variety of fellowship programs support those with financial need. Upward mobility is made possible not by changing the rules of the game but by "creaming" the most talented members of the working class. The creaming process has the dual effect of siphoning off potential leaders from the working class and supporting the belief in equality of opportunity and upward mobility.

There Is No Middle Class

. . . The layer-cake image [of class] encourages a belief in a "center" or a "middle class" that is large and stands between the upper and lower classes. The different groups in the middle may think of themselves as being "better off" than those below them and may see opportunities to move up the "ladder" by improving education, job skills, or income.

This image of class structure is stabilizing, in that it encourages the acceptance of enormous material inequality in American society because of the belief that anyone can improve his or her situation and become one of the "rich and famous." It also encourages greater attention to the small differences between groups and tends to ignore the large differences. For example, many Americans are hardworking men and women who often work two jobs to make ends meet but are limited by these low-wage and no-benefit jobs. These people are often most hostile to the welfare benefits provided for people who are just below them in income. A working poor person gets $12,000 a year for full-time work, whereas a welfare family may get the same amount in total benefits without working. However, these same working poor rarely have their hostility shaped and directed toward the rich, who may be more responsible for the low wages, limited benefits, and inadequate pensions of the working poor.

The belief in a middle class also allows politicians to proclaim their support for tax breaks for what they call the middle class while debating whether the middle class includes those with incomes up to $250,000 a year or only those earning $100,000.

In our conception of class structure, there can be no middle class. Either you have stable, secure resources over time, or you do not. Either you have a stable job and income, or you do not. Either you have secure health insurance and pensions that provide adequate income, or you do not.

Notes

1. Don Stillman, "The Devastating Impact of Plant Relocations." *Working Papers* (July–August 1978): 42–53.
2. Cecelia Burns Stendler, *Children of Brasstown: Their Awareness of the Symbols of Social Class* (Urbana: University of Illinois Press, 1949); Robert G. Simmons and Morris Rosenberg, "Functions of Children's Perceptions of

the Stratification System," *American Sociological Review* 36 (1971): 235–49; Scott Cummings and Del Taebel, "The Economic Socialization of Children: A Neo-Marxist Analysis," *Social Problems* 26 (December 1978): 198–210; Anthony M. Orum and Roberta S. Cohen, "The Development of Political Orientations among Black and White Children," *American Sociological Review* 38 (1973): 62–74; Jeannette F. Tudor, "The Development of Class Awareness in Children." *Social Forces* 49 (1971): 470–76.

3. Harley Shaiken, *Work Transformed: Automation and Labor in the Computer Age* (New York: Holt, Rinehart and Winston, 1985); David F. Noble, *Forces of Production: A Social History of Industrial Automation* (New York: Knopf, 1984).
4. Edward N. Wolff, *Top Heavy: The Increasing Inequality of Wealth in America and What Can Be Done about It* (New York: Twentieth Century Fund, 1996).
5. Jonathan Kozol, *Savage Inequalities: Children in America's Schools* (New York: Harper, 1991).

Class and Race

(2008)

JANIS PRINCE INNISS

America has a long, painful history with race relations but has prided itself on being free of class conflicts. Most Americans—regardless of their actual income—consider themselves middle class. In what is considered the land of opportunity, most people believe that if you work hard, regardless of your beginnings, you can become wealthy.

While there is some discussion in the public arena about race (and to some extent ethnicity), there is less about class. During campaign speeches we hear charges that an opponent is for the rich, at the expense of the common folks. As a presidential candidate in 2008, then-senator Hillary Rodham Clinton addressed the income gap. On November 19, 2007, in a speech titled "Economy: Policy Address on America's Economic Challenges," she made the following comments:

> [T]he gap between the rich and everybody else has only gotten broader.
>
> In 2005, the last year I could find the numbers for, all income gains went to the top 10 percent of households, while the bottom 90 percent saw their incomes decline. That is not the America that I grew up in; that is not the country that I believe is holding out the promise of prosperity for people willing to work hard and take responsibility.
>
> The wealthiest 1 percent of Americans held 22 percent of America's income. That's an astonishing figure, and it is the highest level of income inequality since the beginning of the Great Depression in 1929.

Indeed, the income gap exists and has widened. But what else can we learn about class by digging a little deeper? It is well documented that gender and race intersect with class and that these factors determine our relation to power and privilege.

This essay examines some of the relationships between class and race—by looking at some of the differences in income, wealth, education and occupation by race. I am looking at these two sociodemographic factors for the sake of simplicity, but bearing in mind that the relationships between gender, class, and race are highly interconnected.

Income refers to wages and salaries for work we do. It also refers to money we make on our investments. Income in the U.S. has increased significantly over the

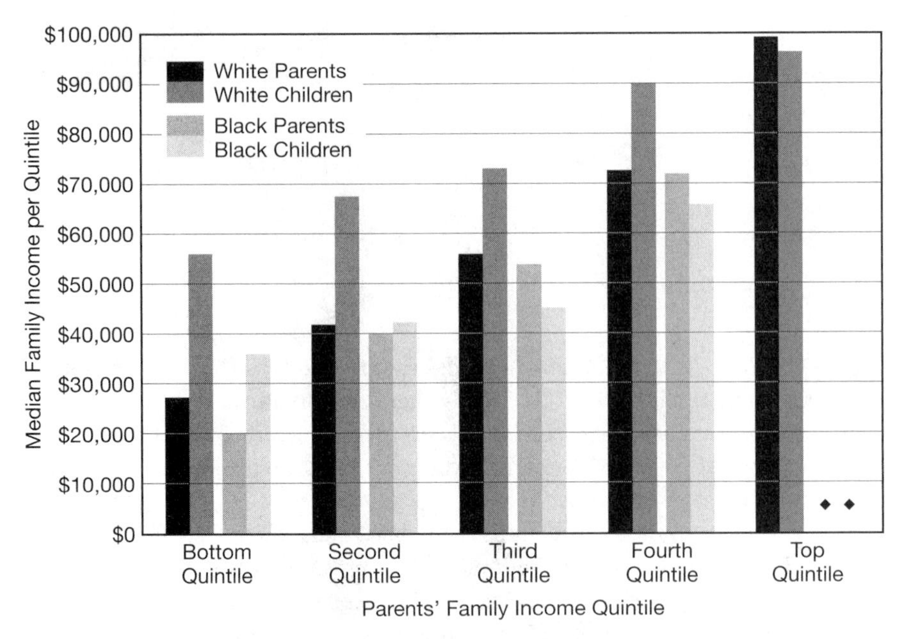

Source: "Economic Mobility of Black and White Families," www.census.gov/hhes/www/income/histinc/ineqtoc.html

FIGURE 1 Children's Income by Race, Compared to Parental Income and Generational Average (2006 Dollars)

**Too few observations to report

past decades for all sectors of workers (not only those in white-collar and professional, managerial occupations but also for blue-collar workers). At the same time however, the divide between the top 5% of wage earners and pretty much everyone else has increased enormously.

A report by the Pew Charitable Trusts entitled "Economic Mobility of Black and White Families" indicates that median family incomes have increased since the 1960s, but that is less true for black families than it is for white families. (These are the only two groups the report addresses due to limitations of the data used.)

Researchers performed an intergenerational analysis and looked at how children fare in comparison to their parents in terms of income. They found that the economic benefits that black middle-class parents enjoy are mostly *not* being matched by their children. In fact, the majority of black children of middle class parents fall *below* their parents in income and economic status, while white children exceed their parents' attainments on those dimensions. Only 31 percent of black children grow up to earn more than their parents, compared to 68 percent of white children in that income range. This decline in income for blacks is found not only among middle-class but also upper-middle-class children.

Even worse, almost half (45 percent) of black children of middle-class parents fall to the very bottom of the income distribution, compared to 16 percent of white

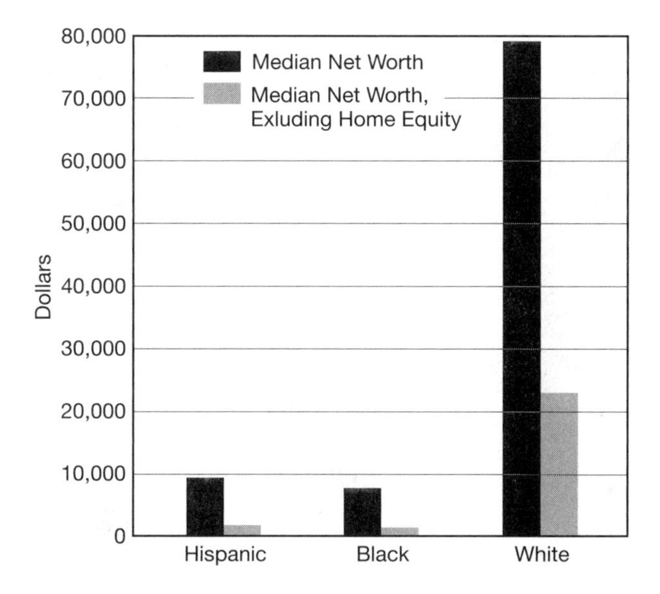

Source: U.S. Census Bureau Net Worth and Asset Ownership of Households: 1995 and 2000.

FIGURE 2 Median Net Worth and Median Net Worth Excluding Home Equity by Race of Householder, 2000 (2000 Dollars)

children. Looking at other income groups, black children fared better in the two lowest income groups, although they are always well below the gains of white children.

Wealth refers to assets such as real estate property, stocks, and bonds. Wealth in the United States is concentrated in the hands of very few people; the top 1 percent of families hold about one third (32.7 percent of the nation's total net worth, and in fact the top 10 percent of families hold about 70 percent of the total net worth.

This means that the majority of people—90 percent of the population—have less than one third of the nation's total net worth!

Data from the U.S. Census Bureau illustrates the relationship between race and economic resources. Black households and Hispanic households held a significantly higher proportion of their net worth in housing than Whites. Black and Hispanic households have a significantly lower proportion in financial assets such as stocks and mutual fund shares compared with White households.

Despite a historically large gap in the high school completion rates between whites and blacks, in 2000, high school completion rates for whites and Asians are pretty close, with Blacks a not very distant third place. Barely half of Hispanics finished high school; this group has the highest dropout rate of any in the United States.

Although a large number of blacks do attend college today, graduation rates are disappointing for this group and for Hispanics. Asians are the only group

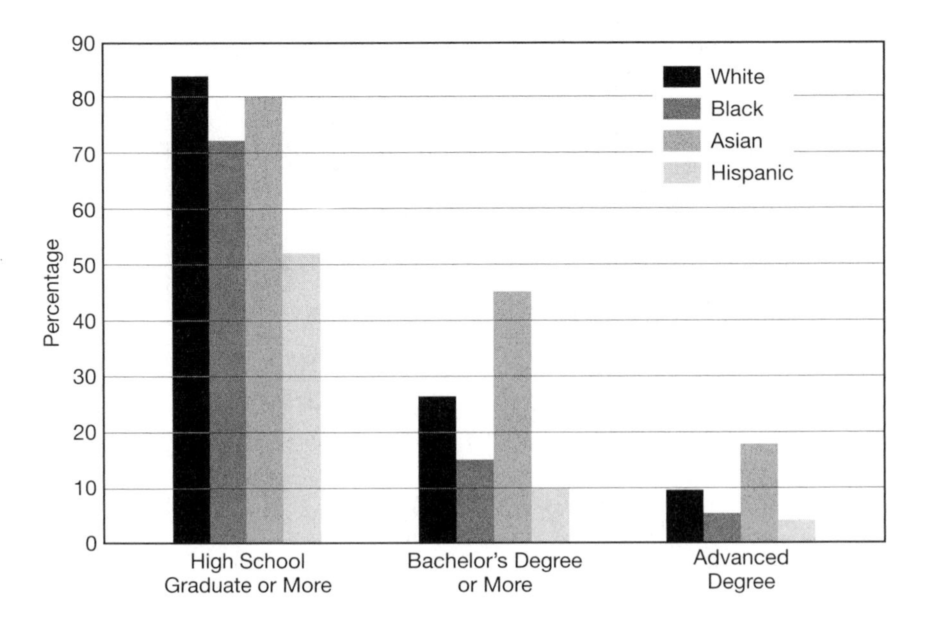

Source: www.census.gov/prod/2002pubs/p23-210.pdf

FIGURE 3 Educational Attainment of Population Over 25 by Race, 2000

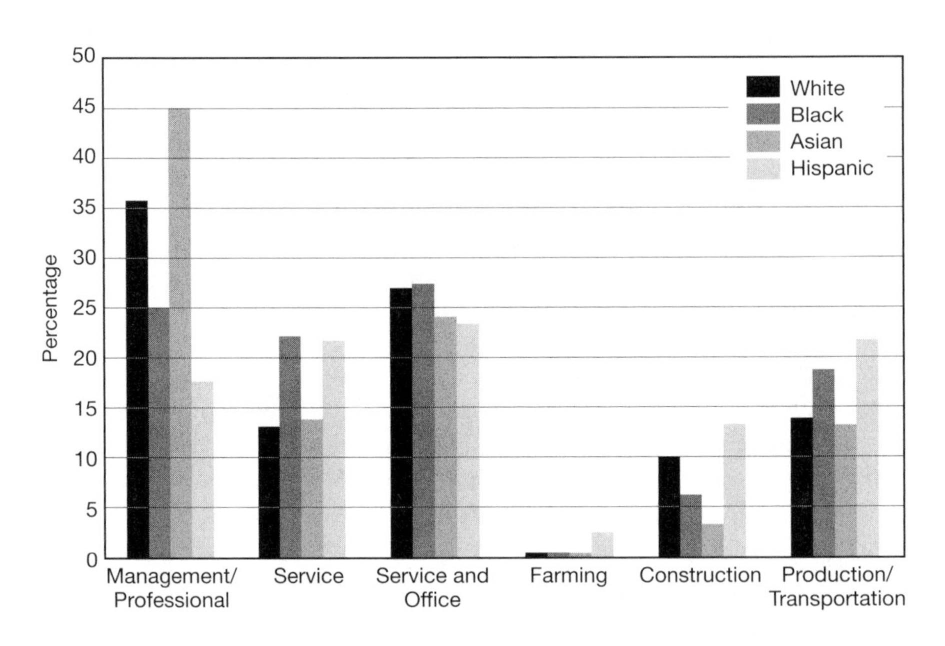

Source: www.census.gov/prod/2003pubs/c2kbr-25.pdf

FIGURE 4 Selected Occupations by Race, 2000

approaching 50 percent of their population having attained a bachelor's degree or higher.

Clearly, education and its relationship to race have an impact on occupation: the types of jobs that people are qualified for and by extension the incomes they can command.

Where do you fall on each of the four dimensions of class—income, wealth, education, and occupation? What role do you think your race plays in your social class standing?

Related Links

Pew Report: www.pewtrusts.org/uploadedFiles/wwwpewtrustsorg/Reports/Economic_Mobility/EMP%20Black%20and%20White%20Families%20ES+Chapter.pdf

New York Times series on class: www.nytimes.com/packages/html/national/20050515_CLASS_GRAPHIC/index_04.html

U.S. Census report on net worth: www.census.gov/prod/2003pubs/p70-88.pdf

Class Consciousness

(2007)

KAREN STERNHEIMER

A few months ago, I got a letter saying that I had won the lottery. No, not that kind of lottery. Not a scam lottery either. I won the kind that gives you a week of jury duty.

So I dutifully showed up at the courthouse to fulfill my civic obligation.

"Jury duty?" a woman asked as I walked out of the parking structure. She must have seen the papers in my hand.

"Yep," I answered.

"Me too," she said. "Have you been here before?" she asked. I said no; she said that she hadn't either.

As we waited in the long security line to enter the courthouse, I noticed that we were among the few white women there. And although she was significantly older than me, our appearances were somewhat similar in other ways: the open-toed shoes revealing manicured feet, slightly cropped pants and short-sleeved shirt under a light sweater. We both carried a tote bag with that day's *Los Angeles Times* sticking out. We were "class" mates.

There were other clues too. The courthouse was located in a working-class neighborhood, where she (correctly) presumed I did not reside.

"How long did it take you to get here?" she asked.

I said not too long, maybe thirty minutes. "From the west side?" she (again, correctly) guessed, and then asked me which streets I took to get there. In Los Angeles, the west side is synonymous with being at least middle class, if not affluent.

Once she confirmed our similar class statuses, she complained that she didn't see any suitable restaurants in the area for lunch. I mentioned that there was a snack bar, and she said there was probably nothing healthy there. I told her that I had the same thought the night before and brought my lunch with me.

Social class is an interesting and complex sociological concept. Based on more than just how much money you have or where you live, it includes things like educational background, occupational prestige, and whether most of your money comes from income earned from a job or from inherited wealth. And as some sociologists argue, cultural preferences may also provide markers about class membership (like what kinds of food you eat and the sort of clothes you wear).

Once we got through security and into the courthouse, we found that the jury room was packed; my new friend and I sat next to each other. In such a crowded space it was all too easy to overhear the numerous conversations taking place. Many revealed the class status of the conversant; a group in front of me discussed how many days their employers paid for jury duty—not an issue for a professor on summer break, a business owner, or someone who does not need to be in the labor force at all.

One of the people in front said he was a mail carrier. In his conversation with the women beside him, he compared the post office's jury duty policy to the transit authority's policy, as he used to be a bus driver. His neighbor mentioned that her friend drives a bus too; from their conversation I learned that wages are much lower now than they had been when the man drove a bus, and that finding a good job with a strong union was tough these days.

Aside from profession, income, neighborhood, and food preferences, our entertainment choices can also be used to demonstrate class status. As the jury room television played *Jerry Springer*, the lady next to me mentioned under her breath that she couldn't understand why anyone would watch such "trash." Later, someone changed the channel and put on an afternoon soap, much to the dismay of the people in front of us.

"Who do they think they are, changing the channel while people are watching?" one woman asked. A man nearby her got up and changed the channel back to the raucous talk show (about who the real father of a teen's baby was). A woman on the other side of me also shook her head and muttered, "I can't believe these people" when it became apparent that the people in front of us really wanted to watch the show.

Now how did my new neighbors know that I wasn't a die-hard Springer fan? Okay, I'm not, but why would they presume that they could criticize the show and not offend me?

My status cues suggested that I wouldn't be someone in Jerry's fan base, but instead someone who reads the newspaper daily (an increasingly small demographic). Plus they overheard me talking to an old grad-school classmate, coincidentally on jury duty too. From our conversation they could surmise other reasons that I would be an unlikely fan of the show: I have an advanced degree and work as a professor.

Some of my neighbors displayed their class status by distancing themselves from the show. And the people in front of me did the same thing in a different way. "Her mother didn't raise her right," one of the women said of the Springer guest, who (supposedly) had no idea who the baby's daddy really was. "Mm-mm," she shook her head, "my momma would have whooped my butt if I was running around with all those guys."

Part of establishing class lines includes differentiating ourselves from others, either those we somehow feel superior to (because of what kinds of popular culture they enjoy, in this case) or those we *think* might feel superior to us ("Who do they think they are?").

But Americans rarely discuss class, maintaining the illusion that we live in a classless society. The mythology of the American Dream tells us that anyone can rise to the top, provided they work hard. Even our use of the word "class" denotes individual rather than collective realities. Saying someone has or doesn't have class is a reflection of their behavior, not a reference to our system of stratification.

Americans often have an easier time noting the impact of race and racial discrimination than understanding the persistence of economic stratification. This is especially challenging because race and class have been so entangled in American life (which is why I purposely haven't explored issues of race in this essay).

Maybe that's because we seldom have opportunities to mingle with people from other social class levels outside of the workplace, and at work stratification may seem normal. Even jury duty, a seemingly perfect possibility for a cross-class gathering, generally excludes those at the top and bottom of the socioeconomic scale.

Those at the bottom may not be registered to vote or have a driver's license, and therefore would be excluded from the pool of potential jurors. Also, people earning minimum wage with no vacation time or benefits might not lose their job if they go on jury duty, but they probably would not get paid and thus could be excused for financial hardship reasons. And as for the wealthy, the threat of a $1,500 fine for failing to appear might not be a big deal (that is, if they couldn't use connections to get themselves excused in the first place).

At the end of the day, the jury room supervisor let us know that none of us would be needed on a case, and we were free to go. I said goodbye to my "class mate," knowing that I would probably never see her again. But I will probably encounter many other "class mates" like her in the future, as America remains in many ways more segregated by class than it is by race.

Class Action in the Media

(2005)

DIANA KENDALL

San Francisco, California:

> They live—and die—on a traffic island in the middle of a busy downtown street, surviving by panhandling drivers or turning tricks. Everyone in their colony is hooked on drugs or alcohol. They are the harsh face of the homeless in San Francisco.
>
> The traffic island where these homeless people live is a 40-by-75 foot triangle chunk of concrete just west of San Francisco's downtown. . . . The little concrete divider wouldn't get a second glance, or have a name—if not for the colony that lives there in a jumble of shopping carts loaded with everything they own. It's called Homeless Island by the shopkeepers who work near it and the street sweepers who clean it; to the homeless, it is just the Island. The inhabitants live hand-to-mouth, sleep on the cement and abuse booze and drugs, mostly heroin. There are at least 3,000 others like them in San Francisco, social workers say. They are known as the "hard core," the people most visible on the streets, the most difficult to help. . . .
>
> Every effort to help the Islanders—from family, probation officers, drug counselors, homeless aid workers—has failed. They have been in and out of hospitals or methadone programs and jails . . . so many times even they have lost count. "We want to get off the street, but I got to tell you true," [Tommy, a homeless man, said]. "Unless they take people like us and put us somewhere we can't keep f—ing up, we're going to keep f—ing up."[1]

How does this excerpt from a newspaper article make you feel about homeless people? Based on this news account, most newspaper readers would have a hard time feeling sympathy for the inhabitants of Homeless Island. To the contrary, a typical reaction to the situation depicted above reported in a *San Francisco Chronicle* series, "Shame of the City," is one of disgust, tinged with "Yeah, that's the sort of homeless people who are the problem"—bums who sleep on the cement, abuse drugs and alcohol, and panhandle for the money it takes to support their habit.

Compare that media-generated account of San Francisco's homeless population with this one, also from a newspaper article:

> "He's OK," Michelle, 48, said of San Francisco Police Officer Matt Maciel one afternoon after he gently told them to move their carts and then asked if they had enough to eat. "He's just doing his job."
>
> Michelle remembers when she might have been the one calling the cops on people leaving needles outside her house. She was born . . . in Colorado . . . and was sexually abused as a child. Her dad was shotgunned to death young, and her mother was a drug addict gone to cancer. But before Michelle crash-landed at the Island five years ago, she worked as a home health aid and wore smart, pressed dresses.
>
> She dreams of getting back to that life. "That cop might be the guy who helps me, or maybe the jail people—it could be anybody," she said, giving Maciel a smile as he drove off. "I just need another chance."[2]

Based on this article, readers might feel some degree of sympathy for the homeless—especially for homeless persons like Michelle. Surprisingly, both of these depictions of the homeless are from the same newspaper and written by the same reporter. The two depictions show how *media framing* of a particular news story or television program often influences how we feel about the people in a story, especially when the subject of the story is related to wealth, poverty, or the future of the middle class. The manner in which class is framed by the media has a major impact on how people feel about class and inequality. For example, most people in the United States are not really *middle class* (since that would be statistically impossible), yet most of us think that we belong in this category—at least partly because the media define the middle class in such a way that most of us can easily self-identify with it.

WHY "FRAMING CLASS"?

My purpose is to demonstrate how newspaper articles and television entertainment programs contribute to the social construction of reality about class in the United States, including the manner in which myths and negative stereotypes about the working class and the poor create a reality that seemingly justifies the superior positions of the upper-middle and upper classes and establishes them as entitled to their privileged position in the stratification system.

Even a cursory look at the media reveals that class clearly permeates media content.[3] Regardless of whether journalists consciously acknowledge the importance of framing class in their analysis of everyday life, this process continually occurs in the millions of articles and television shows that are written and produced each year.

◇ ◇ ◇

...I began to compare information provided by the media about the upper classes with media representations of the working class and the poor. It was evident that journalists and television writers hold elites and their material possessions in greater awe—and encourage their audiences to do likewise—than they do the poor or homeless, who, at best, are portrayed as in need of our pity or, at worst, as doomed by their own shortcomings. I became convinced, in the words of the sociologist Herbert Gans, that "the news especially values the order of the upper-class and upper-middle class sectors of society."[4] ... My primary focus remains on how the media glorify the upper classes, even when they are accused of wrongdoing, but I also demonstrate how framing of stories about the middle, working, and poverty classes may maintain and justify larger class-based inequalities in the United States.

"ALL MEDIA/ALL THE TIME" AND OUR IDEAS ABOUT CLASS

Understanding how the media portray the different social classes in our society is important, because studies have shown that the attitudes and judgments of media audiences may be affected by how the media frame certain issues.[5] Although some may argue that how class is depicted in the media does not matter because each of us can use our own experiences to balance any inaccurate portrayal that we see on television or read in a newspaper or magazine, this contention is not realistic; it assumes that we can distinguish between the realities of the U.S. class structure as it actually exists and the fictionalized version of a perceived reality of class as it is depicted by the mass media.

Framing is an important way in which the media emphasize some ideological perspectives over others and manipulate salience by directing people's attention to some ideas while ignoring others. As such, a frame constitutes a story line or an unfolding narrative about an issue.[6] These narratives are organizations of experience that bring order to events. As such, these narratives wield power, because they influence how we make sense of the world.[7] By the time readers and viewers such as ourselves gain access to media products, those products customarily have gone through an extensive process of review and filtration. In the news industry, for example, the joint efforts of reporters, writers, producers, camera operators, photographers, and many others have framed the available information and produced a construction of social reality that does not necessarily accurately reflect the *real* conditions of social life.... According to the media scholar Gaye Tuchman, "The news frame organizes everyday reality and the news frame is part and parcel of everyday reality.... [It] is an essential feature of news."[8] Both conscious and unconscious motives of media framers play into how the news is framed.

What all of this adds up to with regard to the portrayal of class in the media is that we are not receiving "raw" information or "just" entertainment that accurately reflects the realities of life in different classes; in fact, audiences are receiving formulaic products that have been previously sanitized and schematized so that readers and viewers do not have to think for themselves and do not have to deal with the underlying problems of our society.[9] Today, media framing must be thought of as a process in which frame building and frame setting are important components of what we think of as reality. . . .

By analyzing how the media socially construct meanings about class, we can more clearly see how ideology and everything that passes for knowledge in our society can affect our thinking about inequality and our personal identity in regard to the class structure. Based on a theoretical approach referred to as "the social construction of reality," I argue that we use the information we gain from the media to construct a picture of class and inequality that we come to accept as reality. . . .

Class-based media representations are often taken for granted by viewers and listeners when they see or hear the same ideas repeated frequently.[10] An example is the annual media coverage that accompanies holiday charity toward those who are "down on their luck." This coverage typically has a homogeneous media interpretation as journalists and television entertainment writers give their annual nod to the poor and homeless by writing news stories[11] or television scripts calling for the leading character to serve a Thanksgiving or Christmas meal to the homeless at the local soup kitchen. These media representations suggest that Americans are benevolent people who do not forget the less fortunate. Ironically, the rest of the story line for the "holiday" episode of major television situation comedies typically shows the characters fretting over their own extensive Christmas lists and overindulging at holiday parties, conveying a message widely divergent from the one about unselfishly helping the poor and homeless.

Images of wealth and poverty that are repeatedly depicted by the media may either reinforce readers' and viewers' beliefs about inequality, or these images may challenge those beliefs.[12] This can be true even with regard to a situation comedy or other television program that the viewer knows is fiction. As the communications scholar Linda Holtzman states, "We may say of television, music, or film, 'I know it's not real,' and yet with heavy consumption of the media the repetition of the images will influence us in spite of that understanding."[13] Positive images of wealthy people may make us believe that they are deserving of their wealth; negative images of the poor and homeless may make us believe that they are deserving of their wretched condition. In regard to wealthy celebrities who are constantly featured in media culture, the philosopher Douglas Kellner writes,

"The celebrities of media culture are the icons of the present age, the deities of an entertainment society, in which money, looks, fame, and success are the ideals and goals of the dreaming billions who inhabit Planet Earth."[14] If we accept this dream of fame and fortune, we may engage in voyeurism, vicarious living, and unduly high levels of consumerism, all the while concluding that there is nothing wrong with our society and that our primary concern should be to get rich and avoid being poor—or at least to be solidly middle class but be able to show that we can live as the wealthy and famous do. . . .

◇ ◇ ◇

CONDUCTING THE RESEARCH

Because little prior research has examined media and class, I began my study with newspaper databases, searching for key words such as "working class," "elites," and "middle class" to identify a range of articles in which some specific acknowledgment of class location or socioeconomic status was made. I watched thousands of hours of television entertainment shows, looking specifically for such class-related identifiers as the occupational status of characters, the types and locations of residences in which people lived, and media publicity about the shows that emphasized economic characteristics, such as *Life of Luxury* and *Rich Kids*. Although articles from many newspapers are included in the research, I found that the *New York Times* best reflected what was being printed in newspapers throughout the country; many other papers are affiliated with the *Times* syndicate and publish the same articles within a day or two. . . .

I narrowed my research to newspaper articles and television entertainment shows, because newspapers and television programs are taken for granted as a form of information and entertainment. Although so-called reality series have become increasingly popular in recent years, I have chosen to limit my observation of such shows to those that overtly employ the idea of class, such as *The Simple Life*, which absurdly tries to show rich city girls living a working-class country life among "ordinary people," and *The Apprentice*, in which people compete for top-paying corporate positions. In fact, many "reality" shows are staged and do not indicate the true class position of participants. For instance, in the finale of the first season of ABC's *Bachelorette*, middle-class participants Trista Rehn (a physical therapist) and Ryan Sutter (a firefighter) enjoy a fully televised, multimillion-dollar wedding extravaganza that was in fact paid for by the television network and the show's sponsors.

I divided all of the materials that I had gathered into categories reflecting the different components of the U.S. class structure and also the divisions set forth by well-known sociologists in the field of social stratification. Although there are a variety of views of the American class system, I find a fairly traditional model most useful for explaining the *objective view of class*, because it reflects more closely than some other models what most media typically purport to show about class divisions in this country. According to sociologists, a *class system* is a type of social stratification based on the ownership and control of resources and on the type of work people do.[15] One resource is *income*—the economic gain derived from wages, salaries, income transfers (governmental aid), and ownership of property. Income is most important to those in the middle and lower tiers of the class structure because without it they would not have the means for economic survival. By contrast, *wealth* is the value of all a person's or family's economic assets, including income, personal property, and income-producing property. Some wealthy people do not need to work, because they possess sufficient economic resources—derived from ownership of property, including buildings, land, farms, factories, stocks, bonds, and large bank accounts—to live very well for the duration of their lives and to pass on vast estates to their children and grandchildren.

Because terminology such as "working class" and "upper-middle class" is frequently used by the media, I employed the Gilbert-Kahl model,[16] which divides the United States into six classes—the upper class, the upper-middle class, the middle class, the working class, the working poor, and the poor and homeless—as a basis for analyzing my data. The Gilbert-Kahl model identifies economic variables (such as *occupation*, *income*, and *wealth*), status variables (*prestige*, *association*, and *socialization*), and political variables (*power* and *class consciousness*), which I used to divide my data into categories for analysis. . . .

At the top of the social class hierarchy is the upper (capitalist) class, which constitutes about 1 percent of the U.S. population and comprises the wealthiest and most powerful people, who control the majority of the nation's (and in some cases the world's) wealth. The investment decisions of people in this class shape national and international economies. The upper class includes "owners of substantial enterprises, investors with diversified wealth, heirs to family fortunes, and top executives of major corporations."[17]

Distinctions are sometimes made between "old money" (upper-upper) and "new money" (lower-upper) classes in the sociological literature.[18] Members of the old-money category come from prominent families that have possessed great wealth for several generations. On a national level, names like Rockefeller, Mellon, Du Pont, and Kennedy come to mind. However, many regional elites also are immensely wealthy and pass the benefits of that wealth on to children and grandchildren through gifts and legacies. By contrast, families with "new money" have accumulated vast economic resources during the lifetime of people in the current generation. More recently, this money has come from high-tech industries, investment and banking, top-earning professions, and high-profile careers in sports and entertainment.

Like the upper class, the upper-middle class (about 14 percent of the U.S. population) is identified as privileged in comparison to the middle, working, working poor, and underclasses, in that the upper-middle class is composed primarily of professionals with college and postgraduate degrees. This group includes many top managers of large corporations, business owners, lawyers, doctors, dentists, accountants, architects, and others who earn incomes far above the national average. People in the upper-middle class are often portrayed as having achieved the American Dream. Unlike many in the upper class, however, members of the upper-middle class work to earn a living, and their children must acquire the requisite education if they are to enter well-paid employment, rather than assuming that they will inherit family-owned businesses or diversified stock and bond portfolios.

As compared with the upper-middle class, people in the middle of the middle class (about 30 percent of the U.S. population) are characterized as possessing two-year or four-year college degrees, having more supervision at work, and experiencing less job stability than those in the upper-middle class. Occupational categories include lower-level managers, semiprofessionals, and nonretail sales workers. In the past, middle-class occupations were considered relatively secure and to provide opportunities for advancement if people worked hard, increased their level of education, and gained more experience on the job. Today, however, a number of factors, including escalating housing prices, occupational insecurity, blocked mobility on the job, and a cost-of-living squeeze that has penalized many workers, are causes of concern and much media analysis.

The working class (about 30 percent of the U.S. population) is made up of semiskilled workers such as machine operators in factories ("blue collar" jobs) and some service-sector workers, including clerks and salespeople whose jobs involve routine, mechanized tasks that require little skill beyond basic literacy and brief on-the-job training.[19] Few people in the working class have more than a high school diploma, and many have less, which makes job opportunities for them more scarce in the 2000s. Jobs in fast-food restaurants and "big box" chains such as Wal-Mart have been the largest growth areas of employment for the working class; the segment of the working class made up of semiskilled blue-collar workers in construction and manufacturing has shrunk since the 1950s.

Below the working class in the social hierarchy is the working-poor category (about 20 percent of the U.S. population). Members of the working poor live just above or just below the poverty line. They typically hold unskilled jobs, seasonal migrant jobs in agriculture, lower-paid factory jobs, and minimum-wage service-sector jobs (such as counter help at restaurants). As some people once in the blue-collar sector of the workforce have faced increasing impoverishment and joined the ranks of the working poor, increased media attention has been focused on service workers and the lowest-paid operatives and sales and clerical workers who, despite working full-time and often holding down more than one job, simply cannot make ends meet. At the bottom end of the working class, there is often a pattern of oscillating mobility in which people move back and forth between the working class and the working-poor category.[20]

The poor and homeless (the underclass), about 12 percent of the U.S. population, typically are individuals who are unemployed or are part-time workers caught in long-term deprivation that results from low levels of education and income and from high rates of unemployment. In this category are unskilled workers, many single parents, members of subordinate racial and ethnic groups, persons with mental or physical disabilities, and recent immigrants with low levels of educational attainment.

By using these objective criteria for class, I began to look for recurring frames that have been used over time to describe the lifestyles of people in the upper, middle, and lower classes. It was interesting to see the extent to which these recurring themes could be found, not only over decades but also over centuries in media portrayals. For example, although the harshness of representations of the poor and homeless have been cloaked in more respectable terms of political correctness in recent years, many of the same themes and framing devices are still used when describing the plight of those at the bottom of our society's social, economic, and political ladder. Over the years, there likewise has been an almost fawning acceptance of the rich and famous, even when accused of wrongdoing, that is not found in representations of the working class. By contrast, though most people choose to identify themselves as in the good, solid middle class, media portrayals of this class for the past 150 years have portrayed it as fragile and caught perilously between the rich and the poor. Media representations of the upper class seldom suggest that its members' favored location in the class structure might be short-lived, but depictions of the middle class often portray people in this class as holding on by a thin thread.

. . . [D]iscussions of the rich and famous have captured the interest of journalists from the days of the earliest newspapers to contemporary Internet websites. How the "society page" has changed over time is a reflection of larger societal changes and new information technologies, but it is not an indication that there has been diminished interest in the doings of the wealthy and famous. If anything, just the contrary is true: audiences can increasingly feed around the clock on gossip about those at the top of the economic pyramid. [I found] four positive media frames and their messages: (1) the consensus frame: the wealthy are like everyone else; (2) the admiration frame: the wealthy are generous and caring people; (3) the emulation frame: the wealthy personify the American Dream; and (4) the price-tag frame: the wealthy believe in the gospel of materialism.

However, not all media representations of the top class are positive, and negative framing devices are sometimes used to portray the upper class: (5) the "sour grapes" frame: the wealthy are unhappy and dysfunctional; and (6) the bad-apple frame: some wealthy people are scoundrels. Media coverage of the downfall of some top corporate executives shows how their excessive consumption is of great interest to media audiences even as readers and viewers decry the greedy actions of these "captains of industry." The extent to which some wealthy people believe they can buy anything, including their way out of trouble, is a recurring media frame. How the media frame articles about the wealthy by showing them to be more interesting and more deserving of what they have stands in sharp contrast to portrayals of the poor and that show them as living tedious and less worthy lives.

[A]lthough some framing of persons in poverty and homelessness is sympathetic, much media coverage offers negative images of the poor, showing them as dependent on others (welfare issues) or as deviant in their behavior and lifestyle. A favorite media framing device is exceptionalism framing: "If this person escaped poverty, why can't you?" This approach tells "inspirational" stories about people who have risen from poverty or homelessness to find greater economic solvency and happiness in the class above them. Another framing device, charitable framing, is used by the media to show how we can help the poor at holidays and when disasters occur. Articles and television entertainment story lines using charitable framing focus on the need for a helping hand on "special occasions" but do not suggest that a more focused effort should be made on a daily basis to help alleviate the larger societal problems that contribute to individual problems of poverty, hunger, and homelessness.

[F]ive framing devices [are] used by the media to portray the working class: (1) shady framing: greedy workers, unions, and organized crime; (2) heroic framing: working-class heroes and victims; (3) caricature framing number 1: white-trashing the working class; (4) caricature framing number 2: television's buffoons, bigots, and slobs; and (5) "fading blue collar" framing: out of work or unhappy at work. [M]edia representations of the working class typically do not provide a positive image of that class.

I found [three key frames] frequently employed in media representations of the middle class: middle-class values framing, squeeze framing, and victimization framing. The first of these—middle-class values framing—emphasizes that the core values held by people in the middle class should be the norm for this country and that these values remain largely intact over time despite economic, political, and cultural changes. Within that frame the middle class becomes not only the nation's frame of reference but the ideal model to which people in the United States should aspire, particularly those in the working and poverty classes. However, the other two (seemingly contradictory) frames that I identified are also employed by the media to represent the middle class. Squeeze framing sends the message to media audiences that the middle class is perilously caught between the cost of a middle-class lifestyle and the ability to pay for that lifestyle, whereas victimization framing suggests that many middle-class problems are the result of actions of the upper class and the lower classes, potentially endangering the middle-class way of life.

. . . Since the print media, television, and the Internet have become the primary storytellers of the twenty-first century, we should be concerned about the kinds of stories that are being told and how these socially constructed representations of reality contribute to how we think of ourselves and how they foster an unhealthy ideology that supports the ever-widening chasm between the haves and have-nots in the United States and around the world.

Notes

1. Kevin Fagan, "Shame of the City: Homeless Island," *San Francisco Chronicle*, November 30, 2003, www.sfgate.com (accessed April 11, 2004).
2. Fagan, "Shame of the City: Homeless Island."
3. David Croteau and William Hoynes, *Media/Society: Industries, Images, and Audiences*, 3rd ed. (Thousand Oaks, Calif.: Pine Forge, 2003).
4. Herbert Gans, *Deciding What's News* (New York: Pantheon Books, 1979), 61.
5. See, for example, Robert M. Entman and Andrew Rojecki, *The Black Image in the White Mind: Media and Race in America* (Chicago: University of Chicago Press, 2000); Todd Gitlin, *The Whole World Is Watching* (Berkeley: University of California Press, 1980); Todd Gitlin, *Media Unlimited: How the Torrent of Images and Sounds Overwhelms Our Lives* (New York: Henry Holt, 2003); Shanto Iyengar, *Is Anyone Responsible? How Television Frames Political Issues* (Chicago: University of Chicago Press, 1994); Pippa Norris, Montague Kern, and Marion Just, *Framing Terrorism: The News Media, the Government, and the Public* (New York: Routledge, 2003); Stephen D. Reese, Oscar H. Gandy Jr., and August E. Grant, eds., *Framing Public Life: Perspectives on Media and Our Understanding of the Social World* (Mahwah, N.J.: Lawrence Erlbaum, 2003).
6. William A. Gamson, David Croteau, William Hoynes, and Theodore Sasson, "Media Images and the Social Construction of Reality," *Annual Review of Sociology* 18 (1992): 373–93.
7. Robert K. Manoff, "Writing the News, by Telling the 'Story,'" in *Reading the News*, ed. Robert K. Manoff and Michael Schudson, 197–229 (New York: Pantheon, 1987).
8. Gaye Tuchman, *Making News: A Study in the Construction of Reality* (New York: Free Press, 1978), 193.
9. Max Horkheimer and Theodor W. Adorno, *Dialectic of Enlightenment*, trans. John Cummings (New York: Continuum International, 2002 [1944]).
10. See Gitlin, *The Whole World Is Watching*; Norris, Kern, and Just, *Framing Terrorism*; and Reese, Gandy, and Grant, eds., *Framing Public Life*.
11. William K. Bunis, Angela Yancik, and David Snow, "The Cultural Patterning of Sympathy toward the Homeless and Other Victims of Misfortune," *Social Problems* (November 1996): 387–402.

12. Linda Holtzman, *Media Messages: What Film, Television, and Popular Music Teach Us about Race, Class, Gender, and Sexual Orientation* (London: M. E. Sharpe, 2000).
13. Holtzman, *Media Messages*, 32.
14. Douglas Kellner, *Media Spectacle* (New York: Routledge, 2003).
15. Robert A. Rothman, *Inequality and Stratification: Race, Class, and Gender*, 5th ed. (Upper Saddle River, N.J.: Prentice Hall, 2005).
16. Joseph A. Kahl, *The American Class Structure* (New York: Rinehart, 1957); Dennis Gilbert and Joseph A. Kahl, *The American Class Structure: A New Synthesis* (Homewood, Ill.: Dorsey, 1982); and Dennis Gilbert, *The American Class Structure in an Age of Growing Inequality*, 6th ed. (Belmont, Calif.: Wadsworth, 2003).
17. Gilbert, *The American Class Structure in an Age of Growing Inequality*, 271.
18. W. Lloyd Warner and Paul S. Lunt, *The Social Life of a Modern Community* (New Haven, Conn.: Yale University Press, 1941); Richard P. Coleman and Lee Rainwater, *Social Standing in America: New Dimensions of Class* (New York: Basic, 1978); Diana Kendall, *The Power of Good Deeds: Privileged Women and the Social Reproduction of the Upper Class* (Lanham, Md.: Rowman & Littlefield, 2002).
19. Gilbert, *The American Class Structure in an Age of Growing Inequality.*
20. Gilbert, *The American Class Structure in an Age of Growing Inequality.*

The Disaster of Homelessness

(2007)

SALLY RASKOFF

While listening to a National Public Radio (NPR) report about the 2007 Minnesota bridge collapse, one of the reporter's comments caught my attention. She was describing how a homeless man had come by when she was interviewing people and yelled, "This is my life every day!"

To many, it seems odd that homelessness could be similar to living through a disaster. There are differences that make many of us question that comparison, though. First, disasters are short-lived experiences, yet homelessness is a long-term problem. The longer someone is homeless, the more difficult it is for him or her to move out of it.

Second, there is direct, usually governmental, aid to survivors of disasters, whether natural or otherwise. Much of that aid often goes directly to the people who suffered the loss. However, aid for homelessness goes to organizations, not to the people who suffer the effects.

Third, disaster victims are often seen as blameless. We recognize that the precipitating event came from an outside source. Homeless people, on the other hand, are often blamed for their plight. Indeed, homelessness is one of our country's most typical blame-the-victim scenarios.

Last, in disasters, many people jump up to help those who have suffered. Witness the blanket and blood drives, the food and other donation programs that spring up after disasters like tsunamis and earthquakes. However, most people don't help the homeless person at the freeway off-ramp or on the sidewalk. Aid for homeless causes has been difficult to sustain—often because homeless people appear to be to blame for their circumstances and thus seem less deserving of such help.

Perhaps it would be easier to raise aid for the homeless if people stopped to consider how homeless people resemble victims of a disaster. First, people in both situations certainly experience a breach of norms. When typical rules of society are no longer applicable, people don't know how to behave. This situation of normlessness is what Émile Durkheim meant by anomie. Anomic situations are difficult for the people who exist within them. Because the longer the breach in norms exists, the more upsetting it can be for the people in that situation, most people act to repair those breaches and get to some sense of normalcy as quickly as possible.

If you've ever been through a disaster or been homeless, consider how you might have tried to bring a sense of everyday reality back—and consider how comforting it was if you were successful. In the days after the 1994 Northridge earthquake here in southern California, we had no electricity or water—thus cooking or bathing was nearly impossible. Our first few days after the earthquake were spent sweeping up debris and attempting to make the house look as "normal" as possible. We all felt as if we were acting, but it was comforting to try to pretend that life was indeed "normal."

Second, whether you are homeless or the victim of a disaster, the main tasks with which people occupy themselves are similar. Both homeless people and those who survive disasters spend their time on survival issues: where will their food, shelter, and clothing come from? Bathing is difficult and safety is an issue from both the environment and other people. For example, after the earthquake my family pulled out the camping gear and tried to create a special kind of camping trip by cooking on the Coleman stove. (The kids weren't convinced.)

Bathing was a special challenge since our water was the last utility to return. By the fifth day, I had to go to a friend's house in a functioning neighborhood to take a shower—we were lucky that we had friends who welcomed us. Some years ago my spouse completed emergency training with the fire department and the main message was take care of yourselves, since emergency services probably won't get to you in a timely manner after a major disaster. Thus their advice was to barricade neighborhoods and control the entries and exits—to suppress any looting or robbery activities. If we had had the means, we probably would have gone to a hotel out of the area so that we could have felt as normal as possible as soon as possible.

Third, both for the homeless and for those who have survived a disaster, help is often not helpful at all. Shelters may be available, but they are not perceived as safe or suitable locations to spend one's time. Rebuilding or finding suitable shelter takes time and depends on the resources available. Disaster relief may provide low-interest loans and financial grants to survivors but are often available only to homeowners. Even though both homelessness and disasters have a deep psychological impact on those who experience them, assistance for psychological help is usually not an option unless one has the resources and awareness to seek it out.

Finally, while homelessness isn't considered a "disaster" by most people in our society, disasters can create homeless people—they do destroy homes, after all. The attitudes toward these categories of homelessness are very different. Those of us who study homelessness know that it is a societal disaster and that social factors have a large impact on why people become homeless, but the public does not always see it that way.

While Durkheim's concept of anomie helps us to understand what's happening in the social setting during such situations, Marx's class distinctions and analysis of the ways that power is wielded in society can be useful in explaining why we see these two situations so differently when they are actually quite similar in their experience and impact.

How can we begin to explain these differences in attitudes and assistance? For one thing, homeless people are at the bottom of the class system, while those who are aided by the government and others during disasters are more likely to be at least middle-class. In the hurricanes, earthquakes, and other natural disasters of the last twenty years, homeowners were often given low-interest loans from government agencies like the Federal Emergency Management Agency (FEMA) and the Small Business Administration (SBA) to rebuild their properties and businesses. In some cases, these supplemented insurance payouts and in many areas, the rebuilt areas were actually worth more *after* the disaster than before. A notable exception to this trend is the Katrina aftermath in New Orleans.

Marx's theory can also help us better understand what happened in New Orleans before, during, and after Katrina. The populations most affected were the underclass and working poor who are still suffering the effects of that particular disaster years later. Even if FEMA had been in better working order and there hadn't been as much bureaucratic mismanagement, these poor people likely would have suffered simply because they are poor. Marx would have a lot to say about why the levees were not repaired when the government had the prior knowledge that they were in jeopardy. Why were those projects not identified as a priority? The class distinctions furthered class divisions and exploitation during a natural disaster, enough to create a massive social disaster for one of our most unique cities.

I think the homeless man in Minnesota was right on target: living as a homeless person is like living a disaster every day—but without the assistance and support given to most disaster survivors.

TALK ABOUT IT

1. Do you agree with Perrucci and Wysong's argument that the middle class no longer exists in America? Why or why not?
2. Describe examples of media images of social class you have seen. How do they shape public opinion about class in America?
3. Think about some of your encounters with homeless people. How do others respond to them, or to others in need of assistance?
4. Describe an incident when you encountered people from a different social class. Was the distinction clear? If so, what markers indicated that the people involved had different backgrounds?
5. Why are race and social class so linked in American society? What might change this?

WRITE ABOUT IT

1. Explain Perrucci and Wysong's new model of class in America. Compare and contrast their version with one other model of social class.
2. Choose one of the frames that Kendall identifies, and describe why this frame persists in the media.
3. Apply Perrucci and Wysong's argument that there are only two classes in America with the newly homeless in Raskoff's essay. How might the two-class model work in cases of disaster?
4. Apply Perrucci and Wysong's argument that there are only two classes in America to examples from "Class Consciousness." Does the two-class model apply to everyday interactions, as described in this essay? Include your own everyday experiences in your response.
5. Choose one of Kendall's frames. Is it used more when describing one racial/ethnic group than another? Discuss how and why this links with broader beliefs or stereotypes about that particular racial/ethnic group.

DO IT

1. Construct your own model of social class in America, based on the readings in this section and your own experiences. What defines each level? How does your model differ from more traditional ways of thinking about class and stratification?
2. Interview five people about their views of homeless people. Do their comments express sympathy, derision, or both? Interview five people about their views on the victims of a recent disaster. How do their responses compare? What words do they use to describe one group compared with the other? Analyze the overall differences and similarities in their responses.

3. Choose a television show, news broadcast, or articles online. Watch (or read) for the frames Kendall observed about social class. Do you see any of those frames in your observation? Any other frames about class that Kendall does not mention?
4. Go to a public place such as a mall or a park. What details might reveal the social class of the people you observe? Are there any markers of class that people might display on purpose, such as clothing, jewelry, or other consumer goods?
5. Prince Inniss looks at disparities between black and white children in her analysis of class and race. Go online to find similar data to look at the intersection between race and class in other racial/ethnic groups. Or, find other data that detail how class and race are intertwined in the United States. Illustrate your findings graphically.

7

Gender and Sexuality

Module Goal: ***Examine taken-for-granted assumptions of how we think about gender, sex, and sexual orientation.***

On the surface, gender may seem an obvious social category that needs no further analysis. But gender is more than about being male or female, or the physical characteristics that accompany this distinction. The concept of gender refers to the social constructions that are based on biological sex, arrangements that are rooted in power and that change over time and place.

Because gender is so central to one's personal identity, it might seem innate. Candace West and Don H. Zimmerman argue that gender is actually an accomplishment created through interactions with others. "Doing Gender" borrows from Erving Goffman's work (see Module 3), which considers us all social actors. But we are not simply reading lines and following stage directions in everyday life; whether we are conscious of it or not, we are actively involved in negotiating meaning through our interactions. As you read this selection, think of how you "do gender" through the simplest choices you make—what you wear, how you style your hair, the topics you talk about. Your behavior may sometimes transgress expected "gender roles" as you do gender, reminding us that meanings of gender are dynamic, not static.

Kristen Barber's "The Well-Coiffed Man" explores one example of behavior that challenges traditional notions of masculinity: heterosexual men who visit predominantly female hair salons. Barber explores how salon customers maintain a sense of heterosexual masculinity while patronizing a largely feminized space. Have you had similar experiences where you were one of a few males or females in a particular environment? If so, how did you manage your "outsider" status?

Gender is about more than just group membership: it carries important meanings of power. As you read Barber's selection, consider how the men's comments reflect an awareness of their status and power as heterosexual men. In "Language, Gender, and Power," Sally Raskoff explores the issue of power in everyday language. While we might not be conscious of the importance of the words we use, much of our language is laden with the vestiges of male dominance. How do the words you commonly use reflect meanings of gender?

We can also understand issues of gender by examining how we talk about teen pregnancy. As Janis Prince Inniss discusses in her piece "Back Stage Out in Front: Impressions of Teen Pregnancy," the sexual behavior of boys and men tends to remain "backstage," while teen girls who become pregnant display that they have been sexually active, literally out front. Are there discrepancies in the way sexually active males are discussed, compared with sexually active females?

Sexual orientation is linked with gender. As Barber's interviews indicate, challenging gender expectations can also lead to questions about sexual orientation. Some people choose to keep their sexual orientation secret, particularly in contexts in which gays and lesbians face discrimination. Recent debates have explored whether sexual orientation is biological, genetic, or environmental. In "Does Finger Size Reveal Sexual Orientation?" Sally Raskoff considers some of this research. What sociological factors might prompt researchers to look for physical indicators of sexual orientation?

As you read about gender and sexuality in everyday life, consider the following questions:

1. Why does gender remain such a significant factor in organizing and structuring our society?
2. How do sex and sexual orientation draw on conceptualizations of gender?
3. How are gender, sex, and sexual orientation linked to issues of power?

Doing Gender

(1987)

CANDACE WEST AND DON H. ZIMMERMAN

In the beginning, there was sex and there was gender. Those of us who taught courses in the area in the late 1960s and early 1970s were careful to distinguish one from the other. Sex, we told students, was what was ascribed by biology: anatomy, hormones, and physiology. Gender, we said, was an achieved status: that which is constructed through psychological, cultural, and social means. To introduce the difference between the two, we drew on singular case studies of hermaphrodites (Money 1968, 1974; Money and Ehrhardt 1972) and anthropological investigations of "strange and exotic tribes" (Mead 1963, 1968).

Inevitably (and understandably), in the ensuing weeks of each term, our students became confused. Sex hardly seemed a "given" in the context of research that illustrated the sometimes ambiguous and often conflicting criteria for its ascription. And gender seemed much less an "achievement" in the context of the anthropological, psychological, and social imperatives we studied—the division of labor, the formation of gender identities, and the social subordination of women by men. Moreover, the received doctrine of gender socialization theories conveyed the strong message that while gender may be "achieved," by about age five it was certainly fixed, unvarying, and static—much like sex.

Since about 1975, the confusion has intensified and spread far beyond our individual classrooms. For one thing, we learned that the relationship between biological and cultural processes was far more complex—and reflexive—than we previously had supposed (Rossi 1984, especially pp. 10–14). For another, we discovered that certain structural arrangements, for example, between work and family, actually produce or enable some capacities, such as to mother, that we formerly associated with biology (Chodorow 1978 versus Firestone 1970). In the midst of all this, the notion of gender as a recurring achievement somehow fell by the wayside.

Our purpose in this article is to propose an ethnomethodologically informed, and therefore distinctively sociological, understanding of gender as a routine, methodical, and recurring accomplishment. We contend that the "doing" of gender is undertaken by women and men whose competence as members of society is hostage to its production. Doing gender involves a complex of socially guided perceptual, interactional, and micropolitical activities that cast particular pursuits as expressions of masculine and feminine "natures."

When we view gender as an accomplishment, an achieved property of situated conduct, our attention shifts from matters internal to the individual and focuses on interactional and, ultimately, institutional arenas. In one sense, of course, it is individuals who "do" gender. But it is a situated doing, carried out in the virtual or real presence of others who are presumed to be oriented to its production. Rather than as a property of individuals, we conceive of gender as an emergent feature of social situations: both as an outcome of and a rationale for various social arrangements and as a means of legitimating one of the most fundamental divisions of society.

To advance our argument, we undertake a critical examination of what sociologists have meant by *gender,* including its treatment as a role enactment in the conventional sense and as a "display" in Goffman's (1976) terminology. Both *gender role* and *gender display* focus on behavioral aspects of being a woman or a man (as opposed, for example, to biological differences between the two). However, we contend that the notion of gender as a role obscures the work that is involved in producing gender in everyday activities, while the notion of gender as a display relegates it to the periphery of interaction. We argue instead that participants in interaction organize their various and manifold activities to reflect or express gender, and they are disposed to perceive the behavior of others in a similar light.

We argue that gender is not a set of traits, nor a variable, nor a role, but the product of social doings. . . . What then is the social doing of gender? . . . We claim that gender itself is constituted through interaction.[1] To develop the implications of our claim, we turn to Goffman's (1976) account of "gender display." Our object here is to explore how gender might be exhibited or portrayed through interaction, and thus be seen as "natural," while it is being produced as a socially organized achievement.

GENDER DISPLAY

Goffman contends that when human beings interact with others in their environment, they assume that each possesses an "essential nature"—a nature that can be discerned through the "natural signs given off or expressed by them" (1976, p. 75). . . .

[G]endered expressions might reveal clues to the underlying, fundamental dimensions of the female and male, but they are, in Goffman's view, optional performances. Masculine courtesies may or may not be offered and, if offered, may

1. This is not to say that gender is a singular "thing," omnipresent in the same form historically or in every situation. Because normative conceptions of appropriate attitudes and activities for sex categories can vary across cultures and historical moments, the management of situated conduct in light of those expectations can take many different forms.

or may not be declined (1976, p. 71). . . . Gender depictions are less a consequence of our "essential sexual natures" than interactional portrayals of what we would like to convey about sexual natures, using conventionalized gestures. Our *human* nature gives us the ability to learn to produce and recognize masculine and feminine gender displays—"a capacity [we] have by virtue of being persons, not males and females" (1976, p. 76).

Upon first inspection, it would appear that Goffman's formulation offers an engaging sociological corrective to existing formulations of gender. In his view, gender is a socially scripted dramatization of the culture's *idealization* of feminine and masculine natures, played for an audience that is well schooled in the presentational idiom. To continue the metaphor, there are scheduled performances presented in special locations, and like plays, they constitute introductions to or time out from more serious activities.

There are fundamental equivocations in this perspective. By segregating gender display from the serious business of interaction, Goffman obscures the effects of gender on a wide range of human activities. Gender is not merely something that happens in the nooks and crannies of interaction, fitted in here and there and not interfering with the serious business of life. While it is plausible to contend that gender displays—construed as conventionalized expressions—are optional, it does not seem plausible to say that we have the option of being seen by others as female or male.

The categorization of members of society into indigenous categories such as "girl" or "boy," or "woman" or "man," operates in a distinctively social way. The act of categorization does not involve a positive test, in the sense of a well-defined set of criteria that must be explicitly satisfied prior to making an identification. Rather, the application of membership categories relies on an "if-can" test in everyday interaction (Sacks 1972, pp. 332–35). This test stipulates that if people *can be seen* as members of relevant categories, *then categorize them that way.* That is, use the category that seems appropriate, except in the presence of discrepant information or obvious features that would rule out its use. This procedure is quite in keeping with the attitude of everyday life, which has us take appearances at face value unless we have special reason to doubt (Schutz 1943; Garfinkel 1967, pp. 272–77; Bernstein 1986). . . .

Popular culture abounds with books and magazines that compile idealized depictions of relations between women and men. Those focused on the etiquette of dating or prevailing standards of feminine comportment are meant to be of practical help in these matters. However, the use of any such source *as a manual of procedure* requires the assumption that doing gender merely involves making use of discrete, well-defined bundles of behavior that can simply be plugged into interactional situations to produce recognizable enactments of masculinity and femininity. The man "does" being masculine by, for example, taking the woman's arm to guide her across a street, and she "does" being feminine by consenting to be guided and not initiating such behavior with a man.

[W]e contend [that] doing gender is not so easily regimented (Mithers 1982; Morris 1974). Such sources may list and describe the sorts of behaviors that mark or display gender, but they are necessarily incomplete (Garfinkel 1967, pp. 66–75; Wieder 1974, pp. 183–214; Zimmerman and Wieder 1970, pp. 285–98). And to be successful, marking or displaying gender must be finely fitted to situations and modified or transformed as the occasion demands. Doing gender consists of managing such occasions so that, whatever the particulars, the outcome is seen and seeable in context as gender-appropriate or, as the case may be, gender-*in*appropriate, that is, *accountable.*

GENDER AND ACCOUNTABILITY

If sex category is omnirelevant (or even approaches being so), then a person engaged in virtually any activity may be held accountable for performance of that activity as a *woman* or a *man*, and their incumbency in one or the other sex category can be used to legitimate or discredit their other activities (Berger, Cohen, and Zelditch 1972; Berger, Conner, and Fisek 1974; Berger, Fisek, Norman, and Zelditch 1977; Humphreys and Berger 1981). Accordingly, virtually any activity can be assessed as to its womanly or manly nature. And note, to "do" gender is not always to live up to normative conceptions of femininity or masculinity; it is to engage in behavior *at the risk of gender assessment.* While it is individuals who do gender, the enterprise is fundamentally interactional and institutional in character, for accountability is a feature of social relationships and its idiom is drawn from the institutional arena in which those relationships are enacted. If this be the case, can we ever *not* do gender? Insofar as a society is partitioned by "essential" differences between women and men and placement in a sex category is both relevant and enforced, doing gender is unavoidable.

RESOURCES FOR DOING GENDER

Doing gender means creating differences between girls and boys and women and men, differences that are not natural, essential, or biological. Once the differences have been constructed, they are used to reinforce the "essentialness" of gender. In a delightful account of the "arrangement between the sexes," Goffman (1977) observes the creation of a variety of institutionalized frameworks through which our "natural, normal sexedness" can be enacted. The physical features of social setting provide one obvious resource for the expression of our "essential" differences. For example, the sex segregation of North American public bathrooms distinguishes "ladies" from "gentlemen" in matters held to be fundamentally biological, even though both "are somewhat similar in the question of waste products and their elimination" (Goffman 1977, p. 315). These settings are furnished with dimorphic equipment (such as urinals for men or elaborate grooming facilities for women), even though both sexes may achieve the same ends through the same means (and apparently do so in the privacy of their own homes). . . .

Standardized social occasions also provide stages for evocations of the "essential female and male natures." Goffman cites organized sports as one such institutionalized framework for the expression of manliness. There, those qualities that ought "properly" to be associated with masculinity, such as endurance, strength, and competitive spirit, are celebrated by all parties concerned—participants, who may be seen to demonstrate such traits, and spectators, who applaud their demonstrations from the safety of the sidelines (1977, p. 322).

Assortative mating practices among heterosexual couples afford still further means to create and maintain differences between women and men. For example, even though size, strength, and age tend to be normally distributed among females and males (with considerable overlap between them), selective pairing ensures couples in which boys and men are visibly bigger, stronger, and older (if not "wiser") than the girls and women with whom they are paired. So, should situations emerge in which greater size, strength, or experience is called for, boys and men will be ever ready to display it and girls and women, to appreciate its display (Goffman 1977, p. 321; West and Iritani 1985).

Gender may be routinely fashioned in a variety of situations that seem conventionally expressive to begin with, such as those that present "helpless" women next to heavy objects or flat tires. But, as Goffman notes, heavy, messy, and precarious concerns can be constructed from *any* social situation, "even though by standards set in other settings, this may involve something that is light, clean, and safe" (Goffman 1977, p. 324). Given these resources, it is clear that *any* interactional situation sets the stage for depictions of "essential" sexual natures. In sum, these situations "do not so much allow for the expression of natural differences as for the production of that difference itself" (Goffman 1977, p. 324).

Individuals have many social identities that may be donned or shed, muted or made more salient, depending on the situation. One may be a friend, spouse, professional, citizen, and many other things to many different people—or, to the same person at different times. But we are always women or men—unless we shift into another sex category. What this means is that our identificatory displays will provide an ever-available resource for doing gender under an infinitely diverse set of circumstances.

◇ ◇ ◇

We have sought to show that sex category and gender are managed properties of conduct that are contrived with respect to the fact that others will judge and respond to us in particular ways. We have claimed that a person's gender is not simply an aspect of what one is, but, more fundamentally, it is something that one *does*, and does recurrently, in interaction with others.

What are the consequences of this theoretical formulation? If, for example, individuals strive to achieve gender in encounters with others, how does a culture instill the need to achieve it? What is the relationship between the production of gender at the level of interaction and such institutional arrangements as the division of labor in society? And, perhaps most important, how does doing gender contribute to the subordination of women by men?

◇ ◇ ◇

GENDER, POWER, AND SOCIAL CHANGE

. . . Can we avoid doing gender? . . . It is unavoidable because of the social consequences of sex-category membership: the allocation of power and resources not only in the domestic, economic, and political domains but also in the broad arena of interpersonal relations. In virtually any situation, one's sex category can be relevant, and one's performance as an incumbent of that category (i.e., gender) can be subjected to evaluation. Maintaining such pervasive and faithful assignment of lifetime status requires legitimation.

But doing gender also renders the social arrangements based on sex category accountable as normal and natural, that is, legitimate ways of organizing social life. Differences between women and men that are created by this process can then be portrayed as fundamental and enduring dispositions. In this light, the institutional arrangements of a society can be seen as responsive to the differences—the social order being merely an accommodation to the natural order. Thus if, in doing gender, men are also doing dominance and women are doing deference (cf. Goffman 1967, pp. 47–95), the resultant social order, which supposedly reflects "natural differences," is a powerful reinforcer and legitimator of hierarchical arrangements. . . .

If we do gender appropriately, we simultaneously sustain, reproduce, and render legitimate the institutional arrangements that are based on sex category. If we fail to do gender appropriately, we as individuals—not the institutional arrangements—may be called to account (for our character, motives, and predispositions).

The sex category/gender relationship links the institutional and interactional levels, a coupling that legitimates social arrangements based on sex category and reproduces their asymmetry in face-to-face interaction. Doing gender furnishes the interactional scaffolding of social structure, along with a built-in mechanism of social control. In appreciating the institutional forces that maintain distinctions between women and men, we must not lose sight of the interactional validation of those distinctions that confers upon them their sense of "naturalness" and "rightness."

Gender is a powerful ideological device, which produces, reproduces, and legitimates the choices and limits that are predicated on sex category. An understanding of how gender is produced in social situations will afford clarification of the interactional scaffolding of social structure and the social control processes that sustain it.

References

Berger, Joseph, Bernard P. Cohen, and Morris Zelditch, Jr. 1972. "Status Characteristics and Social Interaction." *American Sociological Review* 37: 241–55.

Berger, Joseph, Thomas L. Conner, and M. Hamit Fisek, eds. 1974. *Expectation States Theory: A Theoretical Research Program.* Cambridge: Winthrop.

Berger, Joseph, M. Hamit Fisek, Robert Z. Norman, and Morris Zelditch, Jr. 1977. *Status Characteristics and Social Interaction: An Expectation States Approach.* New York: Elsevier.

Bernstein, Richard. 1986. "France Jails 2 in Odd Case of Espionage." *New York Times* (May 11).

Chodorow, Nancy. 1978. *The Reproduction of Mothering: Psychoanalysis and the Sociology of Gender.* Los Angeles: University of California Press.

Firestone, Shulamith. 1970. *The Dialectic of Sex: The Case for Feminist Revolution.* New York: William Morrow.

Garfinkel, Harold. 1967. *Studies in Ethnomethodology.* Englewood Cliffs, NJ: Prentice-Hall.

Goffman, Erving. 1967 (1956). "The Nature of Deference and Demeanor." Pp. 47–95 in *Interaction Ritual.* New York: Anchor/Doubleday.

——— 1976. "Gender Display." *Studies in the Anthropology of Visual Communication* 3:69–77.

——— 1977. "The Arrangement Between the Sexes." *Theory and Society* 4:301–31.

Humphreys, Paul, and Joseph Berger. 1981. "Theoretical Consequences of the Status Characteristics Formulation." *American Journal of Sociology* 86:953–83.

Lorber, Judith. 1986. "Dismantling Noah's Ark." *Sex Roles* 14:567–80.

Mead, Margaret. 1963. *Sex and Temperament.* New York: Dell.

——— 1968. *Male and Female.* New York: Dell.

Mithers, Carol L. 1982. "My Life as a Man." *The Village Voice* 27 (October 5):1ff.

Money, John. 1968. *Sex Errors of the Body*. Baltimore: Johns Hopkins.

——— 1974. "Prenatal Hormones and Postnatal Sexualization in Gender Identity Differentiation." Pp. 221–95 in *Nebraska Symposium on Motivation*, Vol. 21, edited by J. K. Cole and R. Dienstbier. Lincoln: University of Nebraska Press.

——— and Anke A. Ehrhardt. 1972. *Man and Woman/Boy and Girl*. Baltimore: John Hopkins.

Morris, Jan. 1974. *Conundrum*. New York: Harcourt Brace Jovanovich.

Rossi, Alice. 1984. "Gender and Parenthood." *American Sociological Review* 49:1–19.

Sacks, Harvey. 1972. "On the Analyzability of Stories by Children." Pp. 325–45 in *Directions in Sociolinguistics*, edited by J. J. Gumperz and D. Hymes. New York: Holt, Rinehart & Winston.

Schutz, Alfred. 1943. "The Problem of Rationality in the Social World." *Economics* 10:130–49.

West, Candace, and Bonita Iritani. 1985. "Gender Politics in Mate Selection: The Male-Older Norm." Paper presented at the Annual Meeting of the American Sociological Association, August, Washington, DC.

Wieder, D. Lawrence. 1974. *Language and Social Reality: The Case of Telling the Convict Code*. The Hague: Mouton.

Zimmerman, Don H., and D. Lawrence Wieder. 1970. "Ethnomethodology and the Problem of Order: Comment on Denzin." Pp. 287–95 in *Understanding Everyday Life*, edited by J. Denzin. Chicago: Aldine.

The Well-coiffed Man

Class, Race, and Heterosexual Masculinity in the Hair Salon (2008)

KRISTEN BARBER

> With all the money modern man has begun to spend on pampering and coiffing himself . . . we might be forgiven for thinking that traditional masculinity has entirely given way. (Salzman, Matathia, and O'Reilly 2005, 38)

Few people know what exactly to make of the metrosexual, a man who turns himself into a project (Brumberg 1997) in the seeming pursuit of the body beautiful. Traditionally associated with women and with gay men, the body beautiful has been tightly linked to the concept of femininity. In her book on *The Male Body*, Bordo (1999) suggests that the media now position men as sexualized objects of the gaze, just as it has done for women. She claims that women, for the first time in recent history, are now encouraged to consume the beautified male bodily form. As a result, Bordo and others (e.g., Salzman, Matathia, and O'Reilly 2005) contend that the sexualization of men in the media and their participation in appearance-enhancing practices destabilize traditional gender dichotomies. This seeming subversion leads Bordo to exclaim, "I never dreamed that 'equality' would move in the direction of men worrying *more* about their looks rather than women worrying less" (1999, 217).

Scholars who study the meaning of *women's* body work help us understand that participation in beauty culture is not rooted solely in gendered relationships, it is tied up with interlocking systems of race, class, gender, sexuality, and age (Battle-Walters 2004; Bordo 1993; Candelario 2000; Clark and Griffin 2007; Cogan 1999; Craig 2006; Furman 1997; Gimlin 1996; Jacobs-Huey 2006; Taub 1999). That is, for women beauty work is often about more than beauty, it is about appropriating and expressing a particular social status by grooming the body in a particular way. Few scholars have examined the meaning of men's participation in beauty culture, however.

In this article, I use a case study of Shear Style,[1] a small hair salon in a Southern California suburb, to explore how men hair salon clients make sense of their partici-

1. The names of the salon, the stylists, and the clients have been changed to protect the privacy of those involved in the study.

pation in beauty work. I find that men at Shear Style empty beauty work of its association with feminized aesthetics and instead construct it as a practice necessary for them to embody a class-based masculinity. But not all men are able to participate in the beauty industry. Rather, it is men with enough disposable income who are able to purchase beauty work and beauty products—or "grooming products" as they are often called for men—that promise to deliver aesthetics compatible with social standards. For the men at Shear Style, preference for "stylish" and "superior" hair embodies expectations of white professional-class masculinity. These men use beauty work to "do difference" (West and Fenstermaker 1995) in a way that distinguishes themselves from white working-class men, while at the same time distancing themselves from the feminizing character of the "women's" hair salon.

LITERATURE REVIEW

Race, Class, Gender, and the Body

In West and Fenstermaker's (1995) work on "doing difference," they describe difference as a methodical, ongoing, and interactional accomplishment. That is, differences along the lines of race, class, and gender are simultaneously experienced and rendered as "normal" and "natural" ways of organizing social life. The body is often a central mechanism through which people appropriate, perform, and negotiate difference. The clothes we wear, the way we style our hair, how we walk, talk, and gesture are all tied up with doing difference. . . .

The beauty industry generates services and products with which women groom their bodies according to social expectations of raced, classed, and sexualized femininities. The hair salon is a key space in the perpetuation of women's body projects. Hair is a social symbol that allows people to associate themselves with others along the lines of race, class, gender, sexuality, and age. Women cut, shape, and dye their hair in ways that express social location (Weitz 2004), and talk about their hair in ways that define their relationships with other women (Gimlin 1996; Jacobs-Huey 2006).

The Hair Salon as a Gendered Space for Women

. . . The hair salon is part of a larger "women's culture" in which women shape their perceptions of self and body, as well as form relationships and social networks (Black 2004; Furman 1997), participate in informal therapy (Black 2004; Sharma and Black 2001; see Kang 2003 on emotional labor in the nail salon), create entrepreneurial opportunities, resist dominant racist frames (Harvey 2005; Harvey-Wingfield 2007), and produce representations of femininity mediated through class (Gimlin 1996), race (Battle-Walters 2004; Candelario 2000; Craig 2006; Jacobs-Huey 2006), and age (Furman 1997). Purchasing beauty work in the salon is one way women accomplish difference and participate in the "naturalizing" of social arrangements.

◇ ◇ ◇

Feminist scholars interested in women, beauty, and the body find that women's participation in beauty work is about relationships, pleasure, and "achiev[ing] a look, and sometimes also a feeling, which is regarded as 'appropriate' in relation to categories of gender, age, sexuality, class and ethnicity" (Black 2004, 11). The hair salon is one space in which women shape their bodies and relationships with others in ways that mark them as members of particular social groups. Since we have long associated beauty work and the hair salon with "women's culture," the hair salon is a space in which men do not venture, or do so infrequently. In this way, "the salon both reflects and reinforces divisions along gender, [as well as] ethnicity and class lines" (Black 2004, 11). Hair salons are for women, barbershops are for men (Lawson 1999). Under this ideological regime, a heterosexual man in a hair salon is an anomaly who transgresses gender boundaries by moving into a women's space and by participating in a beauty practice traditionally associated with women.

Men: From the Laboring Body to the Flannel Suit to the Well-coiffed Man

During the Fordist-era of industrial production, definitions of masculinity were attached to men's ability to perform laborious tasks. We continue to see this today as "scarred and weathered men are seen as more 'manly' and thus socially valuable in many working-class settings and venues" (Paap 2008, 101; see also Paap 2006). For the working class, the literal sweat and blood of men are outward signs of the appropriate performance of masculinity. However, postwar America between 1945 and 1960 saw rapid economic growth, and with it came the corporation and an exponential increase in white-collar jobs. While men's identities continued to be bound up with their jobs, opportunities for intellectual work grew. Many middle-class white men flooded into corporations, trading in their denim work-jumpers for grey flannel suits. As it became necessary for the corporate man to interact with customers and clients, interpersonal skills, personality, and appearance became essential hiring and firing criteria (Luciano 2001).

Luciano (2001) describes how the emphasis on the appearance of middle-class white men emerged from capitalist notions of who a successful professional-class man is. Corporations encouraged these men to package their bodies and personalities for success. Employers correlated softness with Communism, fatness with laziness, and saw baldness as a detriment to sales. Marketers quickly produced sales gimmicks that attached the accomplishment of "professional success" to products such as toupees and pomade, products that had long been considered symbols of vanity, narcissism, and, thus, femininity.

It is no longer enough for some men to work hard, they must also look good. In their discussion of the metrosexual man, Salzman, Matathia, and O'Reilly note the way occupation is tied up with appearance: "In a 2003 poll of American men, 89 percent agreed that grooming is *essential* to the *business world*" (2005, 36; emphasis added). . . .

Thus far, most research on men and hair care has focused on the Black barbershop. This research reveals Black barbershops as spaces for community and the socialization of Black boys into Black men (Alexander 2003; Williams 1993; Wright 1998). In a society that marginalizes Black masculinity, the Black barbershop acts as a safe place for men to congregate, socialize, and reject oppressive stereotyped notions of masculinity. In the Black barbershop, appearance and the cutting of hair are often secondary to the conversations that are important in perpetuating culture and community (Alexander 2003). Research on the Black barbershop and the women's hair salon shows us how race, class, and gender are constructed differently in different spaces.

Unlike the barbershop, the hair salon is not an obvious place in which men participate in the reproduction of masculinity. Certainly it is not a space in which men could create community with other men. Hence, for those men who choose the salon, it is their participation in feminized beauty work that becomes salient. In this article, I seek to address three questions. First, how might men's participation in beauty work be wrapped up with their social locations? Second, how are the men at Shear Style hair salon involved in appropriating an identity that is simultaneously raced, classed, and gendered? And finally, how is their participation in salon hair care tied up with distinction and the doing of difference?

THE STUDY

In this study, I employed both ethnographic methods and in-depth interviews to explore the roles of class, gender, race, and heterosexuality in the purchase of beauty work by men in a small Southern California hair salon, Shear Style. From October 2006 through February 2007, I conducted 40 hours of observations, 15 formal in-depth interviews with men salon clients, and a group interview with three of the four salon stylists.[2] The small size of the salon, with only four work stations in close proximity to each other, made it an ideal space for me to observe client/stylist interaction, talk with men patrons, and recruit interview respondents. I had a number of informal conversations with men as they waited for their appointments or exited the salon. These conversations allowed me to quickly probe men about why they were at the salon and what it was about the salon that retained them as clients. These informal conversations also helped me to structure and refine my questions for the formal interviews.

2. The fourth stylist did not cut men's hair.

THE SALON

The context of Shear Style is important to an understanding of what it means for men to enter the gendered space of the "women's" hair salon. Shear Style is a feminized space marked by pink walls, fresh flowers, and regular cookie samplers. The men at the salon transgress gender boundaries and risk feminization (Kimmel 2001 [1994]) to enter the salon and get their hair cut there. Eleven of the 15 men I interviewed had followed their hairstylists from a prior salon to Shear Style. With its white walls and clean lines, the atmosphere of the previous salon is much more androgynous and, in contrast, Shear Style is understood by the men as "feminine."

Inside the salon, long thin lights snake down from the ceiling. The floors are a dark glossy wood and the walls are painted a dusty pink. On the back wall are old kitchen cabinets that display products for sale such as mousse, hairspray, and hair-wax, as well as jewelry, purses, and Suzanne Somers self-help books. Below these shelves are drawers that store curling-irons and blow-dryers. On Saturdays, the salon is usually at maximum capacity with women everywhere: sitting on the waiting bench, having their hair cut, and working. The salon rings out with the laughter of women as they talk about what is going on in their lives and which celebrity is wearing what.

The men are keenly aware that they are outnumbered in this gendered space, reporting that they rarely see other men in the salon. Hamilton, a 57-year-old white investment manager, points to the women around him as he describes his aversion to the salon, "It's jammed full of housewives . . . and there are bimbos walking around chatting." Hamilton trivializes the salon and the practice of beauty work in the salon by associating it with "bimbos" and "housewives." His privileged position as a white upper-middle-class man likely allows him to feel he has the authority to make such disparaging remarks. Many of my respondents recommended steps the salon could take to better serve its men clients. For example, two men proposed that flat screen televisions be affixed to the walls and tuned to the sports and the news channels. Also, many of the men would like to see available reading material other than "gossip" and bridal magazines. . . .

. . . Neil, a 43-year-old white engineer, describes the salon as a "fairly feminine atmosphere." When I asked him what it is about the salon that makes it "feminine," he told me that you have to "perch" on a cushioned bench while waiting, "and men don't perch." He then gestured toward the maroon, purple, and gold tasseled throw pillows that decorated the bench on which we sat and exclaimed that the "the pillows, food, [and] décor" make him feel he is in a "woman's space." . . . [T]his description allowed Neil to situate himself in contrast to the feminized character of the salon.

The gender composition of the salon's clientele, the lack of amenities for men, and the décor of the salon provides clues to the men that they are in a "women's" space. By articulating an understanding of the space as feminine (see Craig and Liberti 2007), the men set themselves against and create distance from the potentially contaminating "feminine" character of the salon. They contend the salon is not an appropriate space for *them*, as men, despite their regular visits. While the men enter the salon to purchase beauty work from the stylists, they simultaneously maintain a sense of masculinity by distancing themselves from the "feminine" salon and by situating themselves as anomalies in this space.

MEN'S MOTIVATIONS FOR GOING TO THE HAIR SALON

Three themes emerge from this study that help us to understand why the men at Shear Style purchase beauty work in a "women's" hair salon: (1) Because they enjoy the salon as a place of leisure, luxury, and pampering; (2) For the personalized relationships they feel they form with their women stylists; and (3) To obtain a stylish haircut they conflate with white professional-class aesthetics. . . . [T]he men at Shear Style understand the salon as a place important to the appropriation of a white professional-class embodiment, contrast[ing] the salon and the barbershop to differentiate themselves from white working-class masculinity, and resist[ing] feminization while transgressing gender boundaries.

The Pampered Heterosexual Man: Leisure, Luxury, and Touch in the Hair Salon

Bodily pampering, which includes attention to appearance and which takes place within a traditionally feminized space, could be considered a feminized form of leisure. However, the class and race privilege of the men at Shear Style allow them to access this leisure and pleasure without marginalization. The men also maintain a sense of masculinity by marking the salon services as *less* feminine than those offered by nail salons and spas. While they can afford to pay for stylish hair, they would not pay for nail care, for example. Finally, by heterosexualzing the touch that accompanies this pampering the men resist feminization and instead position themselves as heterosexually masculine.

Many of my respondents described the salon as a place of leisure, where they go to relax and pause from their hectic daily lives. The men at Shear Style are professionals who live in a speeded-up metropolis where work and family life collide and compete, and where people's social lives often lose out to the occupational expectations of white-collar "success." The 45 minutes they spend at the salon, waiting and getting their hair cut, is time for themselves, and time to relax and enjoy the services the salon provides. . . .

While many of the men described the salon as a place of leisure, there are any number of places they could go to find time for themselves. So, why do these men choose the gendered space of the "woman's" hair salon? Shear Style provides the men with services that are unique to the salon experience, services that make many of the men feel "pampered" and taken care of. Sharma and Black's interviews with women beauty workers show that "'pampering' was seen as a service which the stressed and hardworking (female) client deserved and needed" (2001, 918). This pampering comes in the form of paid touch, which is a key aspect of the hair salon experience (Furman 1997). . . .

Mack [a 39-year-old white art director] notes that it is in the hair salon where beauty services include physical pleasure. He suggests that the men's barbershop does not include touch that can be described as pleasurable or pampering. In his work on the Black barbershop, Alexander (2003) describes being touched by the barber as *secretly* pleasurable. That is, while he enjoys having the barber touch his scalp, this touch could never be discussed openly as pleasurable since doing so might be interpreted by other men as homoerotic. Comparatively, the heterosocial interactions the men have with their women salon stylists allow the men to access paid touch without their presumed heterosexuality falling under suspicion.

By couching paid touch in heterosexuality, the men position themselves as heterosexual and resist the potential feminization of pampering in a hair salon. They clearly receive pleasure from the scalp massages and shampooing, but state that they enjoy this aspect of pampering solely because they are being touched by a woman. "It's like when you go to get a massage [and] they want to know if you want a man or a woman [masseuse]; I'm like, 'a woman sounds nice,'" Don told me. Sam, a 53-year-old white architect, agrees, "I would say I prefer women. It's kind of like a massage too. They ask, 'do you want a man or a woman?' I always prefer a woman." Don and Sam suggest that a massage from a man would be uncomfortable for them, presumably because it does not fit with their sense of themselves as heterosexual. Therefore, touch in the salon is possible and pleasurable for the men because it is done within the context of a heterosexual interaction. If the men were shampooed by another man, such as a barber, they might not enjoy, or at least discuss, the pampering aspect of paid touch because it could compromise their association with privileged heterosexuality.

Although some of the men classed their hair salon experience by describing it as akin to a "mini spa day," they had not, and declared that they would not, enter a spa. These men define the spa as a place where people (presumably women) purchase services such as pedicures, manicures, facials, massages, body-wraps, and mud-baths. They counterpose their more utilitarian haircut to spa and nail services, which they describe as not a "priority" for them. As one man notes, "I think it's one of those things where I value my spare time so much that it's like when I look at my priorities and things I want to do in my time, [the] spa isn't there." I briefly spoke with a man who was leaving the salon after his haircut; he said that the salon is a nice way to "sneak pampering in while doing something you would have to do anyway." He elaborated by telling me that for professional-class men, paying $45 for a haircut is more acceptable than spending money in a spa or a nail salon because it can be veiled as a necessity. Many of the men admitted that it would probably feel good to get a pedicure, for example, but said such services do not serve a utilitarian purpose and, therefore, cannot be adequately disguised as masculine.

Personalized Relationships and Gendered Care Work

The relationships the men have with their stylists involve both touch and the exchange of personal information. Many of the men at Shear Style have grown attached and loyal to their stylists partially because of relationships they believe they share. . . .

The men appreciate their stylists' seemingly genuine interest in their lives. During my observations, I witnessed the pleasure many of the men receive when their stylists ask them to share what is going on in their personal lives. For example, during my fieldwork, I noted that,

> [A man] was already in the chair when I arrived at the salon. Rosa was cutting his hair and they were chatting away. He seemed comfortable as she talked about her husband and daughter. She asked him about his new baby boy, who was only two months old. I spoke with this man briefly after his haircut. He described the salon as a space in which he felt authentically cared for. He said that it is "fun" to talk with his hairstylist and that they "talk about life." "At the barbershop, they don't care about you," he said. When he left the salon, Rosa pleaded with him to bring his baby with him the next time he came to the salon. He beamed with pride and assured her he would. (Fieldnote: 2/16/2007)

This client reinforces the notion that care work is gendered by claiming that the men in the barbershop "don't care about you." A barber is assumed to not provide care work or emotional labor; instead the men make a distinction whereby the women salon stylists are sincerely interested in the clients' families and want to talk with the men "about life."

Unlike the men, the stylists perceive their relationships with their clients as simply part of the job. They confided that they are not always interested in their clients' lives or families. This demonstrates the way in which beauty work involves the physical labor of cutting and styling hair as well as emotional labor (Black 2004; Sharma and Black 2001). The stylists recognize the care work they perform, as well as the fact that it is not valued as such, claiming that their men clients come to them for a haircut because "it's cheaper than a psychiatrist." The men clients, however, do not see their relationships with their stylists as one-sided; nor do they understand their stylists as paid informal therapists. This is because emotional labor is often taken for granted and naturalized as part of women's essential character (Hochschild 1983; Tancred 1995). This is analogous to domestic employers who see their nannies and housekeepers as part of the family rather than as employees (Hondagneu-Sotelo 2001). Furthermore, the men believe their relationships with their stylists are genuine, not "marred" by economic exchange (Zelizer 2005). By personalizing these relationships, they make invisible the fact that they are paying for *body labor*: both the physical and emotional labor of women beauty workers (Kang 2003).

In the men's discussions of their relationships with their stylists, they not only appropriate women's body work, they also establish themselves as members of a particular class. The men position themselves as "classy" by comparing "salon talk" to barbershop talk and by describing the barbershop as a place for the expression of working-class masculinity in which men talk about ... sports and cars.... One man describes the difference between the salon and the barbershop as "night and day" and explains that, "You have garage talk [read as barbershop talk] and you have salon talk." By describing the conversation in the barbershop as "garage talk," the man genders the two spaces and suggests that traditionally "masculine" topics, which do not include feelings and family, are the only things discussed at the barbershop. Many of the men I spoke with contend that the gendered difference between the barbershop and the hair salon lies in conversation. "[T]he masculine view is that you're supposed to go to a barbershop and get a standard haircut from a man, talk about football, locker rooms, [and] sex," Mack reported. The men prefer the more personal and intimate conversations they have with their stylists to those that take place in the barbershop.

While the men at Shear Style have the option of getting their hair cut in a men's barbershop, they describe the barbershop as a place that does not provide them with *caring* relationships. The value the men place on women as sincere care workers is not surprising given the expectation that women perform emotional labor while providing services. However, by comparing the salon to the barbershop, the men indicate that the barbershop acts to uphold "traditional" notions of masculinity by informally discouraging the sharing of intimate information (Bird 1996). Consequently, they differentiate themselves from what they describe as the white working-class masculinity of barbershop men ... to successfully situate themselves as progressive, professional-class white men.

A Stylish and Classed Haircut

The men at Shear Style also set themselves apart as members of a particular class by describing salon hair care as important to the accomplishment of a "stylish" white professional-class embodiment. They conflate salon hair care with "stylish," customized, and contemporary haircuts. For example, Mack notes, "[If I] want something a little more stylish, I'll come to the salon because the salon develops more current styles [and] different techniques [that are] more relevant." The men understand the salon as a space in which they are able to purchase current trends in hair, and they attribute the ability to deliver this style to the women hairstylists whom they suggest have a "high taste level" and are highly skilled. The men trust their stylists and take comfort in knowing they will get a "good" haircut each and every time they come to the salon. "I know that I'm going to have a consistently good haircut every time I go [to the salon]," one man told me. This consistency gives the men "peace of mind," and alleviates the worry and the stress they feel when they have their hair cut elsewhere.

The men's desires for aesthetic enhancement are potentially threatening to their masculinity since, as men, their sense of self-worth is not supposed to be tied to how they look. To counteract this potential threat, the men claim they do not *want* to look stylish for themselves; rather they *need* to look good to succeed professionally. They construct their purchase of beauty work in the salon as a practice that helps them to compete in the workplace and to persuade their clients that they are professional, responsible, and will do the job well. Tom says,

> I mean, you know, I have clients. That means before they become clients, I have to win them over. Now who are they going to go with? The person who has . . . this great appearance package [pointing to himself] including grooming, style, professionalism, mannerism . . . Who are they going to go with, that person, or are they going to go with somebody who looks like they came in and dressed by accident or [that they are] indifferent about their hair?

Tom equates appearance with professionalism, explaining that he has to look a particular way, which includes "grooming [and] style," to be successful with his business clients. Hamilton also feels pressured because he works with "wealthy clients." "When you walk in a room and there are billionaires sitting there, you need to uphold the same appearance," he told me.

These men suggest that there are unwritten appearance rules in the workplace for men as well as women (Dellinger and Williams 1997) and that these rules require them to purchase beauty work in the hair salon. . . . [T]heir purchase of beauty services in the hair salon becomes about fulfilling what they interpret as expectations of white professional-class masculinity.

Few of these clients directly acknowledge the role class and occupation play in both their desire for and ability to purchase beauty work and "style" in the hair salon. Kerry, a 50-year-old white marketer, first describes the typical male client in the salon as "somebody who has more money than somebody who can only afford 10 dollars." . . .

The men also solidify their class status by again distancing themselves from the masculinity they associate with the "old school" barbershop. They reject the barbershop as a place where men purchase mass produced hairstyles by an out-of-date barber. For example, one man told me, "I think there is a difference; I think she [his stylist] cuts hair a little bit better [than a barber]." A good, stylish haircut is one that is current and modern, and is in contrast with the haircut the men feel they would receive from "old barber[s]." "The male barber is just bad," Hamilton exclaims, "80-year-old barbers who can't see just chop your hair." These men believe that white professional-class men do not need to get their hair cut at the barbershop since they can afford the "superior" and "customized" work of a salon stylist. Rather, they claim that working-class men purchase what they consider the inferior haircuts of the barbershop. As Evan says, "I can't see a mechanic working at, or a grease-monkey working at a Jiffy-Lube, or something like that, going to a shop that charges 65 bucks for a haircut." Evan differentiates the clients of the salon and barbershop in terms of class, and also sets the men salon clients up as superior by derogatorily referring to white working-class men as "grease-monkeys."

The men clients at Shear Style contrast the salon with the barbershop to justify their presence in a "women's" space. They refer to the barbershop as "old" and out of date, allowing them to position themselves in contrast as contemporary stylish men who rightfully seek the beauty work of women. Both the haircuts and the space of the barbershop are associated with an out-of-date style. For example, in justifying his preference for the salon, Mack again connects the barbershop with a passé aggressive and misogynist masculinity,

> [The barbershop's] got the owner's old boxing gloves up on the wall, black and white photos from being in the war, the naugahyde seats, [and] the pile of *Playboys* in the corner . . . I guess it just depends on how machismo I was feeling at the time, if I wanted to go "Grrr" [pretending to be "machismo" as he furrows his brow, grunts, and shakes his head from side to side] and go old school [to the barbershop] or you know, if I wanted to come here [to the salon].

Mack genders the barbershop and describes it is a place of the past with its "black and white photos from the war" and "old school" haircuts. He classes the barbershop by associating it with the cheap material of "naugahyde seats" and with a working-class masculinity that is involved in the physical aspect of war and the aggressive sport of boxing. Neil also classed the barbershop and its customers by describing it as having "no music, vinyl flooring, and *Auto Week* magazines." By contrasting themselves with the traditional "machismo" barbershop which they say does not deliver its supposed working-class customers with "style," the men at Shear Style construct themselves as a class of "new men": progressive, stylish, and professional.

DISCUSSION

. . . By situating salon hair care as necessary for the appropriation of a professional-class whiteness, the men "do difference" in a way that distinguishes them from the white working-class masculinity they associate with the barbershop. The concept of "doing difference" helps us to understand how the men at Shear Style are involved in "naturalizing" the social order along the lines of race and class, and how their purchase of beauty work is tied up with status maintenance. The men at Shear Style "naturalize" the social order by suggesting that working-class men are misogynist and do not value or prioritize style. The men at the salon contrast themselves with this supposed barbershop masculinity to reinforce their status as white middle-class men, and use the hair salon to mark themselves as progressive and stylish men.

In talking about the salon, the men create a binary that pits professional-class white men against working-class white men. They report that they *must* purchase the beauty work of salon hairstylists to appropriately embody and "do" a particular classed-whiteness. As a result, the men's participation in salon hair care does not compromise their masculinity; instead, their stylish hair becomes an outward sign of professional status which sets them apart from white working-class men. The men use "taste" and "priorities" to describe themselves as different from the "mechanic" and the "grease-monkey" who they claim are the typical clients of the barbershop. The men disdain the barbershop and the class status it represents. They describe the barbershop as "old school," traditionally and conservatively masculine, situating salon hair care as for the "new" progressive man. The men create a contemporary, white, professional-class masculinity by transferring traditional masculine characteristics onto, and thus othering, white working-class men (Hondagneu-Sotelo and Messner 1994).

. . . [T]he men at Shear Style—through the purchase and consumption of beauty work—appropriate embodied symbols of educational and cultural capital that distinguish them as raced, classed, sexualized, and gendered. While within a space defined as feminine, the men maintain a sense of masculinity by situating themselves as anomalies in a "women's" salon and by heterosexualizing their interactions with the women hairstylists. This research allows us to see how race and especially class privilege are reproduced by men through the consumption of beauty work, and how this privilege both allows men a "pass" to enter into a "women's" space while protecting them from the powerless aspects associated with the feminine culture of beauty.

References

Alexander, Bryant Keith. 2003. Fading, twisting, and weaving: An interpretive ethnography of the Black barbershop as cultural space. *Qualitative Inquiry* 9 (1): 105–28.

Battle-Walters, Kimberly. 2004. *Sheila's shop: Working-class African American women talk about life, love, race, and hair.* New York: Rowman and Littlefield Publishers, Inc.

Bird, Sharon R. 1996. Welcome to the men's club: Homosociality and the maintenance of hegemonic masculinity. *Gender & Society* 10 (2) 120–32.

Black, Paula. 2004. *The beauty industry: Gender, culture, pleasure.* New York: Routledge.

Bordo, Susan. 1993. *Unbearable weight: Feminism, western culture, and the body.* Berkeley: University of California Press.

———. 1999. *The male body: A new look at men in public and in private.* New York: Farrar, Straus and Giroux.

Brumberg, Joan Jacobs. 1997. *The body project: An intimate history of American girls.* New York: Random House.

Candelario, Ginetta. 2000. Hair race-ing: Dominican beauty culture and identity production. *Meridians: Feminism Race and Transnationalism* 1 (1): 128–56.

Clark, Laura Hurd, and Meridith Griffin. 2007. The body natural and the body unnatural: Beauty work and aging. *Journal of Aging Studies* 21:187–201.

Cogan, Jeanine C. 1999. Lesbians walk the tightrope of beauty. Thin is in but femme is out. *Journal of Lesbian Studies* 3 (4): 77–89.

Craig, Maxine Leeds. 2006. Race, beauty, and the tangled knot of guilty pleasure. *Feminist Theory* 7 (2): 159–77.

Craig, Maxine Leeds, and Rita Liberti. 2007. "'Cause that's what girls do": The making of a feminized gym. *Gender & Society* 21 (5): 676–99.

Dellinger, Kirsten, and Christine L. Williams. 1997. Makeup at work: Negotiating appearance rules in the workplace. *Gender & Society* 11 (2): 151–77.

Furman, Frida Kerner. 1997. *Facing the mirror: Older women and beauty shop culture.* New York: Routledge.

Gimlin, Debra. 1996. Pamela's place: Power and negotiation in the hair salon. *Gender & Society* 10 (5): 505–26.

Harvey, Adia M. 2005. Becoming entrepreneurs: Intersections of race, class, and gender at the Black beauty salon. *Gender & Society* 19 (6): 789–808.

Harvey-Wingfield, Adia. 2007. *Doing business with beauty: Black women, hair salons, and the racial enclave economy.* New York: Rowman and Littlefield Publishers, Inc.

Hochschild, Arlie Russell. 1983. *The managed heart: Commercialization of human feeling.* Berkeley: University of California Press.

Hondagneu-Sotelo, Pierrette. 2001. *Domestica: Immigrant workers cleaning and caring in the shadows of affluence.* Berkeley: University of California Press.

Hondagneu-Sotelo, Pierrette, and Michael A. Messner. 1994. Gender displays and men's power: The "new man" and the Mexican immigrant man. In *Theorizing masculinities*, edited by H. Brod and M. Kaufman. London: Sage Publications.

Jacobs-Huey, Lanita. 2006. *From the kitchen to the parlor: Language and becoming in African American women's hair care.* New York: Oxford University Press.

Kang, Miliann. 2003. The managed hand: The commercialization of bodies and emotions in Korean immigrant-owned nail salons. *Gender & Society* 17 (6): 820–39.

Kimmel, Michael S. 2001 [1994]. Masculinity as homophobia: Fear, shame, and the silence in the construction of gender identity. In *Gender: A sociological reader*, edited by S. Jackson and S. Scott. New York: Routledge.

Lawson, Helene M. 1999. Working on hair. *Qualitative Sociology* 22 (3): 235–57.

Luciano, Lynne. 2001. *Looking good: Male body image in modern America.* New York: Hill and Wang.

Paap, Kris. 2006. *Working construction: Why white working-class men put themselves, and the labor movement, in harm's way.* Ithaca, NY: Cornell University Press.

———. 2008. Power and embodiment: Comment on Anderson. *Gender & Society* 22 (1): 99–103.

Salzman, Marian, Ira Matathia, and Ann O'Reilly. 2005. *The future of men.* New York: Palgrave MacMillan.

Sharma, Ursula, and Paula Black. 2001. Look good, feel better: Beauty therapy as emotional labor. *Sociology* 35 (4): 913–31.

Tancred, Peta E. 1995. Women's work: A challenge to the sociology of work. *Gender, Work and Organization* 2 (1): 11–20.

Taub, Jennifer. 1999. Bisexual women and beauty norms: A qualitative examination. *Journal of Lesbian Studies* 3 (4): 27–36.

Weitz, Rose. 2004. *Rapunzel's daughters: What women's hair tells us about women's lives.* New York: Farrar, Straus and Giroux.

West, Candace, and Sarah Fenstermaker. 1995. Doing difference. *Gender & Society* 9 (1): 8–37.

Williams, Louis. 1993. The relationship between a Black barbershop and the community that supports it. *Human Mosaic* 27: 29–33.

Wright, Earl II. 1998. More than just a haircut: Sociability within the urban African American barbershop. *Challenge: A Journal of Research on African American Men* 9:1–13.

Zelizer, Viviana. 2005. *The purchase of intimacy.* Princeton, NJ: Princeton University Press.

Language, Gender, and Power

(2007)

SALLY RASKOFF

Have you ever noticed the gendered nature of the English language? If you take a close look, words highlight some important features of our culture.

Take the word "seminal" (as in "seminal work" or "seminal idea"). We use this word to credit people with creating work so important that it has changed the way we think about something. Seminal work inspires many others as well.

Seminal is durative of the word semen; as in human reproduction, seminal work has gone forth and multiplied much like sperm does if it is successful in merging with an egg (or ovum) and conception occurs.

Why don't we use "ovular" in the same way? Ova are the female equivalent to sperm and are just as responsible for the creation of a new being. Although there are many more sperm created in the time it takes for one ovum to move through its cycle, both are responsible for creating new life. We could say that someone has created an ovular idea that then inspires others to go forth and develop other ideas based on that one ovular thought.

Likewise, think of how we address people formally. We refer to most men as "Mr." Traditionally, women's courtesy titles have been "Miss" or "Mrs." Now women can be called "Ms."—thus women have three titles, "Miss" (single woman or girl), "Mrs." (married woman), or "Ms." (grown woman, marital status undetermined) while men have just the one (grown man, marital status irrelevant). Have you wondered why women have the three and men only the one? Why don't men have titles that indicate their marital status?

Now, let's consider curse words. Some are gender neutral, such as referring to one's posterior. Some are specifically reserved for women, such as the short b-word indicating a crabby female (as opposed to a female dog) and the c-word or the p-word, which are references to women's genitals. Even if the words are aimed at men or women, these terms often refer to women negatively.

Perhaps one's mother is the target of the insult, whether through having a child outside marriage, another b-word, or as a willing or unwilling intercourse participant, as in "mother" f-word as an active verb. Or, as the f-word itself does, the word invokes the act of intercourse and ties the act of penetration as a potentially violent action.

Of course, curse words aren't always intended as insults, since many people use them for fun or for teasing their friends. Some women use some of them as a term of empowerment (the c-word or the first b-word mentioned above).

But this applies only if they utter them, not if they are labeled with them by others (especially men). This is similar to the n-word and our current social debate over who (and if anyone) can use it; most recognize that when African Americans say it, it means something wholly different than when others, especially whites, say it.

The f-word in particular has many uses—both as a noun and a verb—but it does connect sex and violence, not just as a threat against women but also against gay men. Gay men have other words directed at them, many of which refer to them as feminine (or even female) or suggest violence.

Sociology helps explain these word choices. Rather than anomalies or coincidences, they reflect our society's power structure.

If you think about power and gender in this society, it quickly becomes clear that as a group, men dominate women. Men are the gender group with power in this society, not women. This is why important ideas that spawn other works (not to mention Nobel Prizes) are called seminal and not ovular. Traditionally, men have received credit, even if women were involved in their creation.

Why is marital status such a big deal for women and not for men? Not so long ago in this country, women were considered property; their title indicated who was responsible for this woman, father or husband. During the women's movement in the 1960–70s when many women no longer wished to be identified by their marital status, "Ms." was created as contraction of "Miss" and "Mrs."

Why do curse words refer to body parts and pejorative references to women? Because in a society characterized by male power, one doesn't insult a male directly; one must refer to inferior things, such as crude references to body parts considered "dirty" and to people who are less than masculine according to that society's norms.

In dominant American culture, masculinity is defined as being assertive, aggressive, strong, a leader, and heterosexual. This is what R. W. Connell refers to as "hegemonic masculinity" in the classic book *Gender and Power*.[1] Hegemonic masculinity insists that men be dominant over others in society to prove that they are "real men."

"Emphasized femininity," Connell's counterpart to hegemonic masculinity, encourages women to be passive, nurturing, caring, mothering, and otherwise subordinate. Yes, our definitions of masculine and feminine change over time and place, yet these ideals are primary in our media and in how we socialize children. Note also how gay men are equated with women and thus set aside from the more powerful group of heterosexual men.

Our language reflects our society—the words I have discussed here all distinguish between men and women—all to reinforce and maintain the gendered hierarchy of power.

---

1. Connell, R. W. (1987). *Gender and Power: Society, the Person, and Sexual Politics*. Stanford, CA: Stanford University Press. [*Editor's note*]

Backstage Out in Front: Impressions of Teen Pregnancy

(2007)

JANIS PRINCE INNISS

The mere mention of teenage pregnancy evokes strong emotions, including sorrow, dismay, disgust, and pity. There is an impression that pregnant teenage girls have "fallen from grace," as pregnancy is an oh-so-visible indication that they have been sexually active—an idea that makes many people shudder. The fact that the boys and men who partner in these pregnancies are (mostly) absolved of the scorn reserved for pregnant girls is an indication that the double standard about sex and sexuality remains.

We know that many teenagers are sexually active; data from the Youth Risk Behavior Surveillance (YRBS) indicate that almost half (47%) of all U.S. high school students admit to having had sexual intercourse. Some teens do not use birth control, as additional data from the YRBS indicate: Of the 33.9% who had been sexually active three months before the survey, more than a third of them (37.2%) had not used a condom and only a scant 17.6% (the respondent or their partner) had used birth control pills to prevent pregnancy before their last sexual encounter. Not surprisingly, a number of these teenage girls became pregnant.

In 2002, the U.S. teen pregnancy rate was 76.4 pregnancies per 1,000 females aged 15–19. The pie chart on page 200 represents the outcomes of these 757,000 pregnancies. Data from the Centers for Disease Control and Prevention (CDC) indicate that a little more than half of teens aged 15–19 who became pregnant gave birth to their babies. Although 16% of these teens suffered fetal losses, 28% aborted them.

The sociological concept of impression management is useful in thinking about teen pregnancy. Impression management might be defined as caring what others think; it is being aware of how we are seen by others and attempting to influence (consciously or not) how we are perceived and ultimately treated. According to sociologist Erving Goffman, who developed the concept of impression management, we have front and backstage lives. Front stage refers to those occasions when we are "onstage" in formal roles, in "public" creating or maintaining a particular impression of ourselves.

Backstage is, like the backstage of a theater, where we are our "private selves"; the place where people put on makeup and get dressed in preparation for being onstage. Backstage is where the real story—and not just what we want others to think, know, or feel about us—resides. So using this lens to consider pregnant teens, we recognize that unless it is common knowledge that a teenager has had

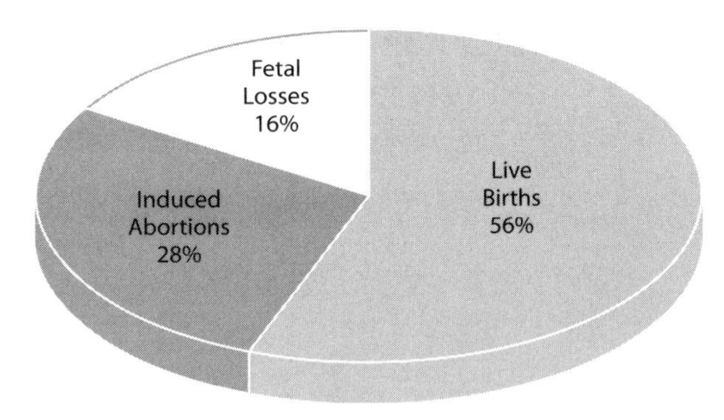

Source: www.cdc.gov/nchs/data/nvsr/nvsr49/nvsr49_04.pdf

FIGURE 1 Teen Pregnancy Outcomes, Ages 15–19

an abortion or that she was pregnant and gave up a baby for adoption, she may continue to be perceived as a "good girl," or at least maintain whatever public image she had before she became pregnant.

Notice the double standard again. When it comes to sex, girls and women are seen as *either* virtuous *or* promiscuous, but neither label is typically applied to males. This either or dichotomy acts as a constraint on female sexuality. Can you see how? Sexual activity and pregnancy may remain backstage for such girls and onlookers are likely to maintain whatever impressions they had of them, despite the girls' experiences with sex and pregnancy. On the other hand, a pregnant girl cannot hide her pregnancy backstage, because it is literally out in front! Consequently, impressions about her are bound to include this titillating knowledge.

I was very surprised to learn from CDC data that in the United States the highest teenage birth rates of the last 64 years were in the 1950s. As indicated in the line graph below, the 2000 U.S. birth rate of 48.7 is almost exactly *half* of the 1957 rate of 96.3!

What factors do you think contributed to this change in birth rate? Our impression that teen pregnancy is "new" may be related to the fact that the majority (70%) of teenagers who give birth today are unmarried. The opposite was true in the 1950s when teen pregnancies frequently *resulted* in marriage, and in general, people married and had children at earlier ages than they do today. Many of us have the impression that there was little or no premarital sex, teen pregnancies, or births out of wedlock in the "old days," but these data suggest that marriage helped to create that perception.

I know adults who became parents as teens, but this information is usually kept backstage. Typically, do you count the age difference between parents and their children, even when parents seem relatively young? I do not, and on a few occasions have been surprised to learn that someone—sometimes even a family member—I have known for a long time was a teen parent. With time, marriage,

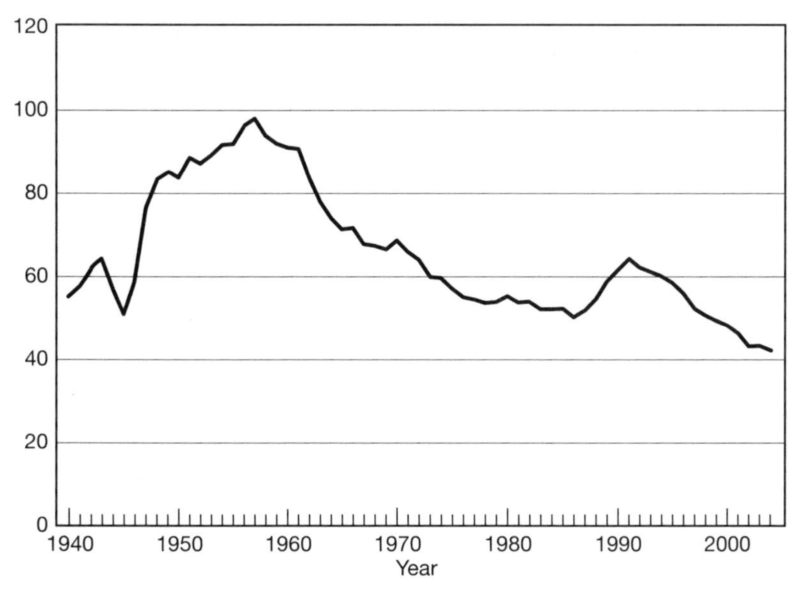

Source: www.cdc.gov/nchs/data/nvsr/nvsr49/nvsr49_10.pdf

FIGURE 2 Teenage Birth Rates, 1940–2004

and the tacit agreement of the community, many adults are able to have their teen pregnancies "move" backstage.

But many people, including teen parents, delay marriage much longer now than during the 1950s. Should they remain unmarried? How do you think today's teen parents will be perceived in ten or more years?

Related Links

Youth Risk Behavior Surveillance (YRBS): www.cdc.gov/mmwr/PDF/SS/SS5505.pdf

Centers for Disease Control and Prevention (CDC): www.cdc.gov/nchs/products/pubs/pubd/hestats/teenpreg1990-2002/teenpreg1990-2002.htm

www.cdc.gov/nchs/data/nvsr/nvsr49/nvsr49_10.pdf

www.cdc.gov/nchs/data/nvsr/nvsr55/nvsr55_01.pdf

Allen Guttmacher Institute: www.guttmacher.org/pubs/tgr/05/1/gr050107.html

Does Finger Size Reveal Sexual Orientation?

(2007)

SALLY RASKOFF

Do you think you can tell a person's sexual orientation just by looking at them? A 2007 *New York* magazine article by David France suggests that there are physical characteristics that indicate one's sexual orientation as straight, gay, or lesbian. Lately, research has focused on such markers as a person's finger length and fingerprint density, the direction that hair swirls on one's head, and left- or righthandedness.

According the researchers France cites, finger length, or more specifically the ratio of the second digit (index or pointer finger) to the fourth digit (ring finger), can indicate sexual orientation for both men and women, although in opposite patterns. Men with a smaller ratio (index fingers are shorter than their ring fingers) would indicate a heterosexual orientation while men with a larger ratio (index fingers longer than their ring fingers) would indicate a homosexual orientation. Alternatively, women with a larger ratio, those deemed heterosexual, would have longer index fingers and women with a smaller ratio (index finger shorter than ring finger) would be lesbian.

Did you stop reading here to look at your fingers or your hair? I did when I first heard the story on NPR's *Talk of the Nation.*

The article has received a lot of media attention (including from *The Colbert Report*), which seemed to assume that these patterns are real and reliable. Thus the public who hears about this research might assume that one can identify people's sexual orientation by their relative finger lengths and hair swirls.

As a sociologist, this news story has me wondering what the researchers actually said and, if indeed these are valid and reliable findings, how strong these supposed patterns are.

Looking up related peer-reviewed research on my campus library's webpage, I found many articles relating to these issues. Many of them do find statistically significant differences in these characteristics between those who identify as heterosexual, gay, or lesbian; but it took me a while to find the details on the strength of these patterns. But depending on the characteristic in question, the significance of these patterns is not overwhelming.

Let's start with handedness. A study published in 2003 by Richard Lippa found that homosexual men have an 82% greater chance than heterosexual men

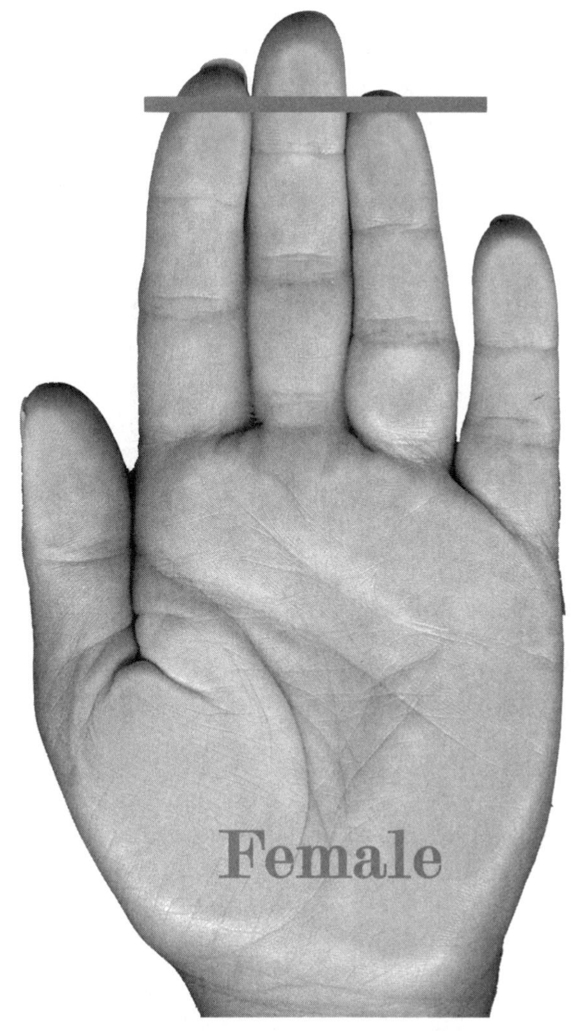

Female Hand: index finger longer than ring finger.

of being non-righthanded (lefthanded or ambidextrous).[1] This is a statistically significant difference based on his research finding that 11.4% of heterosexual men and 19% of homosexual men are non-righthanded. His findings for women were not significant.

Regarding the finger length issue, studies have found differences depending on gender, ethnicity, and which hand one is looking at. A comprehensive analysis of this research published in 2005 highlights that in the five studies they analyzed,

1. Richard Lippa. (2003). "Handedness, Sexual Orientation, and Gender-Related Personality Traits in Men and Women." *Archives of Sexual Behavior* 32, 103–114.

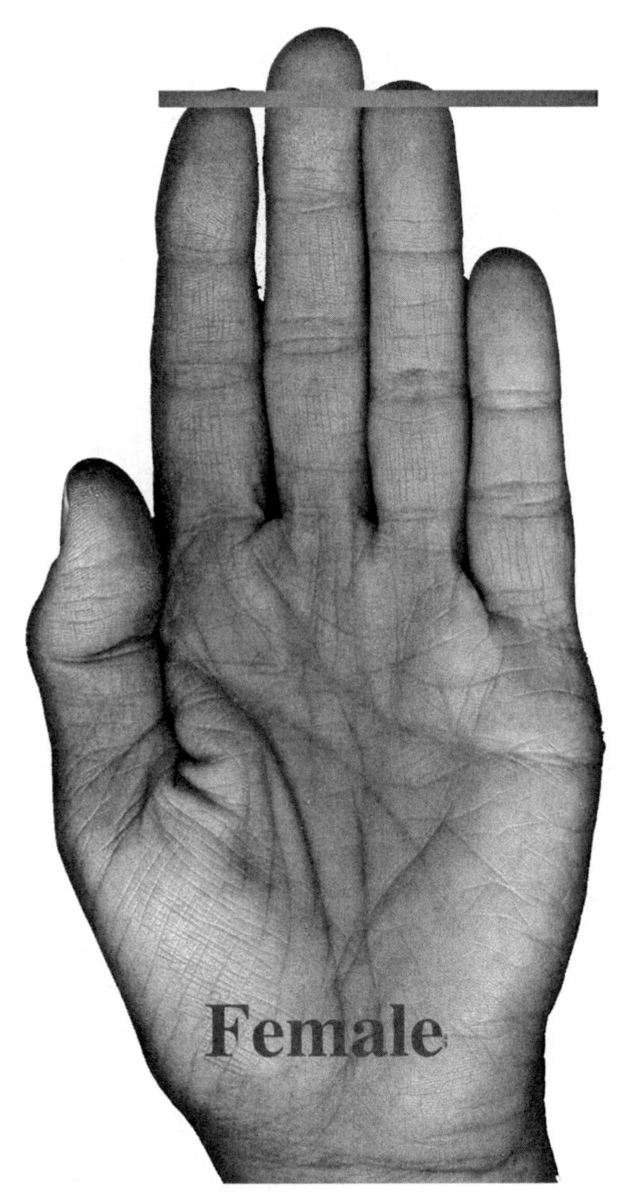

Female Hand: index and ring fingers same length.

there is more variation in the finger length ratio among heterosexual people than there is among homosexual people.[2]

Many of these studies are done to assess whether genetics or in-utero conditions have a greater effect on human development. Another study of finger length

2. Dennis McFadden, et al. (2005). "A Reanalysis of Five Studies on Sexual Orientation and the Relative Length of the Second and Fourth Fingers (the 20:40 Ratio)." *Archives of Sexual Behavior* 34, 341–56.

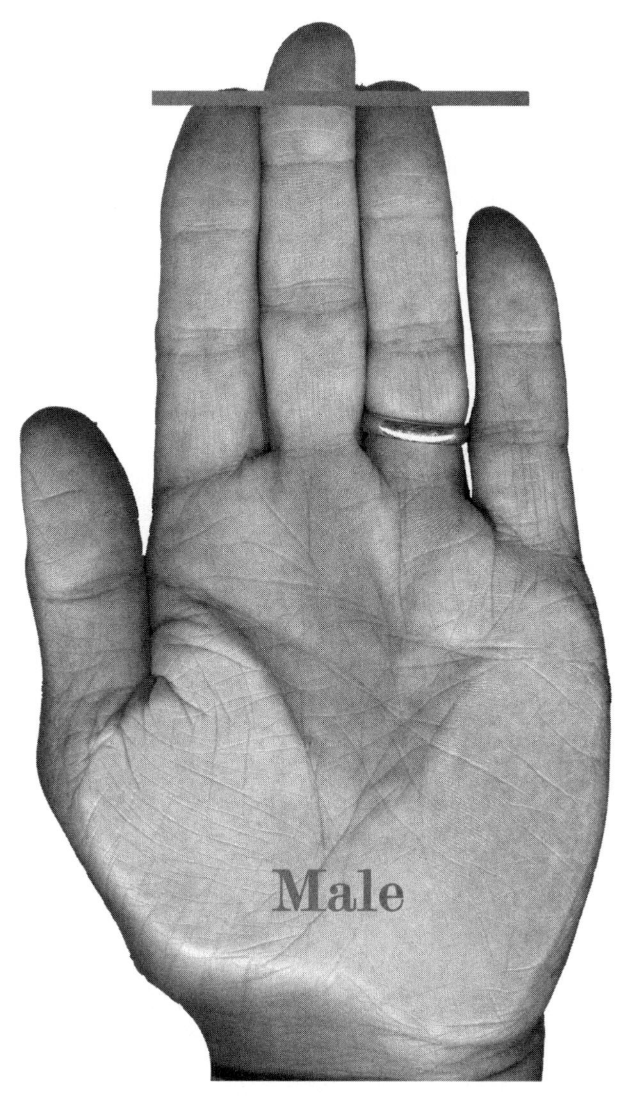

Male Hand: index finger longer than ring finger.

used a sample of identical twins (who of course have identical genes) to assess the role of genetics versus the "prenatal environment." The researchers tested seven twin pairs who were "discordant" for sexual orientation (one twin was heterosexual and the other homosexual in orientation), and five twin pairs who have "concordant" (the same) sexual orientation. Their findings did indicate a statistically significant difference in ratios for both the left and right hands, with the heterosexual twins having greater ratios between their second and fourth fingers than their homosexual twins.

If you look closely at the twin data, however, you'll see that the differences in ratios are not overwhelming. In the analysis of data from five previous studies, the ratios for each gender group were also not overwhelmingly different across sexual orientation groups.

All in all, my journey into the actual research did show that there are some interesting physical differences across groups. However, those patterns can easily be misinterpreted and applied in inappropriate ways. Just because the researchers found statistically significant differences does not mean that having a particular finger ratio indicates homosexuality. For example, in the handedness study, while gay men may have a higher chance of being non-righthanded compared to straight men, it does not follow that lefthanded men are gay—keep in mind that less than 20% of men in *either* group are non-righthanded!

Studies on finger length ratios and the other characteristics alleged to be associated with sexual orientation are vulnerable to the same kind of interpretation error. If you look at your index and ring fingers and assess which is longer, does this indicate your sexual orientation? Some people might question their sexual orientation once they hear of this research and identify their own finger ratio. However, this is a misuse of this research and a misinterpretation of the data. While many straight men and lesbian women may have shorter index fingers relative to ring fingers, there will be plenty of straight men and lesbian women who have comparatively longer index fingers. Likewise, there are many gay men and straight women with same length or longer index fingers, there are also gay men and straight women with shorter index fingers.

When I see news items that mention relationships like these, I know that it's a good idea to see what the researchers actually said and if the public hears the same story. The media's job of translating the scientific world for the public is a difficult task and is sometimes impossible considering the lack of scientific expertise of most reporters, restrictions on time, the need to avoid scientific language, and the wish to have the simplest explanation of very complex phenomena. Since the media are often more concerned with generating the most sensational headline than it is with relaying information accurately, it is imperative that we educate ourselves to assess research studies ourselves and to identify the most accurate information in them.

Having established that there are statistically significant patterns in finger length, does this mean that homosexuality creates different finger lengths? Or that finger length ratios create homosexuality? Remember, these studies cannot support a strong causal relationship between these characteristics and homosexual orientation because of the high levels of variation within groups. This brings to mind an important phrase you may have heard in sociology or other classes: correlation is not causation.

Related Links

New York magazine article: nymag.com/news/features/33520/

David France's article with pictures: www.davidfrance.com/gayness.pdf

National Public Radio story:
www.npr.org/templates/story/story.php?storyId=11422189

TALK ABOUT IT

1. Discuss some ways you have observed people "doing gender."
2. Have you ever observed men in traditionally female settings or women in traditionally male settings? How did they navigate in "foreign" territory?
3. How do fears about being perceived as being gay encourage people to adhere to gender norms?
4. Women are frequently called "girls" in everyday conversations. Why does this happens more often than referring to men as "boys"?
5. Discuss examples of how girls and women who are sexually active are more readily stigmatized than men. How does our use of language further exemplify this tendency?

WRITE ABOUT IT

1. Following Raskoff's "Language, Gender, and Power," identify five words that are rooted in gender. How do these words reflect gender and power? How do they enable us to "do gender" as West and Zimmerman describe?
2. Barber's study examines how men clarify their sense of masculinity when approaching a "boundary" of femininity. Can you think of other gender boundaries? Under what circumstances do men and women confront what might seem cross-gendered behavior?
3. How does homophobia shape our perception of gender? How might Barber's respondents have been influenced by homophobia, even if none of them held any prejudice toward gay individuals?
4. What were your perceptions of teen pregnancy before reading Prince Inniss's essay? Were you surprised by the downward trend in teen pregnancy? Why do many people believe that teens are more likely to get pregnant now than in the 1950s, even though the reverse is true?
5. Discuss the double standard that exists between males and females who are sexually active. Tie your ideas to any two readings from this section.

DO IT

1. Observe friends, family, or other people in a public place such as a mall or a park. Notice how they "do gender" in their everyday behavior.
2. Interview five people on their perception and use of gendered language. Choose a few specific words and ask them to describe what the words mean to them. Do any of your respondents note the gendered nature of these words?

3. Choose a television show that contains openly gay or lesbian characters. Do the characters behave in a stereotypical way or challenge gender boundaries? Why are these characters portrayed as they are? How do their representations shape perceptions about gays and lesbians?
4. Find one journal article containing details of a study that Raskoff describes in her essay on sexual orientation. What method does it use? What findings does it claim? Are the findings are plausible given the data they present? Why or why not?
5. Compare statistics on teen pregnancy with discussions of teen pregnancy in news articles. Does the word choice, focus, and imagery in the articles contradict or support the actual long-term trends? Describe your impression of the coverage of teen pregnancy.

8

Race and Ethnicity

Module Goal: ***Understand the meanings of race and ethnicity, and the power these distinctions still carry.***

It might be tempting to think of race simply as the color of one's skin, but race in America has a much more complex set of meanings. Historically, the definition has shifted and changed, and although segregation is no longer legal, the effects of our past caste system still linger.

"Racial Formation" by Michael Omi and Howard Winant explores how definitions of race have shifted throughout America's history. As you will see, race is not something we are born with, but is instead collectively constructed and rooted in the structural organization of society. This is true today, more than four decades after the passage of civil rights legislation.

Definitions of race become murky for people with multiracial heritage. Many standardized forms now allow people to identify themselves as multiracial, but in the past individuals were expected to choose a singular racial identity. In "Black and White or Rainbow Colors," Janis Prince Inniss discusses how the golfer Tiger Woods, who is of multiracial heritage, is still regarded by many simply as African American.

Because race relations can be controversial, many people would prefer not to discuss these issues at all and leave our troubled past behind us. The comedian Stephen Colbert jokes that he doesn't see race; would it be better for society if none of us did either? C. N. Le discusses the perils of ignoring the issue of race in "Racial Tensions and Living in a Color-blind Society." What might be the result of becoming "color-blind"?

Race is closely linked to the concept of ethnicity, the cultural connection that groups share through language, customs, cuisine, and often religion. Historically, ethnic groups have also been defined as races; in the nineteenth century, the Irish were considered a separate race from the British, and Jews, Italians, and Slavs were all considered distinct races. Today members of these groups are typically defined as white, with their ethnicity a secondary and often optional identifier.

In "The Cost of a Costless Community," Mary C. Waters explores how and why people claim an ethnic label, as well as the ramifications of doing so in contrast to an identity based on race. Do you identify strongly with a particular ethnic group? If so, are there any social costs to doing so? How does this identity shape your everyday life?

Sometimes we choose a temporary ethnicity that has nothing to do with our family's heritage. Do you know anyone who "becomes Irish" for one day in March? Janis Prince Inniss discusses the meaning of cultural traditions such as St. Patrick's Day in "Celebrating St. Patrick's Day." Are there any ethnic celebrations you regularly enjoy? If so, how do they shape your sense of identity?

As you read about race and ethnicity in everyday life, consider the following questions:

1. How is race defined? How and why has this definition shifted over time?
2. What are the social and political costs of becoming "color-blind"?
3. What are the social and political costs of ethnic identity? How do these costs compare with those associated with racial identity?

Racial Formation

(1994)

MICHAEL OMI AND HOWARD WINANT

In 1982–83, Susie Guillory Phipps unsuccessfully sued the Louisiana Bureau of Vital Records to change her racial classification from black to white. The descendant of an 18th-century white planter and a black slave, Phipps was designated "black" in her birth certificate in accordance with a 1970 state law which declared anyone with at least 1/32nd "Negro blood" to be black.

The Phipps case raised intriguing questions about the concept of race, its meaning in contemporary society, and its use (and abuse) in public policy. Assistant Attorney General Ron Davis defended the law by pointing out that some type of racial classification was necessary to comply with federal record-keeping requirements and to facilitate programs for the prevention of genetic diseases. Phipps's attorney, Brian Begue, argued that the assignment of racial categories on birth certificates was unconstitutional and that the 1/32nd designation was inaccurate. He called on a retired Tulane University professor who cited research indicating that most Louisiana whites have at least 1/20th "Negro" ancestry.

In the end, Phipps lost. The court upheld the state's right to classify and quantify racial identity.[1]

Phipps's problematic racial identity, and her effort to resolve it through state action, is in many ways a parable of America's unsolved racial dilemma. It illustrates the difficulties of defining race and assigning individuals or groups to racial categories. It shows how the racial legacies of the past—slavery and bigotry—continue to shape the present. It reveals both the deep involvement of the state in the organization and interpretation of race, and the inadequacy of state institutions to carry out these functions. It demonstrates how deeply Americans both as individuals and as a civilization are shaped, and indeed haunted, by race.

Having lived her whole life thinking that she was white, Phipps suddenly discovers that by legal definition she is not. In U.S. society, such an event is indeed catastrophic.[2] But if she is not white, of what race is she? The *state* claims that she is black, based on its rules of classification,[3] and another state agency, the court, upholds this judgment. But despite these classificatory standards which have imposed an either-or logic on racial identity, Phipps will not in fact "change color." Unlike what would have happened during slavery times if one's claim to whiteness was successfully challenged, we can assume that despite the outcome of her legal challenge, Phipps will remain in most of the social relationships she had occupied before the trial. Her socialization, her familial and friendship networks, her cultural orientation, will not change. . . .

A crucial dimension of the Phipps case is that it illustrates the inadequacy of claims that race is a mere matter of variations in human physiognomy, that it is simply a matter of skin color. But if race cannot be understood in this manner, how *can* it be understood? . . . Our goal in this chapter [is] to offer the outlines of a theory of race and racism.

WHAT IS RACE?

There is a continuous temptation to think of race as an *essence*, as something fixed, concrete, and objective. And there is also an opposite temptation: to imagine race as a mere *illusion*, a purely ideological construct which some ideal non-racist social order would eliminate. It is necessary to challenge both these positions, to disrupt and reframe the rigid and bipolar manner in which they are posed and debated, and to transcend the presumably irreconcilable relationship between them.

. . . [L]et us propose a definition: *race is a concept which signifies and symbolizes social conflicts and interests by referring to different types of human bodies*. Although the concept of race invokes biologically based human characteristics (so-called "phenotypes"), selection of these particular human features for purposes of racial signification is always and necessarily a social and historical process. In contrast to the other major distinction of this type, that of gender, there is no biological basis for distinguishing among human groups along the lines of race.[4] Indeed, the categories employed to differentiate among human groups along racial lines reveal themselves, upon serious examination, to be at best imprecise, and at worst completely arbitrary.

If the concept of race is so nebulous, can we not dispense with it? Can we not "do without" race, at least in the "enlightened" present? This question has been posed often, and with greater frequency in recent years.[5] An affirmative answer would of course present obvious practical difficulties: it is rather difficult to jettison widely held beliefs, beliefs which moreover are central to everyone's identity and understanding of the social world. So the attempt to banish the concept as an archaism is at best counterintuitive. But a deeper difficulty, we believe, is inherent in the very formulation of this schema, in its way of posing race as a *problem*, a misconception left over from the past, and suitable now only for the dustbin of history.

A more effective starting point is the recognition that despite its uncertainties and contradictions, the concept of race continues to play a fundamental role in structuring and representing the social world. The task for theory is to explain this situation. It is to avoid both the utopian framework which sees race as an illusion we can somehow "get beyond," and also the essentialist formulation which sees race as something objective and fixed, a biological datum.[6] Thus we should think of race as an element of social structure rather than as an irregularity within it; we should see race as a dimension of human representation rather than an illusion. These perspectives inform the theoretical approach we call racial formation.

RACIAL FORMATION

We define *racial formation* as the sociohistorical process by which racial categories are created, inhabited, transformed, and destroyed. . . .

From a racial formation perspective, race is a matter of both social structure and cultural representation. Too often, the attempt is made to understand race simply or primarily in terms of only one of these two analytical dimensions.[7] For example, efforts to explain racial inequality as a purely social structural phenomenon are unable to account for the origins, patterning, and transformation of racial difference.

Conversely, many examinations of racial difference—understood as a matter of cultural attributes *à la* ethnicity theory, or as a society-wide signification system, cannot comprehend such structural phenomena as racial stratification in the labor market or patterns of residential segregation.

An alternative approach is to think of racial formation processes as occurring through a linkage between structure and representation. Racial *projects* do the ideological "work" of making these links. *A racial project is simultaneously an interpretation, representation, or explanation of racial dynamics, and an effort to reorganize and redistribute resources along particular racial lines.* Racial projects connect what race *means* . . . and the ways in which both social structures and everyday experiences are racially *organized*, based upon that meaning. Let us consider this proposition, first in terms of large-scale or macro-level social processes, and then in terms of other dimensions of the racial formation process.

Racial Formation as a Macro-Level Social Process

To *interpret the meaning of race is to frame it social structurally.* Consider for example, this statement by Charles Murray on welfare reform:

> My proposal for dealing with the racial issue in social welfare is to repeal every bit of legislation and reverse every court decision that in any way requires, recommends, or awards differential treatment according to race, and thereby put us back onto the track that we left in 1965. We may argue about the appropriate limits of government intervention in trying to enforce the ideal, but at least it should be possible to identify the ideal: Race is not a morally admissible reason for treating one person differently from another. Period.[8]

Here there is a partial but significant analysis of the meaning of race: it is not a morally valid basis upon which to treat people "differently from one another."

We may notice someone's race, but we cannot act upon that awareness. We must act in a "color-blind" fashion. This analysis of the meaning of race is immediately linked to a specific conception of the role of race in the social structure: it can play no part in government action, save in "the enforcement of the ideal." No state policy can legitimately require, recommend, or award different status according to race. This example can be classified as a particular type of racial project in the present day U.S.—a "neoconservative" one.

Conversely, *to recognize the racial dimension in social structure is to interpret the meaning of race*. Consider the following statement by the late Supreme Court Justice Thurgood Marshall on minority "set-aside" programs:

> A profound difference separates governmental actions that themselves are racist, and governmental actions that seek to remedy the effects of prior racism or to prevent neutral government activity from perpetuating the effects of such racism.[9]

Here the focus is on the racial dimensions of *social structure*—in this case of state activity and policy. The argument is that state actions in the past and present have treated people in very different ways according to their race, and thus the government cannot retreat from its policy responsibilities in this area. It cannot suddenly declare itself "color-blind" without in fact perpetuating the same type of differential, racist treatment.[10] Thus, race continues to signify difference and structure inequality. Here, racialized social structure is immediately linked to an interpretation of the meaning of race. This example too can be classified as a particular type of racial project in the present-day U.S.—a "liberal" one.

To be sure, such political labels as "neoconservative" or "liberal" cannot fully capture the complexity of racial projects, for these are always multiply determined, politically contested, and deeply shaped by their historical context. Thus, encapsulated within the neoconservative example cited here are certain egalitarian commitments which derive from a previous historical context in which they played a very different role, and which are rearticulated in neoconservative racial discourse precisely to oppose a more open-ended, more capacious conception of the meaning of equality. Similarly, in the liberal example, Justice Marshall recognizes that the contemporary state, which was formerly the architect of segregation and the chief enforcer of racial difference, has a tendency to reproduce those patterns of inequality in a new guise. Thus he admonishes it (in dissent, significantly) to fulfill its responsibilities to uphold a robust conception of equality. . . .

◇ ◇ ◇

Racial Formation as Everyday Experience

One of the first things we notice about people when we meet them (along with their sex) is their race. We utilize race to provide clues about *who* a person is. This fact is made painfully obvious when we encounter someone whom we cannot conveniently racially categorize—someone who is, for example, racially "mixed" or of an ethnic/racial group we are not familiar with. Such an encounter becomes a source of discomfort and momentarily a crisis of racial meaning.

Our ability to interpret racial meanings depends on preconceived notions of a racialized social structure. Comments such as, "Funny, you don't look black," betray an underlying image of what black should be. We expect people to act out their apparent racial identities; indeed we become disoriented when they do not. The black banker harassed by police while walking in casual clothes through his own well-off neighborhood, the Latino or white kid rapping in perfect Afro patois, the unending *faux pas* committed by whites who assume that the non-whites they encounter are servants or tradespeople, the belief that non-white colleagues are less qualified persons hired to fulfill affirmative action guidelines, indeed the whole gamut of racial stereotypes—that "white men can't jump," that Asians can't dance, etc., etc.—all testify to the way a racialized social structure shapes racial experience and conditions meaning. Analysis of such stereotypes reveals the always present, already active link between our view of the social structure—its demography, its laws, its customs, its threats—and our conception of what race means.

... Everybody learns some combination, some version, of the rules of racial classification, and of her own racial identity, often without obvious teaching or conscious inculcation. Thus are we inserted in a comprehensively racialized social structure. Race becomes "common sense"—a way of comprehending, explaining, and acting in the world. . . .

Under such circumstances, it is not possible to represent race discursively without simultaneously locating it, explicitly or implicitly, in a social structural (and historical) context. Nor is it possible to organize, maintain, or transform social structures without simultaneously engaging, once more either explicitly or implicitly, in racial signification. Racial formation, therefore, is a kind of synthesis, an outcome, of the interaction of racial projects on a society-wide level. . . .

Since racial formation is always historically situated, our understanding of the significance of race, and of the way race structures society, has changed enormously over time. The processes of racial formation we encounter today, the racial projects large and small which structure U.S. society in so many ways, are merely the present-day outcomes of a complex historical evolution. The contemporary racial order remains transient. By knowing something of how it evolved, we can perhaps better discern where it is heading. We therefore turn next to a historical survey of the racial formation process, and the conflicts and debates it has engendered.

FROM SCIENCE TO POLITICS

It has taken scholars more than a century to reject biologistic notions of race in favor of an approach which regards race as a *social* concept. This trend has been slow and uneven, and even today remains somewhat embattled, but its overall direction seems clear. At the turn of the century Max Weber discounted biological explanations for racial conflict and instead highlighted the social and political factors which engendered such conflict.[11] W. E. B. Du Bois argued for a sociopolitical definition of race by identifying "the color line" as "the problem of the 20th century."[12] Pioneering cultural anthropologist Franz Boas rejected attempts to link racial identifications and cultural traits, labelling as pseudoscientific any assumption of a continuum of "higher" and "lower" cultural groups.[13] Other early exponents of social, as opposed to biological, views of race included Robert E. Park, founder of the "Chicago school" of sociology, and Alain Leroy Locke, philosopher and theorist of the Harlem Renaissance.[14]

Perhaps more important than these and subsequent intellectual efforts, however, were the political struggles of racially defined groups themselves. Waged all around the globe under a variety of banners such as anticolonialism and civil rights, these battles to challenge various structural and cultural racisms have been a major feature of 20th-century politics. The racial horrors of the 20th century—colonial slaughter and apartheid, the genocide of the Holocaust, and the massive bloodlettings required to end these evils—have also indelibly marked the theme of race as a political issue *par excellence*.

As a result of prior efforts and struggles, we have now reached the point of fairly general agreement that race is not a biologically given but rather a socially constructed way of differentiating human beings. While a tremendous achievement, the transcendence of biologistic conceptions of race does not provide any reprieve from the dilemmas of racial injustice and conflict, nor from controversies over the significance of race in the present. Views of race as socially constructed simply recognize the fact that these conflicts and controversies are now more properly framed on the terrain of politics. By privileging politics in the analysis which follows we do not mean to suggest that race has been displaced as a concern of scientific inquiry, or that struggles over cultural representation are no longer important. We do argue, however, that race is now a preeminently political phenomenon. Such an assertion invites examination of the evolving role of racial politics in the U.S. This is the subject to which we now turn.

[DICTATORSHIP AND DEMOCRACY]

For most of its existence both as European colony and as an independent nation, the U.S. was a *racial dictatorship.* From 1607 to 1865—258 years—most non-whites were firmly eliminated from the sphere of politics . . . After the Civil War there was the brief egalitarian experiment of Reconstruction which terminated ignominiously in 1877. In its wake followed almost a century of legally sanctioned segregation and denial of the vote, nearly absolute in the South and much of the Southwest, less effective in the North and far West, but formidable in any case.[15] These barriers fell only in the mid-1960s, a mere quarter-century ago. Nor did the successes of the black movement and its allies mean that all obstacles to their political participation had now been abolished. Patterns of racial inequality have proven, unfortunately, to be quite stubborn and persistent.

It is important, therefore, to recognize that in many respects, racial dictatorship is the norm against which all U.S. politics must be measured. The centuries of racial dictatorship have had three very large consequences: first, they defined "American" identity as white, as the negation of racialized "otherness"—at first largely African and indigenous, later Latin American and Asian as well.[16] This negation took shape in both law and custom, in public institutions and in forms of cultural representation. It became the archetype of hegemonic rule in the U.S. It was the successor to the conquest as the "master" racial project.

Second, racial dictatorship organized . . . the "color line" rendering it the fundamental division in U.S. society. The dictatorship elaborated, articulated, and drove racial divisions not only through institutions, but also through psyches, extending up to our own time the racial obsessions of the conquest and slavery periods.

The transition from a racial dictatorship to a racial democracy has been a slow, painful, and contentious one; it remains far from complete. A recognition of the abiding presence of racial dictatorship, we contend, is crucial for the development of a theory of racial formation in the U.S. . . .

Racial rule can be understood as a slow and uneven historical process which has moved from dictatorship to democracy, from domination to hegemony. In this transition, hegemonic forms of racial rule—those based on consent—eventually came to supplant those based on coercion. Of course, before this assertion can be accepted, it must be qualified in important ways. By no means has the U.S. established racial democracy at the end of the century, and by no means is coercion a thing of the past. . . .

WHAT IS RACISM?

Since the ambiguous triumph of the civil rights movement in the mid-1960s, clarity about what racism means has been eroding. The concept entered the lexicon of "common sense" only in the 1960s. Before that, although the term had surfaced occasionally,[17] the problem of racial injustice and inequality was generally understood in a more limited fashion, as a matter of prejudiced attitudes or bigotry on the one hand,[18] and discriminatory practices on the other.[19] Solutions, it was believed, would therefore involve the overcoming of such attitudes, the achievement of tolerance, the acceptance of "brotherhood," etc., and the passage of laws which prohibited discrimination with respect to access to public accommodations, jobs, education, etc. The early civil rights movement explicitly reflected such views. . . .

The later 1960s, however, signalled a sharp break with this vision. The emergence of the slogan "black power" (and soon after, of "brown power," "red power," and "yellow power"), the wave of riots that swept the urban ghettos from 1964 to 1968, and the founding of radical movement organizations of nationalist and Marxist orientation, coincided with the recognition that racial inequality and injustice had much deeper roots. They were not simply the product of prejudice, nor was discrimination only a matter of intentionally informed action. Rather, prejudice was an almost unavoidable outcome of patterns of socialization which were "bred in the bone," affecting not only whites but even minorities themselves.[20] Discrimination, far from manifesting itself only (or even principally) through individual actions or conscious policies, was a structural feature of U.S. society, the product of centuries of systematic exclusion, exploitation, and disregard of racially defined minorities.[21] It was this combination of relationships—prejudice, discrimination, and institutional inequality—which defined the concept of racism at the end of the 1960s.

. . . If the "institutional" component of racism were so pervasive and deeply rooted, it became difficult to see how the democratization of U.S. society could be achieved, and difficult to explain what progress had been made. The result was a levelling critique which denied any distinction between the Jim Crow era . . . and the present. . . . The result of the "inflation" of the concept of racism was thus a deep pessimism about any efforts to overcome racial barriers, in the workplace, the community, or any other sphere of lived experience. An overly comprehensive view of racism, then, potentially served as a self-fulfilling prophecy.

The distinct, and contested, meanings of racism which have been advanced over the past three decades have contributed to an overall crisis of meaning for the concept today. Today, the absence of a clear "common sense" understanding of what racism means has become a significant obstacle to efforts aimed at challenging it. . . . Whites tend to locate racism in color consciousness and find its absence color-blindness. In so doing, they see the affirmation of difference and racial identity among racially defined minority students as racist. Non-white students, by contrast, see racism as a system of power, and correspondingly argue that blacks, for example, cannot be racist because they lack power. . . .

Given this crisis of meaning, and in the absence of any "common sense" understanding, does the concept of racism retain any validity? If so, what view of racism should we adopt? . . .

We employ racial formation theory to reformulate the concept of racism. Our approach recognizes that racism, like race, has changed over time. It is obvious that the attitudes, practices, and institutions of the epochs of slavery, say, or of Jim Crow, no longer exist today. Employing a similar logic, it is reasonable to question whether concepts of racism which developed in the early days of the post–civil rights era, when the limitations of both moderate reform and militant racial radicalism of various types had not yet been encountered, remain adequate to explain circumstances and conflicts a quarter-century later.

Racial formation theory allows us to differentiate between race and racism. The two concepts should not be used interchangeably. We have argued that race has no fixed meaning, but is constructed and transformed sociohistorically . . . through the necessary and ineluctable link between the structural and cultural dimensions of race in the U.S. . . .

A racial project can be defined as *racist* if and only if it *creates or reproduces structures of domination based on essentialist categories of race.* Such a definition recognizes the importance of locating racism within a fluid and contested history of racially based social structures and discourses. Thus there can be no timeless and absolute standard for what constitutes racism, for social structures change and discourses are subject to rearticulation. Our definition therefore focuses instead on the "work" essentialism does for domination, and the "need" domination displays to essentialize the subordinated.

Further, it is important to distinguish racial awareness from racial essentialism. To attribute merits, allocate values or resources to, and/or represent individuals or groups on the basis of racial identity should not be considered racist in and of itself. Such projects may in fact be quite benign.

Consider the following examples: first, the statement, "Many Asian Americans are highly entrepreneurial"; second, the organization of an association of, say, black accountants.

The first racial project, in our view, signifies or represents a racial category ("Asian Americans") and locates that representation within the social structure of the contemporary U.S. (in regard to business, class issues, socialization, etc.). The second racial project is organizational or social structural, and therefore must engage in racial signification. Black accountants, the organizers might maintain, have certain common experiences, can offer each other certain support, etc. Neither of these racial projects is essentialist, and neither can fairly be labelled racist. Of course, racial representations may be biased or misinterpret their subjects, just as racially based organizational efforts may be unfair or unjustifiably exclusive. If such were the case, if for instance in our first example the statement in question were "Asian Americans are naturally entrepreneurial," this would by our criterion be racist. Similarly, if the effort to organize black accountants had as its rationale the raiding of clients from white accountants, it would by our criterion be racist as well.

Without question, any abstract concept of racism is severely put to the test by the untidy world of reality. To illustrate our discussion, we analyze the following examples, chosen from current racial issues because of their complexity and the rancorous debates they have engendered:

- Is the allocation of employment opportunities through programs restricted to racially defined minorities, so-called "preferential treatment" or affirmative action policies, racist? Do such policies practice "racism in reverse"? We think not, with certain qualifications. Although such programs necessarily employ racial criteria in assessing eligibility, they do not generally essentialize race, because they seek to overcome specific socially and historically constructed inequalities.[22] Criteria of effectiveness and feasibility, therefore, must be considered in evaluating such programs. They must balance egalitarian and context-specific objectives, such as academic potential or job-related qualifications. . . .
- Is all racism the same, or is there a distinction between white and non-white versions of racism? We have little patience with the argument that racism is solely a white problem, or even a "white disease."[23] The idea that non-whites cannot act in a racist manner, since they do not possess "power," is another variant of this formulation.

  For many years now, racism has operated in a more complex fashion than this, sometimes taking such forms as self-hatred or self-aggrandizement at the expense of more vulnerable members of racially subordinate groups.[24] Whites can at times be the victims of racism—by other whites or non-whites—as is the case with anti-Jewish and anti-Arab prejudice. Furthermore, unless one is prepared to argue that there has been no transformation of the U.S. racial order over the years, and that racism consequently has remained unchanged . . . it is difficult to contend that racially defined minorities have attained no power or influence, especially in recent years.

  Having said this, we still do not consider that all racism is the same. This is because of the crucial importance we place in situating various "racisms" within the dominant hegemonic discourse about race. [B]lack supremacy may be an instance of racism, just as its advocacy may be offensive, but it can hardly constitute the threat that white supremacy has represented in the U.S. . . . All racisms, all racist political projects, are not the same.

- Is the redrawing—or gerrymandering—of adjacent electoral districts to incorporate large numbers of racially defined minority voters in one, and largely white voters in the other, racist? Do such policies amount to "segregation" of the electorate? Certainly this alternative is preferable to the pre-Voting Rights Act practice of simply denying racial minorities the franchise. But does it achieve the Act's purpose of fostering electoral equality across and within racial lines? In our view such practices, in which the post-1990 redistricting process engaged rather widely—are vulnerable to charges of essentialism. They often operate through "racial lumping," tend to freeze rather than overcome racial inequalities, and frequently subvert or defuse political processes through which racially defined groups could otherwise negotiate their differences and interests. . . .

In summary, the racism of today is no longer a virtual monolith, as was the racism of yore. Today, racial hegemony is "messy." The complexity of the present situation is the product of a vast historical legacy of structural inequality and invidious racial representation, which has been confronted during the post-World War II period with an opposition more serious and effective than any it had faced before. . . .

Notes

1. *San Francisco Chronicle*, 14 September 1982, 19 May 1983. Ironically, the 1970 Louisiana law was enacted to supersede an old Jim Crow statute which relied on the idea of "common report" in determining an infant's race. Following Phipps's unsuccessful attempt to change her classification and have the law declared unconstitutional, a legislative effort arose which culminated in the repeal of the law. See *San Francisco Chronicle*, 23 June 1983.
2. Compare the Phipps case to Andrew Hacker's well-known "parable" in which a white person is informed by a mysterious official that "the organization he represents has made a mistake" and that ". . . [a]ccording to their records . . . , you were to have been born black: to another set of parents, far from where you were raised." How much compensation, Hacker's official asks, would "you" require to undo the damage of this unfortunate error? See Hacker, *Two Nations: Black and White, Separate, Hostile, Unequal* (New York: Charles Scribner's Sons, 1992) pp. 31–32.
3. On the evolution of Louisiana's racial classification system, see Virginia Dominguez, *White By Definition: Social Classification in Creole Louisiana* (New Brunswick: Rutgers University Press, 1986).

4. This is not to suggest that gender is a biological category while race is not. Gender, like race, is a social construct. However, the biological division of humans into sexes—two at least, and possibly intermediate ones as well—is not in dispute. This provides a basis for argument over gender divisions—how "natural," etc.—which does not exist with regard to race. To ground an argument for the "natural" existence of race, one must resort to philosophical anthropology.
5. "The truth is that there are no races, there is nothing in the world that can do all we ask race to do for us. . . . The evil that is done is done by the concept, and by easy—yet impossible—assumptions as to its application." (Kwame Anthony Appiah, *In My Father's House: Africa in the Philosophy of Culture* [New York: Oxford University Press, 1992].) Appiah's eloquent and learned book fails, in our view, to dispense with the race concept, despite its anguished attempt to do so; this indeed is the source of its author's anguish. We agree with him as to the non-objective character of race, but fail to see how this recognition justifies its abandonment. This argument is developed below.
6. We understand essentialism as *belief in real, true human, essences, existing outside or impervious to social and historical context.* We draw this definition, with some small modifications, from Diana Fuss, *Essentially Speaking: Feminism, Nature, & Difference* (New York: Routledge, 1989) p. xi.
7. Michael Omi and Howard Winant, "On the Theoretical Status of the Concept of Race" in Warren Crichlow and Cameron McCarthy, eds., *Race, Identity, and Representation in Education* (New York: Routledge, 1993).
8. Charles Murray, *Losing Ground: American Social Policy, 1950–1980* (New York: Basic Books, 1984), p. 223.
9. Justice Thurgood Marshall, dissenting in *City of Richmond v. J. A. Croson Co.*, 488 U.S. 469 (1989).
10. See, for example, Derrick Bell, "Remembrances of Racism Past: Getting Past the Civil Rights Decline." in Herbert Hill and James E. Jones, Jr., eds., *Race in America: The Struggle for Equality* (Madison: The University of Wisconsin Press, 1993) pp. 75–76; Gertrude Ezorsky, *Racism and Justice: The Case for Affirmative Action* (Ithaca: Cornell University Press, 1991) pp. 109–111; David Kairys, *With Liberty and Justice for Some: A Critique of the Conservative Supreme Court* (New York: The New Press, 1993) pp. 138–41.
11. See Weber, *Economy and Society*, Vol. I (Berkeley: University of California Press, 1978), pp. 385–87; Ernst Moritz Manasse, "Max Weber on Race," *Social Research*, Vol. 14 (1947) pp. 191–221.
12. Du Bois, *The Souls of Black Folk* (New York: Penguin, 1989 [1903]), p. 13. Du Bois himself wrestled heavily with the conflict between a fully socio-

historical conception of race, and the more essentialized and deterministic vision he encountered as a student in Berlin. In "The Conservation of Races" (1897) we can see his first mature effort to resolve this conflict in a vision which combined racial solidarity and a commitment to social equality. See Du Bois, "The Conservation of Races," in Dan S. Green and Edwin D. Driver, eds., *W. E. B. Du Bois on Sociology and the Black Community* (Chicago: University of Chicago Press, 1978) pp. 238–49; Manning Marable, *W. E. B. Du Bois: Black Radical Democrat* (Boston: Twayne, 1986) pp. 35–38. For a contrary, and we believe incorrect, reading see Appiah, *In My Father's House: Africa in the Philosophy of Culture* (New York: Oxford University Press, 1992), pp. 28–46.

13. A good collection of Boas's work is George W. Stocking, ed., *The Shaping of American Anthropology, 1883–1911: A Franz Boas Reader* (Chicago: University of Chicago Press, 1974).

14. Robert E. Park's *Race and Culture* (Glencoe, IL: Free Press, 1950) can still provide insight; see also Stanford H. Lyman, *Militarism, Imperialism, and Racial Accommodation: An Analysis and Interpretation of the Early Writings of Robert E. Park* (Fayetteville: University of Arkansas Press, 1992); Locke's views are concisely expressed in Alain Leroy Locke, *Race Contacts and Interracial Relations*, ed. Jeffrey C. Stewart (Washington, DC: Howard University Press, 1992), originally a series of lectures given at Howard University.

15. Especially when we recall that until around 1960, the majority of blacks, the largest racially defined minority group, lived in the South.

16. Toni Morrison, *Playing in the Dark: Whiteness and the Literary Imagination* (Cambridge, MA: Harvard University Press, 1992); Richard Drinnon, *Facing West: The Metaphysics of Indian-Hating and Empire-Building* (Minneapolis: University of Minnesota Press, 1980); Michael Paul Rogin, *Fathers and Children: Andrew Jackson and the Subjugation of the American Indian* (New York: Knopf, 1975).

17. For example, in Magnus Hirschfeld's prescient book *Racism* (London: Victor Gollancz, 1938).

18. This was the framework, employed in the crucial study of Myrdal and his associates; see Gunnar Myrdal, *An American Dilemma: The Negro Problem and Modern Democracy*, 20th Anniversary Edition (New York: Harper and Row, 1962 [1944]). See also the articles by Thomas F. Pettigrew and George Fredrickson in Pettigrew et al., *Prejudice: Selections from The Harvard Encyclopedia of American Ethnic Groups* (Cambridge, MA: The Belknap Press of Harvard University, 1982).

19. On discrimination, see Frederickson in ibid. In an early essay which explicitly sought to modify the framework of the Myrdal study, Robert K. Merton recognized that prejudice and discrimination need not coincide,

and indeed could combine in a variety of ways. See Merton, "Discrimination and the American Creed," in R. M. McIver, ed., *Discrimination and National Welfare* (New York: Harper and Row, 1949).

20. Gordon W. Allport, *The Nature of Prejudice* (Cambridge, MA: Addison-Wesley, 1954) remains a classic work in the field; see also Philomena Essed, *Understanding Everyday Racism: An Interdisciplinary Theory* (Newbury Park, CA: Sage, 1991). A good overview of black attitudes toward black identities is provided in William E. Cross, Jr., *Shades of Black: Diversity in African-American Identity* (Philadelphia: Temple University Press, 1991).
21. Stokely Carmichael and Charles V. Hamilton first popularized the notion of "institutional" forms of discrimination in *Black Power: The Politics of Liberation in America* (New York: Vintage, 1967), although the basic concept certainly predated that work. . . .
22. This view supports Supreme Court decisions taken in the late 1960s and early 1970s, for example in *Griggs v. Duke Power*, 401 U.S. 424 (1971). We agree with Kairys that only ". . . [F]or that brief period in our history, it could accurately be said that governmental discrimination was prohibited by law" (Kairys, *With Liberty and Justice For Some*, p. 144).
23. See for example, Judy H. Katz, *White Awareness: Handbook for Anti-Racism Training* (Norman: University of Oklahoma Press, 1978).
24. To pick but one example among many: writing before the successes of the civil rights movement, E. Franklin Frazier bitterly castigated the collaboration of black elites with white supremacy. See Frazier, *Black Bourgeoisie: The Rise of a New Middle Class in the United States* (New York: The Free Press, 1957).

Black and White or Rainbow Colors

Tiger Woods and the "One-Drop Rule" (2007)

JANIS PRINCE INNISS

Recently, golfer Tiger Woods and his wife, Elin Nordegren, became parents. Given that Nordegren is white and Swedish, this announcement made me wonder what if anything would be made of the race of any of the members of this young family. I thought about this because ten years ago, a then twenty-one-year-old Woods had already captured the prestigious Masters title and the minds of many Americans. Despite all of this, Woods was the subject of heated debate in diverse forums because he expresses a preference *not* to be identified as African American.

I recognized that trouble was brewing when the African-American host of a popular, nationally syndicated radio program repeated the statement Woods made on the Oprah Winfrey show that he was "Cablinasian." Woods said that he had made up the term "Cablinasian" to describe his racial background, and preferred not to be called African American. The radio host criticized Woods and suggested that African Americans would reject Woods unless he explained himself. The host was right: Woods later felt the heat for daring not to be described as African American.

One week later, the Reverend Jesse Jackson expressed sympathy for Woods. By rejecting the label African American, Jackson said, the golfer had no base upon which to stand. Woods had said that his background is African American, Asian, Caucasian, and Native American; just as white Americans might describe themselves as French, English, and Italian, for example. At the time, the media described Woods as the first African American and Asian American to win a major golf tournament and various writers quantified each aspect of his background.

I fully understood the need for African Americans to claim Tiger Woods. He is a young man who excels at a sport synonymous with white upper-class privilege. Woods had just set a record by becoming the youngest Masters champion. Because we are bombarded by images of African Americans (particularly young males) committing various heinous acts, there is a steady call for more positive role models. Woods would seem a perfect antidote to many negative representations of our youth, so when he rejected an African American identity it seemed as if he had abandoned those with the greatest need. Woods's claim about the diversity of his heritage seemed like a rejection of African Americans, or even a form of self-delusion.

This controversy takes place within the context of historical racism and prejudice against people of African descent in the United States. The hatred for persons of African descent was so encompassing that for years having just "one drop" of "black" blood was as an invitation to subhuman treatment. In pre-Civil War America, white "masters" frequently raped African women they considered their property; any resulting offspring were classified as black, as enslavers did not want to bestow humane status to this group of "mixed" race people. Thus, the "one-drop rule" was born—anyone possessing even "one drop" of African blood was "black."

The persistent denial of non-African roots of African Americans and the "minority" roots of whites is a legacy of such racist ideology. We have become used to simplistic racial categories (black *or* white, for example) as a shorthand way of navigating the world. It seems that for Woods, his Native American and African-American father and Thai, Chinese, and white mother could not have produced an African-American child. It's sort of like saying that yellow, green, and purple make purple, and not a fourth color consisting of all of its parts.

One argument advanced against recognizing multiracial identities emphasizes that Tiger Woods and others who are (noticeably) of African descent will be seen and treated by most Americans as African American, regardless of their mixed racial heritage. Whatever Woods chooses to call himself, because of the color of his skin he may be subject to what many consider the racist comments of people like Frank Urban "Fuzzy" Zoeller. Zoeller, a professional golfer playing at the same Masters tournament that Woods was about to win, referred to Woods as "that little boy" and said that Woods should not request that they "serve fried chicken . . . or collard greens or whatever the hell they serve" at next year's Masters' dinner.

Social factors have incredible power to shape how we think about the world and about ourselves. Woods's attempt to construct his own, and therefore new, racial identity is a fascinating example of the relationship between our private ideas and societal norms such as the "one-drop rule." For going against the norm, Woods received a variety of informal sanctions—and this may be at least one reason why he has not publicly discussed his being "Cablinasian" again, and has certainly not referred to it when he discusses the birth of his daughter.

Usually, we think of race as "fixed" and presume that the racial classifications we are familiar with are "real" and "natural" without thinking about their origins, functions, or consequences. Racial classifications are seen as absolute biological categories, rather than the social constructs they are. As social constructs, racial classifications will change and have changed over time. This is one example that encourages us to think about *why* racial categorizations in the United States are the way they are, and under what circumstances they change. Can you think of what, if any, benefits there are to things remaining the same versus changing?

Racial Tensions and Living in a Color-blind Society

(2008)

C. N. LE

In many ways, Asian Americans have achieved notable levels of socioeconomic mobility and success in American society. Nonetheless, despite (or perhaps because of) these successes, Asian Americans still confront ongoing instances of hostility, exclusion, and discrimination.

Asian American students continue to face various obstacles in being treated fairly and justly on college campuses, whether it relates to dealing offensive "satire" or being violently attacked.

Some might be tempted to say that these were isolated incidents but as *New American Media* summarizes, these kinds of incidents are actually quite commonplace on college campuses around the country:

> In recent months, incidents have proven this is not the tolerant and highly-evolved society we thought. Hate crimes against Asian students, racial remarks masked under the term "satire," and institutional discrimination—are just a few causes triggering racial tension on college campuses. . . .
>
> On January 21, Martin Luther King, Jr. Day, Kyle Descher, a Korean American, headed out to a bar with his roommate after a Washington State University football victory over Oregon. Minutes after hearing a racial slur from one of three unknown men, Descher is "sucker-punched" in an unprovoked attack. Doctors add three titanium plates to Descher's broken jaw and it's wired shut. . . .
>
> In [the University of Pennsylvania's quarterly student magazine *The Punch Bowl* winter 2008 edition's] "Where Asians Don't Belong" section, staffers listed Math 104, in a panties drawer, on the basketball court, at a frat party, and behind the wheel. Imagine why the staff didn't make jokes with the same glee for all the places African Americans "don't belong." In their defense, *Punch Bowl* editors said some of the writers of the "satirical" issue were Asian Americans themselves, even posing in photos poking fun at APIs.

The article goes on to list several other racially-charged incidents around the country involving a broad range of groups of color.

It would be great if there were positive aspects of our attempts to alleviate racial inequality. Alas, these incidents only highlight what many scholars have been saying all along—as we move forward into the twenty-first century, racism and racial prejudice are still alive and well in American society.

One difference between its nature today versus that of one hundred years ago is that in many ways, racism is now expressed in "color-blind" terms. That is, racists now apparently think that racial equality has been achieved (they'll point to Asian-American socioeconomic achievements as one example), so it's perfectly fine to make fun of Asian Americans and other groups because we're all equal now—we're all on a level playing field nowadays, so everybody is fair game.

In other words, this is what it means to live in a color-blind society these days—historical legacies of systematic racism are completely ignored or "whitewashed" and we all pretend that all racial groups are perfectly equal. Or alternatively, racists act on their resentment that minorities have apparently achieved "equality" and physically attack those minorities.

Unfortunately, I predict that this climate of "color-blind" prejudice will get worse before it gets better, especially as globalization continues to reshape American society, the American economy, and as a result the assumption of American superiority around the world.

As Americans, particularly many white Americans, continue to economically struggle as we enter a recession, and as demographic and cultural shifts take place all around them, their fears, frustrations, and anger will inevitably boil over. It's likely that verbal and physical attacks on convenient scapegoats such as Asian Americans will continue.

I want to be optimistic and hopefully I'm wrong, but as these recent incidents show, racial tensions seem to be on the rise, not on the decline.

Related Links

Asian Nation website:
www.asian-nation.org/headlines/2007/01/another-anti-arab-student-attack/

Report on campus violence:
news.newamericamedia.org/news/view_article.html?article_id=8ac72542d58e957a0d8be5dca8084b4b

The Costs of a Costless Community

(1990)

MARY C. WATERS

What does claiming an ethnic label mean for a white middle-class American? Census data and my interviews suggest that ethnicity is increasingly a personal choice of whether to be ethnic at all, and, for an increasing majority of people, of which ethnicity to be. An ethnic identity is something that does not affect much in everyday life. It does not, for the most part, limit choice of marriage partner (except in almost all cases to exclude non-whites). It does not determine where you will live, who your friends will be, what job you will have, or whether you will be subject to discrimination. It matters only in voluntary ways—in celebrating holidays with a special twist, cooking a special ethnic meal (or at least calling a meal by a special ethnic name), remembering a special phrase or two in a foreign language. However, in spite of all the ways in which it does not matter, people cling tenaciously to their ethnic identities: they value having an ethnicity and make sure their children know "where they come from."

In this chapter I suggest two reasons for the curious paradox posed by symbolic ethnicity. First, I believe it stems from two contradictory desires in the American character: a quest for community on the one hand and a desire for individuality on the other. Second, symbolic ethnicity persists because of its ideological "fit" with racist beliefs.

... Even among those who have a homogeneous background and do not need to choose an ancestry to identify with, it is clear that people do choose to keep an ethnic identity. And until recently many social scientists who have attempted to understand this persistence of ethnic identity have looked at the nature of the particular ethnic groups—extolling the virtue of particular strands of the ethnic culture worth preserving. Yet if one looks at ethnicity almost as though it were a product one would purchase in the marketplace ... one can see that symbolic ethnic identity is an attractive product.

Part of the reason that ethnicity is so appealing to people is evident in the reasons people give to the question of *why* they "like being ethnic." Being ethnic makes them feel unique and special and not just "vanilla," as one respondent put it. They are not like everyone else. At the same time, being ethnic gives them a sense of belonging to a collectivity. It is the best of all worlds: they can claim to be unique and special while simultaneously finding the community and conformity with others that they also crave. But that "community" is of a type that will not interfere with a person's individuality. The closest this type of ethnic identity brings a person to "group activity" is something like a Saint Patrick's Day parade. It is not as if these people belong to ethnic voluntary organizations or gather as a group in churches or neighborhood or union halls. They work and reside within the mainstream of American middle-class life, yet they retain the interesting benefits—the "specialness" of ethnic allegiance.

[T]he very idea that Americans have of "community" is very much tied up in their minds with ethnicity. Ethnicity is sometimes defined as family writ large. The image that people conjure up of "community" is in part one based on common origins and interests. The concrete nature of those images in America is likely to be something like a small town or an ethnic ghetto, while in many other parts of the world this sense of peoplehood or community might be realized through nationalist feelings. The idea of being "American" does not give people a sense of one large family, the way that being French does for people in France. In America, rather than conjuring up an image of nationhood to meet this desire, ethnic images are called forth.

The immensely popular book *Habits of the Heart*[1] exemplifies the invocation of ethnicity as an example of community. The authors diagnose the problems with Americans as stemming from a lack of community—a community that people really want, but lack even a language to talk about, because it challenges the independence they have traditionally valued. Bellah et al. mourn the passing of the strong ethnic ties that vanish as Americans move into the middle class. . . .

This is the essential contradiction in American culture between individuality and community. . . . And I think this is the best way to understand the symbolic ethnicity I have described—it gives middle-class Americans at least the appearance of both: conformity with individuality; community with social change. And as an added bonus—which almost ensures its appeal to Americans—the element of choice is also there. . . .

Over and over again people told me that they liked keeping an ethnic identity because it gave them a sense of who they were, where they had come from, and,

1. Bellah, Robert N., et al. (1985). *Habits of the Heart: Individualism and Commitment in American Life.* Berkeley: University of California Press. [*Editor's note*]

as one respondent said, made them "more interesting." And the more unusual your ancestry sounds, the more "interesting" you are. . . .

Symbolic ethnicity is thus not something that will easily or quickly disappear, while at the same time it does not need very much to sustain it. The choice itself—a community without cost and a specialness that comes to you just by virtue of being born—is a potent combination.

SYMBOLIC ETHNICITY AND RACE

But what of the consequences of this symbolic ethnicity? Is it a harmless way for Saturday suburban ethnics to feel connected and special? Is it a useful way to unite Americans by reminding us that we are all descended from immigrants who had a hard time and sacrificed a bit? Is it a lovely way to show that all cultures can coexist and that the pluralist values of diversity and tolerance are alive and well in the United States?

The answer is yes and maybe no. Because aside from all of the positive, amusing, and creative aspects to this celebration of roots and ethnicity, there is a subtle way in which this ethnicity has consequences for American race relations. After all, in much of this discussion the implicit and sometimes explicit comparison for this symbolic ethnicity has been the social reality of racial and ethnic identities of America's minority groups. For the ways in which ethnicity is flexible and symbolic and voluntary for white middle-class Americans are the very ways in which it is not so for non-white and Hispanic Americans.

Thus the discussions of the influence of looks and surname on ethnic choice would look very different if one were describing a person who was one-quarter Italian and three-quarters African-American or a woman whose married name changed from O'Connell to Martinez. The social and political consequences of being Asian or Hispanic or black are not symbolic for the most part, or voluntary. They are real and often hurtful.

So for all of the ways in which I have shown that ethnicity does not matter for white Americans, I could show how it does still matter very much for non-whites. Who your ancestors are does affect your choice of spouse, where you live, what job you have, who your friends are, and what your chances are for success in American society, if those ancestors happen not to have been from Europe. Whether this is a temporary situation, and the experience of non-whites in America will follow the same progression as the experience of these white ethnic groups, has been one of the central questions in American social science writing on this subject. The question, then, of whether ethnic groups such as Italians and Poles are in some way the same as minority groups such as Chicanos and blacks is a complicated one—both analytically and politically. Analytically, social scientists have tried to assess the assimilation process of white ethnics and non-white groups to ascertain whether the American opportunity structure will open up for non-whites. Politically, this issue is also an important one—especially with the development of affirmative action legislation and the Voting Rights Act, which moved to provide legal protection and special attention to what were defined as "minority groups" subject to discrimination, as opposed to ethnic groups who were not. Stephen Steinberg (1981) and others writing on the ethnic revival of the 1970s argue quite strongly that the self-conscious organization of white ethnics on the basis of their ethnicity was a racist response to the civil rights movement of the 1960s and 1970s and to celebrations of racial and ethnic identities by non-white groups.

Michael Novak, author of *The Rise of the Unmeltable Ethnics*,[2] was the conservative leader of the white ethnic movement of the 1970s. He tries to answer the criticism that white ethnics are anti-black and "going back to their ethnicity" in order to oppose the black power movement. He writes: "The new ethnicity is the nation's best hope for confronting racial hatred. A Pole who knows he is a Pole, who is proud to be a Pole, who knows the social costs and possibilities of being a Polish worker in America, who knows where he stands in power, status and integrity—such a Pole can face a black militant eye to eye" (294). Novak really could not have been more wrong here, but not only for the most obvious reason. In the context of the content of the rest of his book and the debates of the early 1970s, Novak was wrong because the "new white ethnics" *were* in opposition to the black power movement, and various other developments that came out of the civil rights movement. And Novak's own work was read then and can be read now as fanning the flames of racial division at the time.

But the other sense in which Novak is wrong in this passage is in part a result of some of the developments of the new ethnicity movement of the 1970s. A Polish-American who "knows he is a Pole, who is proud to be a Pole, who knows the social costs and possibilities of being a Polish worker" is less able to understand the experience of being black in America precisely because of being "in touch with his own ethnicity." That is because the nature of being a Pole in America is as I have described it—lacking in social costs, providing enjoyment, and chosen voluntarily.

. . . The reality is that white ethnics have a lot more choice and room for maneuver than they themselves think they do. The situation is very different for members of racial minorities, whose lives are strongly influenced by their race or national origin regardless of how much they may choose not to identify themselves in ethnic or racial terms. Yet my respondents did not make a distinction between their own experience of ethnicity as a personal choice and the experience of being a member of a racial minority.

People who assert a symbolic ethnicity do not give much attention to the ease with which they are able to slip in and out of their ethnic roles. It is quite natural to them that in the greater part of their lives, their ethnicity does not matter.

2. Novak, Michael. (1973). *The Rise of the Unmeltable Ethnics: Politics and Culture in the Seventies*. New York: Macmillan.

They also take for granted that when it does matter, it is largely a matter of personal choice and a source of pleasure.

The fact that ethnicity is something that is enjoyed and will not cause problems for the individual is something people just accept. This also leads to the belief that all ancestries are equal—more or less interchangeable, but that you should be proud of and enjoy the one you have. . . .

This approach to their own ethnicity leads to a situation where whites with a symbolic ethnicity are unable to understand the everyday influence and importance of skin color and racial minority status for members of minority groups in the United States. This lack of understanding of the difference between the experience of ethnicity for white Americans and the implications of ethnicity for members of racial minorities was made quite clear in an interchange in the "Dear Abby" newspaper column. The following debate is between two Irish-Americans and two Asian-Americans on the issue of whether or not it is polite to inquire about an individual's ethnic background. The Irish-Americans cannot understand why the Asian-Americans are offended:

> Dear Abby,
>
> Regarding "100 Percent American," the American of Oriental descent who complained that within five minutes of being introduced to a Caucasian, he was asked, "What are you?": You replied that it was rude to ask personal questions at any time, but because the average Caucasian doesn't know a Chinese from a Japanese, Cambodian, Vietnamese, Korean or a Thai, the question seemed reasonable—but it was still rude.
>
> Rude? I disagree. Inquiries about a person's roots are not necessarily rude. It shows a sincere interest in their heritage.
>
> The Orient is a rich and diverse geography. The face of an Oriental reveals his heritage. His looks tell of a passage through villages, cultures and languages—but which ones? His story is probably quite fascinating. I don't think it is rude to observe that such a face has a rich ancestry. I think it is a positive component of international understanding.
>
> AN AMERICAN NAMED FINN

Abby replied:

> My mail was heavy on this one. Without exception, all writers of Oriental descent resented being asked, "What are you?" shortly after being introduced. A typical letter:
>
> Dear Abby,
>
> I, too, am 100 percent American and because I am of Asian ancestry, I am often asked, "What are you?" It's not the personal nature of this question that

bothers me, it's the question itself. This query seems to question my very humanity. "What am I?" Why I am a person like everyone else!

Another question I am frequently asked is, "Where did you come from?" This would be an innocent question, when one Caucasian asks it of another, but when it is asked of an Asian, it takes on a different tone . . .

A REAL AMERICAN

Dear Abby,

Why do people resent being asked what they are? The Irish are so proud of being Irish, they tell you before you even ask. Tip O'Neill has never tried to hide his Irish ancestry.

JIMMY

(*San Francisco Chronicle*, February 28, 1986)

I was struck when I read this by how well it summarized the ways in which I found that the symbolic ethnicity of my respondents related to their ideas about racial minorities in our society. "An American Named Finn" cannot understand why Asians are not as happy to be asked about their ancestry as he is because he understands his ethnicity and theirs to be separate but equal. Everyone has to come from somewhere—his family from Ireland, another's family from Asia—each has a history and each should be proud of it. But the reason he cannot understand the perspective of the Asian-American is that all ethnicities are not equal, all are not symbolic, costless, and voluntary. And that is where the subtle effect of symbolic ethnicity on American race relations develops.

The people I interviewed were not involved in ethnic organizations and were not self-consciously organized on the basis of their ethnicity. However, I do think that the way they experience their ethnicity creates a climate leading to a lack of understanding of the ethnic or racial experience of others. People equated their European ancestral background with the backgrounds of people from minority groups and saw them as interchangeable.

Thus respondents told me they just did not see why blacks and Mexican-Americans were always blaming things on their race or their ethnicity. . . .

Others denied, especially, that blacks were experiencing discrimination, citing examples of when affirmative action policies had hurt them or their families as "reverse discrimination." . . .

Part of the tradition handed down as part of an ethnic ancestry are the family stories about ancestors having faced discrimination in the past. In fact, a large part of what people want to pass on to their children is the history of discrimination and struggle that ancestors faced when first arriving in the United States. All of my respondents were sure that their ancestors had faced discrimination when they first came to the United States. Many had heard stories about it within their families, some had read about it in history books, but all were sure it had happened. It was also one of the most important things mentioned to me by parents when they talked about what they wanted their children to know about their ethnic ancestry. . . .

This type of interpretation of history contributes to the problems middle-class Americans of European origin have in understanding the experiences of their contemporary non-white fellow citizens. The idea that the Irish were forced to sit at the back of a bus (when, in 1840?) in a sense could be seen to bring people together. The message of such a belief is that all ethnicities are similar and all will eventually end up successful. If the Irish had to sit at the back of the bus sometime in the past, and now being Irish just means having fun at funerals, then there is hope for all groups facing discrimination now. But, of course, if the Irish did not need legislation to allow them into the front of the bus, then why do blacks? If the Irish could triumph over hardships and discrimination through individual initiative and hard work, then why the need for affirmative action and civil rights legislation?

It is clear that people have a sense that being an immigrant was hard, that society did not accept their groups, and that now discrimination and prejudice is much less than it was before. People also believe that blacks, Hispanics, and Asians are still in a somewhat earlier stage. But, on the other hand, beliefs that the discrimination faced by Irish, Italians, and Serbs was the same both in degree and in kind as that faced by non-whites sets the stage for resentment of any policies that single out racial minorities.

In this sense the process and content of symbolic ethnicity tend to reinforce one another. If invoking an ethnic background is increasingly a voluntary, individual decision, and if it is understood that invoking that background is done for the enjoyment of the personality traits or rituals that one associates with one's ethnicity, then ethnicity itself takes on certain individual and positive connotations. The process and content of a symbolic ethnicity then make it increasingly difficult for white ethnics to sympathize with or understand the experience of a non-symbolic ethnicity—the experience of racial minorities in the United States.

THE FUTURE OF SYMBOLIC ETHNICITY

This analysis suggests both that symbolic ethnicity persists because it meets a need Americans have for community without individual cost and that a potential societal cost of this symbolic ethnicity is in its subtle reinforcement of racism. Perhaps this is an inherent danger in any pluralist society. The celebration of the fact that we all have heritages implies an equality among those heritages. This would obscure the fact that the experiences of non-whites have been qualitatively and quantitatively different from those of whites.

It is true that at the turn of the century Italians were considered by some to be non-whites. It is also true that there were signs in many East Coast cities prohibiting the Irish from applying for jobs or entering establishments. The discrimination faced by Jews was even greater. They were excluded from certain neighborhoods, organizations, and occupations. Yet the degree of discrimination against white European immigrants and their children never matched the systematic, legal and official discrimination and violence experienced by blacks, Hispanics, and Asians in America. The fact that whites of European ancestry today can enjoy an ethnicity that gives them options and brings them enjoyment with little or no social cost is no small accomplishment. But does it mean that in time we shall have a pluralist society with symbolic ethnicity for all Americans?

[S]ymbolic ethnicity is not just something associated with generational movement. It is also very much dependent on social mobility. As long as racial or ethnic identity is associated with class stratification, or as long as ascriptive characteristics are used to assign rewards in society, ethnic identity will be much more complex than individual choice and selective personal and familial enjoyment of tradition.

The effects of changes in American immigration law make it difficult at times to distinguish developments owing to generational mobility from those owing to social and economic mobility. This is because the social and economic mobility of white ethnics in the twentieth century coincided with the drastic reduction in immigration from European sources—which means that the cohorts of Poles and Italians advancing socially and generationally have not been followed by large numbers of fresh immigrants who take over unskilled jobs and populate ethnic ghettos. Thus when the socially mobile children and grandchildren of the original immigrants left the urban ghettos and unskilled jobs for college and the suburbs in the 1950s and 1960s, blacks, Hispanics, and Asians took their places. The social mobility that makes a symbolic ethnicity possible for these whites might have looked very different if the supply of new immigrants from Europe had not been drastically curtailed.

This also makes it difficult to generalize from the experience of these white ethnic groups to the experiences of the largely non-European immigrants arriving since the 1965 immigration law. There is definitely evidence of social mobility and increasing intermarriage among the second- and among the small number of third-generation Asian-Americans. There is also evidence of social mobility and intermarriage among Hispanics. However, both of these groups are different from groups of European origin in that there is a continuing supply of new immigrants who take the place of the older generations in the ethnic neighborhoods and occupations. Middle-class third-generation Mexican-Americans may enjoy some of the same intermittent and voluntary aspects of ethnic identity as Italian-Americans, but the existence of a strong first-generation ethnic community, as well as of continued discrimination in housing and employment against Hispanics, would probably impose constraints on such upwardly mobile third-generation Mexican-Americans that it would not on Italian-Americans.

Given the fact that the structural conditions and trends that give rise to symbolic ethnicity are continuing, I would expect that symbolic ethnicity will continue to characterize the ethnicity of later-generation whites. The individual and familial construction of the substance of that ethnicity, along with increasing intermarriage, means that the shared content of any one ethnicity will become even more diluted. Consequently there will be increased dependence on the mass media, ethnic stereotypes, and popular culture to tell people how to be Irish or Italian or Polish.

The paradox of symbolic ethnicity is that it depends upon the ultimate goal of a pluralist society and at the same time makes it more difficult to achieve that ultimate goal. It is dependent upon the concept that all ethnicities mean the same thing—that enjoying the traditions of one's heritage is an option available to a group or individual—but that such a heritage should not have any social costs associated with it. The options of symbolic ethnicity involve choosing among elements in one's ancestry and choosing when and if voluntarily to enjoy the traditions of that ancestry. However . . . the individuals who enjoy a symbolic ethnicity for themselves do not always recognize the options they enjoy or the ways in which their own concepts of ethnicity and uses of those concepts constrain and deny choice to others.

Americans who have a symbolic ethnicity continue to think of ethnicity—as well as race—as being biologically rooted. They enjoy many choices themselves, but they continue to ascribe identities to others—especially those they can identify by skin color. Thus a person with a black skin who had some Irish ancestry would have to work very hard to decide to present him or herself as Irish—and in many important ways he/she would be denied that option. The discussion of racial intermarriage makes this point clearly—racial identity is understood by these respondents as an inherited physical aspect of an individual, not as a social construct. Thus respondents exhibit contradictory ideas about minorities in American society—they are clear that there is a fundamental difference between a white ethnic and a black person when the issue is intermarriage in their own families. On the other hand, they do not understand why blacks seem to make such a big deal about their ethnicity. They see an equivalence between the African-American and, say, Polish-American heritages.

So symbolic ethnicity only works for some ancestries—the pluralist ideal of an equality of heritages is far from a reality in American life. But at the same time, the legacy of symbolic ethnicity is to imply that this equality exists. The political result of that ideological legacy is a backlash against affirmative action programs that recognize and try to redress the inequalities in our society.

The ultimate goal of a pluralist society should be a situation of symbolic ethnicity for all Americans. If all Americans were free to exercise their "ethnic option" with the certainty that there would be no costs associated with it, we could all enjoy the voluntary, pleasurable aspects of ethnic traditions in the way my respondents describe their own enjoyments. It is important not to romanticize the traditional white ethnic group. In addition to its positive aspects, it was experienced as extremely constricting and narrow by many people. There are parts of these past ethnic traditions that are sexist, racist, clannish, and narrow-minded. With a symbolic ethnic identity an individual can choose to celebrate an ethnic holiday and refuse to perpetuate a sexist tradition that values boys over girls or that channels girls into domestic roles without their consent. The selective aspects of a symbolic ethnicity are in part what make it so enjoyable to so many individuals.

Currently, however, we are far removed from a position where this freedom is available for all. As the Asian-Americans who wrote to Dear Abby make clear, there are many societal issues and involuntary ascriptions associated with nonwhite identities. The developments necessary for this to change are not individual but societal in nature. Social mobility and declining racial and ethnic sensitivity are closely associated. The legacy and the present reality of discrimination on the basis of race or ethnicity must be overcome before the ideal of a pluralist society where all heritages are treated equally and are equally available for individuals to choose or discard at will is realized. It is a sad irony that the enjoyment and individual character of their own ethnicity contributes to the thinking that makes these middle-class whites oppose the very programs designed to achieve that reality.

Celebrating St. Patrick's Day

Symbolic Ethnicity
(2008)

JANIS PRINCE INNISS

I'm seeing green! St. Patrick's green, that is. Everywhere. At the grocery store. At Wal-Mart. At the mall. At my gym. Surely you've seen the decorations and a variety of green products such as carnations, bagels, greeting cards, frosted cupcakes—and even the Chicago River!

My introduction to St. Paddy's Day came when I lived in New York City; fitting because New York is home to one of the biggest parades, with millions of onlookers. Irish soldiers began the parade in New York in 1762 and it has grown to include more than 150,000 people from a variety of Irish organizations. It is the largest parade in New York, even bigger than the Macy's Thanksgiving Day parade.

Is there a parade in your city? Chicago, Boston, and Savannah, along with a variety of other cities around the world, have St. Patrick's Day parades. In the United States, St. Patrick's Day is a religious holiday celebrated for centuries by the Irish on March 17 during Lent. Although the details about his early life differ, Patrick is said to have died on March 17, 460 A.D., and most scholars agree that he introduced Christianity to Ireland. Traditionally, Irish families' St. Patrick Day's celebration involved attending church in the morning and then—with the restriction against eating meat lifted for the occasion—feasting on bacon and cabbage in the evening. The focus on St. Patrick's Day as a religious holiday in Ireland has remained that way until recently; it was only in the 1970s that pubs were allowed to remain open on this day.

Why do Irish Americans celebrate St. Patrick's Day? This celebration is an example of symbolic ethnicity, characterized by a need to hold on to the culture of the immigrant generation, coupled with a pragmatic desire not to let this culture interfere with everyday life. The "old" culture is converted into ethnic symbols that must be simple enough to be shared by many people and easily understood. Many whites in the United States who maintain ethnic identities do so only in symbolic ways that take little time and minimally affect their everyday lives. Ethnicity, then, becomes highly individualized and expressive, although it has little or no impact on day-to-day living. Their ethnicity is tied to voluntary and arguably superficial events such as dishes cooked and holidays celebrated; for many, St. Patrick's Day can be understood in this context.

Mary Waters, author of "The Costs of a Costless Community" [reproduced in this volume], theorizes that the element of choice available to white ethnics makes symbolic ethnicity appealing. Although their ethnicity does not affect their lives in any crucial ways, Waters argues that it is important to white ethnics because ethnicity combines two important aspects of life. First, ethnicity connotes individuality—a feeling of being special that sets one apart from others. Second, it provides a sense of community, albeit a loosely knit one. This sense of community does not infringe on or restrict personal lives. Attending a St. Patrick's Day parade, for example, allows Irish Americans to feel a part of the Irish American community, but when the parade is over there's no stipulation that their lives have to be guided by Irish tradition or culture.

The traditional Irish focus on the religious aspects of St. Patrick's Day stands in sharp contrast to the festive American counterpart. Right now, we have a unique opportunity to notice the tensions between the religious and the celebratory aspects of St. Patrick's Day. In 2008, Holy Week—the week before Easter that includes Palm Sunday and Good Friday, which memorializes the last week of Jesus' life—began on Sunday, March 16. This means that St. Patrick's Day fell on Holy Monday. Many church officials in the United States asked parade organizers to refrain from holding their parades on this day in deference to Holy Monday. Some cities such as Philadelphia and Milwaukee had early parades, but the New York parade and many others continued as always on March 17.

Interestingly, St. Patrick's is celebrated by many Americans who are *not* Irish. Almost three quarters (71.8%) of Americans 18–24 years old will celebrate the day, and although 34.5 million Americans claim to have Irish ancestry, this number clearly does not account for all of those taking part in the celebrations. This leads to a staggering amount of money spent on the festivities—$3.6 billion, according to the National Retail Foundation.

Why do you think so many people with no Irish heritage celebrate St. Patrick's Day? Clearly, the symbols (partying and wearing green) are simple enough to be shared by many people.

Related links

National Retail Federation:
www.nrf.com/modules.php?name=News&op=viewlive&sp_id=483

U.S. Census Data: www.census.gov/Press-Release/www/releases/archives/facts_for_features_special_editions/006328.html

TALK ABOUT IT

1. As a child, when were you first aware of the concept of race? What event brought race to your attention?
2. What might be different in the United States if race had not been so intertwined with power?
3. How are ethnic identities different from racial identities? How are they linked?
4. How would you describe your racial or ethnic identity? Does your racial or ethnic identity defy simple classification?
5. Race can be a difficult concept to talk about in the United States, but ignoring the concept sometimes means ignoring the existence of racism. How should Americans discuss the issue of race?

WRITE ABOUT IT

1. Research a law that supported racial discrimination in American history but has since been overturned. What lingering effects of that law can we observe today, even though the law may no longer be in effect?
2. Think of an ethnic celebration that you or others have enjoyed. Why do people continue to celebrate this day? How does this celebration relate to the points made by Waters and/or Prince Inniss? Are there any social costs that might reduce celebrants' social status by participating?
3. Pick an individual with a multiethnic or multiracial background—yourself, a friend, or someone in the public eye. How does this individual classify him or herself racially and/or ethnically? How do others classify this person? Is there a difference? Discuss whether racial or ethnic classification matters today on a personal or public level.
4. Discuss racial or ethnic stereotypes that some might regard as positive traits. How can these assumptions be damaging, even if they suggest a talent or skill?
5. Has society become color-blind? Why or why not? What are the benefits and limitations of becoming a color-blind society?

DO IT

1. Interview five people and show them pictures of ten people. Ask your interviewees to decide the race of the people in each picture, and then ask them how they determined the race of each person. What factors did they use? What did they overlook? What does this tell us about the ways we construct meanings of race?

2. Interview five people about their ethnic backgrounds. Ask them whether they choose to share this information with others, and how they feel about being part of this ethnic group. How do your findings compare with Mary Waters's analysis of optional ethnicities?
3. On your favorite television show, how many characters are members of racial or ethnic minorities? How racially integrated is this show? Is the race or ethnicity of any of the characters made more salient than others'? Analyze the overall meaning of race and/or ethnicity in this show.
4. Observe people on your campus or in a public place such as a park or a mall. Do people appear to socialize with those of similar racial and/or ethnic backgrounds? If so, why do is this the case? How did you determine whether the people were of similar racial or ethnic backgrounds?
5. Create a video of people discussing their ideas on the importance of race today. What do their ideas tell us about the ways in which race matters? Apply your findings to the ideas of any of the authors in this section.

9

Social Institutions

Module Goal: ***To understand the role social institutions—family, work, religion, education, and government—play in our everyday lives.***

Think of all the various social institutions that have shaped your life. Chances are you took your first breath in a hospital, part of the healthcare system. You might have gone home with your family, another form of a social institution. Was there a religious ritual performed shortly after your birth? If so, there's another social institution in your history. Later you went to school, representing another social institution, education. Chances are you began no later than age five or six and remained in school until you were in your teens, thanks to compulsory education laws enacted and enforced by the government, another social institution. Do you have a job? Have you ever made a purchase? If so, you have been part of our economic system.

All these different institutions have formal and informal rules that have shaped your behavior. Most obviously, your family and teachers likely taught you how you should behave and what you need to know to be part of society. Your family and teachers were governed by laws that attempt to shape your experiences: parents can be charged with child abuse if authorities believe that children are being severely mistreated, and accreditation boards determine what teachers should teach.

Social institutions all serve important functions in socializing members of a society and in managing various aspects of social life. They all include specific rules, patterns, and expectations for society's members. These rules often regulate members' behavior and provide consequences for those who do not abide by the rules. Institutions keep society operating, like the various components of a machine. Yet as we will see, sometimes parts of this social machine do not work together as well as they could. Sometimes the operation of one social institution creates difficulties for other institutions.

Let's start with the arguably most important social institution, the family. Though families are private and personal, they are essential for organizing social life and for socializing its members. Unlike most other social institutions, families are *primary groups*—small groups marked by a great deal of interpersonal interaction. While most other social institutions have formal rules and might include bureaucratic methods of organization, families are much more informal (yet are not outside the reach of formal organizations, as noted above).

Arlie Russell Hochschild, author of "The Overextended Family," has studied families for several decades. In this selection, she details some of the challenges families face and how family members cope with them. Many families are under severe economic stress. As you read this selection, consider how one social institution may impair the smooth function of other social institutions, in this case the economic system and the family. What can be done to make these social institutions work together more efficiently?

The most important function of the family is to nurture and provide for children. Yet in order to provide economically, many parents must hire others to care for children while they are at work. In "Who Cares for America's Babies?" Janis Prince Inniss discusses how the policies of other social institutions—the government and the workplace—affect childcare. Like Hochschild, Prince Inniss encourages us to consider how social institutions can create policies that better serve young children and ultimately American society.

Although holding a stressful job can create challenges for families, *not* having a job can create even bigger problems. Despite following the advice of staying in school and getting a college degree, many people have found that economic stability remains illusory. In "White Collar Downward Mobility," Barbara Ehrenreich explores the difficulty many well-educated people find in the workforce, challenging the belief that our economic system works for those willing to work hard and earn a degree. As you read this selection, consider how this social institution might change to provide more opportunity for people who are highly educated and motivated.

You've likely heard the axiom that *who* you know is more important than *what* you know. In "Getting a Job," Bradley Wright discusses the informal mechanisms people use to find work. Think about how Wright's conclusions compare with Ehrenreich's. What do these selections tell us about our economic system?

Our educational system is another vital social institution, teaching students how to become productive members of society, important information about the society, and how to get along with others. When schools don't work, these lessons might not be effectively transmitted.

If it is difficult for the highly educated to achieve economic stability, it is nearly impossible for those without a quality education. Jonathan Kozol has written numerous books about inequality within American schools and the problems in the way this social institution is structured. In "Hitting Them Hardest When They're Small," Kozol discusses letters students sent to him after he visited a school in the

South Bronx, a neighborhood in New York City. As you read his piece, consider the shortcomings of our educational system, as well as the broader implications for our society if we do not make changes to this vital social institution. As C. N. Le discusses in "Globalization and Higher Education," some American students have chosen to study overseas, in part because the costs of higher education have risen so sharply. How will problems in our educational system affect us in the global marketplace of the future?

Religious institutions also play an important role in society, providing members with a variety of moral lessons regulating their behavior, and promoting conformity. Religious organizations can also provide social connections and support for their members in ways that other social institutions do not. In "Bridging the Gap," Greg C. Stanczak discusses how religious activity can lead to greater community involvement and participation in movements dedicated to social change.

Some people become suspicious when movements take on a religious fervor, particularly if these movements isolate followers from others. Branding a group a cult is a way to discredit the group and to highlight the dangers it might pose to its followers and others. In "What Is a Cult?" Kathleen Lowney explores how and why this term used. What distinguishes a legitimate religion from a cult? Would you consider the terrorist group that perpetrated the attacks on September 11, 2001, a cult?

In the immediate aftermath of the attacks on the World Trade Center and the Pentagon, most Americans looked to the government to respond. Government represents another important social institution, creating and enforcing laws designed to protect its citizens. Since the attacks, public debate has raged on how to respond best and to prevent future attacks. A small but vocal group insists that the events of September 11 were part of an internal conspiracy. In "The Sociology of Conspiracy," I examine why conspiracy theories emerge when they do, and how these theories unwittingly reinforce the notion of government as an infallible social institution. As you read this essay, think about other conspiracy theories you might have heard and how they are related to this social institution.

As you think about social institutions in everyday life, consider the following questions:

1. What social institutions have put a strain on families? What might alleviate this strain?
2. How can our social institutions better prepare our workforce for the realities of the twenty-first century? How can workplace policies improve both our productivity and family stability?
3. What can be done to strengthen our educational institutions? What long-term problems are associated with ineffective educational institutions?
4. What role does religion play in politics and social movements?
5. What specific government policies affect other social institutions? How might these policies be changed to improve these social institutions?

The Overextended Family

(1997)

ARLIE RUSSELL HOCHSCHILD

If work [is] sometimes a refuge from troubled family lives, it [is] also a place where conflicts originating in the home [are] discussed, debated, and subjected to sympathetic scrutiny and where possible solutions were devised and tested. A case in point was Vivian Goodman, a slow-speaking, dignified woman of forty-two whom I interviewed. . . . She lowered herself into a chair opposite me, as if before a judge, and immediately began to describe why she was struggling to free herself of the 11 P.M. to 7 A.M. shift and get on the 7 A.M. to 3 P.M. shift. At stake was a rekindled love affair with another Amerco worker, Emmanuel, who was holding down a 5:30 A.M. to 1:30 P.M. shift. Both worked ten to fifteen hours a week of overtime.

To begin with, everything she said was about time:

> It's not easy. Emmanuel comes home at two-thirty in the afternoon, and I'm already gone to work. If I work overtime, that means I work until 10 A.M. and come home when he's gone.

Having divorced her husband ten years earlier, Vivian had been building a new life with the recently divorced Emmanuel for ten months. "He is my life," she said simply. "He's very kind. We seldom quarrel." But only weeks before, her plans had taken a disastrous turn. Emmanuel moved out because, as she explained it, "my children made it hard for him to be there. I live with my two children from my previous marriage. They should be on their own, but they aren't."

Though Vivian separated from her first husband when her son Tim, now nineteen, was small, Tim continued to cling to memories of his father and of moments of family vacation fun long forgotten by Vivian. She had reconciled with her husband several times, each time raising her son's hopes. "Of course, Tim doesn't know about the affairs his father had with other women, the terrible fights we had. I can't convince Tim that we will never be that family again." Tim had rejected a series of his mother's boyfriends, and most recently, Emmanuel. When Emmanuel was around, Tim became moody and pugnacious. Emmanuel was understanding, but the boy's persistent rudeness finally wore him down.

Vivian's daughter, Tracy, twenty-one, had gradually come to accept Emmanuel. They had even planted a vegetable garden together behind Vivian's trailer;

and for her birthday, Emmanuel had given her a blue jacket he knew she coveted. Tracy liked the idea of Emmanuel's moving in, until she learned Emmanuel wanted to incorporate Emerald, his own daughter from a previous marriage, into their family. As Vivian described the situation,

> Having missed her real dad, she wanted Emmanuel to be her new dad, a dad for herself. She was jealous. She thought Emmanuel treated Emerald like a queen. We were building two new rooms onto the trailer, and Tracy says to me, "You're just building the extra rooms so you can bring *Emerald* in."

Vivian had been protective of Emmanuel's relationship with his daughter and had tried desperately to include her in a blended family. "Emmanuel only got to see Emerald every other weekend, so I didn't want to make plans that interfered with that," she explained. Once when she, Emmanuel, and Emerald went to a restaurant, Emmanuel sat on the same side of the table as Vivian. Noting that Emerald felt pushed away, Vivian prompted Emmanuel, "Go sit next to Emerald."

In the same gentle spirit, Vivian tried to blend into her contentious fold tattered pieces of her own extended "family." She took in Tracy's jobless boyfriend, who according to the hard-working Emmanuel, lolled about the house "doing nothing." She also took in her ex-husband's adopted sister, who had been sexually abused by her ex-husband's father. For six months, she housed two nephews who were avoiding their drunken father. Soon after, she also took under her wing Tracy's closest friend, a young woman who had been abused by her mother's boyfriend. In effect, Vivian was running a refuge to protect the young against the old, children against parents or parent surrogates. She carried a heavy caseload of broken hearts, opening her home to those who needed a safe place, a bed, a meal, or a sympathetic ear. So she worked one shift plus overtime at the plant, a second as a housewife-mother at home, plus overtime as Mother Teresa for a troubled circle of family and friends.

Emmanuel loved Vivian for her big heart and claimed to share her vision of home as a shelter for loved ones in need. But he had little patience for the long waits for the bathroom on rushed mornings, the beer missing from the refrigerator when he was about to watch a game on TV, the tools mislaid from his own workbench when he had a few rare hours for the projects he loved, and, most of all, the lack of time with Vivian.

He simply didn't feel up to sharing Vivian's caseload. He admired her for it but increasingly wanted to assert his own needs, to come first—or at least second—in her community of needy relations. Amid the mad traffic of refugees at home, and with Vivian spending even more hours at Amerco, Emmanuel felt there was little left for him.

So he began to stop off a bit longer at the neighborhood bar after work—and that turned out to be only the beginning. "I thought he was with his brothers and sisters," Vivian told me, "and they were there some of the time, but so was a certain other somebody."

> Eventually, he had an affair with her. One time the mistress called me and tried to justify what she'd done by saying, "*You're* never home." It was true. I *was* never home. I took all the overtime I could get. I wasn't home because I didn't want to be home. The problem was that I was trying to take care of us all and I couldn't.

From childhood on, Emmanuel had had a lot of relatives around the house; he was used to that. What was hard, he claimed, was seeing the "lost lambs" Vivian brought in take advantage of her in her own house while he felt powerless to intervene. "Emmanuel says the kids mistreat me. Well," said Vivian, "they do have their whiny little tantrums, but I've learned to live with them." When Emmanuel finally moved out, his last words to her were "I can't stand to see you wash Tracy's boyfriend's dirty socks."

The problem seemed to be threefold. First, many people, including Emmanuel, came to Vivian in need of help. Second, Vivian herself didn't really have anyone at home to turn to when life became too much for her. Third, Emmanuel's own long hours took him out of the show at home, though no one defined this as a problem. Without Emmanuel to rely on, Vivian turned to friends at work instead. And Emmanuel eventually retreated into an affair. Vivian was devastated. As she recounted,

> I haven't talked to Emmanuel about his affair and I don't think I will. If it happens again, it happens again. It's over and Emmanuel told me that it would never happen again. Well, my ex told me that, too. But this time, it was more than I could bear. I lost thirty-six pounds. The doctor gave me nerve pills. I took them, went into the bathroom at work, and zonked out for two hours at a stretch. I missed my overtime. My coworkers knew Emmanuel was seeing someone. They see. They know. I had girls come back and tell me, "The whole department is worried about you."
>
> My kids realized how much his leaving hurt me. I felt like I had no control. The kids were making decisions. Emmanuel was making decisions. Amerco was making decisions for all of us. I felt I was being buried. In the middle of all this, I had to come to work. I had to function. But you know, coming to work helped.

Work was the one place where Vivian could feel supported in her misery. She was surrounded by an audience of coworkers who offered sympathy, warnings, tales of their own—who gave rather than took. Coworkers told her to eat more, to change her medication, to tell Emmanuel off, to have (or not have) a fling herself. At lunch, on breaks, or over beers after work, coworkers talked among themselves about whether a carousing louse like Emmanuel deserved a kind-hearted woman like Vivian, or whether Vivian had pushed Emmanuel out by paying too much attention to too many other people. It was so unfair that men did so much damage, some said, and then when a few good women like Vivian tried to repair it, they got left for their trouble. Whatever the point of view, these were the conversations—which once might have taken place in a neighbor's kitchen or over the backyard fence—that helped Vivian weather her crisis at home.

FEMININE COMMUNITY AND COMPANY POLICY

Many of the men I interviewed took pride in helping others, but no one told a story remotely similar to Vivian's. At work and at home, most Amerco men saw themselves primarily as wage earners, and their care of others was likely to seem "extra." In general, offering and receiving personal help in and outside of the office, reaffirming bonds of friendship, or building community were more common activities for women than for men. As Amerco hired more women, it adapted to, and built upon, the female culture women brought to work. Just as Vivian Goodman took in needy people at home, so too did Vicky King feel it natural to take them in at work. Vicky's informal caseload was made up of management trainees, secretaries in her office, and other workers in trouble. Even as home was being "masculinized," managed as an efficient "workplace" where personal needs were to be displaced, repressed, or deferred, the workplace was being "feminized" through a management philosophy that stressed trust, team building, and courtesy to the internal customer.

There was a key difference, however, in the extent of workplace "feminization" between top-tier salaried workers and factory wage laborers. Asked about their family lives, top executives, male and female, scarcely mentioned grandparents, aunts, uncles, or cousins. "Family" to them meant the *nuclear* family—mother, father, and children. In interviews with factory workers, male and female, a vast array of relative's names—extending far beyond the nuclear family—popped up all the time. Partly, this was because Amerco factory workers generally came from the Spotted Deer area while most Amerco managers had moved to Spotted Deer from somewhere else. Partly, working-class family ties simply seemed to connect a wider circle of kin.

If one could speak of family and friends as an informal domestic "welfare system," there were more welfare workers among factory personnel than among managers. At the top, "family needs" were likely to be taken care of by paid services—babysitters, summer camps, retirement communities—or by housewives. At the factory level, family needs were likely to be met by family members, and usually by working women like Vivian. So the temporal "cutbacks" at home caused by ever longer workdays at Amerco caused more obvious suffering for those at the bottom than at the top.

The changes at Amerco in recent years only exacerbated this situation. Total Quality, which emphasized cooperation and mutual aid within the workplace, was extended to the factory floor; family-friendly policies that emphasized these same goals at home were not. These corporate decisions, when added to increasing amounts of required (and often desired) overtime, created the framework within which Vivian's terrible dilemma was being played out.

Improving work-family balance was not an issue easily raised on the factory floor. After all, for a lone individual to contest the terms of the "normal" workday, given the company's power, was unlikely, and few were doing it. Even the harshest policies went unchallenged. According to the rules on absenteeism in Amerco plants, if a worker was late for any reason, familial or otherwise, a note went into her file. If she was late again, she would be punished with unpaid days off. It may seem paradoxical that Amerco punished workers who needed time by giving them more time, but punitive suspension was only the first of three steps that led inexorably toward dismissal. Three such suspensions in one year and a worker was fired.

Many mothers of young children came up against these absentee rules when medical emergencies arose. As one described it,

> The kids have been sick all winter. Todd has the chicken pox now. Two weeks ago, Teddy got pneumonia and they put him in the hospital. We called up my supervisor and asked for some time off so I could stay with Teddy. But he said no. I took three sick days and then some vacation days, and they put a note in my file. But I can't take my kids to my mom or my mother-in-law every time they get sick. They both work, too. And besides, when Teddy is sick, he wants me, not anyone else.

In another case, the son of a single mother needed surgery, but because she had already used up her sick days and her vacation days, she chose to wait six months to schedule the surgery so she could arrange a day off. In response to this delay, her son's doctor threatened to press charges of child abuse. In another instance, the coworkers of a single father at Amerco covered for him each night during fifteen-minute extensions of his thirty-minute break so that he could drive to his house and put his ten-year-old daughter, home alone, to bed. On discovering this arrangement, his supervisor stopped the practice. The supervisor in a third case threatened to fire a mother who left work to care for a daughter with a dangerously high fever.

One factory-employed mother was written up for absenteeism for quite a different reason:

> I had to take a day off to go to family court to help my husband get custody of his two daughters [by a previous marriage]. Between us, we have five. Family court is like a green-stamp store, you wait all day. It was two-thirty before we got out. All the days I came into work late because of court, my boss wrote me up. I lost three days of pay. I went through the chain of command in the plant and out of the plant to an executive in Industrial Relations at headquarters. They all told me, "We're sorry, but you took the time off."

Nine out of ten examples of work-family balance crises that came up in my interviews with hourly working parents concerned sick children. But while medical emergencies were fairly clear-cut, the difficult issue of what might be called semichronic problems—children who were depressed, failing in their studies, isolated, or hanging around with the wrong kids—which cried out for more time and parental attention, were rarely raised at all.

Outside of emergencies, however, most working parents were not complaining much about the encroachments of work time. For one thing, parents needed the money. But for Becky Winters, work was also a way of avoiding quarrels. For Vivian, it was a way of distancing herself from her demanding "caseload" at home. And for one of their coworkers, Dolores Jay, work was an escape route from family violence. One day she pointed to the wood-trimmed wall of the small office in the plant where I was conducting interviews and said,

> See the boards along the wall here? My husband would check if there was dust on them and beat me if he found any. He'd measure the space between the coffee table and the wall, and if it wasn't exactly twenty-one inches on each side, he'd get violent. One time he came home on leave from the navy. He hadn't seen me or our year-old baby. I was taking a shower and my husband came into the bathroom, pushed back the shower curtain, and handed me the baby. He'd beaten him. I laid the baby on the bed. He didn't cry for hours. My husband wouldn't let me out of the house. He sat on the front porch, so I couldn't get help. I just sat there over the baby because I didn't have a phone, didn't have anyone I could call. I couldn't go anywhere! After a few hours, my son started moving. I think he thought I did it. I've had problems with my son ever since.

Help for Dolores came through her husband's workplace. A coworker of his called the navy chaplain, who in turn called Dolores's father. He then sent Dolores a one-way ticket back home.

As it was for Dolores Jay, work can become a place to hide and recover from traumatic experiences, and home the place where the trauma takes place. Another woman who worked in the plant discovered that her husband was having an affair long known to her best friends. "That's what I do all day at work," she said. "Toss it back and forth in my mind. How could he? And why didn't they tell me?" In such cases, work became a "recovery room" in which to heal from or at least contemplate with some degree of calm the bruises of life suffered outside. In other cases, work can be a means of trying to avoid the trauma in the first place. For example, the wife of one man was taken to the hospital, half-dead from hemorrhaging with a stillborn child. The distraught husband called his wife's friend from the hospital to tell her the news and then drove back to work. His wife's friend marched up to his workstation, clapped him firmly on the shoulder, and said, "She *needs* you. Go!" Embarrassed at himself, the husband later humbly thanked his wife's friend for helping him do the right thing at such an important moment.

The structure of work time with its rotating shifts and its overtime exacerbated the very problems people thought they were fleeing home to escape. With Amerco's help tens of thousands of individual "time scarcity" cycles were being set in motion. The more overtime Vivian Goodman took, for example, the more demands her children made and the more Emmanuel withdrew. The more they demanded and he withdrew, the harder it became for Vivian to be home, and the more overtime she worked. Only when Emmanuel moved out, precipitating a crisis, did Vivian even begin to imagine that there was a cycle to be broken and to explore ways out.

Joann Redman, another of Vivian's coworkers, experienced an extreme version of this cycle. The mother of a four-year-old, she worked nine-hour days, six days a week, to pay for seventy-seven acres of land, a camper truck, and a $40,000 boat the family had been out on once all summer. As Joann explained,

> My father sometimes worked twenty hours at the plant and would be back four hours later. My mother worked a lot of doubles, too. So I had to cook and take care of my brother, which I hated. Now, I guess I'm doing the same. This past year, I worked twelve hours a day for eight months, rotating shift.

Her husband Paul often found these hours hard to handle. Since they had so little time together, she didn't want to waste it cooking at home.

> We take the kids to Burger King, McDonald's, Friendly's. We went out last night because my sisters were in town. We had some drinks and dinner. That was the first time we'd been out with no kids in over a year. Paul really loosened up. He was surprised. He said, "I . . . am . . . having . . . a . . . good . . . time!"

Most of all, her long hours were hard on her four-year-old son, Lewis. Given her schedule, Joann saw Lewis only one day a week for any length of time, and that changed how she treated him.

> I'm not going to spend that day being the bad guy. So I let Lewis get away with a lot. I'm paying for it now, because he's become a rude brat. Not to Paul, just to me.

Joann had herself been alternately neglected and indulged by workaholic parents. Just as she'd been given toys and ice cream instead of parental time, so she gave gifts to Lewis to substitute for missing time. Complicating matters further was the fact that Paul's two children, aged eleven and nine, lived with the Redmans every other weekend.

> There are days I resent paying for Paul's two kids. I resent being the "dad" who works long hours. I felt guilty that I went back to work when Lewis was six weeks old, back to twelve-hour days, six-day weeks. I'm like my dad who missed a big part of my growing up. But maybe it's worth it. I want to give this seventy-seven acres to Lewis and my stepchildren.

What worried Joann about her overwork, about being "the dad," was that she didn't quite know why she was doing it. None of her explanations satisfied her. "The money's nice; but it's not worth it when you live at work," she concluded. But at the same time, she wasn't changing her hours. For a while, as she brooded about this, she fell into a private after-work ritual:

> When I work the 3 P.M. to 11 P.M. shift, Paul and Lewis are asleep by the time I'm home. I went through a period when I'd stop at the store to buy a six-pack of beer, put it in the car, and drive around for an hour on old country roads, pull up a half-mile from the house, sit and drink maybe two beers. I'd ask myself, "Is this really what I want? Do I want to uproot Lewis and be a single mother? Do I want to be free?" Paul didn't know I did this, and I got scared on those country roads by myself. I'd forget about it until the next time, and then I'd do it again. For a long time, I thought I was losing my mind.

At work, Becky Winters found some solace from the pain of her traumatic divorce. Vivian Goodman found relief from her rescue missions at home. But Joann Redman, who worked an even longer day, couldn't figure out why she was working so hard. It made me wonder how many other people were driving around their own "country roads" at midnight, asking themselves why their lives are the way they are, never quite grasping the link between their desire for escape and a company's desire for profit.

Who Cares for America's Babies?

(2008)

JANIS PRINCE INNISS

As a faculty member at a large university (that is, I have a good job with health benefits), if I adopt or give birth to a baby, I am entitled to about three months (twelve weeks to be exact) of leave. That means that if I work right up to the time I give birth, I can return to work when my baby is three months old.

Today, returning to work a few months after having a baby is not at all unusual. Have a look at the figure below. I would be like many first-time mothers of infants, more of whom return to work than do not. Over the last several decades, increasing numbers of women return to work after giving birth, and they do so sooner and sooner after giving birth. Of the 1961–1965 cohort of first-time mothers who worked during their pregnancy, only 17 percent went back to work when their babies were three months old. In fact, at that time, only a quarter of mothers went back to work when their babies were twelve months old. The trend of mothers returning to work accelerated in the early 1980s, when about half of all mothers with babies over three months old had returned to work. Beginning in the late 1990s, between 60 and 80 percent of women who worked during pregnancy returned to work three to twelve months after having their first babies. What do you think explains such a change in women's participation in the labor force after giving birth?

Across the world, countries handle parental leave quite differently. The United States and Australia are the only two industrialized countries in the world without paid maternity leave, although Australia offers 52 weeks of unpaid leave to all working women, in comparison to the twelve weeks *eligible* women get in the United States. In the United Kingdom, women are entitled to 52 weeks of maternity leave, 39 of which may be paid. This is true regardless of how long they have been employed. Women in Canada look forward to seventeen to eighteen weeks of maternity leave, with at least 55 percent of their salary, while parents in Sweden can share sixteen months of parental leave at 80 percent pay.

I should point out that the three months I could spend with my baby would be unpaid. I would have to use some or all of my accrued sick or vacation time to remain in a paid status for some or all of that time, and of course if I had amassed more leave, I could use that to stay home longer. I am guaranteed these three months of leave every 12 months as a result of the Family and Medical Leave Act (FMLA), passed in 1993. FMLA was passed to allow American workers job security when they have to attend to family and medical care needs. Once they meet

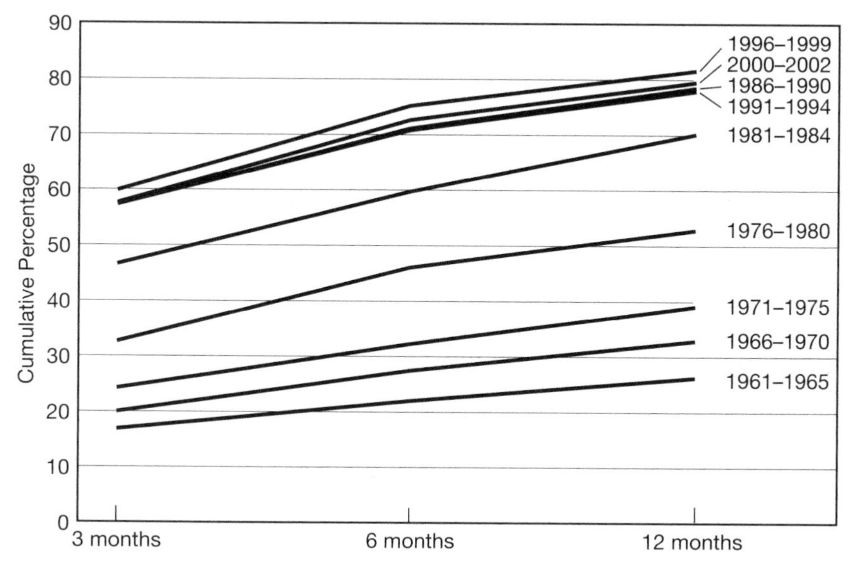

Source: www.census.gov/prod/2008pubs/p70-113.pdf

Percentage of Women Working after the Birth of Their First Child

the FMLA criteria, employers cannot deny FMLA leave nor can its use be a reason for termination.

My husband is also eligible for FMLA leave, since it is available for both men and women. I was surprised to learn that FMLA does not apply to all American workers, however. I learned about this when a relative told me that because she worked at a small firm, she would get no maternity leave. FMLA does not apply to employers of fewer than 50 employees. With little vacation or sick leave available, my relative returned to work when her daughter was a few weeks old, leaving her baby with a sitter.

How many children are being cared for by people other than their parents in the United States? The figure above shows that the majority of children in childcare are in centers. This is true even for infants and toddlers, of whom 53 percent and 60 percent, respectively, are in centers.

The implications of mothers of infants returning to work early are many, and are not only personal. Clearly, family economics is a major factor, as is work productivity. But beyond that, think about an issue like breastfeeding that may seem highly personal. In the United States there are no federal workplace protections for breastfeeding women, while in other countries there are. Breastfeeding is easier for mothers at home with their babies and has many advantages for mother and baby, including reducing infant mortality; the health benefits or costs associated with breastfeeding affect more than any individual family. Can you think of some ways that illness affects society?

Average Monthly Percentage of Children in Child Care by Age Category and Type of Care (Federal Fiscal Year 2006)

Age Group	Child's Home	Family Home	Group Home	Center
Infants (0 to <1 yr)	7%	35%	5%	53%
Toddlers (1 yr to <3 yrs)	6%	28%	6%	60%
Preschool (3 yrs to <6 yrs)	5%	25%	4%	66%
School Age (6 yrs to <13 yrs)	11%	34%	5%	50%
13 years and older	21%	48%	3%	28%
All Ages	7%	30%	5%	58%

Source: U.S Dept of Health and Human Services

As a contrast to U.S. policies, I have briefly described a few models of how motherhood and paid work are combined from different countries. Thinking of these, whose responsibility do you think it is to help women combine motherhood and paid work? Is it a personal responsibility? That of society? One for employers to tackle? At what point does a problem faced by millions move from an individual problem to a societal one?

Related links

Global picture of family leave:
unstats.un.org/unsd/demographic/products/indwm/ww2005/tab5c.htm

Maternity leave in the U.K.:
www.direct.gov.uk/en/Parents/Moneyandworkentitlements/Parentalleaveandpay/DG_10029285

U.S. Family and Medical Leave Act: www.dol.gov/esa/whd/fmla/

MSNBC story on work/family balance: www.msnbc.msn.com/id/16907584

American Academy of Pediatrics (AAP) statement on breastfeeding:
aappolicy.aappublications.org/cgi/content/full/pediatrics;115/2/496

[White-collar Downward Mobility]

(2005)

BARBARA EHRENREICH

Because I've written a lot about poverty, I'm used to hearing from people in scary circumstances. An eviction notice has arrived. A child has been diagnosed with a serious illness and the health insurance has run out. The car has broken down and there's no way to get to work. These are the routine emergencies that plague the chronically poor. But it struck me, starting in about 2002, that many such tales of hardship were coming from people who were once members in good standing of the middle class—college graduates and former occupants of mid-level white-collar positions. One such writer upbraided me for what she saw as my neglect of hardworking, virtuous people like herself.

> Try investigating people like me who didn't have babies in high school, who made good grades, who work hard and don't kiss a lot of ass and instead of getting promoted or paid fairly must regress to working for $7/hr., having their student loans in perpetual deferment, living at home with their parents, and generally exist in debt which they feel they may never get out of.

Stories of white-collar downward mobility cannot be brushed off as easily as accounts of blue-collar economic woes, which the hard-hearted traditionally blame on "bad choices": failing to get a college degree, for example, failing to postpone child-bearing until acquiring a nest egg, or failing to choose affluent parents in the first place. But distressed white-collar people cannot be accused of fecklessness of any kind; they are the ones who "did everything right." They earned higher degrees, often setting aside their youthful passion for philosophy or music to suffer through dull practical majors like management or finance. In some cases, they were high achievers who ran into trouble precisely because they had risen far enough in the company for their salaries to look like a tempting cost cut. They were the losers, in other words, in a classic game of bait and switch. And while blue-collar poverty has become numbingly routine, white-collar unemployment—and the poverty that often results—remains a rude finger in the face of the American dream.

I realized that I knew very little about the mid- to upper levels of the corporate world, having so far encountered this world almost entirely through its low-wage, entry-level representatives. I was one of them—a server in a national chain restaurant, a cleaning person, and a Wal-Mart "associate"—in the course of researching an earlier book, *Nickel and Dimed: On (Not) Getting By in America*.[1] Like everyone else, I've also encountered the corporate world as a consumer, dealing with people quite far down in the occupational hierarchy—retail clerks, customer service representatives, telemarketers. Of the levels where decisions are made—where the vice presidents, account executives, and regional managers dwell—my experience has been limited to seeing these sorts of people on airplanes, where they study books on "leadership," fiddle with spreadsheets on their laptops, or fall asleep over biographies of the founding fathers.[2] I'm better acquainted with the corporate functionaries of the future, many of whom I've met on my visits to college campuses, where "business" remains the most popular major, if only because it is believed to be the safest and most lucrative.[3]

But there have been growing signs of trouble—if not outright misery—within the white-collar corporate workforce. First, starting with the economic downturn of 2001, there has been a rise in unemployment among highly credentialed and experienced people. In late 2003, when I started this project, unemployment was running at about 5.9 percent, but in contrast to earlier economic downturns, a sizable portion—almost 20 percent, or about 1.6 million—of the unemployed were white-collar professionals.[4] Previous downturns had disproportionately hit blue-collar people; this time it was the relative elite of professional, technical, and managerial employees who were being singled out for media sympathy. In April 2003, for example, the *New York Times Magazine* offered a much-discussed cover story about a former $300,000-a-year computer industry executive reduced, after two years of unemployment, to working as a sales associate at the Gap.[5] Throughout the first four years of the 2000s, there were similar stories of the mighty or the mere midlevel brought low, ejected from their office suites and forced to serve behind the counter at Starbucks.

Today, white-collar job insecurity is no longer a function of the business cycle—rising as the stock market falls and declining again when the numbers improve.[6] Nor is it confined to a few volatile sectors like telecommunications or technology,

1. (2001). New York: Metropolitan Books. [*Editor's note*]

2. Even fiction—my favorite source of insight into cultures and times remote from my own—was no help. While the fifties and sixties had produced absorbing novels about white-collar corporate life, including Richard Yates's *Revolutionary Road* and Sloan Wilson's *The Man in the Gray Flannel Suit*, more recent novels and films tend to ignore the white-collar corporate work world except as a backdrop to sexual intrigue.

3. National Center for Educational Statistics, http://nces.ed.gov/pubs2004/2004018.pdf.

4. According to the Bureau of Labor Statistics, women are only slightly more likely than men to be unemployed—6.1 percent compared to 5.7 percent—and white women, like myself, are about half as likely as black women to be unemployed (www.bls.gov).

5. Jonathan Mahler, "Commute to Nowhere," *New York Times Magazine*, April 13, 2003.

6. I was particularly enlightened by Jill Andresky Fraser's *White Collar Sweatshop: The Deterioration of Work and Its Rewards in Corporate America* (New York: Norton, 2001) and Richard Sennett's *The Corrosion of Character: The Personal Consequences of Work in the New Capitalism* (New York: Norton, 1998).

or a few regions of the country like the rust belt or Silicon Valley. The economy may be looking up, the company may be raking in cash, and still the layoffs continue, like a perverse form of natural selection, weeding out the talented and successful as well as the mediocre. Since the midnineties, this perpetual winnowing process has been institutionalized under various euphemisms such as "downsizing," "right-sizing," "smart-sizing," "restructuring," and "de-layering"—to which we can now add the outsourcing of white-collar functions to cheaper labor markets overseas.

In the metaphor of the best-selling business book of the first few years of the twenty-first century, the "cheese"—meaning a stable, rewarding, job—has indeed been moved. A 2004 survey of executives found 95 percent expecting to move on, voluntarily or otherwise, from their current jobs, and 68 percent concerned about unexpected firings and layoffs.[7] You don't, in other words, have to lose a job to feel the anxiety and despair of the unemployed.

7. Harvey Mackay, *We Got Fired! And It's the Best Thing That Ever Happened to Us* (New York: Ballantine, 2004), p. 94.

Getting a Job

Weak Social Ties and Online Connections (2008)

BRADLEY WRIGHT

Last summer my wife was looking for a summer job, and she did the usual things—read employment bulletins and sent out applications. Ultimately, though, she got a job through an acquaintance. We see this person a few times a year, and she heads up an administrative unit here on campus. My wife applied, got the job, and we all lived happily after.

This story illustrates the somewhat cynical mantra of all job seekers that it's not what you know but who you know. Sociologists call this phenomenon the strength of weak ties.

A "weak" social tie, in everyday language, is an acquaintanceship—someone with whom you are familiar but not too close. In contrast, a "strong" tie would be a good friend or close family member, someone with whom you interact a lot. An "absent" tie would be someone you know but don't really have any kind of relationship with.

In a famous sociological study, Mark Granovetter interviewed several hundred businesspeople and asked them how they got their jobs. Seventeen percent reported learning about their jobs from a close friend (strong tie), 28% reported learning about it from someone they barely knew (absent tie), and a full 56% of the respondents reported learning about it from an acquaintance (weak tie).[1]

It's a bit of a paradox: Why are acquaintances, people we sort of know, more important in the job search process than our close friends and family? Our strong ties, after all, care about us more and would be much more willing to help us.

The answer, according to Granovetter, is that weak ties are a unique social resource: they connect us with a wider set of social networks than do social ties. Your acquaintances each have their own strong ties—family and friends to whom they are very close. Through your acquaintances, you gain access to their strong ties—and to the social networks to which they belong. All social networks offer various resources, such as information about job opportunities, and so by connecting with a greater number of social networks, via weak social ties, you gain access to more possible employment opportunities.

Strong ties, in contrast, connect us with fewer social networks. Your best friend in the world would probably do anything for you, but chances are that the

---

1. Mark Granovetter, "The Strength of Weak Ties," *American Journal of Sociology* 78 (1973): 1360–80.

two of you know many of the same people. As such, it's not that your close friends and family don't want to help you in a job search; it's just that they have less to offer because you probably already know about most of the contacts they have. You already share many of the same networks. So, there's a tradeoff: Strong ties are more willing and available to offer help, but weak ties typically have more resources to offer.

In this context, it's interesting to think about the many social ties created by the Internet. About a year ago, I started blogging, and through that I have had contact with dozens, if not hundreds, of people with similar personal and research interests. Likewise, most college students have Facebook accounts in order to keep track of their friends and make friends with their friends' friends (got that?). As a result of this online networking, this generation may have more casual social ties than any before.

The question, then, becomes the nature of these online ties. Granovetter studied fairly conventional acquaintances—people you see in person at, for example, work or social gatherings. Online acquaintances are different. If I met some of the people I know from online, I don't think that I would even recognize them. Yes, we've exchanged many comments on our blogs, and I know a fair amount of information about them—how they think, what they do—but I've never met them in person.

Would these online ties be as useful in a job search? The answer is . . . I don't know. The focus of these online relationships is social networking, getting to know each other pretty much for the sake of getting to know each other. The interactions with these people tend to be more social—what you're doing, what interests you have in common. I'm not sure how often instrumental concerns come up. In everyday conversation, it's easy to drop in the information that you're looking for a job, but it might fit more awkwardly in online interactions.

Perhaps more important, though, is that the social networks and resources offered by online connections are often too distant to be of much value. For example, one of the people I interact with online lives in Kenya. Now, he may know of great job opportunities for me and be very willing to help, but unless I'm willing to relocate to Africa they don't do me much good. This may be why in-person acquaintances remain so important—by virtue of meeting them face-to-face, you occupy the same physical location, at least briefly. Chances are, therefore, that the social resources they have to offer would also be close and thus of greater value.

So, do you want to get a job? Make sure to let your acquaintances know, since they may be very helpful. Your online connections might be as well, but probably not as much.

Hitting Them Hardest When They're Small

(2005)

JONATHAN KOZOL

Dear Mr. Kozol," said the eight-year-old, "we do not have the things you have. You have Clean things. We do not have. You have a clean bathroom. We do not have that. You have Parks and we do not have Parks. You have all the thing and we do not have all the thing. . . . Can you help us?"

The letter, from a child named Alliyah, came in a fat envelope of 27 letters from a class of third grade children in the Bronx. Other letters that the students in Alliyah's classroom sent me registered some of the same complaints. "We don't have no gardens," and "no Music or Art," and "no fun places to play," one child said. "Is there a way to fix this Problem?" Another noted a concern one hears from many children in such overcrowded schools: "We have a gym but it is for lining up. I think it is not fair." Yet another of Alliyah's classmates asked me, with a sweet misspelling, if I knew the way to make her school into a "good" school—"like the other kings have"—and ended with the hope that I would do my best to make it possible for "all the kings" to have good schools.

The letter that affected me the most, however, had been written by a child named Elizabeth. "It is not fair that other kids have a garden and new things. But we don't have that," said Elizabeth. "I wish that this school was the most beautiful school in the whole why world."

Elizabeth had very careful, very small, and neatly formed handwriting. She had corrected other errors in her letter, squeezing in a missing letter she'd initially forgotten, erasing and rewriting a few words she had misspelled. The error she had left unaltered in the final sentence therefore captured my attention more than it might otherwise have done.

"The whole why world" stayed in my thoughts for days. When I later met Elizabeth I brought her letter with me, thinking I might see whether, in reading it aloud, she'd change the "why" to "wide" or leave it as it was. My visit to her class, however, proved to be so pleasant, and the children seemed so eager to bombard me with their questions about where I lived, and why I lived there rather than New York, and who I lived with, and how many dogs I had, and other interesting questions of that sort, that I decided not to interrupt the nice reception they had given me with questions about usages and spelling. I left "the whole why world" to float around unedited and unrevised within my mind. The letter itself soon found a resting place up on the wall above my desk.

In the years before I met Elizabeth, I had visited many elementary schools in the South Bronx and in one northern district of the Bronx as well. I had also made a number of visits to a high school where a stream of water flowed down one of the main stairwells on a rainy afternoon and where green fungus molds were growing in the office where the students went for counseling. A large blue barrel was positioned to collect rain-water coming through the ceiling. In one make-shift elementary school housed in a former skating rink next to a funeral parlor in another nearly all-black-and-Hispanic section of the Bronx, class size rose to 34 and more; four kindergarten classes and a sixth grade class were packed into a single room that had no windows. Airlessness was stifling in many rooms; and recess was impossible because there was no outdoor playground and no indoor gym, so the children had no place to play.

In another elementary school, which had been built to hold 1,000 children but was packed to bursting with some 1,500 boys and girls, the principal poured out his feelings to me in a room in which a plastic garbage bag had been attached somehow to cover part of the collapsing ceiling. "This," he told me, pointing to the garbage bag, then gesturing around him at the other indications of decay and disrepair one sees in ghetto schools much like it elsewhere, "would not happen to white children."

A friend of mine who was a first-year teacher in a Harlem high school told me she had 40 students in her class but only 30 chairs, so some of her students had to sit on windowsills or lean against the walls. Other high schools were so crowded they were forced to shorten schooldays and to cut back hours of instruction to accommodate a double shift of pupils. Tens of thousands of black and Hispanic students were in schools like these, in which half the student body started classes very early in the morning and departed just before or after lunch, while the other half did not begin their schoolday until noon.

Libraries, once one of the glories of the New York City system, were either nonexistent or, at best, vestigial in large numbers of the elementary schools. Art and music programs had for the most part disappeared as well. "When I began to teach in 1969," the principal of an elementary school in the South Bronx reported to me, "every school had a full-time licensed art and music teacher and librarian." During the next decade, he recalled, "I saw all of that destroyed."

School physicians were also removed from elementary schools during these years. In 1970, when substantial numbers of white children still attended New York City's schools, 400 doctors had been present to address the health needs of the children. By 1993, the number of doctors had been cut to 23, most of them part-time—a cutback that affected most acutely children in the city's poorest neighborhoods where medical provision was perennially substandard and health problems faced by children most extreme. . . .

Political leaders in New York tended to point to shifting economic factors, such as a serious budget crisis in the middle 1970s, rather than to the changing racial demographics of the student population, as the explanation for these steep declines in services. But the fact of economic ups and downs from year to year, or from one decade to the next, could not convincingly explain the permanent short-changing of the city's students, which took place routinely in good economic times and bad, with bad times seized upon politically to justify these cuts while, in the good times, losses undergone during the crisis years had never been restored.

"If you close your eyes to the changing racial composition of the schools and look only at budget actions and political events," says Noreen Connell, the director of the nonprofit Educational Priorities Panel in New York, "you're missing the assumptions that are underlying these decisions." When minority parents ask for something better for their kids, she says, "the assumption is that these are parents who can be discounted. These are kids that we don't value."

The disrepair and overcrowding of these schools in the South Bronx "wouldn't happen for a moment in a white suburban school district like Scarsdale," says former New York State Commissioner of Education Thomas Sobol, who was once the superintendent of the Scarsdale schools and is now a professor of education at Teachers College in New York. "I'm aware that I could never prove that race is at the heart of this if I were called to testify before a legislative hearing. But I've felt it for so long, and seen it operating for so long, I know it's true. . . ."

During the 1990s, physical conditions in some buildings had become so dangerous that a principal at one Bronx school, which had been condemned in 1989 but nonetheless continued to be used, was forced to order that the building's windows not be cleaned because the frames were rotted and glass panes were falling in the street, while at another school the principal had to have the windows bolted shut for the same reason. These were not years of economic crisis in New York. This was a period in which financial markets soared and a new generation of free-spending millionaires and billionaires was widely celebrated by the press and on TV; but none of the proceeds of this period of economic growth had found their way into the schools that served the truly poor.

I had visited many schools in other cities by this time; but I did not know children in those schools as closely as I'd come to know, or soon would know, so many of the children in the New York City schools. So it would be these children, and especially the ones in elementary schools in which I spent the most time in the Bronx, whose sensibilities and puzzlements and understandings would impress themselves most deeply on my own impressions in the years to come, and it would be their questions that became my questions and their accusations and their challenges, when it appeared that they were making challenges, that came to be my own.

In a social order where it seems a fairly common matter to believe that what we spend to purchase almost anything we need bears some connection to the worth of what we get, a look at what we think it's in our interest to invest in children like Alliyah may not tell us everything we need to know about the state of educational fair play within our nation, but it surely tells us *something* about what we think these kids are worth to us in human terms and in the contributions they may someday make to our society. At the time I met Alliyah in the school-year 1997–1998, New York's Board of Education spent about $8,000 yearly on the education of a third grade child in a New York City public school. If you could have scooped Alliyah up out of the neighborhood where she was born and plunked her down within a fairly typical white suburb of New York, she would have received a public education worth about $12,000 every year. If you were to lift her up once more and set her down within one of the wealthiest white suburbs of New York, she would have received as much as $18,000 worth of public education every year and would likely have had a third grade teacher paid approximately $30,000 more than was her teacher in the Bronx.

The dollars on both sides of the equation have increased since then, but the discrepancies between them have not greatly changed. The present per-pupil spending level in the New York City schools is $11,700, which may be compared to a per-pupil spending level in excess of $22,000 in the well-to-do suburban district of Manhasset. The present New York City level is, indeed, almost exactly what Manhasset spent per pupil 18 years ago, in 1987, when that sum of money bought a great deal more in services and salaries than it can buy today. In dollars adjusted for inflation, New York City has not yet caught up to where its wealthiest suburbs were a quarter-century ago.

Even these numbers that compare the city to its suburbs cannot give an adequate impression of the inequalities imposed upon the children living in poor sections of New York. For, even within the New York City schools themselves, there are additional discrepancies in funding between schools that serve the poorest and the wealthiest communities, since teachers with the least seniority and least experience are commonly assigned to schools in the most deeply segregated neighborhoods. . . .

None of this includes the additional resources given to the public schools in affluent communities where parents have the means to supplement the public funds with private funding of their own, money used to build and stock a good school library for instance, or to arrange for art and music lessons or, in many of these neighborhoods, to hire extra teachers to reduce the size of classes for their children.

This relatively new phenomenon of private money being used selectively to benefit the children only of specific public schools had not been noted widely in New York until about ten years ago when parents of the students at a public school in Greenwich Village in Manhattan raised the funds to pay a fourth grade teacher, outside of the normal budget of the school, when class size in the ourth grade otherwise was likely to increase from 26 to 32, which was the average class size in the district at the time but which, one of the parents said, "would have a devastating impact" on her son. The parents, therefore, collected $46,000—two thirds of it, remarkably, in just one night—in order to retain the extra teacher.

The school in Greenwich Village served a population in which less than 20 percent of students were from families of low income, a very low figure in New York . . . The Greenwich Village school, moreover, was already raising a great deal of private money—more than $100,000 yearly, it was now revealed—to pay for music, art, and science programs and for furniture repairs.

The chancellor of the New York City schools initially rejected the use of private funds to underwrite a teacher's pay, making the argument that this was not fair to the children in those many other schools that had much larger classes; but the district later somehow came up with the public funds to meet the cost of hiring the extra teacher, so the parents won their children the advantage they had sought for them in any case.

As it turned out, the use of private subsidies to supplement the tax-supported budgets of some schools in affluent communities was a more commonly accepted practice than most people in the city's poorest neighborhoods had known. The PTA at one school on the Upper West Side of Manhattan, for example, had been raising nearly $50,000 yearly to hire a writing teacher and two part-time music teachers. At a school in a middle-class section of Park Slope in Brooklyn, parents raised more than $100,000 yearly to employ a science teacher and two art instructors. In yet another neighborhood, parents at an elementary school and junior high had raised more than $1 million, mostly for enrichment programs for their children.

In principle, the parents in poor neighborhoods were free to do fund-raising too, but the proceeds they were likely to bring in differed dramatically. The PTA in one low-income immigrant community, for instance, which sponsored activities like candy sales and tried without success to win foundation grants, was able to raise less than $4,000. In the same year, parents at P.S. 6, a top-rated elementary school serving the Upper East Side of Manhattan, raised $200,000. The solicitation of private funds from parents in communities like this had come to be so common, said the president of the New York City Board of Education, "you almost expect a notice from the schools saying there's going to be tuition." A good deal of private money, moreover, as the *Times* observed, was "being collected under the table" because parents sometimes feared that they would otherwise be forced to share these funds with other schools. "We can do it," said the leader of the parent group at one of the schools where lavish sums of private money had been raised, "but it is sad that other schools that don't have a richer parent body can't. It really does make it a question of haves and have-nots."

In view of the extensive coverage of this new phenomenon not only by New York City papers but by those in other cities where the same trends are observed, it is apparent that this second layer of disparities between the children of the wealthy and the children of the poor is no secret to the public any longer.

Yet, even while they sometimes are officially deplored, these added forms of inequality have been accepted with apparent equanimity by those who are their beneficiaries.

"Inequality is not an intentional thing," said the leader of the PTA in one of the West Side neighborhoods where parents had been raising private funds, some of which had been obtained as charitable grants. "You have schools that are empowered and you have schools that have no power at all. . . . I don't bear any guilt for knowing how to write a grant," he said, a statement that undoubtedly made sense to some but skirted the entire issue of endemic underbudgeting of public schools attended by the children of poor people who did not enjoy his money-raising skills or possible connections to grant makers.

A narrowing of civic virtue to the borders of distinct and self-contained communities is now evolving in these hybrid institutions which are public schools in that they benefit from the receipt of public funds but private in the many supplementary programs that are purchased independently. Boutique schools within an otherwise impoverished system, they enable parents of the middle class and upper middle class to claim allegiance to the general idea of public schools while making sure their children do not suffer gravely for the stripped-down budgets that have done great damage to poor children like Alliyah.

In New York City, affluent parents pay surprisingly large sums of money to enroll their youngsters in extraordinary early-education programs, typically beginning at the age of two or three, that give them social competence and rudimentary pedagogic skills unknown to children of the same age in the city's poorer neighborhoods. The most exclusive of the private preschools in New York, which are known to those who can afford them as the "Baby Ivies," cost as much as $22,000 for a full-day program. Competition for admission to these pre-K schools is so intense that "private counselors" are frequently retained, at fees as high as $300 hourly, according to the *Times,* to guide the parents through the application process.

At the opposite extreme along the economic spectrum in New York are thousands of children who receive no preschool opportunity at all. Exactly how *many* thousands is almost impossible to know. Numbers that originate in governmental agencies in New York and other states are incomplete and imprecise and do not always differentiate with clarity between authentic pre-K programs that have educative and developmental substance and those less expensive childcare arrangements that do not. But even where states do compile numbers that refer specifically to educative preschool programs, it is difficult to know how many of the children who are served are of low income since admissions to some of the state-supported programs aren't determined by low income or they are determined by a complicated set of factors of which poverty is only one.

There is another way, however, to obtain a fairly vivid sense of what impoverished four-year-olds receive in segregated sections of our cities like the Bronx.

This is by asking kids themselves while you are with them in a kindergarten class to tell you how they spent their time the year before—or, if the children get confused or are too shy to give you a clear answer, then by asking the same question to their teacher.

"How many of these children were in pre-K programs last year or the last two years?" I often ask a kindergarten teacher.

In middle- and upper-class suburbs, a familiar answer is "more than three quarters of them," "this year, almost all of them," or "virtually all. . . ." In poor urban neighborhoods, by comparison, what I more often hear is "only a handful," "possibly as many as a fourth," "maybe about a third of them got *something* for one year. . . ."

Government data and the estimates of independent agencies tend to substantiate the estimates of principals and teachers. Of approximately 250,000 four-year-olds in New York State in 2001–2002, only about 25 percent, some 60,000, were believed to be enrolled in the state-funded preschool program—which is known as "Universal Pre-K" nonetheless—and typically in two-and-a-half-hour sessions rather than the more extended programs children of middle-class families usually attend. Then too, because these figures were not broken down by family income levels and because the program did not give priority to children of low income, it was difficult to know how many children in the poorest neighborhoods had been excluded from the program.

Head Start, which is a federal program, is of course much better known than New York's Universal Pre-K and it has a long track-record, having been created 40 years ago by Congress at a time when social programs that expanded opportunities for children of low income were not viewed with the same skepticism that is common among many people who set public policy today. In spite of the generally high level of approval Head Start has received over the years, whether for its academic benefits or for its social benefits, or both, 40 percent of three- and four-year-olds who qualified for Head Start by their parents' income were denied this opportunity in 2001, a percentage of exclusion that has risen steeply in the subsequent four years. In some of the major cities, where the need is greatest, only a tiny fraction of low-income children in this age bracket are served. In New York City, for example, less than 13,000 four-year-olds were served by Head Start in 2001; and, in many cases, Head Start was combined with Universal Pre-K, so the children served by Head Start on its own were relatively few.

There are exceptions to this pattern in some sections of the nation. In Milwaukee, for example, nearly every four-year-old is now enrolled in a preliminary kindergarten program, which amounts to a full year of all-day preschool education, prior to a second kindergarten year for five-year-olds, according to the superintendent of Milwaukee's schools. In New Jersey, full-day pre-K programs have been instituted for all three- and four-year-olds in 31 low-income districts, one of the consequences of a legal action to reduce inequities of education in that state. More commonly in urban neighborhoods, large numbers of children have received no preschool education and they come into their kindergarten year without the minimal social skills that children need in order to participate in class activities and without even such very modest early-learning skills as knowing how to hold a pencil, identify perhaps a couple of shapes or colors, or recognize that printed pages go from left to right. A first grade teacher in Boston pointed out a child in her class who had received no preschool and, as I recall, had missed much of his kindergarten year as well, and introduced me to the boy so I could sit beside him for a while and derive my own conclusions, then confirmed my first impression when she told me in a whisper, "He's a sweetheart of a baby but knows almost absolutely nothing about anything that has to do with school!"

In third grade, these children are introduced to what are known as "high-stakes tests," which in many urban systems now determine whether students can or cannot be promoted. Children who have been in programs like the "Baby Ivies" since the age of two have been given seven years of education by this point, nearly twice as many as the children who have been denied these opportunities; yet all are required to take, and will be measured and in many cases penalized severely by, the same examinations.

Which of these children will receive the highest scores—those who spent the years from two to four in lovely little Montessori schools and other pastel-painted settings in which tender and attentive grown-ups read to them from storybooks and introduced them for the first time to the world of numbers, and the shapes of letters, and the sizes and varieties of solid objects, and perhaps taught them to sort things into groups or to arrange them in a sequence, or to do those many other interesting things that early-childhood specialists refer to as prenumeracy skills, or the ones who spent those years at home in front of a TV or sitting by the window of a slum apartment gazing down into the street? There is something deeply hypocritical in a society that holds an inner-city child only eight years old "accountable" for her performance on a high-stakes standardized exam but does not hold the high officials of our government accountable for robbing her of what they gave their own kids six or seven years before.

There are obviously other forces that affect the early school performance of low-income children: levels of parent education, social instability, and frequently undiagnosed depression and anxiety that make it hard for many parents I have known to take an active role in backing up the efforts of their children's teachers in the public schools. Still, it is all too easy to assign the primary onus of responsibility to parents in these neighborhoods. (Where were these parents educated after all? Usually in the same low-ranking schools their children now attend.) In a nation in which fairness was respected, children of the poorest and least educated mothers would receive the most extensive and most costly preschool preparation, not the least and cheapest, because children in these families need it so much more than those whose educated parents can deliver the same benefits of early learning to them in their homes.

The "Baby Ivies" of Manhattan are not public institutions and receive no subsidies from public funds. In a number of cities, on the other hand, even this last line of squeamishness has now been crossed and public funds are being used to underwrite part of the costs of preschool education for the children of the middle class in public institutions which, however, do not offer the same services to children of the poor. Starting in spring 2001, Chicago's public schools began to operate a special track of preschool for the children of those families who were able to afford to pay an extra fee—nearly $6,000—to provide their children with a full-day program of about 11 hours, starting at the age of two if parents so desired. In a city where 87 percent of students in the public schools were black or Hispanic, the pay-for-preschool program served primarily white children.

. . . At some of the well-known private prep schools in the New York City area, tuition and associated costs are typically more than $20,000. In their children's teenage years [parents] sometimes send [their children] off to boarding schools like Andover or Exeter or Groton, where tuition, boarding, and additional expenses rise to more than $30,000. Often a family has two teenage children in these schools at the same time; so they may be spending over $60,000 on their children's education every year. Yet here I am one night, a guest within their home, and dinner has been served and we are having coffee now; and this entirely likable, and generally sensible, and beautifully refined and thoughtful person looks me in the eyes and asks me whether you can really buy your way to better education for the children of the poor.

Civility, of course, controls these situations. One rarely gets to give the answer one would like to give in social settings of this kind. And sometimes, too, the people who have asked these questions make it apparent, in an almost saddened afterthought, that they are not appeased entirely by the doubts they've raised, because before the evening's over and once every other argument is made and the discussion at long last begins to wind down to its end, a concessionary comment seems to find its way into the conversation. "Well, that's how it is. . . . Life isn't fair. . . . We do the best we can, in other ways. . . ." Sometimes, then, a charitable activity is named. "Our daughter's private school insists that every student do a service project for one year. . . ." "They tutor children at an elementary school in one of the disadvantaged neighborhoods . . . ," or something else that's decent, philanthropic, and sincere like that, which smoothes the edges of the evening.

References to service programs, mentoring and tutoring and such, provide at least a hint of what fair-minded people often wish that they could do on a more comprehensive basis if the means for doing it did not seem so politically complex or threaten to exact too high a toll on their immediate self-interest. Most honest grown-ups, after all, do not really get a lot of solace out of saying that "life isn't fair," especially if they can see the ways they benefit from the unfairness they deplore. Most also understand that a considerably higher level of taxation for our public schools, if equitably allocated on the basis of real need, would make it possible for far more children from poor neighborhoods to enter the admissions pool for the distinguished colleges and universities their own children attend. Some of their children might encounter stiffer competition. Children like Alliyah might get in instead.

There are others, however, who appear to suffer no uneasiness at all about these contradictions and appear to be convinced—at least, it *sounds* as if they are—that money well-invested in the education of the children of their social class makes perfect sense while spending on the same scale for the children of the very poor achieves, at best, only some marginal results, or maybe none at all. "An equal society," President George W. Bush told the National Urban League in August of 2001, would begin with "equally excellent schools." Simply increasing federal assistance to the public schools, however, had not been effective, he told his audience. It was, he said, like "pumping gas into a flooded engine," by which he seemed to mean that inner-city "engines" (schools) had too much gas (too many dollars flooding them already.

It was an odd metaphor, I thought. It would have been fair to ask the president how schools like Phillips Academy or Exeter or Andover, the latter of which he had himself attended, were able to absorb some $30,000 yearly for each pupil without "flooding" their own engines. Did they have perhaps a bigger engine to begin with? Did the beautifully developed infrastructure of these schools permit them to deploy large sums of money more effectively than did the schools with rotting window frames and no school libraries? "I'll believe money doesn't count the day the rich stop spending so much on their own children," says former New York City principal Deborah Meier, who subsequently became the principal of an elementary school in Boston; but Mrs. Meier's commonsense reaction is resisted widely among those who are in power now in Washington.

It is sometimes claimed by those who share the president's beliefs that it is possible to point to certain urban districts in which annual per-pupil spending now approximates the levels found in some adjacent middle-class communities but that the children in these districts still do not perform at nearly the same levels as the children in these neighboring communities. Highly selective examples commonly are used to press this point; and the subsequent argument is made that these examples demonstrate "the limited effects" of higher levels of investment in the education of low-income children.

There are several reasons why I've never found this a convincing argument. First, it tends to obviate almost all recognition of the consequences of the previous decades of low funding in these districts: the cumulative deficits in school construction and in infrastructure maintenance, for instance. It also ignores the deficits in preschool education and the effects of prior years of mediocre schooling on the educational levels of the parents of the children in these neighborhoods. Nor does it even contemplate the multiple effects of concentrated poverty and racial isolation in themselves.

Equitable funding levels under these conditions would not merely approximate the spending levels found in wealthier communities; they would far exceed them. And the benefits to be derived from equitable funding could not properly be measured on a short-term basis, since it would take many years before the consequences of so many prior years of organized shortchanging of the children, and their parents and grandparents, in a segregated district could be plausibly reversed. The examples of high-spending urban districts used to press the case against increasing our investment in poor children are, in any case, atypical. Nationwide, the differential in per-pupil spending between districts with the highest numbers of minority children and those with the fewest children of minorities amounts to more than $25,000 for a typical class in elementary school. In Illinois, the differential grows to $47,000, in New York to more than $50,000. From any point of elemental fairness, inequalities like these are unacceptable.

Those who search for signs of optimism often make the point that there are children who do not allow themselves to be demoralized by the conditions we have seen but do their work and keep their spirits high and often get good grades and seem, at least, to have a better chance than many of their peers to graduate from high school and go on to college—and, in any case, whether they do or not, refuse to let themselves be broken or embittered by the circumstances they may face.

I have portrayed a number of such powerfully resilient children in my recent book about the South Bronx, *Ordinary Resurrections*, and in an earlier book titled *Amazing Grace*. Other writers have portrayed such children elsewhere. There are also academic studies that examine qualities of character in inner-city children who transcend the difficult conditions of their lives, stumble at times, face disappointment and discouragement, but nonetheless persist against the odds and ultimately manage to prevail.

These expectations are not simply those, moreover, that can be attributed to the ambitions and the value systems of the parents of these children but are rooted in demonstrable advantages in what their schools provide to them: experienced instructors, reasonably small classes, well-appointed libraries, plenty of computers with sophisticated software, at the secondary level often college-level history and literature and science programs, and extensive counseling facilities, as well as the aesthetic benefits of cheerful buildings and nice places to have lunch and, in a lot of secondary schools, lovely quadrangles and courtyards where the adolescents can relax and work with one another in small groups and, especially important for the younger children, green expansive spaces to go out and play at recess so that they return to class invigorated and refreshed.

This nation can afford to give clean places and green spaces and, as one of Alliyah's classmates put it, "fun places to play" to virtually every child in our public schools. That we refuse to do so, and continue to insist that our refusal can be justified by explanations such as insufficiency of funds and periodic "fiscal crises" and the like, depends upon a claim to penury to which a nation with our economic superfluity is not entitled. If we were forced to see these kids before our eyes each day, in all the fullness of their complicated and diverse and tenderly emerging personalities, as well as in their juvenile fragility, it would be harder to maintain this myth. Keeping them at a distance makes it easier.

Globalization and Higher Education

(2008)

C. N. LE

Sociologists and other scholars around the world are talking about how the world in general and American society in particular are becoming increasingly globalized. But to many students, these concepts are rather vague and abstract. With that in mind, I'd like to use two examples—Asian/Asian American culture and higher education—to illustrate how globalization works in our society these days.

The first example concerns a Chinese-born immigrant who was educated in the United States, became infatuated with American culture, and then went back to China to start an American-style college for Chinese students. In December 2007, the *Los Angeles Times*[1] described the school:

> The school's faculty of about 700 includes 119 foreign instructors, mainly from the U.S. They teach English, history and literature and help students with debate club, cheerleading and marching band—things unheard of in this country.
>
> [Shawn] Chen went to the United States in 1985 and got a master's degree in education at Linfield College in Oregon. After attending a typical no-frills, monochrome college in China, he basked in campus life in the Pacific Northwest. . . . Chen was so taken by American culture he named his children Brandon and Brenda, after the two characters in the early 1990s TV hit "Beverly Hills, 90210."

In illustrating one example of globalization, this story is a great example of Asian Americans using their cross-national cultural ties to achieve success for both sides of their identity in Asia and America. In the process their "foreignness" is an asset, rather than a liability.

The second example also involves Asian Americans, higher education, and international migration—but in the opposite direction. We know that the competition to get into the top colleges and universities is quite intense these days. With that in mind, many Korean American students have decided to skip the U.S.

1. Don Lee, "Chinese School Is Rah-Rah for U.S.-Style Campus," *Los Angeles Times*, December 4, 2007.

entirely and instead attend top universities in South Korea. *JoongAng Daily*, a Korean newspaper, described one American student's experience:[2]

> A year ago, 19-year-old Korean-American Choi Joo-eun chose Korea's Yonsei University over the prestigious University of California system in her home state. Having gotten into both UC San Diego and UC Irvine, she had earned a place in two schools even many California teenagers dream of entering.
>
> So far she has no regrets. On campus, she takes classes taught entirely in English while spending her spare time learning Korean culture and language. Off campus, Choi, who had never visited Korea before deciding to study here, keeps busy building a new network of friends and pursuing her dream of working for the United Nations one day.

The article highlights the many advantages associated with such a process—reconnecting with one's ancestral ethnic roots, exposure to an international climate, and becoming bilingual in English and Korean. But as the last line of the quote above reveals, there can also be loneliness and cultural adjustment issues for those studying overseas.

This particular trend of Korean Americans "going back" to Korean schools is likely to accelerate in the coming years, as globalization continues to evolve and permeate more of American society.

But as the article points out, being Korean American does not automatically mean that you will have an easy time in Korea; being Asian and Asian American are two different things.

Nonetheless, being Korean American does provide another avenue of personal and academic enrichment, and that can be seen as an asset rather than a liability as we move forward into the twenty-first century.

Related links

Los Angeles Times story on Chinese school: www.latimes.com/business/la-fi-university4dec04,1,4893525.story?coll=la-default-underdog

JoongAng Daily story on Korean-American students: joongangdaily.joins.com/article/view.asp?aid=2887771

2. "Korean-Americans Come 'Home' to University," *JoongAng Daily*, March 24, 2008.

Bridging the Gap

The Split between Spirituality and Society (2006)

GREGORY C. STANCZAK

SPIRITUAL BUT NOT RELIGIOUS

It is hard not to slip into talking about spirituality and religion in dichotomous ways. . . . Once seen as complementary components of an integrated whole, religion and spirituality are increasingly interpreted as two distinct phenomena that may share occasional overlap but, for the most part, represent two diametrically opposed philosophies or feelings. The ubiquitous phrase "I'm spiritual, not religious" is most likely heartfelt for scores of Americans; however, it has become reified by detractors of spiritual individualism as a new foreboding standard, a cultural idiom of an individualized and rootless society.[1]

Robert Bellah and his colleagues in *Habits of the Heart* crystallize this perception around a new prototype dubbed "Sheilaism" after one of their interview subjects, Sheila Larson. From this perspective, church and community appear less important than experience and feeling.[2] Sheilaism soon became symptomatic of a social and cultural eclecticism in which spirituality was offered, perhaps more enticingly, in bookstores, coffee shops, television shows, and even diet fads. The gloomy prognosis was that institutional religion would wither.[3] When given these dichotomous options, it seems that spirituality would have slim potential for social change beyond its effects on religious competition and self-help hucksterism.[4] But can individuals really support such a nihilistic view of individualistic spiritual motivations among their fellow Americans? One empirically convincing answer is that they may not have to.

DEFINING SPIRITUALITY

If spirituality and religion overlap, and those who are spiritual tend to also be the same as those who are religious, what is the analytical difference between the two? How might one distinguish between spirituality and religion without artificially segregating them from each other? While undoubtedly these types of questions are batted around with much more frequency and eloquence in rabbinical schools, seminaries, and religion departments, a recently renewed debate is taking place in the social sciences, where some of the most significant definitional exploration is fomenting.[5] Summarizing a decade of conceptual work, spirituality is very often discussed as a "search for the sacred."[6] This phrase may sound overly simplistic, but it elegantly captures the core elements of a quest and of a transcendent order without adding too many doctrinal or social parameters. Of course, under this broad umbrella fall a diverse spectrum of practices, rituals, beliefs, and social contextual influences through which individuals negotiate a personal connection.

A more specifically active definition suggests that spirituality involves the "paths people take in their efforts to find, conserve, and transform the sacred in their lives."[7] Spirituality, as a search for the sacred, is not static but multidimensional, not only about finding but also about sustaining and sometimes creatively re-creating one's construction of the sacred. . . .

Additionally, while nearly all of the current conceptual definitions of spirituality allow for or even expect a compatibility with religion, they also acknowledge the broad ways in which the sacred can be perceived in, or extended to include, otherwise mundane objects, interpersonal relationships, or even, as these cases here will attest, social structural patterns such as poverty or racial discrimination. As such, spirituality, whether found in the synagogue or on the beach at sunset, has seemingly limitless applications and sources. Spirituality, then, is the active and sometimes creatively fluid attempts by individuals and groups to connect with the sacred.

There are two other dimensions to consider as well. First, spirituality is often pragmatic. Robert Wuthnow, in his study of spirituality throughout the second half of the twentieth century, argued that practice-oriented spirituality—the spirituality of the day-to-day, disciplined, and focused attempts at connection with the sacred—salvages the individual quests from the often disparaging "seeker" phenomenon of contemporary religious homelessness.[8] Practice concretizes this wandering, selfish search in practical ways that give spiritual substance, beyond moods and whims, to the profound experiences of individuals in their everyday lives. Wuthnow's practice-oriented emphasis acknowledges that through this practice day-to-day life fuses with spirituality in ways that provide a greater integration of the sacred into mundane activities or spaces.

Second, spirituality is affective or emotionally felt. In certain ways, the affective component of spiritual connection parallels the faddishly popular argument for emotions as a form of intelligence. Spiritual intelligence allows for useful traits beyond the rational standards of traditional intellectual intelligence.[9] As with intelligence, emotional resources can be crafted and honed in ways that provide an extra edge in finding meaning and developing creative solutions to life's challenges. Emotions and feelings provide one additional link between individuals and their perceptions and actions within the social world around them.[10]

This affective level can be surprisingly unexpected in practice and can produce surprisingly unexpected consequences in action.

[This chapter explores the] ways that [these threads] contribute to the understanding of socially active spirituality. First, spirituality is *transcendent*, or at least somehow directed toward communicating with something subjectively perceived to be sacred. Second, spirituality is an *active* and *ongoing* process that not only seeks out the sacred but also maintains and even changes it in one's life. Third, spirituality is *multidimensional*—traditional and/or creative, individual and/or collective. Fourth, spirituality is *unlimited* in its experience and is bound neither to time nor place nor objects, but rather is accessible in all aspects of life. Fifth, spirituality is *pragmatic*. It is both a resource and is resourceful, and as such it can be honed and utilized through active practice by individuals throughout their lives. Finally, spirituality is *emotional*, connecting individuals to their lived environments in deeply affective ways.

DEFINING SOCIAL CHANGE

The remainder of this [chapter] is devoted to unpacking the connections between the flexibility and situatedness of spirituality as it relates to social change. For the purposes of this study, "social action," "social activism," "social change," and at times "social justice" are all colloquial shorthand terms that respondents used to refer to different levels of the same basic principle: service work in society—whether on the local, the institutional, the regional, the state, or the global level—that is strategically focused and at times mandated by deeply held transcendent values to bring about change in this world. The term "social action" is most often applied to the classically considered direct service work of volunteer agencies, such as feeding the hungry, serving the poor, and administering to the sick. Of course, these somewhat cliché phrases at times take on highly complex organizational casts when dealing with the complicated issues that face modern communities.

. . . Spirituality directed toward social action is similar in many ways to other forms of spirituality, yet not all spirituality is engaged for social action and change—at least not in the way they are conceptualized here. In other words, I am not considering evangelical spiritualities that strictly profess that saving individual souls through conversion will change the world. Whether or not they are right, my interest falls upon those who act upon their spirituality explicitly to bring about changes in communities, in social or religious policies, in social services, or individually, even when it does not assume religious conversion. This form of spirituality is uniquely constructed through various social and subjective influences that merge a spirituality of the soul with a spirituality of the streets. Although the convergence of spirituality and the streets fits a contemporary social milieu, considering an earlier example grounds this analysis as more than a current trend.

◇ ◇ ◇

MIDCENTURY MODERNS

. . . [T]he natural affiliation between individual spiritual experiences and social change is by no means a recent development.[11] Across millennia and throughout cultures, radical social shifts have been the products of divinely interpreted revelations or collectively defended definitions of the transcendent "Truths" about the universe. Even within the presumably "secular" twentieth century, when conventional social wisdom championed modernism's reign and rationality characteristically shaped the United States' domestic technological and scientific development, [a spiritual perspective reveals] a very different trajectory and set of guiding principles that set the texture of social and political affairs.

[Let's consider] the Greatest Generation. As a whole, this cohort is characterized as deeply sacrificial for family and nation, courageously fighting a noble war or selflessly contributing in other ways at home. Symbolically they collectively personify and embody the staid prosperity that followed the hard times of the Great Depression. They are reconstructed through our mediated memory nostalgically and monolithically as conventional white suburban families that upheld consensual American values such as hard work and community.[12] We do not often think of this Greatest Generation as a spiritual generation in today's terms. Religious, yes, but spiritual, no.[13]

While religious affiliations were strong, members of the Greatest Generation, broadly speaking, were not known as being expressive with their personal feelings or indulgent with their experiences. Tom Brokaw's best-selling book *The Greatest Generation* set as its sole objective the documentation of personal stories by the aging members of this generation, particularly stories of war and sacrifice.[14] These stories have had an impact among family members who were often unable to draw out emotional recollections from their own parents, grandparents, aunts, or great uncles.

The same may be suggested of stories of intimately personal spiritual experiences.[15] For many of the people that I interviewed, their religious upbringing was very formulaic—a social duty performed on Saturdays or Sundays or in the form of a prayer before meals. Few had deeply expressive or individually compelling experiences growing up and fewer still witnessed, either in person or through stories, the connection between spiritual experience and social change.

However, [there is a] real possibility that a socially directed spirituality was present among an active and influential set of individuals during the middle part of the century. Not only was it present, for some it was actively applied to efforts of great proportion. . . . After all, spiritual experiences have been bubbling up throughout the history of the United States, and it stands to reason that other cyclical patterns, whether publicly acknowledged or not, effect change in other times and other places as well.[16]

◇ ◇ ◇

A SPIRITUAL RESOURCE

Apart from the seemingly broad social and historical shifts in spirituality and religion that mark reawakenings or organizational schisms in religious institutions, it is equally important to understand spirituality in its everyday manifestations that incrementally foster change locally and, at times, globally. From this perspective, spirituality is an individual and collective social resource that, while shaped and molded by social and cultural contexts, exists in the hearts and minds of some people in ways that are similar to other cultural tools used to make sense in the world and to make choices about how to act within that world. Spirituality is more aptly considered an internal yet socially shaped variable that affects individual motivations and creative innovations in actively striving for social change.[17] At times throughout history, spirituality has been constituted and wielded as a mighty tool, as was the case with the outstanding revolutionary figures of the twentieth century. More often, the effects of this spiritual tool have been local and the efforts not always so dramatically successful, although no less profound.

SPIRITUAL MARKETS

If we consider spirituality as a social resource, contemporary contexts provide a rich backdrop for accumulating these resources. One common contemporary metaphor compares the diverse religious landscape and the competition between Christian churches (and even non-Christian organizations) to a marketplace where rationally informed shoppers browse around until they find what religion they want to consume.[18] Consumption of religion from this point of view is rationally determined; the costs and benefits of attending one religious congregation are weighed much like any other decision that we make in everyday life, such as where to send our children to school or which medical insurance plan would best serve our needs.[19] Religion, in this case, is a far cry from the irrational and overly emotional delusions that early social theorists suggested. For some, religion in this marketplace becomes trivialized, reduced to whims and fads alongside any number of other lifestyle accessories.[20] Religion as an institution becomes a commodity in the service of a therapeutic society, interested primarily in self-development, expressive individualism, and a narcissistic quest for personal satisfaction.[21] Self-help groups, popular psychology, and spiritual products become booming industries in a society that continually seeks to reinvent itself one person at a time.[22]

The residual effects of this cultural trend toward therapeutic consumption spill throughout society as spirituality becomes a cultural currency. We can see this in the marketing of tell-all autobiographies, the hawking of confessional talk shows, and even in the advertising of political campaigns; all emphasize openness, sharing, and publicly exposing the wounds of our lives in an effort to heal them with the balm of full disclosure. When former President Bill Clinton released an autobiography detailing his childhood as well as his personal and public life while in office, it was touted as the most intimately revealing self-examination of any past president. Clinton was both derided and championed as a creature of his times, a new introspective public figure who discussed personal demons openly. To his critics, this was nothing but self-indulgent egoism, while his supporters credited his vulnerability and forthrightness.[23] Not surprisingly, in an act of synchronicity that illustrates the overlap of this trend between politics, media, and commodities, one of the former president's first stops on his book tour was the Oprah Winfrey show, a show that at its apex regularly dedicated portions of the hour to "Finding Your Spirit." In a market where competing daytime television programs include a show in which a self-proclaimed "medium" speaks to deceased relatives of audience members, Winfrey's introspective feel-good spirituality more closely defines the cultural, and now political, mainstream.

The spirituality of therapeutic pop culture, if we think back to the multidimensional and pragmatic aspects of our working definition, cannot be thought of as universally trivialized or universally revitalizing. While the question "What would Buffy do?" shouts out one particularly contemporary meaning,[24] the dangling keychain question of "What would Jesus do?" is equally telling of the way in which spirituality is both a faddishly individual fashion accessory and an individual imperative to constantly remind oneself of the spiritual considerations in life's choices.[25] Whether Christian punk rockers, primetime demons, or Deepak Chopra's latest best-seller are discussed jokingly, derisively, or concertedly, contemporary spirituality seems to be an unavoidable part of the popular culture detritus about which all of us can contribute our own two cents.

Confessions and self-reflections—both secular and spiritual—are part of the ubiquitous backdrop in contemporary culture and have created an atmosphere that allows for and perhaps even encourages a very public exploration of the experiential, emotional, and spiritual elements of life. The stories that I have collected illuminate one small corner of this broader arena and give voice to the ongoing ways in which a very different, critical spirituality has always been part and parcel of the American religious, civic, and popular experience.[26] Although hard to imagine from this current milieu, openly expressing that spiritual component was—and sometimes still is—seen as unbecoming, inappropriately intimate, or a matter to be relegated to private and even hidden moments of life.[27] Yet the current expressive backdrop of mainstream culture allows for greater empirical exploration of the ways in which spiritual connections are utilized in everyday life.

SHIFTING SPIRITUAL BORDERS

In the incredibly hot and dry eastern communities of greater Los Angeles, I met up with Werner Marroquin, an organizing member of La Asociación Nacional Salvadoreño-Americana, or SANA. SANA was created as a civic organization among Salvadorans living in southern California but, much more than that, Marroquin envisions SANA as a cultural repository of Salvadoran art, music, poetry, and dance, as well as a place to sustain the stories of migrants who fled the civil war at home. He explains, "We want to be able to be reminding our community that once we were persecuted. Once we were hungry. Once we were cold, and there were good hands that opened their hearts to us, and feed us, and treat us well, and gave us a space to sleep, and gave us food to eat." This history not only provides a sense of rootedness to his children and others growing up in the United States, and increasingly being born here, it also provides a moral lesson. Marroquin adds, "I think it's important for my kids to know that they were persecuted once and they have to be sensitive to future generations of immigrants, to future conflicts that are going to come, because I don't think they're going to end. And they have to have a sense of solidarity."

While having one foot still planted metaphorically in El Salvador, Marroquin is firmly committed to civic participation in his new home. He intimately knows the struggles of living underground in the United States from the days before he became a citizen. But being a citizen does not mean renouncing this past identity. Marroquin says, "We don't want to jump [into being American] with no first name or last name and with not a face and with not a history. We want to jump in there by saying who we are."

A large part of who Marroquin is involves his spiritual ties to the blended identity of the national and transcendent aspects being Salvadoran. Although Marroquin is Protestant, he feels a keen affiliation with the Catholic culture that is inseparable from his sense of Salvadoran identity. Part of this identity is symbolically represented through the World Savior statue of Jesus that stands in the national cathedral in San Salvador. Marroquin sees this as neither Catholic nor exclusively Salvadoran, but rather as a representation with which all Christians can affiliate. However, the iconic role of this statue as a Salvadoran representation of both national and spiritual identity inspired a group of patrons in Los Angeles to fund a replica of the statue, hand crafted in El Salvador. When it was complete, the Salvadoran artisans said they would ship it to Los Angeles by air. Yet Marroquin asked, "What would Jesus do in our times?" He continued, "Would he take an airplane or would he walk a path that thousands of sisters and brothers have taken?" The answer to that question by the migrant and religious community in Los Angeles was resounding. He would walk.

Marroquin took part in the overland journey to bring the replica of the World Savior to Los Angeles across the path that migrants and displaced Salvadorans traveled not that long ago. This, Marroquin said, would be the migrants' vindication. When the statue finally arrived, SANA planned a massive event in a downtown park. Thousands attended. Cultural identity blended with spiritual feelings of awe and the blossoming of a new form of civic community that Marroquin had envisioned all along. Not only was this a moment of raising self-esteem within the Salvadoran community, Marroquin said, "it reminds us of the work that we need to do, the challenges that we also oppose, the bitterness of our human condition that we need to be striving [against] every day. It's all kinds of specific and concrete things." When asked what his experience of this event felt like spiritually, Marroquin replied, "there's an energy that glows and nobody can escape it. . . . The energy is very positive and kind of cleans you out."

Marroquin, in trying to establish a new network of civic participation among Salvadorans now living in America, utilized a spirituality of in-betweeness. This spirituality, while drawing upon Catholic traditions in El Salvador, resonated beyond that strictly religious group as a potent symbol of nation, of community, and of common experience and produced a new sacred effervescence within the community. The statue pulled in symbolic representations that were not seen as gross commodities or secular tricks to attract attendance. As Marroquin claimed, "It's no longer, 'Ah, this [statue] is just a piece of wood.' That's the cynical piece in our hearts." Instead, this piece of wood transformed into a new representation of past and future, of old and new, of spirituality and civic society, and the broader social historical trends of war and migration that continually overlap with spiritual and religious change. The qualitatively distinguishing addition of this diffuse spirituality is both personally affective as well as communally integrative, fostering community bonds and civic engagement, as well as promoting social change.

FEELING CONNECTED

If, as Marroquin's example illustrates, the spiritual and the civic are inseparable in the ways they are lived, why is it that they are often discussed separately? In many ways—as with the discussion of religion and spirituality—some find it easier to think in specifics, in blacks and whites and binary codes, about how the world or how spirituality actually works. Perhaps this is because of the simplicity of this design, or, more likely, it is because so much of our world has been, and to a large degree still is, interpreted along a series of gross distinctions. Dichotomies such as culture and religion, sacred and profane, individual and collective, rational and nonrational, public and private, even male and female have shaped and, for many people, constrained the direction and extent of spiritual experiences.

One compelling binary tension that has received attention throughout the past generation is the private versus public role of religion in political and civic life. This distinction is particularly salient when considering stories of spiritually engaged social action. There is a notable and somewhat schizophrenic disjuncture between spirituality and the public sphere that is affected primarily by modern public discourse—of secular governments, intellectuals, and religious bodies.

There are sound reasons for remaining cautious of overlapping church and state sympathies. Yet while there is a considerable amount of attention paid to maintaining a divisional purity between religious spheres and the sphere of civil society, underneath this discourse the connections continue to be made both by individuals and organizations alike. In fact, the frameworks that establish a binary model of secular society versus spirituality simply do not fit the experiences of the people that I spoke with or the ways in which their spirituality was acted upon. Instead, spirituality, as an individual resource, is better equipped to navigate and negotiate both miniscule and monumental decisions.

The individuals interviewed in this study engaged in subtle yet profound ongoing actions within their communities that produced a society that, on one level, retained the veneer of a division between religion and society while, on another level, actively pursued connections between the two. SANA, for example, hosted an event that through some eyes may have appeared profoundly religious. Yet Marroquin's assessment of the role of the World Savior replica was that, while it clearly centered around religious symbolism, it was inseparable from the civic community that took root around the event and could be read as a social event by community members of all faiths. These interpretations vary, but the distinct split between what is religious and what is social is no longer clear.

As the boundaries of our society begin to blur, the ongoing subterraneous connections between spirituality and social action reemerge publicly in creative and examinable ways. If we acknowledge that spirituality can be more than just private, individualized narcissism with little connection to social life—and it seems much of the concern over contemporary spirituality is actually a veiled concern for individualistic spirituality—then . . . spirituality must also be considered in its hybrid form as a social, shared, and potentially consequential resource for social change.

INSPIRING A CHANGE

When turning more directly to social change, it should be kept in mind that this discussion of spirituality does not deny or preclude the organizational strengths of religion. Although the focus will be on spirituality, the contributions of religion have slipped substantively into the academic vernacular for understanding the way in which institutional agents usher in social change or stabilize social equilibrium and are complementary to this argument.

The civil rights movement was one notable episode of dramatic social change in which religious organizations played a central role. Aldon Morris, in his rich chronicling of the movement, suggested that the Southern Christian Leadership Conference acted in many ways as a decentralized network of southern black churches.[28] As such, it had at its disposal the various organizational resources that churches as social institutions provide, resources such as church halls, communication networks, and trained leaders. These were invaluable assets in the successful mobilization of the participants and the economic feasibility of thrown-together volunteers who needed physical spaces in which to meet and social networks through which to solicit support.[29]

Yet spirituality infused this process. Beyond the organizational resources such as leadership networks or meeting halls, churches had a significant amount of moral authority within society that conferred legitimacy upon the movement as a whole as well as the civil disobedience that movement volunteers orchestrated and implemented throughout the South. The perceived transcendence of religion that leaders so powerfully conjured up and that traditional hymns so gently impart—in other words, the spiritually felt component of religion—sets religious indignation apart from the legal-rational, institutional authority of jurisprudence and politics. For those who take this transcendence as real, religion can both stabilize and legitimize some actions while standing in judgment of others in ways that prompt or even necessitate change. This transcendent mandate was something the Reverend Martin Luther King Jr. was well aware of, and his personal charisma carried this religious call in ways that could capture the religious and the nonreligious alike. In the revival-style meetings that followed in the footsteps of the social gospel movement generations earlier, King preached an inner-worldly, moral command for social engagement, suggesting that "any religion that professes to be concerned with the souls of men [*sic*] and is not concerned with the slums that damn them, the economic conditions that strangle them, and the social conditions that cripple them is a dry-as-dust religion."[30]

The transcendent components of the civil rights movement were particularly consequential on an individual basis, in part, because of the charismatic dexterity of King for inspiring personal passions, but also (especially for many of the white participants who had discovered their calling for social justice issues) because it was the first time in their lives that religion had been connected to a dramatic confrontation with society rather than simply a private and subtle confirmation of the status quo. Religion, through spiritual experience, became much more internally charged and externally active for these individuals.

Just as the emotional energies that religion at times elicits can be used collectively to mobilize mass constituencies and create a sense of moral authority and shared identity, the same may be true on the individual level. It is this individual resource that will be explored here as motivation for, sustainability in, and creative innovation of social change.[31] In fact, it has been suggested that out of these spiritual experiences, individuals may interpret a sense of efficacy in their efforts, an elevated confidence, or a feeling of personal control over external circumstances that is qualitatively different from other forms of experience.[32]

A sense of efficacy or control is a crucial component in understanding why people decide whether or not to take action over a particular issue. Both apathy and engagement often hinge upon the perception of efficacy. As mentioned earlier, shifts in contemporary society have created a perceived narcissistic individualism that has led to the fragmentation of self-involved spirituality. In fact, it has been argued that Americans do not participate in civic life to the same degree as past generations.[33] Interestingly, the two casualties of the so-called self-indulgent turn in culture—spirituality and civic participation—may actually benefit from each other in discernable and regenerative ways.

First, spirituality has not been fully explored as a significant spark for the shift in perspective toward personal and collective efficacy within social movement analyses or social change in general. Yet this is crucial for success. Frances Piven and Richard Cloward, in their contemporary classic, *Poor People's Movements*, argue that "the social arrangements that are ordinarily perceived as just and immutable must come to be seen as unjust and mutable."[34] When individuals can turn this corner in their heads, new actions, previously thought untenable or out of reach, now appear quite achievable and even necessary.[35] Seen from this perspective alone, the creative potential of spirituality for social action can be read as a distinct subjective resource that, while often embedded within other institutional religious resources, requires additional attention as a significant variable in its own right.

On the other hand, while individual spiritual experience can spark the vision of a better society, acting upon this experience confers an authenticity of action itself and expunges doubts and uncertainties. Just as the blurred dichotomies discussed above have allowed for various hybrids such as spiritually informed social action to reemerge both publicly and academically, they also produce destabilizing questions. . . . Humans question various aspects of their previously taken-for-granted social knowledge, such as religious institutional doctrine and history, and their understanding of the world becomes a set of hypotheses rather than known Truths.[36] For some, this may result in apathy about civic or religious participation, while for others it opens up possibilities for the newly directed social action . . .

ENGAGING SPIRITUALITY

The perceived bifurcation of spirituality and religion has produced a divide that pits private spirituality against many other social or productive elements of modern life, including civic participation and working for social change. In other words, religions do social services and spirituality does the soul. This divide is not completely an artificial one, but it is an overstated one. Whereas religion is primarily collective, public, and shared, spirituality is simultaneously collective *and* individual, public *and* private, shared *and* internally intimate. Spirituality is neither one nor the other of these pairings, but both. It is this fluid quality that, if understood as an already occurring, individually nurtured social resource, has vast potential socially and analytically.

Notes

1. Wade Clark Roof, *Spiritual Marketplace: Baby Boomers and the Remaking of American Religion* (Princeton, NJ: Princeton University Press, 1999); Richard P. Cimino and Don Lattin, *Shopping for Faith: American Religion in the New Millennium* (New York: Jossey-Bass, 1998).
2. Robert N. Bellah et al., *Habits of the Heart: Individualism and Commitment in American Life* (Berkeley: University of California Press, 1985), 221.
3. Jose Casanova, *Public Religions in the Modern World* (Chicago: University of Chicago Press, 1994), 35–39, provides an excellent synopsis of different branches of secularization theses, one of which is the privatization model in which religion recedes to the family or the bounded space of the church, temple, or synagogue, but has little influence on larger arenas of public life.
4. Penny Long Marler and C. Kirk Hadaway, "'Being Religious' or 'Being Spiritual' in America: A Zero-Sum Proposition?" *Journal for the Scientific Study of Religion* 41 (2002): 289–300; Zinnbauer et al., "Religion and Spirituality: Unfuzzying the Fuzzy," *Journal for the Scientific Study of Religion* 36 (1997): 549–564.
5. Robert K. C. Forman, "What Does Mysticism Have to Teach Us about Consciousness?" *Journal of Consciousness Studies* 5 (1998): 185–201; Daniel A. Helminiak, *Spiritual Development: An Interdisciplinary Study* (Chicago: Loyola University Press, 1987); Helminiak, *The Human Care of Spirituality: Mind as Psyche and Spirit* (Albany: State University of New York Press, 1996); Kenneth I. Pargament et al., "The Many Meanings of Religiousness: A Policy Capturing Approach," *Journal of Personality* 63 (1995): 954–83. "The Many Meanings of Religiousness"; Zinnbauer et al., "Religion and Spirituality."
6. Kenneth I. Pargament, *The Psychology of Religion and Coping: Theory Research, Practice* (New York: Guilford Press, 1997).
7. Zinnbauer et al., "Religion and Spirituality," 909.
8. Robert Wuthnow, *Christianity in the Twenty-First Century: Reflections on the Challenges Ahead* (New York: Oxford University Press, 1993), 168–198.
9. Robert A. Emmons, *The Psychology of Ultimate Concerns: Motivation and Spirituality in Personality* (New York: Guilford Press, 1999).
10. Jack M. Barbalet, *Emotion, Social Theory, and Social Structure: A Macrosociological Approach* (New York: Cambridge University Press, 1998), xvi.

11. I use the term "natural affiliation" in a conscious way that reflects my assumptions about spiritually profound moments, human nature, and the social construction of our lived environments. This is based upon sociological and cultural assumptions rather than personal or theological ones. Peter Berger, *The Sacred Canopy: A Sociological Theory of Religion* (Garden City, NY: Doubleday, 1967); Christian Smith, *Moral, Believing Animals: Human Personhood and Culture* (New York: Oxford University Press, 2003).
12. In *America's Crisis of Values: Reality and Perception* (Princeton, NJ: Princeton University Press, 2004), Wayne E. Baker points out that American values such as egalitarianism and individualism are often projected onto an idealized past as a way to critique the contemporary and debatable "crisis" in contemporary American values.
13. In *Protestant Catholic Jew* (Garden City, NJ: Anchor Books, 1955), Will Herberg's classic assessment of mid-twentieth-century American life attested to the religious adherence of this generation and the salience that it had for a nation still experiencing growing pains from the waves of immigration at the turn of the nineteenth to twentieth century.
14. Tom Brokaw, *The Greatest Generation* (New York: Random House, 1998).
15. Robert Orsi's *Thank You St. Jude: Women's Devotion to the Patron Saint of Hopeless Causes* (New Haven: Yale University Press, 1996) is a wonderful account of immigrant women during this period of transition that sensitively unpacks the spiritual lives of devotees of Saint Jude.
16. At different times and influenced by different social constraints or encouragements, this spiritual expression has flourished or been decried as regressive irrationality—and often times both. Jon Butler, *Awash in a Sea of Faith: Christianizing the American People* (Cambridge, MA: Harvard University Press, 1990); Roger Finke and Rodney Stark, *The Churching of America, 1776–1990: Winners and Losers in Our Religious Economy* (New Brunswick, NJ: Rutgers University Press, 1992); Rodney Stark and Roger Finke, *Acts of Faith: Explaining the Human Side of Religion* (Berkeley: University of California Press, 2000); Ann Taves, *Fits, Trances, and Visions: Experiencing Religion and Explaining Religion from Wesley to James* (Princeton, NJ: Princeton University Press, 1999). Peter Berger, *The Desecularization of the World: Resurgent Religion and World Politics* (Grand Rapids, MI: William B. Eerdmans Publishing Co., 1999) assesses the contemporary cycle of religious resurgence.
17. My approach here is cultural and I view spirituality as a particular element of culture that is similarly constituted. By culture, I mean the dual meaningful processes that are both "medium and outcome." Anthony Giddens, *The Constitution of Society* (Cambridge, MA: Polity Press, 1984), 25. The active cultural influence is from Ann Swidler,

"Culture in Action: Symbols and Strategies," *American Sociological Review* (1986).

18. Prema Kurien, "Becoming American by Becoming Hindu," in *Gatherings in Diaspora: Religious Communities and the New Immigrants* (Philadelphia: Temple University Press, 1998), suggests that Indian immigrant communities in Los Angeles construct congregational models in order to fulfill the needs of religious and cultural preservation in their new home, pass down traditions to a new generation, and foster networks that were based on religious community rather than solely on business and status groupings.
19. Finke and Stark, *Churching*; Roof, *Spiritual Marketplace*; Stark and Finke, *Acts of Faith.*
20. Wade Clark Roof, *A Generation of Seekers* (San Francisco: HarperSanFrancisco, 1993).
21. Christopher Lasch, *The Culture of Narcissism: American Life in the Age of Diminishing Expectations* (New York: Norton, 1979).
22. *Publishers Weekly* (December 6) notes that in 2004 religion/self-help was the most successful subcategory of books on religion. Micki McGee, *Self-Help, Inc.* (New York: Oxford University Press, 2005).
23. Two *New York Times* reviews mirror this divide with Michiko Kakutani on June 20, 2004, excoriating the "self-serving" mess of reflections by the "avatar of his [baby boomer] generation," while, three days later, Larry McMurtry lobbed softer comparisons to reflective literary figures admitting that this was the "richest American presidential autobiography."
24. Jana Riess, *What Would Buffy Do: The Vampire Slayer as Spiritual Guide* (New York: Jossey-Bass, 2004). This question riffs off the common "Jesus question" but substitutes the film and television character Buffy the Vampire Slayer, who has attained a cultlike following among some viewers.
25. Colleen McDannell, *Material Christianity: Religion and Popular Culture in America* (New Haven, CT: Yale University Press, 1995).
26. Robert Bellah, *The Broken Covenant: American Civil Religion in a Time of Trial* (New York: Seabury Press, 1975); Richard W. Fox, *Jesus in America: Personal Savior, Cultural Hero, National Obsession* (San Francisco: HarperSanFrancisco, 2004). David Morgan, *Protestants and Pictures: Religion, Visual Culture, and the Age of American Mass Production* (New York: Oxford University Press, 1999) provides a wonderful visual history.
27. In *St. Jude*, Orsi illustrates the profound and complex spiritual relationships women throughout the early to middle parts of the twentieth century

often secretly maintained with Saint Jude. Jude became a confidant and receptacle for their concerns and desires that they were unable to legitimately express elsewhere. Harvey Cox, *Fire from Heaven: The Rise of Pentecostal Spirituality and the Reshaping of Religion in the Twenty-first Century* (Reading, MA: Addison-Wesley, 1995), notes the sensation caused by Pentecostals throughout the twentieth century, specifically noting the provocative racial and gender relations at the Azusa Street revival.

28. Aldon Morris, *The Origins of the Civil Rights Movement: Black Communities Organizing for Change* (New York: Free Press, 1984), 77–99.

29. Christian Smith, *Disruptive Religion: The Force of Faith in Social Movements* (New York: Routledge, 1996), compiled a list of organizational and cultural resources that religious institutions bring to the table in aiding social movements or facilitating social change. These include organizational resources, shared identity, social and geographic positioning, privileged legitimacy, institutional self-interest, and, perhaps most significantly for this conversation, transcendent motivations.

30. Quoted in Morris, *Civil Rights*, 97.

31. Myra Marx Ferree, "The Political Context of Rationality: Rational Choice Theory and Resource Mobilization," in *Frontiers in Social Movement Theory* (New Haven, CT: Yale University Press, 1992), 32, suggests that acknowledging that "all people do behave impulsively and irrationally at times *enriches* the account of rationality that can be given by including the individual and organizational problems of anticipating, managing, and reacting to such tendencies." Ferree is making the case for anticipating destructive, although emotionally satisfying, episodes of impulsive behavior such as reactions to taunting or beatings. However, I want to suggest that this impulsive experience may also be used constructively in ways that link positive experiences to social change.

32. Fredrick C. Harris, *Something Within: Religion in African-American Political Activism* (New York: Oxford University Press, 1999); Douglas A. Marshall, "Behavior, Belonging, and Belief: A Theory of Ritual Practice," *Sociological Theory* 20 (2002): 360–380; Mark R. Warren, *Dry Bones Rattling: Community Building to Revitalize American Democracy* (Princeton, NJ: Princeton University Press, 2001); Richard L. Wood, *Faith in Action: Religion, Race, and Democratic Organizing in America* (Chicago: University of Chicago Press, 2002).

33. Robert D. Putnam, *Bowling Alone: The Collapse and Revival of American Community* (New York: Simon and Schuster, 2000).

34. Frances F. Piven and Richard Cloward, *Poor People's Movements* (New York: Pantheon, 1977), 12. See also Doug McAdam, *Political Process and the Development of Black Insurgency, 1930–1970* (Chicago: University of Chicago Press, 1999).

35. Social movement literature of the past half century, much like recent analyses of religion, has battled to rationalize collective actions previously explained away by or derided as irrational. For social movement discussions of this critique, see Ferree, *Political Context*; James M. Jasper, "The Emotions of Protest: Affective and Reactive Emotions in and around Social Movements," *Sociological Forum* 13 (1998): 397–424; Laura Pulido, "The Sacredness of 'Mother Earth': Spirituality, Activism and Social Justice," *Annals of the Association of American Geographers* 88 (1998): 719–723. For religion, see Robert Orsi, "Is the Study of Lived Religion Irrelevant to the World We Live In?" *Journal for the Scientific Study of Religion* 42 (2003):169–174. And see Smith, *Disruptive Religion*, for a combination of the two.
36. Anthony Giddens, *Modernity and Self-Identity: Self and Society in the Late Modern Age* (Stanford, CA: Stanford University Press, 1991), 3, states, "all knowledge [now] takes the form of hypotheses: claims which may very well be true, but which are in principle always open to revision and may have at some point to be abandoned." Similarly, Michel de Certeau, *The Practice of Everyday Life* (Berkeley: University of California Press, 1984), 179, suggests, "There are now too many things to believe and not enough credibility to go around." It is this lack of credibility that some find fulfilled through action.

What Is a Cult?

(2008)

KATHLEEN LOWNEY

I admit it, I'm a political junkie. Campaign season is my favorite time of the year. And the 2008 presidential campaign was quite a ride, wasn't it? We saw the rise of Huck's Army, heard Obama Girl sing about her crush, watched McCainiacs be thrilled at their candidate's stunning comeback, and witnessed the persuasiveness that a ringing phone at 3 A.M. might have had with Texas and Ohio voters.

But I'm not just an avid consumer of political news; as a sociologist, I'm also a media analyst. And something has been bothering me as this presidential campaign has played out: the frequency with which blogs and mainstream news outlets such as ABC News, *Time* magazine, and the *Los Angeles Times* talked about the "cult of Obama."

It's the word "cult" that troubles me. Media commentators seem to imply that the enthusiasm and energy of the president's supporters, their commitment to his vision for America, the world, and each other, is somehow worrisome and menacing.

It's made me realize once again that sociology is not only a way of thinking about the social world we live in, but that as sociologists, we talk in a distinct—and distinctive—way. For students learning sociology, I think that learning our sociological way of talking can sometimes be hard. Doesn't it seem like sometimes we sociologists use a lot of words to make some rather simple points? I think that too once in a while! I believe, however, that it's sociologists' scientific preciseness that fuels our wordiness—at least, that is my hope!

"Cult" is one of those words that means one thing to sociologists and often quite different things to nonsociologists. Here's how the text for my Sociology of Religion class defines it:

> A *cult* is similar to a sect in its rejection of the religious patterns and formulations of denominations—or of whatever the society's dominant form(s) of religion happens to be. Cult members were either not attracted to dominant religious groups in the first place or, like sectarians, became disenchanted with commonly accepted religious forms. The cult differs from the sect, however, in that it does not call for a return to the original, pure religion, but rather emphasizes the new—a new revelation or insight provided by a supernatural power, say, or the rediscovery of an old revelation that had

been lost and unknown for many years (and which is, therefore, new to this age).[1]

But is this what you think about when you hear the word "cult"? I doubt it. Since the 1970s, popular culture, led by the press, has come to define the word as a religion that many people do not like; one that uses recruitment techniques unlike many traditional Protestant denominations (i.e., "brainwashing") in order to ensnare impressionable young adults. Cults are often portrayed as being "alien" to the United States, run by manipulative messianic figures who are really all about lavishly spending the money their followers raise.

In fact, this pop culture definition of "cult" has even altered our sociological vocabulary. Nowadays sociologists of religion tend to use the term "new religious movement" instead of "cult" because we recognize how pervasive the pop culture definition has become.

So when commentators write about the "cult of Obama," they are both tapping into this negative connotation and simultaneously helping it to persist. I find it interesting that it is Senator Obama's followers who have come under such media scrutiny and not, for example, Mike Huckabee's army of college-age activists. Barack Obama was the upstart, the unexpected Democratic candidate. Because of his father's nationality, some critics questioned his patriotism and citizenship.

If words matter—and as a sociologist, I absolutely believe that they do—how social institutions such as the press talk can shape the public's social construction of reality. Words like "cult" are now perceived to be, in our culture, inflammatory. So the next time you read a headline or hear political commentators talk about "the cult of Obama," think about it for a moment. What is that reporter/analyst trying to get you to believe? And perhaps more important, why? How does such a negative construction of President Obama's followers shape the political environment of this presidential campaign? Who might the construction help?

Related links

ABC News story: abcnews.go.com/Nightline/Vote2008/story?id=4313643&page=1

Time magazine story: www.time.com/time/printout/0,8816,1710721,00.html

Los Angeles Times op-ed:
www.latimes.com/news/opinion/la-oe-stein8feb08,0,3418234.column

Obamassiah website: obamamessiah.blogspot.com/

1. Ronald L. Johnstone, *Religion in Society: A Sociology of Religion,* Eighth Edition (Prentice Hall, 2007), p. 78.

The Sociology of Conspiracy

(2007)

KAREN STERNHEIMER

For the past several years, the anniversary of the September 11th attacks has brought introspection and examination into what happened on that terrible day.

A story in the *Los Angeles Times* charged that the Central Intelligence Agency (CIA) did not have an adequate plan to deal with the threat of terrorism before the 2001 events. For those who read the 9-11 Commission Report, published in 2004, this new information should not be a big surprise. In all this, what remains hard to understand is how a band of thugs could penetrate the security of the world's sole superpower.

Some people have such a hard time accepting this idea that they reject the notion that a terrorist cell was behind the attacks. Instead, they passionately believe that both the devastation of that day and the explanation that followed was part of a grand conspiracy—an American conspiracy.

The History Channel has devoted two hours of programming to examine some of the claims of conspiracy buffs. Rather than discussing such claims (which have gotten more than enough attention on the Internet already), I find it more interesting to consider how common conspiracy theories are in popular culture. Why is this so?

Sociologists refer to conspiracy theories as a form of collective behavior, similar to urban legends, rumors, and panics. We engage in this behavior together, and it gains traction as it appeals to more and more people. Sociologists seek to understand how and why groups create meaning through claiming that conspiracies have taken place.

The creation of the Internet has definitely greased the wheels of collective behavior. One of the most fascinating things about collective behavior is that it often starts from the grassroots level, from everyday people rather from those in positions of power. In fact, the very distance from the centers of power fuels conspiracy theories.

Let's think about some other conspiracy theories. Some people claim that the Holocaust never happened. Perhaps the most famous conspiracy theory is based on the premise that President John F. Kennedy's assassination was the work of insiders.

The public's willingness to entertain such theories differs tremendously. For most people, even *questioning* the reality that millions of civilians were murdered during World War II is incredibly offensive. But there's something about Kennedy's assassination that makes millions question the findings of the Warren Commission Report. Why does one conspiracy theory seem outlandish, while another one seems plausible?

Imbalance of power is a key ingredient. It is not hard to believe that a powerful regime or dictator could slaughter a group of people with little or no social power, as sadly has happened time and again in human history.

But the opposite is much harder to believe: an individual or group with little power harming someone with significantly more power and status doesn't make sense. It challenges what we think we know about the social order.

So the Kennedy assassination—apparently the work of a lone gunman who by all reports was, to put it kindly, unsuccessful in his other ventures—seems hard to believe. That a charismatic, larger-than-life leader of the free world could be brought down by a "nobody" has fueled conspiracy theorists for over forty years. Although solid evidence refutes the idea of a conspiracy, I admit to entertaining this notion myself. I now see that I fell into the power imbalance trap too.

In my defense, I also grew up during the 1970s, when network television routinely featured programs about the Bermuda Triangle, Bigfoot, the Loch Ness monster, and other supernatural "secrets." The Kennedy assassination was also a big topic during the decade that featured the Watergate cover-up and made many Americans question how much the government could be trusted. In the early 1970s, Skylab, a precursor to today's international space station, actually fell to earth (which is terrifying if you're a kid!), and faith in the government fell as well.

Flash forward more than twenty-five years, and you can see why people still might have trouble believing the government. Congress and President George W. Bush's approval ratings declined significantly as the war in Iraq became increasingly unpopular and as no weapons of mass destruction were found. Conspiracy claims make sense during a time when mistrust and anger toward the government run high.

It is difficult to accept that our powerful military could not protect us that September day. For some, it is easier to believe that our government is all-powerful (even if that power is abused) than it is to believe that the government is flawed. Our Cold War military build-up made us feel almost invincible, and September 11th challenged that assumption. In a strange way, conspiracy theories prop up the belief in an all-powerful America. Perhaps clinging to this idea is less upsetting than facing what actually transpired that day.

Related links

Los Angeles Times story: articles.latimes.com/2007/aug/22/nation/na-cia22

The 9-11 Commission Report: www.9-11commission.gov/

Warren Commission Report (Kennedy Assassination):
www.archives.gov/research/jfk/warren-commission-report/

TALK ABOUT IT

1. What role, if any, should businesses play in helping employees to balance their work and family obligations? How might family leave policies better serve employees?
2. How might employee productivity be affected by family issues? How might employers benefit from assisting employees in dealing with family issues?
3. If you were to look for a job today, what factors would you need to consider in your search? How would you go about your search? What factors might help or hinder you?
4. How is religion more than a private issue in American life? In what way does religion influence other social institutions?
5. How would you have defined a cult before reading Lowney's essay? How would you describe a cult now? Are there groups not often regarded as cults that might fit your new definition?
6. Discuss examples of social change that religious groups have been part of in recent years.
7. Choose one conspiracy theory and discuss why believers might continue to challenge the official explanation of an event despite evidence supporting the official explanation.
8. Why do so many American schools continue to lack funding for basic materials?
9. How has your educational experience been affected by globalization, based on the points in Le's essay?
10. Choose one social institution not discussed in this module. How does it help shape and organize society? How does it affect your everyday life?

WRITE ABOUT IT

1. What do work and family life have in common? How can they complement one another? Create problems with one another? Use examples from Hochschild's essay in your response.
2. What makes it easier for some people to find high-paying jobs than others? Consider Ehrenreich's and Wright's points in your response.
3. What is the "American Dream"? How might social institutions make this dream more feasible for some than others? Use two selections from this module to support your response.
4. Discuss the challenges working mothers face. What changes led to the growth in mothers' working outside of the home, as Prince Inniss's piece discusses?

5. Choose a group that some might describe as a cult. Does it meet the sociological definition? If so, how? If not, why not? What effect has this labeling had on the group?
6. Choose one social movement that was aided by religious institutions and/or spiritual beliefs. How did the participants' beliefs affect the movement? What might have been different if religion and/or spirituality had *not* been part of this movement?
7. Describe one conspiracy theory that has wide support but that evidence disputes. Why do the believers think that officials have lied to them? What does this conspiracy theory say about peoples' faith in social institutions?
8. Why does faith in social institutions rise and fall? Discuss one reason why trust in a specific social institution rose or fell at a particular time in history.
9. Discuss your reaction to Kozol's description of the students in schools that need basic resources. Compare a school Kozol describes to one you attended. Are they different? Similar? How do these experiences with the institution of education affect the people within it, beyond just the quality of their education?
10. How can globalization enhance the institutions of higher education? What challenges might globalization present in education?

DO IT

1. Interview five people who have jobs and children. How do they balance their responsibilities? If married, how do the spouses balance responsibilities between them? Analyze their responses and compare them to Hochschild's interviewees.
2. Read Barbara Ehrenreich's *Bait and Switch*—in its entirety. Conduct an experiment similar to Ehrenreich's. Apply for professional-level jobs over the course of several weeks, utilizing all the resources you can. Describe the resources you have access to and how they might help you in this process. What factors helped you in this process? What limitations did you face? Did you get interviews? Job offers? How much time and money did you spend in the process? Discuss how people without access to the same resources might fare in their job searches.
3. Apply Wright's idea about the strength of weak social ties in finding a job. Replicate the experiment from question 2, this time using Internet resources only, including any online social networks you belong to. Describe how this process worked. Did you get information about jobs or about jobs in your area? How do your findings relate to Wright's points?
4. Find unemployment statistics for the nation, your state, and the nearest major city. How do these rates vary in factors such as age, gender, and race?

What do these numbers indicate about the likelihood of people in your region finding work?

5. Consider the statistics listed in Prince Inniss's selection on working mothers. Research why the numbers have increased significantly in the past forty years. How have social institutions changed along with the labor force?
6. Search online to find a website or online community devoted to a conspiracy that challenges the official explanation of an event. Analyze the word choice, imagery, and rationales proponents use. Why does this group insist that we are being deceived? What does this tell us about their belief in the social institution in question? How isolated is this group? Does it fit Lowney's definition of a cult?
7. Interview five people who are very involved in a religious or spiritual group. Determine how their involvement creates civic engagement, as Stanczak describes in his selection.
8. Arrange a visit to a school in an affluent area of your community. Describe the facilities, the students, and the materials. Now visit a school in a low-income area and make the same observations. How do the schools differ? What would Kozol say about any disparities?
9. Find data on your school's enrollment. What proportion are international students? Interview five international students. What are they studying? What motivated them to study abroad? Do they hope to return to their native country or remain here? How do they describe the cultural differences in being a student here and in their home country? What does your analysis tell us about the globalization of education?
10. Interview five students who have spent a term studying abroad. What motivated them to study in the country they chose? Did their experience surprise them in any way? How do they describe cultural differences in being a student as a foreigner? What does your analysis tell us about the globalization of education?

10

Social Change

Module Goal: ***Understand how population shifts and social movements create changes in society.***

Why do societies change? Sometimes sociopolitical events like wars or other conflicts create large-scale changes as well as smaller ripple effects for many years to come. Sometimes people actively struggle to create change and devote time, resources, and energy to social movements. At other times, change happens gradually, spurred by shifts in population patterns such as a baby boom or an influx of immigrants.

Sometimes change happens because populations change. Consider what sociologists call the *cohort effect*: when a large group of people shares a common experience at a critical time in their lives, they might collectively develop a new worldview. In "Generations X, Y and Z," Duane F. Alwin examines whether attitudes about gender, sex, and race are evolving because of younger generations, addressing several reasons that attitudes about social issues change. Why have attitudes about these issues shifted over time?

Populations change as a result of immigration too. The United States is essentially a nation of immigrants, yet immigration remains a matter of intense public debate. As hard as it might be to believe today, in the early years of the republic Americans actually encouraged others, particularly from Western Europe, to resettle here. For some people, immigration today means unwelcome change, perhaps new cultural practices or languages that sound unfamiliar. Others are concerned that new immigrants will be a societal drain with few skills to offer. In "Black Ethnicity," Janis Prince Inniss discusses immigrant groups that are frequently overlooked in public discussions about immigration. As you read her piece, consider common stereotypes and misconceptions about immigrants.

Another major fear people have about immigrants is that they bring crime to their new country. In "Rethinking Crime and Immigration," Robert J. Sampson challenges these assumptions about immigrants and crime. Continue to think about these popular beliefs as you read Sally Raskoff's "Statistics and Myths about Immigrants." Why is the fear of immigrants, and the social change they may bring with them, so pervasive?

In many cases social change is more than a "natural" evolution of thought; it is the result of hard work and personal sacrifice by those who fervently believe in a cause. For example, changes in ideas about racial equality did not simply evolve on their own; they were the result of years of participation in the civil rights movement, a movement in which people were arrested, beaten, and killed in the quest for social change. Sociologists study this and other movements to understand what motivates people to participate, and what factors make movements successful. In "Social Movements and the Environment," I examine how historical context makes movements more successful at some times than others. What factors have led more people to take environmental concerns seriously in recent years?

After reading the last nine modules, you should have a good idea of how societies are organized and stratified. But you should not conclude that societies are fixed and unchanging. Even large social institutions like governments and educational systems can change.

Societies change in part because people take action, refusing to accept that "this is just the way things are." These everyday realities are not static; change is possible if people take the steps necessary to rethink everyday interactions and how social institutions operate.

As you consider social change in everyday life, think about the following questions:

1. Is your generation changing society? How? What changes *should* your generation make?
2. How do fears about immigrants compare to reality?
3. What role do social movements play in creating social change? How might you mobilize others to create change?

Generations X, Y, and Z

Are They Changing America? (2002)

DUANE F. ALWIN

The Greatest Generation saved the world from fascism. The Dr. Spock Generation gave us rebellion and free love. Generation X made cynicism and slacking off the hallmarks of the end of the 20th century. In the media, generation is a popular and all-purpose explanation for change in America. Each new generation replaces an older one's zeitgeist with its own.

Generational succession is increasingly a popular explanation among scholars, too. Recently, political scientist Robert Putnam argued in *Bowling Alone* [excerpted in this volume] that civic engagement has declined in America even though individual Americans have not necessarily become less civic minded. Instead, he argues, older engaged citizens are dying off and being replaced by younger, more alienated Americans who are less tied to institutions such as the church, lodge, political party and bowling league.

Next to characteristics like social class, race, and religion, generation is probably the most common explanatory tool used by social scientists to account for differences among people. The difficulties in proving such explanations, however, are not always apparent and are often overshadowed by the seductiveness of the idea. Generational arguments do not always hold the same allure once they are given closer scrutiny.

Changes in the worldviews of Americans result not only from the progression of generations but also from historical events and patterns of aging. For example, generational replacement seems to explain why fewer Americans now than 30 years ago say they trust other people, but historical events seem to explain why fewer say they trust government. Similarly, historical events in interaction with aging (or life cycle change) may explain lifetime changes in church attendance and political partisanship better than generational shifts.

EXPLAINING SOCIAL CHANGE

Some rather massive changes over the past 50 years in Americans' attitudes need explaining. Consider this short list of examples:

- In 1977, 66 percent said that it is better if the man works and the woman stays home; in 2000, only 35 percent did.

- In 1972, 48 percent said that sex before marriage is wrong; in 2000, 36 percent did.
- In 1972, 39 percent said that there should be a law against interracial marriage; in 2000, 12 percent did.
- In 1958, 78 percent said that one could trust the government in Washington to do right; in 2000 only 44 percent did.

Do changes in beliefs and behaviors reflect the experiences of specific generations, do they occur when Americans of all ages change their orientations, or do they result from something else? Although the idea of generational succession is promising and useful, it also has problems that may limit it as an all-purpose explanation of social change.

SOME PRELIMINARIES

Before we begin to deconstruct the idea of generational replacement we need to clarify a few issues. The first is that when sociologists use the term *generation* it can refer to one of three quite different things:

1. All people born at the same time.
2. A unique position within a family's line of descent (as in the second generation of Bush presidents).
3. A group of people self-consciously defined, by themselves and by others, as part of an historically based social movement (as in the "hippie" generation).

There are many examples in the social science literature of all three uses, and this can create a great deal of confusion. Here I refer mainly to the first use, measuring generation by year of birth. Demographers prefer to use the term cohort. Either way the reference is to the historical period in which people grow to maturity. I use the terms cohort and generation more or less interchangeably.

When sociologists are discussing social change in less precise terms, they may refer to generations in a somewhat more nuanced, cultural sense. Generations in this usage do not necessarily map neatly to birth years. Rather, the distinction between generations is a matter of quality, not degree, and their exact time boundaries cannot always be easily identified. It is also clear that statistically there is no way to identify cohort or generation effects unequivocally. The interpretation of generational differences depends entirely on one's ability or willingness to make some rather hefty assumptions about other processes, such as how aging affects attitudes, but as we shall see, we can nonetheless develop reasonable conclusions.

COHORT REPLACEMENT

Cohort replacement is a fact of social life. Earlier-born cohorts die off and are replaced by those born more recently. The question is: do the unique formative experiences of cohorts become distinctively imprinted onto members' worldviews, making them distinct generations over the course of their lifetimes, or do people of all cohorts adapt to change, remaining pliable in their beliefs throughout their lives?

When historical events mainly affect the young, we have the makings of a generation. Such an effect—labeled a cohort effect—refers to the outcomes attributable to having been born in a particular historical period. When, for example, people describe the Depression generation as particularly thrifty, they imply that the experience of growing up under privation permanently changed the economic beliefs and style of life of people who grew to maturity during that time.

Unique events that happen during youth are no doubt powerful. Certainly, some eras and social movements, like the Civil Rights era and the women's movement, or some new ideologies (e.g. Roosevelt's New Deal) provide distinctive experiences for youth during particular times. As Norman Ryder put it, "the potential for change is concentrated in the cohorts of young adults who are old enough to participate directly in the movements impelled by change, but not old enough to have become committed to an occupation, a residence, a family of procreation or a way of life."

To some observers, today's younger generations—Generation X and its younger counterpart—display a distinctive lack of social commitment. The goals of individualism and the good life have replaced an earlier generation's involvement in social movements and organizations. Is this outlook simply part of being young, or is it characteristic of a particular generation?

Each generation resolves issues of identity in its own way. In the words of analyst Erik Erikson, "No longer is it merely for the old to teach the young the meaning of life . . . it is the young who, by their responses and actions, tell the old whether life as represented by the old and presented to the young has meaning; and it is the young who carry in them the power to confirm those who confirm them and, joining the issues, to renew and to regenerate or to reform and to rebel."

Such reasoning about generational replacement is not new. Eighteenth- and nineteenth-century social philosophers from David Hume to Auguste Comte linked the biological succession of generations to change in society. As early as 1835, the statistician Adolphe Quetelet wrote about the importance of taking year of birth into account when examining human development. In the 1920s, the German sociologist Karl Mannheim wrote an often-cited treatise on "the problem of generations," arguing that having shared the same formative experiences contributed to a generation's unique worldview, which remained a powerful force in their lives. In Mannheim's words, "Even if the rest of one's life consisted of one long process of negation and destruction of the natural worldview acquired in youth, the determining influence of these early impressions would still be predominant."

Before we accept this way of understanding change, however, we should consider other possibilities. One is that people change as they get older, which we call an effect of aging. The older people get, for example, the more intensely they may hold to their views. America, as a whole, may be becoming more politically partisan because the population is getting older—an age effect. Another possibility is that people change in response to specific historical events, what sociologists call period effects. The Civil Rights movement, for example, may have changed many Americans' ideas about race, not just the views of the generation growing up in the 1960s. The events of September 11, 2001, likely had an effect on the entire nation, not just those in the most impressionable years of youth.

A third possibility is that the change is located in only one segment of society. Members of the Roman Catholic faith, for example, may be the most responsive to the current turmoil over the sexual exploitation of youth by some priests in ways that hardly touch the lives of Protestants. Let us weigh these possibilities more closely, looking at the issues raised by Putnam in *Bowling Alone.*

CHANGES IN SOCIAL CONNECTEDNESS AND TRUST

It is often relatively easy to construct a picture of generational differences by comparing data from different age groups in social surveys and polls, but determining what produced the data is considerably more complex.

Take, for example, one of the key empirical findings of Putnam's analysis: the responses people give to the question of whether they trust their fellow human beings. The General Social Survey (administered regularly to a nationwide, representative sample of American residents since 1972) asks the following question: "Do you think most people would try to take advantage of you if they got the chance, or would they try to be fair?" Figure 1 presents the percentage of respondents in each set of cohorts who responded that people would try to be fair. The results show that birth cohorts were consistently different from one another, the recent ones being more cynical about human nature. There has been little change in this outcome over the years except insofar as new generations replaced older ones. These results reinforce the Putnam thesis, that the degree of social connectedness in the formative years of people's generation shapes their sense of trust.

Still, I would note some problems with these conclusions. First, generational experiences are not the only factors that differentiate these four groups; they also differ by age. Second, these data do not depict the young lives of the cohorts born before 1930 (who were 42 years of age or older in 1972), so we have little purchase on their beliefs before 1972. Third, there is remarkable growth in trust among the Baby Boom cohorts—those born from 1947 to 1962—over their midlife

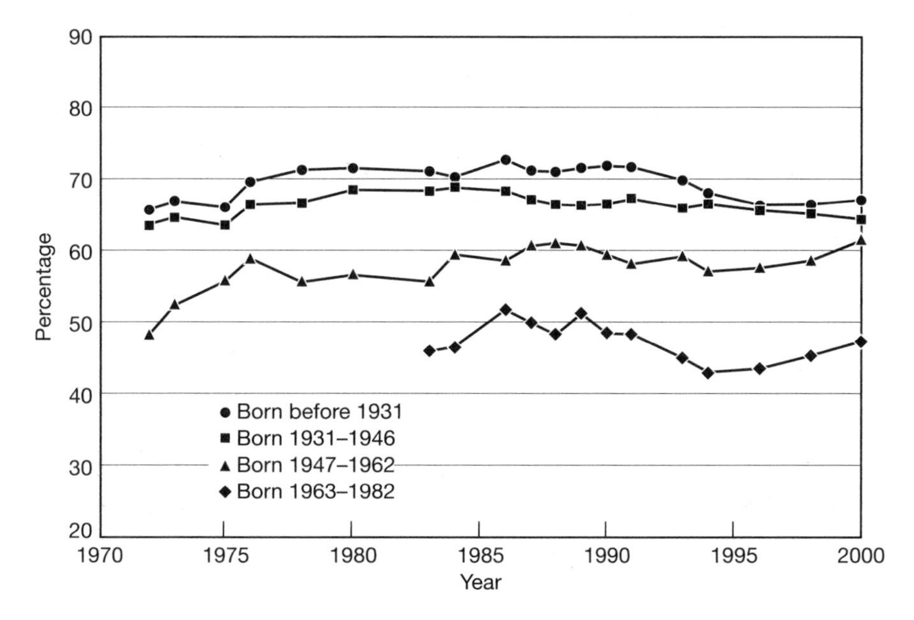

Source: Alwin, Duane F. "Generations X,Y, and Z: Are They Changing America?" *Contexts*, Winter 2002, vol. 1, no. 4.

FIGURE 1 Percentage of U.S. Population Who Believe "Most People Try to Be Fair"

period, and in 2000 they had achieved a level of trust on a par with earlier cohorts. Finally, even the most recent cohorts (the lowest line in the figure) show some tendency to gain trust in recent years. The point is that while the data appear to show a pattern of generational differences—less trust among more recent cohorts—age might be just as plausible an explanation of the differences: trust goes up as people mature.

There may be more than one way to explain changes in Americans' trust of people, but generations do not explain changes in Americans' trust of government. In 1958 the National Election Studies (NES) began using the following question: "How much of the time do you think you can trust the government in Washington to do what is right—just about always, most of the time, or only some of the time?"

There are two important things to note about figure 2. First, there are hardly any differences among birth cohorts who say most of the time or always in their responses to this question; the lines are virtually identical. Thus, generational replacement explains none of the very dramatic decline of trust in government. That decline may be better explained by historical events that affected all cohorts—the Vietnam War, the feminist movement, or the Watergate and Whitewater scandals—and there is little basis for arguing that more recent cohorts are more alienated from government than those born earlier (Note that affirmations of trust in government rose dramatically right after 9/11.)

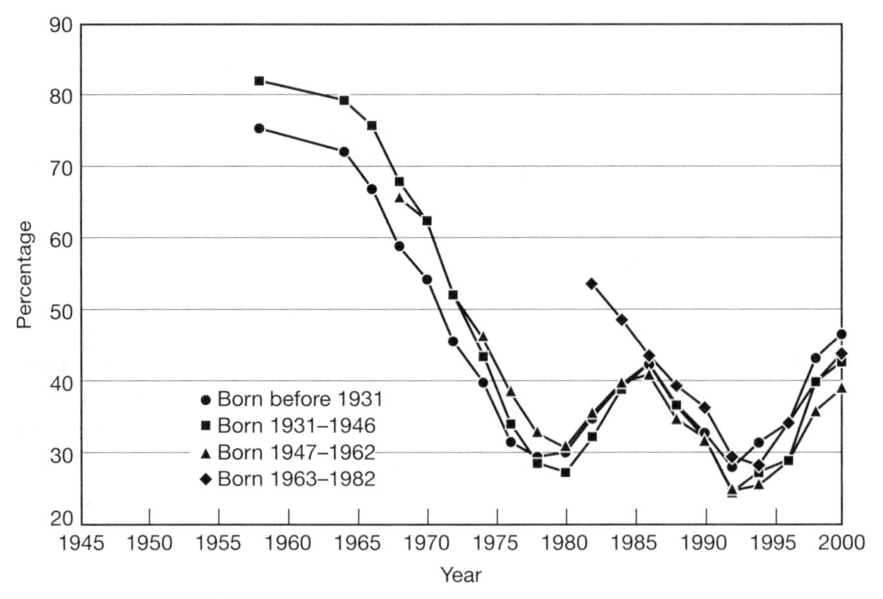

Source: Alwin, Duane F. "Generations X,Y, and Z: Are They Changing America?" *Contexts*, Winter 2002, vol. 1, no. 4.

FIGURE 2 Percentage of U.S. Population Who Believe "You Can Trust the Government in Washington to Do What Is Right"

TRENDS IN CHURCH ATTENDANCE

Reports of attendance at religious services may provide the best example of the complexities of generational analysis. Regarding church attendance, Putnam states that "trends in religious life reinforce rather than counterbalance the ominous plunge in social connectedness in the secular community."

From 1972 through 2000, the General Social Survey has asked random samples of the American public to report how often they attend religious services. These data (not shown here) suggest some important cohort differences in attendance patterns. The Greatest Generation (those born from 1915 to 1930), as well as those born earlier, typically report attending church services something like 25 weeks per year or about half the time. By contrast, people born after the Second World War say they attend church substantially less often. Generation X members report attending services fewer than 15 weeks per year. Consequently, as the earlier cohorts of church attenders die off and are replaced by those less likely to attend church, it could be reasoned that society as a whole will become decidedly less observant.

This interpretation matches the kind of conclusions drawn by Putnam and others who decry modern life as devoid of communal ties. However, these results might be explained, fully or partly, by aging. Typically, after a youthful period of church avoidance, people participate more regularly in religious activities. One common explanation, thus, is that levels of religious participation reflect the effects of aging or the life cycle rather than generation and that the higher levels of involvement reported by cohorts born earlier has as much to do with their age as it does with their generation.

Clearly, more recent generations report less church attendance than earlier ones, but within particular generations, reports of attendance increase over the years. The picture is clouded, however, by Catholic-Protestant differences. Members of the Roman Catholic faith (25 percent of the U.S. population) account for virtually all the decline in reported church attendance in American society between the 1970s and the 1990s. Typical Catholic attendance, some 35 weeks per year in the early 1970s, had declined to 23 weeks per year nearly 30 years later. Much of the decline was due to cohort replacement—younger, less active Catholics replacing the more active Catholics who had died. Most religion scholars attribute the change to the profound differences between Vatican policy on the reproductive rights of women and the views of many lay Catholics. Among Protestants, by contrast, the level of reported church attendance did not change significantly over this period; if anything, it increased. While less active youngsters replace more active older people among Protestant groups, too, that trend is entirely counterbalanced by more active attendance as each generation gets older.

These examples do not do justice to the complex and substantive issues Putnam has raised about civic engagement and social participation, but the case of church attendance points out the difficulties in making strong claims about cohort replacement.

POLITICAL PARTISANSHIP AND THE AGING OF THE BABY BOOMERS

There is yet another possible combination of generation and history: cohort differences may change over time. Take the example of whether or not people identify with a political party. Since 1952, the NES have asked the question: "Generally speaking, do you consider yourself a Republican, Democrat, Independent, or what?" Figure 3 presents data on the percentage of the American public who identify with either of the two major political parties. The earliest born cohorts—the top line—are clearly the most loyal to the major political parties. The two most recent generations—the Baby Boomers (those born 1947 to 1962) and the so-called Generation X (those born 1963 to 1980) are least likely to identify with the two major parties.

These trends, however, are not entirely stable. Throughout most of their lives, the Baby Boomers have been distinctively independent, but beginning in the early 1980s, they began a new trend, which might reflect the "aging of the Baby Boom generation." With time they have become much less independent and in fact more likely to affiliate with the Republican Party. What once appeared to be generational differences have gradually eroded.

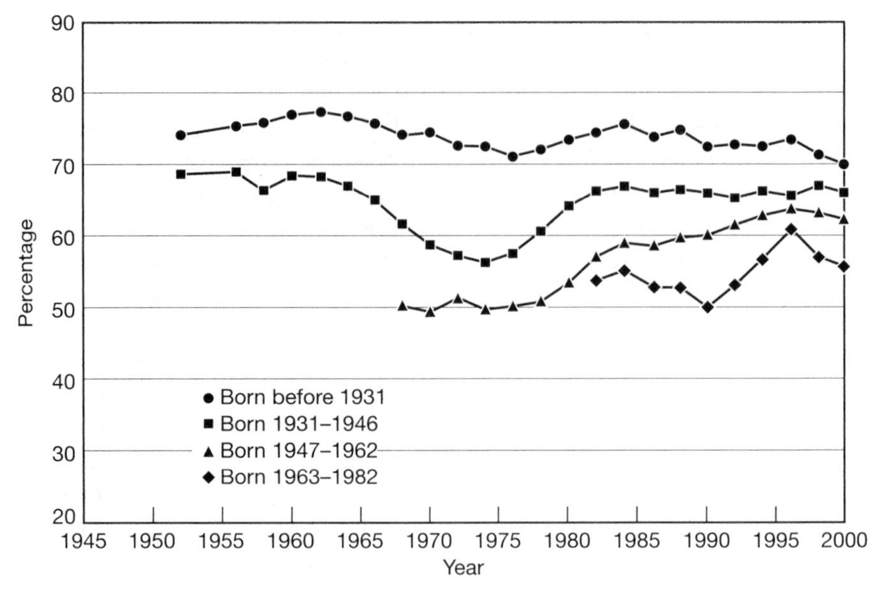

Source: Alwin, Duane F. "Generations X,Y, and Z: Are They Changing America?" *Contexts*, Winter 2002, vol. 1 , no. 4.

FIGURE 3 Percentage of U.S. Population Identifying with One of the Two Major Political Parties

GENERATIONS AND SOCIAL CHANGE

Society reflects, at any given time, the sum of its generations. Where one set of cohorts is especially large—like the Baby Boomers—its lifestyle dominates the society as it passes through the life course. Baby Boomers' taste in music and clothes, for example, disproportionately influence the whole culture. However, in cases where there are no major differences among generations (as in the example of trust in government), then generational succession cannot explain social change.

Where generations persistently differ, however, their succession will produce social change. Certainly, if the more recent generations have less affiliation and involvement with traditional religious groups, this will lead to social change, at least until they develop their own form of religiosity.

Because of the Baby Boomer generation's sheer size, its liberal positions on political and social issues will probably shape beliefs and behavior well into the new century, as Boomers replace the generations that came before. But even here, the Baby Boomers' distinctiveness may wane under the influence of historical events and processes of aging. Baby Boomers, for example, may be growing more conservative with age. This argues in favor of an alternative to the generational view: Generations do not necessarily differ in the same ways over time; individuals are not particularly consistent over their lives; and social change results as much from shifts in individual lives due either to aging or historical events.

The most extensive effort to date to identify the presence of generational effects on social change is the work of James Davis, the founder of the General Social Survey. Analyzing how liberal or conservative survey respondents were across a range of social attitudes, Davis found a general trend in the liberal direction across cohorts—a broad turn he calls the "great 'liberal' shift since World War II." But Davis also found a different tendency within the generations, a "conservative trend between the early and late 1970s and a liberal 'rebound' in the 1980s." Generational change aside, there were historical changes, too. Sometimes those historical changes counterbalance the generational shifts.

The existence of generation effects may depend very much on when one takes the snapshot of generational differences, and how generations differ may depend on which groups in society one examines. All fair warnings for the next essay you read on Generations X, Y or Z.

Recommended Resources

Alwin, Duane F. "The Political Impact of the Baby Boom: Are There Persistent Generational Differences in Political Beliefs and Behavior?" *Generations* 22 (Spring 1998): 46–54. Uses the National Election Studies to document cohort change in political beliefs and behavior over the past 50 years.

Alwin, Duane F., and Ryan J. McCammon. "Generations, Cohorts, and Social Change." In *Handbook on the Life Course*, edited by Jeylan Mortimer and Michael Shanahan. New York: Kluwer Academic / Plenum Publishers, 2002. A recent detailed review of the scholarly literature on stability and change of individuals, cohorts and society from the perspective of life course theory.

Davis, James A. "Patterns of attitude change in the USA: 1972–1994." In *Understanding Change in Social Attitudes*, edited by B. Taylor and K. Thomson. Brookfield, VT: Dartmouth, 1996. The most exhaustive empirical examination of cohort effects and intra-cohort change on social attitudes and beliefs.

Erikson, Erik H. "Youth: Fidelity and Diversity." *Daedalus* 117 (1988): 1–24. A classic statement on the dilemmas and opportunities of youth.

Mannheim, Karl. "The Problem of Generations." In *Essays in the Sociology of Knowledge*; edited by P. Kecskemeti. Boston: Routledge & Kegan Paul, 1952. (Original work published in 1927). A modern classic which examines the concept of generation and generational replacement.

Mason, William M., and Stephen E. Fienberg. *Cohort Analysis in Social Research: Beyond the Identification Problem.* New York: Springer-Verlag, 1985. A standard reference on the difficulties of drawing inferences about cohort effects in repeated cross-sectional research designs.

Putnam, Robert D. *Bowling Alone: The Collapse and Revival of American Community.* New York: Simon & Schuster, 2000. Argues on the basis of massive amounts of data that individual differences in social connectedness and trust depend heavily on cohort placement.

Ryder, Norman B. "The Cohort as a Concept in the Study of Social Change." *American Sociological Review* 30 (December 1965): 843–61. A carefully crafted demographer's perspective on the concept of cohort in understanding social change.

Black Ethnicity

The Foreign-born in America (2008)

JANIS PRINCE INNISS

Recently I completed an online form that asked for my race. Not that unusual. What was unusual is that there were 15 choices! Among other options, I could choose from:

- ☐ Black–African
- ☐ Black–African American
- ☐ Black–Jamaican
- ☐ Black–Caribbean
- ☐ Black–West Indian
- ☐ Black–Tanzanian
- ☐ Black–Haitian
- ☐ Black–Nigerian

There is much that is noteworthy about this list, but I will focus on one aspect of it: The list was made long mostly by the writer's wish to accommodate a variety of foreign-born blacks.

What does the term foreign-born mean? The U. S. Census Bureau definition of the foreign born includes all people residing in the United States who are not American citizens at birth, immigrants, legal nonimmigrants (such as refugees and students), and people who are living in the U.S. illegally. According to the bureau, the largest number of foreign-born persons living the United States in the first half of the 20th century was 14.2 million in 1930 (11.6 percent of the total population at that time), although in 1910 the largest *proportion* of foreign-born persons living in the United States was 14.7 percent. The last thirty years or so have been marked by increasing numbers and proportions of foreign-born persons in the United States; in 2000, there were 28.4 million foreign-born people estimated to be living in the United States. This figure is exactly twice as many as the previous high period in 1930, and this time the foreign-born were estimated to be 10.4 percent of the total population—the highest proportion since 1930.

Of course, the United States is not the only country hosting immigrants. We live in a world of tremendous movement. According to the *New York Times*, in 2005 about 190 million people lived outside of their countries of birth.

Among the millions of foreign-borns living in the United States are black people from all over the world. In fact, the proportion of foreign-born blacks among blacks in the United States has risen to 7.8 percent from 1.3 percent between 1970 and 2000. Black immigrants come from all over the world but are primarily from the Caribbean and Africa. Haiti, Jamaica, and the Dominican Republic are the top three countries of origin of black immigrants in the United States. And where do the foreign-born tend to live? New York, New Jersey, Texas, Florida, California, and Illinois host most of the foreign-born population in general, and this is true for the black foreign-born population as well. Florida has experienced the most growth in the number of foreign-born blacks in the last thirty years, although with a quarter of its black population being foreign-born, New York is now home to the largest share of this group.

To state what is not always obvious: All black people in America are not African Americans. Some have become American citizens, and others have not. Black immigrants do not necessarily see themselves as having much in common with African Americans, and vice versa. They may have grown up in widely differing circumstances—"third world" versus North American countries and all their attendant disparities—so why would we expect them to be the same? Given that Americans of different races often find themselves focused on their differences despite their many similarities, why would a group of newly (or even not so newly) arrived immigrants be assumed to share much with African Americans?

This discussion is not meant to ignore that on *American* soil, with regard to race, and regardless of place of birth, blacks may encounter identical experiences. I recognize there may be no difference in the ways that people with dark skin are perceived or treated. Similarly, the reference to recent historical differences between African American and foreign-born blacks is meant to diminish neither shared African origins nor the overlap in current sociopolitical concerns.

A recent study reported in the *Journal of Blacks in Higher Education* found that for blacks, having foreign-born parents is related to attending selective colleges and universities. Based on data from twenty-eight such institutions, researchers found that 27 percent of blacks students had at least one foreign-born parent—a significantly higher percentage than the national average. As we might imagine given the data presented earlier on the origins of the black foreign-born, this study found that 43 percent of these students had Caribbean roots and 29 percent were of African parentage. Many of us—including sociologists—focus on the race of blacks to the exclusion of ethnicity *among* blacks. With the naming of all immigrants of African descent "black/African American," our ethnicity becomes subsumed beneath our race, propelling race to dominant status.

Findings such as these highlight the role of ethnicity in all its complexity and remind us that race is *not* all that matters.

Related links

Census report on foreign-born individuals:
www.census.gov/prod/2002pubs/p23-206.pdf

New York Times story on global migration:
www.nytimes.com/ref/world/20070622_CAPEVERDE_GRAPHIC.html#

Population Reference Bureau report on foreign-born blacks in the United States:
www.prb.org/Articles/2002/ForeignBornMakeUpGrowingSegmentofUSBlackPopulation.aspx

Journal of Blacks in Higher Education study:
www.jbhe.com/news_views/56_race_sensitive_not_helping.html

Rethinking Crime and Immigration

(2008)

ROBERT J. SAMPSON

The summer of 2007 witnessed a perfect storm of controversy over immigration to the United States. After building for months with angry debate, a widely touted immigration reform bill supported by President George W. Bush and many leaders in Congress failed decisively. Recriminations soon followed across the political spectrum.

Just when it seemed media attention couldn't be greater, a human tragedy unfolded with the horrifying execution-style murders of three teenagers in Newark, N.J., attributed by authorities to illegal aliens.

Presidential candidate Rep. Tom Tancredo (R–Colorado) descended on Newark to blame city leaders for encouraging illegal immigration, while Newt Gingrich declared the "war at home" against illegal immigrants was more deadly than the battlefields of Iraq. National headlines and outrage reached a feverish pitch, with Newark offering politicians a potent new symbol and a brown face to replace the infamous Willie Horton, who committed armed robbery and rape while on a weekend furlough from his life sentence to a Massachusetts prison. Another presidential candidate, former Tennessee senator Fred Thompson, seemed to capture the mood of the times at the Prescott Bush Awards Dinner: "Twelve million illegal immigrants later, we are now living in a nation that is beset by people who are suicidal maniacs and want to kill countless innocent men, women, and children around the world."

Now imagine a nearly opposite, fact-based scenario. Consider that immigration—even if illegal—is associated with *lower* crime rates in most disadvantaged urban neighborhoods. Or that increasing immigration tracks with the broad *reduction* in crime the United States has witnessed since the 1990s.

Well before the 2007 Summer of Discontent over immigration, I proposed we take such ideas seriously. Based on hindsight I shouldn't have been surprised by the intense reaction to what I thought at the time was a rather logical reflection. From the right came loud guffaws, expletive-filled insults, angry web postings, and not-so-thinly veiled threats. But the left wasn't so happy either, because my argument assumes racial and ethnic differences in crime not tidily attributable to material deprivation or discrimination—the canonical explanations.

Although Americans hold polarizing and conflicting views about its value, immigration is a major social force that will continue for some time. It thus pays to reconsider the role of immigration in shaping crime, cities, culture, and societal change writ large, especially in this era of social anxiety and vitriolic claims about immigration's reign of terror.

SOME FACTS

Consider first the "Latino Paradox." Hispanic Americans do better on a wide range of social indicators—including propensity to violence—than one would expect given their socioeconomic disadvantages. To assess this paradox in more depth, my colleagues and I examined violent acts committed by nearly 3,000 males and females in Chicago ranging in age from 8 to 25 between 1995 and 2003. The study selected whites, blacks, and Hispanics (primarily Mexican-Americans) from 180 neighborhoods ranging from highly segregated to very integrated. We also analyzed data from police records, the U.S. Census, and a separate survey of more than 8,000 Chicago residents who were asked about the characteristics of their neighborhoods.

Notably, we found a significantly lower rate of violence among Mexican-Americans compared to blacks and whites. A major reason is that more than a quarter of those of Mexican descent were born abroad and more than half lived in neighborhoods where the majority of residents were also Mexican. In particular, first-generation immigrants (those born outside the United States) were 45 percent less likely to commit violence than third-generation Americans, adjusting for individual, family, and neighborhood background. Second-generation immigrants were 22 percent less likely to commit violence than the third generation. This pattern held true for non-Hispanic whites and blacks as well. Our study further showed living in a neighborhood of concentrated immigration was directly associated with lower violence (again, after taking into account a host of correlated factors, including poverty and an individual's immigrant status). Immigration thus appeared "protective" against violence.

Consider next the implications of these findings when set against the backdrop of one of the most profound social changes to visit the United States in recent decades. Foreign immigration to the United States rose sharply in the 1990s, especially from Mexico and especially to immigrant enclaves in large cities. Overall, the foreign-born population increased by more than 50 percent in 10 years, to 31 million in 2000. A report by the Pew Hispanic Center found immigration grew most significantly in the mid-1990s and hit its peak at the end of the decade, when the national homicide rate plunged to levels not seen since the 1960s. Immigrant flows have receded since 2001 but remain high, while the national homicide rate leveled off and seems now to be creeping up. Both trends are compared over time in figure 1.

The pattern upends popular stereotypes. Among the public, policy makers, and even many academics, a common expectation is that the concentration of immigrants and the influx of foreigners drive up crime rates because of the assumed propensities of these groups to commit crimes and settle in poor, presumably disorganized communities. This belief is so pervasive that in our

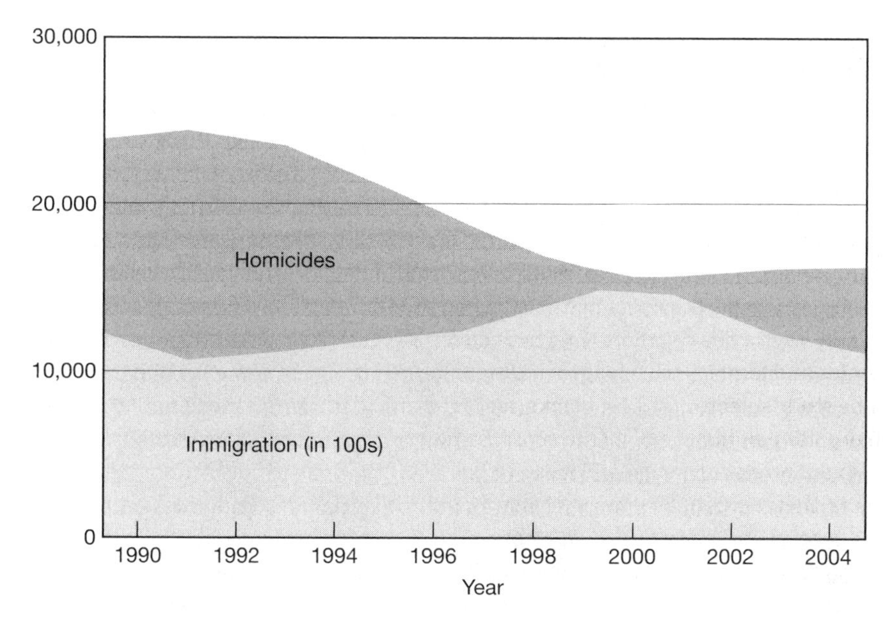

Source: Sampson, Robert J, "Rethinking Crime and Immigration," *Contexts*, vol. 7, no. 1, pp 28–33.

FIGURE 1 Immigration Flows and Homicide Trends: U.S. Total, 1990–2004 (Three-Year Averages)

Chicago study the concentration of Latinos in a neighborhood strongly predicted perceptions of disorder no matter the actual amount of disorder or rate of reported crimes. And yet immigrants appear in general to be less violent than people born in America, particularly when they live in neighborhoods with high numbers of other immigrants.

We are thus witnessing a different pattern from early 20th century America, when growth in immigration from Europe, along with ethnic diversity more generally, was linked with increasing crime and formed a building block for what became known as "social disorganization" theory. New York today is a leading magnet for immigration, yet it has for a decade ranked as one of America's safest cities. Crime in Los Angeles dropped considerably in the late 1990s (45 percent overall) as did other Hispanic influenced cities such as San Jose, Dallas, and Phoenix. The same can be said for cities smack on the border like El Paso and San Diego, which have long ranked as low-crime areas. Cities of concentrated immigration are some of the safest places around.

COUNTERPOINT

There are criticisms of these arguments, of course. To begin, the previous figure juxtaposes two trends and nothing more—correlation doesn't equal causation. But it does demonstrate the trends are opposite of what's commonly assumed, which is surely not irrelevant to the many, and strongly causal, claims that immigration increases crime. Descriptive facts are at the heart of sound social science, a first step in any causal inquiry.

Perhaps a bigger concern is that we need to distinguish illegal from legal immigration and focus on the many illegal aliens who allegedly are accounting for crime waves across the country—the "Newark phenomenon." By one argument, because of deportation risk illegal immigrants are afraid to report crimes against them to the police, resulting in artificially low official estimates in the Hispanic community. But no evidence exists that reporting biases seriously affect estimates of the homicide victimization rate—unlike other crimes there is a body. At the national level, then, the homicides committed by illegal aliens in the United States are reflected in the data just like for everyone else. The bottom line is that as immigrants poured into the country, homicides plummeted. One could claim crime would decrease faster absent immigration inflows, but that's a different argument and concedes my basic point.

There is also little disputing that in areas and times of high legal immigration we find accompanying surges of illegal entrants. It would be odd indeed if illegal aliens descended on areas with no other immigrants or where they had no pre-existing networks. And so it is that areas of concentrated immigration are magnets for illegal concentration. Because crime tends to be negatively associated with undifferentiated immigration measures, it follows that we can disconfirm the idea that increasing illegal immigration is associated with increasing crime.

Furthermore, our Chicago study did include both legal and illegal immigrants. I would estimate the illegal status at roughly a quarter—but in any case no group was excluded from the analysis. The other important point is that the violence estimates were based on confidential self-reports and not police statistics or other official sources of crime. Therefore, police arrest biases or undercounts can't explain the fact that first generation immigrants self-report lower violence than the second generation, which in turn reports less than the third generation.

So let us proceed on the assumption of a substantial negative association across individuals, places, and time with respect to immigration and violence. What potential mechanisms might explain the connections and are they causal? Thinking about these questions requires attention be paid to confounding factors and competing explanations.

Social scientists worry a lot about selection bias because individuals differ in preferences and can, within means, select their environments. It has been widely hypothesized that immigrants, and Mexicans in particular, selectively migrate to the United States on characteristics that predispose them to low crime, such as motivation to work, ambition, and a desire not to be deported. Immigrants may also come from cultures where violence isn't rewarded as a strategy for establishing reputation (to which I return below).

This scenario is undoubtedly the case and central to the argument—social selection is a causal mechanism. Namely, to the extent that more people predisposed to lower crime immigrate to the United States (we now have some 35 million people of foreign-born status), they will sharply increase the denominator of the crime rate while rarely appearing in the numerator. And in the neighborhoods of U.S. cities with high concentrations of immigrants, one would expect on selection grounds alone to find lower crime rates. Selection thus favors the argument that immigration may be causally linked to lower crime.

Another concern of social scientists is common sources of causation, or "competing" explanations. One candidate is economic trends. After all, potential immigrants respond to incentives and presumably choose to relocate when times are better in their destinations. Although a legitimate concern, economics can't easily explain the story. Depending on the measure, economic trends aren't isomorphic with either immigration or crime at either the beginning or end of the time series. Real wages were declining and inequality increasing in the 1990s by most accounts, which should have produced increases in crime by the logic of relative deprivation theory, which says that income gaps, not absolute poverty, are what matters. Broad economic indicators like stock market values did skyrocket but collapsed sharply while immigration didn't.

Scholars in criminology have long searched for a sturdy link between national economic trends and violence, to little avail. The patterns just don't match up well, and often they're in the opposite direction of deprivation-based expectations. The best example is the 1960s when the economy markedly improved yet crime shot up. Don't forget, too, the concentrated immigration and crime link remains when controlling for economic indicators.

Finally, the "Latino Paradox" in itself should put to rest the idea that economics is the go-to answer: Immigrant Latinos are poor and disadvantaged but at low risk for crime. Poor immigrant neighborhoods and immigrant-tinged cities like El Paso have similarly lower crime than their economic profile would suggest.

Competing explanations also can't explain the Chicago findings. Immigrant youths committed less violence than natives after adjustment for a rich set of individual, family, and neighborhood confounders. Moreover, there's an influence of immigrant concentration beyond the effects of individual immigrant status and other individual factors, and beyond neighborhood socioeconomic status and legal cynicism—previously shown to significantly predict violence. We estimated male violence by age for three types of neighborhoods (below, figure 2):

- "Low-risk," where a very high percentage of people work in professional and managerial occupations (90th percentile), few people hold cynical attitudes about the law and morality (10th percentile), and there are no immigrants;
- "High-risk," where professional/managerial jobs are scarce, cynicism is pervasive, and there are also no immigrants;
- "High-risk, immigrant neighborhoods," defined by similarly low shares of professional/managerial workers and high legal cynicism, but where about one-half of the people are immigrants.

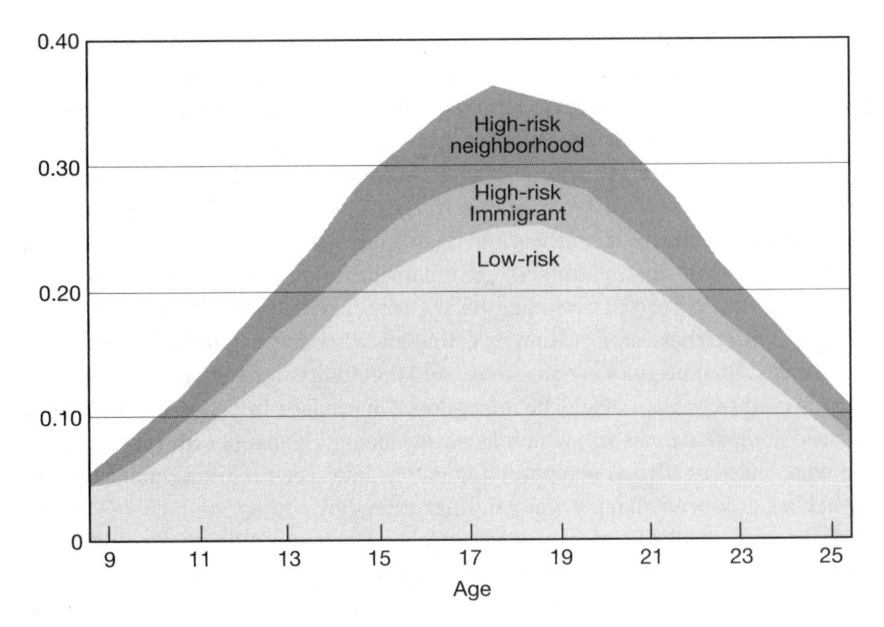

Source: Sampson, Robert J, "Rethinking Crime and Immigration," *Contexts*, vol. 7, no. 1, pp 28–33.

FIGURE 2 Estimated Probability of Violence by Third-Generation Males in Chicago Neighborhoods

The estimated probability an average male living in a high-risk neighborhood without immigrants will engage in violence is almost 25 percent higher than in the high-risk, immigrant neighborhood, a pattern again suggesting the protective, rather than crime-generating, influence of immigrant concentration.

Finally, we examined violence in Chicago neighborhoods by a foreign-born diversity index capturing 100 countries of birth from around the world. In both high- and low-poverty communities, foreign-born diversity is clearly and strongly linked to lower violence. Concentrated poverty predicts more violence (note the high poverty areas above the prediction line) but violence is lower as diversity goes up for low- and high-poverty neighborhoods alike. Interestingly, the link between lower violence and diversity is strongest in the most disadvantaged neighborhoods.

CRIME DECLINES AMONG NON-HISPANICS

A puzzle apparently remains in how immigration explains the crime decline among whites and blacks in the 1990s. One agitated critic, for example, charged that my thesis implies that for every Mexican entering America a black person would have to commit fewer crimes. But immigration isn't the only cause of the crime decline. There are many causes of crime—that declines ensued for blacks and whites doesn't in itself invalidate the immigration argument.

This critique also exposes a misconception about immigrant diversity. Immigration isn't just about Mexicans, it's about the influx of a wide range of different groups. The previous figure, for example, represents 100 countries, a conservative template for many places. In cities such as Los Angeles and New York, immigrant flows are erasing simple black-white-brown scenarios and replacing them with a complex mixture of immigrant diversity.

Even the traditionally black-white city of Chicago reflects evidence of immigration's broad reach. When we looked at whites and blacks we still found surprising variation in generational status, with immigration protective for all racial/ethnic groups except Puerto Ricans/other Latinos. In fact, controlling for immigrant generation reduced the gap between African Americans and whites by 14 percent, implying one reason whites have lower levels of violence than African Americans is that whites are more likely to be recent immigrants. The pattern of immigrant generational status and lower crime is thus not just restricted to Latinos, and it extends to helping explain white-black differences as well.

Added to this is substantial non-Latino immigration into the United States from around the world, including Russia, Poland, India, and the Caribbean, to name just a few countries. Black and white populations are increasingly characterized by immigrants (Poles and Russians among whites in Chicago, for example, and Caribbeans and West Africans among blacks in New York). According to Census 2000, the Chicago area has more than 130,000 Polish immigrants, so we aren't talking about trivial numbers.

Perhaps more important, focusing on the "what about whites and blacks" question misses the non-selection-based component of a broader immigration argument. We're so used to thinking about immigrant adaptation (or assimilation) to the host society we've failed to fully appreciate how immigrants themselves shape the host society. Take economic revitalization and urban growth. A growing consensus argues immigration revitalizes cities around the country. Many decaying inner-city areas gained population in the 1990s and became more vital, in large part through immigration. One of the most thriving scenes of economic activity in the entire Chicagoland area, for example, second only to the famed "Miracle Mile" of Michigan Avenue, is the 26th Street corridor in Little Village. A recent analysis of New York City showed that for the first time ever, blacks' incomes in Queens have surpassed whites', with the surge in the black middle class driven largely by the successes of black immigrants from the West Indies. Segregation and the concentration of poverty have also decreased in many cities for the first time in decades.

Such changes are a major social force and immigrants aren't the only beneficiaries—native born blacks, whites, and other traditional groups in the United States have been exposed to the gains associated with lower crime (decreases in segregation, decreases in concentrated poverty, increases in the economic and civic health of central cities, to name just a few). There are many examples of inner-city neighborhoods rejuvenated by immigration that go well

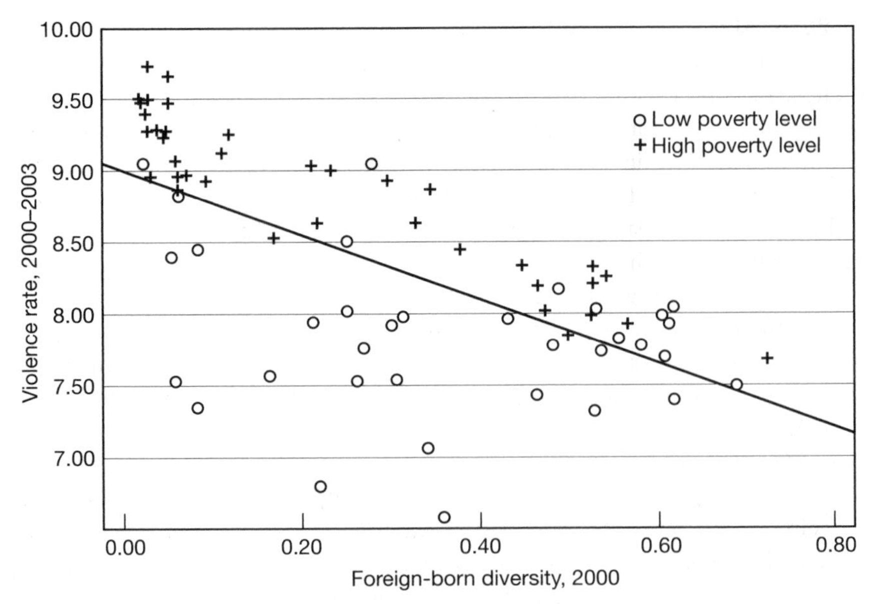

Source: Sampson, Robert J, "Rethinking Crime and Immigration," *Contexts*, vol. 7, no. 1, pp 28–33.

FIGURE 3 Violence and Diversity in Chicago Neighborhoods

beyond Queens and the Lower West Side of Chicago. From Bushwick in Brooklyn to Miami, and from large swaths of south central Los Angeles to the rural South, immigration is reshaping America. It follows that the "externalities" associated with immigration are multiple in character and constitute a plausible mechanism explaining some of the variation in crime rates of all groups in the host society.

There are important implications for this line of argument. If it is correct, then simply adjusting for things like economic revitalization, urban change, and other seemingly confounding explanations is illegitimate from a causal explanation standpoint because they would instead be mediators or conduits of immigration effects—themselves part of the pathway of explanation. Put differently, to the extent immigration is causally bound up with major social changes that in turn are part of the explanatory process of reduced crime, estimating only the net effects of immigration will give us the wrong answer.

CULTURAL PENETRATION AND SOCIETAL RENEWAL

A related cultural implication, while speculative and perhaps provocative, is worth considering. If immigration leads to the penetration into America of diverse and formerly external cultures, then this diffusion may contribute to less crime if these cultures don't carry the same meanings with respect to violence and crime.

It's no secret the United States has long been a high-violence society, with many scholars positing a subculture or code of the streets as its main cause. In one influential version, shared expectations for demanding respect and "saving face" lead participants in the "street culture" of poor inner cities to react violently to perceived slights, insults, and otherwise petty encounters that make up the rounds of daily life. But according to the logic of this theory, if one doesn't share the cultural attribution or perceived meaning of the event, violence is less likely. Outsiders to the culture, that is, are unlikely to be caught in the vicious cycles of interaction (and reaction) that promote violence.

The massive penetration of immigrant (particularly, but not only, Mexican) populations throughout the United States, including rural areas and the South, can properly be thought of as a diffusion-like process. One possible result is that over time American culture is being diluted. Some of the most voracious critiques of immigration have embraced this very line of argument. Samuel Huntington, in one well-known example, claims the very essence of American identity is at stake because of increasing diversity and immigration, especially from Mexico. He may well be right, but the diagnosis might not be so bad if a frontier mentality that endorses and perpetuates codes of violence is a defining feature of American culture.

A profound irony in the immigration debate concedes another point to Huntington. If immigration can be said to have brought violence to America, it most likely came with (white) Irish and Scottish immigrants whose cultural traditions emphasizing honor and respect were defended with violent means when they settled in the South in the 1700s and 1800s. Richard Nisbett and Dov Cohen have presented provocative evidence in favor of this thesis, emphasizing cultural transmission in the form of Scotch-Irish immigrants, descendants of Celtic herdsman, who developed rural herding communities in the frontier South. In areas with little state power to command compliance with the law, a tradition of frontier justice carried over from rural Europe took hold, with a heavy emphasis on retaliation and the use of violence to settle disputes, represented most clearly in the culture of dueling.

In today's society, then, I would hypothesize that immigration and the increasing cultural diversity that accompanies it generate the sort of conflicts of culture that lead not to increased crime but nearly the opposite. In other words, selective immigration in the current era may be leading to the greater visibility of competing non-violent mores that affect not just immigrant communities but diffuse and concatenate through social interactions to tamp down violent conflict in general. Recent findings showing the spread of immigration to all parts of America, including rural areas of the Midwest and South, give credence to this argument. The Willie Hortonization of illegal aliens notwithstanding, diversity and cultural conflict wrought by immigration may well prove healthy, rather than destructive, as traditionally believed.

Recommended Resources

Richard Nisbett and Dov Cohen. *Culture of Honor: The Psychology of Violence in the South* (Westview, 1996). A fascinating take on the cultural roots of violence in the United States, including the culture of honor posited to afflict the South disproportionately and traced to European immigration.

Eyal Press. "Do Immigrants Make Us Safer?" *New York Times Magazine* December 3, 2006. A *New York Times* writer considers the questions raised in this article, taking to the streets of Chicago.

Rubén G. Rumbaut and Walter A. Ewing. "The Myth of Immigrant Criminality and the Paradox of Assimilation: Incarceration Rates among Native and Foreign-Born Men" (Immigration Policy Center, 2007). A recent synthesis of the empirical facts on immigration and crime, with a special focus on incarceration.

Thorsten Sellin. *Culture Conflict and Crime* (Social Science Research Council, 1938). Widely considered the classical account of immigration, culture, and crime in the early part of the 20th century.

Statistics and Myths about Immigrants

(2008)

SALLY RASKOFF

A friend sent me an email that I found very alarming. Although I consider this person a friend, we have never really talked about politics. But I was still surprised when the missive below came from her.

Her email was obviously a chain letter expressing frustration about California's problems, allegedly due to illegal immigrants. The content of the "evidence" is supposed to be from the *Los Angeles Times* and lists many statistics that lay blame for scary and negative situations squarely upon illegal immigrants.

From the *L.A. Times*

1. 40% of all workers in L.A. County (L.A. County has 10.2 million people) are working for cash and not paying taxes. This was because they are predominantly illegal immigrants, working without a green card.
2. 95% of warrants for murder in Los Angeles are for illegal aliens.
3. 75% of people on the most wanted list in Los Angeles are illegal aliens.
4. Over 2/3 of all births in Los Angeles County are to illegal alien Mexicans on Medi-Cal, whose births were paid for by taxpayers.
5. Nearly 35% of all inmates in California detention centers are Mexican nationals here illegally.
6. Over 300,000 illegal aliens in Los Angeles County are living in garages.
7. The FBI reports half of all gang members in Los Angeles are most likely illegal aliens from south of the border.
8. Nearly 60% of all occupants of HUD properties are illegal.
9. 21 radio stations in L.A. are Spanish speaking.
10. In L.A. County 5.1 million people speak English, 3.9 million speak Spanish. (There are 10.2 million people in L.A. County).

(All 10 of the above are from the Los Angeles Times)

Less than 2% of illegal aliens are picking our crops, but 29% are on welfare.

Over 70% of the United States' annual population growth (and over 90% of California, Florida, and New York) results from immigration.

29% of inmates in federal prisons are illegal aliens.

We are a bunch of fools for letting this continue

HOW CAN YOU HELP?

Send copies of this letter to at least two other people 100 would be even better.

As a sociologist who teaches statistics, I could not let this go without a response. While I included in my email response a tactful discussion of the reasons why these statistics are problematic, I'd like to invite you to help identify what the problems are with this message.

I'll start with the source—stating that these came from the *Times* isn't sufficient to give them credibility. No date, page, research source, or author is mentioned. These could have come from an advertisement in that newspaper or, more likely, never appeared there to begin with. Searching the *Los Angeles Times* online, even with quotes from the text, no connections appear.

Many of the statistics are illogical: "95% of warrants for murder" are for "illegal aliens"? The 95% is a big red flag. Few human patterns, especially crime patterns, are so simple that there can be an easy explanation.

Other statistics mentioned are more about prejudice than serious social problems—for example, "21 radio stations in L.A. are Spanish speaking."

Since these statistics are all about Los Angeles and California, the research reported by the Public Policy Institute of California provides a good contrast to these figures. In their June 2008 "Just the Facts" report on "Immigrants in California," they state that "Immigration has directly accounted for 40% of the state's population growth since 2000," which is a much lower figure than the e-mail's purported 90%.

Finally, checking the text of the email on Snopes.com, a site devoted to investigating urban legends and hoaxes, this message has quite a history, and has been circulating since 2006.

Questioning such email forwards, and considering the accuracy and sources of information that come our way, are crucial steps in critical thinking and forging a pathway based on accuracy rather than ignorance. The email tells us more about anxieties surrounding population changes than immigration itself; rather than simply a concern about new residents, the email suggests that those immigrating are a threat to those of us already here. The threat felt is not just physical (concerns about crime) but also cultural (concerns about language). For many who are upset about both legal and illegal immigration, the fear is about social and cultural change and what the future might hold in a society that might look and sound different from today.

Related links

Public Policy Institute of California facts on immigration:
www.ppic.org/content/pubs/jtf/JTF_ImmigrantsJTF.pdf

Snopes.com debunking of email: www.snopes.com/politics/immigration/taxes.asp

Social Movements and the Environment

(2009)

KAREN STERNHEIMER

Would you break the law to protect the environment? Tim DeChristopher, a twenty-seven-year-old college student, did. At a December 2008 Bureau of Land Management auction in Utah where public land was on the block, DeChristopher bid $1.79 million to buy 22,000 acres of land, in order to prevent oil companies from drilling there. The problem: he didn't *have* $1.79 million—not many college students do!

Supporters sent Tim donations, but he did not raise the $1.79 million. In the end that didn't matter, since the United States Secretary of the Interior Ken Salazar invalidated the results of the auction and reclaimed the public land for the public.

Sociologists study what makes people decide to get involved in social movements. Why, for instance, are some people willing to risk going to jail, as DeChristopher could have, for a cause when others do not decide to take action? Sociologists also examine why certain movements gain traction at some times but not others. What has put the environmental cause on many Americans' radar?

The environment was a significant point of debate during the 2008 presidential race: global warming, clean energy, and our dependence on foreign oil were major campaign issues.

It certainly wasn't always this way. When the former White House Press Secretary Ari Fleischer was asked in 2001 about whether Americans should change our lifestyles to conserve energy, he answered, "That's a big no."

I can recall the last big energy crisis when I was a kid in the 1970s. In 1973 an oil crisis began when OPEC embargoed oil delivery to the United States. Gas prices spiked, and Congress enacted the National Maximum Speed Law (remember when highway speed limits were 55 mph?) in order to save gas. Conservation was a big deal, and public service announcements reminded us to focus on saving water. Restaurants would dim their lights and serve water only upon request.

Environmental disasters at places like the Three Mile Island nuclear facility and discovery of tons of toxic waste at Love Canal, a neighborhood in Niagara Falls, New York, also raised public awareness about protecting the environment.

Then, in the 1980s, regulations thought to impede business were repealed, and Americans were encouraged to focus on individual success. When I was in high school during the mid-'80s, anything that smacked of the '60s or '70s (read: any social cause) was considered lame. A faint mural of something called the ecology club was painted over, and membership dwindled to a few people before it too faded away.

Gas prices declined during this decade, SUVs were invented, and shows like *Dallas* and *Dynasty* (both about oil tycoons) celebrated extreme wealth, materialism, and individualism. Environmental disasters seemed a thing of the past (or of the far away—at Chernobyl, in the remote Soviet Union). The environment seemed a quaint hippie topic, and derogatory terms like "treehugger" and "eco-terrorist" derided people who sought to protect the environment.

So what factors have led to our contemporary concern about environmental issues? According to resource mobilization theory, social movements are most successful when they manage to garner sufficient resources like money, volunteers, media attention, and, perhaps most centrally, legitimacy. Collaborating with other organized groups can build coalitions to maximize resources.

But a lot of environmental activists worked very hard before getting widespread recognition. For instance, scientists studied global warming for many years before government officials and the population at large considered it to be an urgent problem. Former Vice President Al Gore gave many speeches on this issue before his 2006 documentary *An Inconvenient Truth* won an Academy Award. What turned the tide?

One of the best ways to gain widespread support for a social movement is to convince the general public that without action, their lives will change for the worse. For example, skyrocketing energy costs mobilized people who might not otherwise be concerned with environmental issues. When our wallets are in danger, we can spring into action very quickly. Couple this tendency with a growing number of high-profile supporters across the ideological spectrum, such as T. Boone Pickens, who made a good deal of his fortune in oil, and it becomes easier to convince people that the problem is significant and that something should be done.

But this does not explain why some people take significant personal risks to support a cause. I might recycle, drive a fuel-efficient car, and walk instead of drive in my neighborhood, but these actions don't have a great personal cost. In fact, my city provides special recycling bins that they pick up with the trash, my fuel-efficient car was cheaper than others that get worse mileage, and I like to take walks. So these actions actually *benefit* me.

What sociological explanations might help us understand why Tim DeChristopher and others like him are willing to take personal risks to support a cause?

Related links

Tim DeChristopher's website: www.bidder70.org

Los Angeles Times story on DeChristopher: www.latimes.com/news/science/environment/la-na-lease-activist18-2009jan18,0,7527533.story

TALK ABOUT IT

1. Discuss how Sampson's, Raskoff's, and Prince Inniss's selections challenge stereotypes about immigration.
2. Why do you think immigrants, both legal and illegal, are blamed for many social problems today?
3. Why are some groups of immigrants highly visible and central in public debate, while others, specifically those white and black, tend to remain less central in these debates?
4. What social changes can you identify within your lifetime? What political, historical, and social factors created them?
5. What social movements have had the most success in recent years? How were the leaders of these movements able to achieve their goals? What can future social movements learn from their examples?

WRITE ABOUT IT

1. Find an online article arguing that immigration has had a negative impact on society. Compare and contrast its points to selections from in this section.
2. Choose one immigrant group (this can include one not mentioned in this section). What political, economic, or social factors led this group to leave their countries of origin? Discuss how immigration involves more than personal, individual choices.
3. Discuss a nonimmigrant group that has been blamed for recent social changes. How is public perception of this group different from other immigrant groups? How is it similar?
4. Using resource mobilization theory, describe how you would advise the social movement of your choice to achieve their goals.
5. What type of social change might motivate you to take action? Describe the risks and sacrifices you would or would not be willing to make in support of this cause. What factors would entice you to increase your participation in a social movement?

DO IT

1. Find five to ten online articles that discuss immigration. Analyze their word choice, tone, and assumptions. How do the points in these articles compare with the selections in this section?
2. Interview someone who has immigrated to this country. Ask them about what factors in their home country motivated them to leave, focusing on

political, economic, or other social factors. What specific personal changes has he or she experienced since immigrating? How have they been able to assimilate into their new community?

3. Watch an episode of a television show from a previous decade on DVD or online. Besides fashion and hairstyles, what significant changes do you notice between then and now? What political, economic, or other social factors are behind these changes?
4. Visit a community that has a large population of new immigrants, paying special attention to the shops and customs in this area. Describe your findings. Research the history and recent trends within this community. Has the ethnic composition changed? What political, economic, and social factors might be behind these changes? What are the trends in income and crime in this community?
5. Interview someone who is active in a local social movement. What are the movement's goals? How does he or she attempt to accomplish these? What motivated your interviewee to get involved? What risks or sacrifices has he or she made in order to create social change?

CREDITS

Duane F. Alwin: "Generations X, Y, and Z: Are They Changing America?" *Contexts*, Fall/Winter 2002, Vol. 1, No. 4, pp. 42–51. Copyright © 2002, The American Sociological Association. Reprinted by permission of University of California Press.

Kristen Barber: "The Well-coiffed Man: Class, Race, and Heterosexual Masculinity in the Hair Salon," *Gender & Society*, Vol. 22, No. 4, pp. 455–61, 463–76. Copyright © 2008, Sociologists for Women in Society. Reprinted by permission of Sage Publications.

Joel Best: "Scary Numbers," *More Damned Lies and Statistics: How Numbers Confuse Public Issues*, pp. 63–69, 74–77, 83–87. Copyright © 2004, The Regents of the University of California. Reprinted by permission of University of California Press.

Barbara Ehrenreich: Introduction from *Bait and Switch: The Futile Pursuit of the American Dream* by Barbara Ehrenreich. Copyright © 2005 by Barbara Ehrenreich. Reprinted by arrangement with Henry Holt and Company, LLC.

Erving Goffman: From *The Presentation of Self in Everyday Life* by Erving Goffman, copyright © 1959 by Erving Goffman. Used by permission of Doubleday, a division of Random House, Inc.

Arlie Hochschild: "The Overextended Family" from *The Time Bind: When Work Becomes Home and Home Becomes Work* by Arlie Russell Hochschild. Copyright © 1997 by Arlie Russell Hochschild. Reprinted by arrangement with Henry Holt and Company, LLC.

Diana Kendall: "Class Action in the Media," from *Framing Class: Media Representations of Wealth and Poverty in America*, pp. 1–6, 10–20. Copyright © 2005 by Rowman & Littlefield Publishers, Inc. Reprinted by permission of the publisher.

Jonathan Kozol: From *The Shame of the Nation* by Jonathan Kozol, copyright © 2005 by Jonathan Kozol. Used by permission of Crown Publishers, a division of Random House, Inc.

Meika Loe and Leigh Cuttino: "Grappling with the Medicated Self: The Case of ADHD College Students," *Symbolic Interaction*, Summer 2008, Vol. 31, No. 3, pp. 303–23. Copyright © 2008, Society for the Study of Symbolic Interaction. Reprinted by permission of University of California Press.

C. Wright Mills: "The Promise" from *Sociological Imagination*, pp. 5–11. Copyright © 1959 by Oxford University Press, Inc. Reprinted by permission of Oxford University Press, Inc.

Michael Omi and Howard Winant: "Racial Formation," from *Racial Formation in the United States: From the 1960s to the 1990s*, pp. 53–61, 64–76. Copyright © 1994 by Michael Omi and Howard Winant. Reproduced with permission of Taylor & Francis Group LLC—Books in the format Textbook via Copyright Clearance Center.

Patrick F. Parnaby and Vincent F. Sacco: "Fame and Strain: The Contributions of Mertonian Deviance Theory to an Understanding of the Relationship Between Celebrity and Deviant Behavior," *Deviant Behavior*, Vol. 25, 2004, pp. 2–3, 5–16, 23–26. Copyright © 2004 Routledge. Reprinted by permission of the publisher (Taylor & Francis Group, www.informaworld.com).

Robert Perrucci and Earl Wysong: "Class in America," from *The New Class Society: Goodbye American Dream?* 2nd Edition, pp. 1–6, 21–30, 34–40. Copyright © 2008 by Rowman & Littlefield Publishers, Inc. Reprinted by permission of the publisher.

In **Perrucci/Wysong: Don Stillman:** "The Devastating Impact of Plant Relocations," *Working Papers* 5, July/August 1978 (Policy Studies Institute), pp. 42–43.

Robert D. Putnam: "Civic Participation." Reprinted with the permission of Simon & Schuster, Inc., from *Bowling Alone: The Collapse and Revival of American Community* by Robert D. Putnam, pp. 48–63. Copyright © 2000 by Robert D. Putnam. All rights reserved.

Robert J. Sampson: "Rethinking Crime and Imagination," *Contexts*, February 2008, Vol. 7, No. 1, pp. 42–51. Copyright © 2008, The American Sociological Association. Reprinted by permission of University of California Press.

Juliet B. Schor: "The Visible Lifestyle" [edited] from *The Overspent American: Why We Want What We Don't Need* by Juliet B. Schor. Copyright © 1998 by Juliet Schor. Reprinted by permission of HarperCollins Publishers.

Gregory C. Stanczak: "Bridging the Gap: The Split between Spirituality and Society," *Engaged Spirituality: Social Change and American Religion*. Copyright © 1998 by Rutgers, the State University. Reprinted by permission of Rutgers University Press.

Mary C. Waters: "The Costs of a Costless Community," *Ethnic Options: Choosing Identities in America*, pp. 147, 151–68. Copyright © 1990, The Regents of the University of California. Reprinted by permission of University of California Press.

In **Waters:** As seen in DEAR ABBY by Abigail Van Buren a.k.a. Jeanne Phillips and founded by her mother Pauline Phillips. © 1986 Universal Press Syndicate. Reprinted with permission. All rights reserved.

Max Weber: "Bureaucracy" from *Max Weber: Essays in Sociology*, edited by H. H. Gerth and C. Wright Mills, pp. 196–200, 204. © 1948 H. H. Gerth and C. Wright Mills. Reprinted by permission of Oxford University Press, Inc.

Candace West and Don H. Zimmerman: "Doing Gender," *Gender & Society,* Vol. 1, No. 2, pp. 125–27, 129–30, 133, 135–40, 145–51. Copyright © 1987, Sociologists for Women in Society. Reprinted by permission of Sage Publications.

James Q. Wilson and Robert Kelling: "Broken Windows," © James Q. Wilson, reprinted from *The Atlantic,* March 1982. Reprinted with permission.